India's Rise as an Asian Power

SOUTH ASIA IN WORLD AFFAIRS SERIES

T.V. Paul, Series Editor

TITLES IN THE SERIES

Afghan Endgames: Strategy and Policy Choices for America's Longest War
Hy Rothstein and John Arquilla, editors

The Engagement of India: Strategies and Responses
Ian Hall, Editor

Globalization and India's Economic Integration
Baldev Raj Nayar

India's Rise as an Asian Power: Nation, Neighborhood, and Region
Sandy Gordon

Pakistan's Counterterrorism Challenge
Moeed Yusuf, Editor

Vying for Allah's Vote: Understanding Islamic Parties, Political Violence, and Extremism in Pakistan
Haroon K. Ullah

India's Rise as an Asian Power

Nation, Neighborhood, and Region

SANDY GORDON

Georgetown University Press / Washington, DC

Library of Congress Cataloging-in-Publication Data

Gordon, A. D. D.
India's rise as an Asian power : nation, neighborhood, and region / Sandy Gordon.
pages cm. -- (South Asia in world affairs series)
Includes bibliographical references and index.
ISBN 978-1-62616-110-8 (hardcover : alk. paper) -- ISBN 978-1-62616-074-3 (pbk. : alk. paper)
1. India--Politics and government--21st century. 2. India--Economic conditions--21st century. 3. National security--India. 4. India--Foreign relations. 5. India--Foreign economic relations. 6. India--Foreign relations--South Asia. 7. South Asia--Foreign relations--India. I. Title.
DS449.G67 2014
327.54--dc23

2014000936

♾ This book is printed on acid-free paper meeting the requirements of the American National Standard for Permanence in Paper for Printed Library Materials.

15 14 9 8 7 6 5 4 3 2 First printing

Printed in the United States of America

MANAN VATSYAYANA / AFP / Getty Images

To Flora, Solomon, Robin, Dashiell, and others who may come along

CONTENTS

	Preface	ix
	Author's Note on Currency Conversion	xi
	Abbreviations	xiii
	Introduction	xvii
CHAPTER 1	Governance and the "Hybrid Inheritance"	1
CHAPTER 2	Enmeshed Dissonance in South Asia	43
CHAPTER 3	South Asian Dissonance, Global Factors, and Global Power Competition	79
CHAPTER 4	Wider Regional Implications	111
CHAPTER 5	The Government Response: Domestic Governance and Security	155
CHAPTER 6	External Strategies and Challenges: From Neighborhood to Region	181
	Conclusion	207
	Bibliography	213
	About the Author	245
	Index	247

PREFACE

This book has had a long gestation dating back to the beginning of the 1990s. At that time, I had an Australian government defense fellowship at the Australian National University (ANU). The outcome was *India's Rise to Power: In the Twentieth Century and Beyond* (London: Macmillan, 1995). My thanks are due to Professor Desmond Ball of the ANU for inviting me to undertake that work.

In it, I sought to explain what I saw as India's failure to rise rapidly to power given its megapopulation status. I did so in terms of the constraints India then confronted due to its sprawling domestic polity; difficult South Asian neighborhood; emerging environmental issues; flawed policies in education, defense industry, and technological acquisition; and limited progress with economic liberalization. I described India in this setting as acting according to a "weak-strong" paradigm. I concluded that even though India would likely become a declared nuclear power, its rise as an Asian and global power would be delayed till somewhat later in the twenty-first century.

Over a decade later I was kindly invited by Professor Peter Grabosky to take up a research position with the Centre of Excellence in Policing and Security (CEPS) at the Regulatory Institutions Network (RegNet), ANU. My thanks are due to Peter and my other colleagues at CEPS and RegNet, including Professor Roderic Broadhurst, who took over from Peter as head of CEPS on his retirement. My brief at RegNet was to cover governance, terrorism, and transnational crime. This focus reflected the fact that during the years between my first sojourn at ANU and my second, I had been, among other things, head of intelligence at the Australian Federal Police, equivalent to the Federal Bureau of Investigation in the United States.

On returning to ANU, however, I was still keen to revisit my work on India. I decided to do this by again looking at the issue of India's rise to power, only this time with a greater emphasis on governance issues, especially corruption, terrorism, and crime. This work was furthered by a fellowship with the Institute for Defence Studies and Analysis (IDSA) in New Delhi in 2009. My thanks are due to the then director and colleagues at IDSA for the assistance they provided and the fruitful discussions I had. I also received help from several members of the Central Bureau of Investigation and National Investigation Agency. My thanks to them as well.

My renewed interest in India predated the global financial crisis (GFC) in 2008. At that time, India was widely perceived as a rapidly emerging power and a potential "swing state" in the Asia-Pacific strategic context. This was due to the fact that economic growth had shown remarkable progress since liberalization was first commenced in 1991, with growth persistently in the range of 7 percent to 9 percent. With the lingering GFC and other bottlenecks, however, growth has recently fallen to just over 5 percent. At the same time, there has been an escalation in so-called megacorruption—or at least that has been the public perception. Confidence in India and its imminent rise to power has somewhat diminished as a consequence. Concern about governance and corruption and their role in retarding India's growth is in the air, so to speak. In that sense, I hope this book is timely and useful.

In order to be so, it seeks not just to be analytical but also prescriptive, especially in its final two chapters. I am highly conscious that, as a non-Indian, I am entering potentially difficult terrain in offering prescriptions to those who actually run India and are far better informed than myself about the problems and constraints that confront them. I am also conscious that in prescribing strategies for "India," I am prescribing them not for a country, which cannot, of course, make and carry out policy, but rather for a vast array of policymakers right across India.

I put forward two points by way of explanation. First, the so-called strategies prescribed here are only meant to be heuristic. They are strategies that might sensibly be prescribed (or so I believe) were there such a single policy entity as "India" capable of carrying them out. In that sense they are an intellectual exercise to see what might be done given the analysis carried out in the first four chapters of the book and given Voltaire's "best of all possible worlds."

Second, my hope is that by prescribing strategies, I can contribute to a discussion of what India's broad priorities should be. In saying that, I am not naive enough to suppose that policymakers in India will necessarily have the time or inclination to read this book. But hopefully some others may, and it may therefore enter the debate of ideas that usually precedes significant change.

As well as the people named above, I would like to thank those associated with the South Asia project at Georgetown University Press, especially Professor T. V. Paul, Don Jacobs, and Deborah Weiner who have been unfailingly courteous and helpful.

Finally, I would like to thank my wife Sue, who not only put up with my engagement for long hours on this project when I was supposed to be enjoying retirement with her, but also read parts of it and gave exacting comments on it.

Author's Note on Currency Conversion

At times amounts are expressed in the Indian term *crore* of rupees, meaning units of ten million rupees. Where amounts are translated into US dollars, the exchange rate will be approximate and will vary according to when the information came to hand. This is because the rupee-dollar exchange fluctuated markedly during the time it took to write this book, from about forty rupees to the dollar to the current rate of about sixty. All dollars are US dollars unless otherwise stated.

Abbreviations

ABM	antiballistic missile
ADR	Association for Democratic Reform
AFSPA	Armed Forces Special Powers Act
ANA	Afghan National Army
ANP	Afghan National Police
APEC	Asia-Pacific Economic Cooperation forum
ARF	ASEAN Regional Forum
ASEAN	Association of South East Asian Nations
ASEM	Asia-Europe Meeting
BCIM	Bangladesh-China-India-Myanmar Forum for Regional Cooperation
BIMSTEC	Bay of Bengal Initiative for Multi-Sectoral Technical and Economic Cooperation
BJP	Bharatia Janata Party
BPL	below poverty line
BRICS	Brazil, Russia, India, China, and South Africa
BSF	Border Security Force
CAG	Office of the Comptroller and Auditor General
CBI	Central Bureau of Investigation
CCS	Cabinet Committee on Security
CINCPAC	Commander-in-Chief, Pacific (US Navy)
CMP	Common Minimum Program

CRPF	Central Reserve Police Force
CT	counterterrorism
CVC	Central Vigilance Commission
DMK	Dravida Munnetra Kazhagam
DOT	Department of Telecommunications
EAS	East Asia Summit
ED	Enforcement Directorate
EU	European Union
FDI	foreign direct investment
FIR	first information report
FRCA	Foreign Contribution Regulation Act
FTA	free-trade agreement
GDP	gross domestic product
GFI	global financial integrity
HuJI	Harkat-ul-Jihad al-Islami
IAS	Indian Administrative Service
IB	Intelligence Bureau
ICBM	intercontinental ballistic missile
ICT	information and communications technology
IFIOR	International Forum on the Indian Ocean Region
IM	Indian Mujahideen
IMF	International Monetary Fund
IONS	Indian Ocean Naval Symposium
IOR	Indian Ocean Region
IORA	Indian Ocean Rim Association
IPS	Indian Police Service
ISI	Inter-Services Intelligence Directorate (Pakistan)
ISRO	Indian Space Research Organisation
J-e-M	Jaish-e-Mohammed
LeT	Lashkar-e-Toiba
LOC	line of control (between Indian and Pakistani Kashmir)
MAC	Multi-Agency Centre
MEA	Ministry of External Affairs

MFN	most-favored nation
MGG	Mekong-Ganga Group
MGNREGS	Mahatma Gandhi National Rural Employment Guarantee Scheme
MHA	Ministry of Home Affairs
MOD	Ministry of Defence
NATGRID	National Intelligence Grid
NATO	North Atlantic Treaty Organization
NCB	Narcotics Control Bureau
NCTC	National Counter-Terrorism Centre
NDA	National Democratic Alliance
NeGP	National Electronic Governance Plan
NIA	National Investigation Agency
NRI	non-resident Indian
NSA	national security adviser
NSC	National Security Council
NSG	National Security Guard
NSS	national sample survey
NTB	nontariff barrier
PAC	Provincial Armed Constabulary
PDS	Public Distribution System
PLAN	People's Liberation Army (Navy)
POTA	Prevention of Terrorism Act
RAW	Research and Analysis Wing
RIMPAC	Exercise Rim of the Pacific
RRF	Rapid Response Force
RSS	Rashtriya Swayamsevak Sangh
RTI	Right to Information Act
SAARC	South Asian Association for Regional Cooperation
SAFTA	South Asia Free Trade Agreement
SCO	Shanghai Cooperation Organisation
SIMI	Students Islamic Movement of India
SLBM	submarine-launched ballistic missile

SLOCS	sea-lanes (or lines) of communication
SMAC	Subsidiary Multi-Agency Centre
TADA	Terrorism and Disruptive Activities Act
TI	Transparency International
UAPA	Unlawful Activities Prevention Act
UBS	United Bank of Switzerland
UID	Unique Identification
UNESCO	United Nations Educational, Scientific, and Cultural Organization
UNODC	United National Office on Drugs and Crime
UPA	United Progressive Alliance
USPACOM	US Pacific Command
WTO	World Trade Organization

INTRODUCTION

There is now a rich vein of scholarship analyzing India's global rise in the context of its relations with its South Asian neighbors.[1] This book not only follows in that tradition, but also adds to it by seeking to explain India's global performance and potential at least partly in terms of the linkage between its domestic problems and its difficult South Asian milieu.[2]

This focus on strategic enmeshment at what we refer to as the neighborhood[3] level, and its role in mediating power, is in a sense the flip side of the liberal approach in international relations. Liberals argue that economic interdependence and globalization tend to minimize the risks of conflict by raising its costs. Economic enmeshment is also said to lower the profile of the state. In the case of India's place in its neighborhood, however, economic engagement has tended to be minimal and strategic enmeshment, often of a negative kind, pronounced. Given historical and strategic animosities in South Asia, the role of globalization is also often negative rather than positive. As pointed out by Norris M. Ripsman and T. V. Paul, while the role of globalization in more stable parts of the globe tends to diminish the role of the state, emphasis on the state is maintained or even enhanced in difficult subregions such as South Asia.[4]

Ironically, while the role of the state is enhanced in these circumstances, its autonomy is often diminished. In India, difficult neighborhood conditions have led to the adoption of a continental defense and security posture. This posture tends to restrain India's behavior on the wider international stage, at least in terms of the traditional view of how power is exercised. Such neighborhood conditions also provide bait for outside powers, including for potential competitors of India such as China. India's core strategy of "strategic autonomy" is thus constrained.[5]

India's other core strategy of "inclusive growth" is also impeded by cross-border problems and the poor state of governance in India itself.[6] Cross-border problems and the general malaise they have caused in South Asia have prevented the region progressing economically and socially into one in which all, including India, can "rise on the same tide." Governance problems within India limit the capacity of the state to alleviate poverty and enhance human capacity at the grassroots level. They also contribute to neighborhood strategic enmeshment by means of a negative feedback loop. Regionally and globally, these problems have created a sense of skepticism about India and its prospects.

The focus of this book on the domestic and neighborhood spheres and how they intersect differs from most other attempts to analyze India's rise to power, which tend to concentrate on higher levels of the international system. The work further departs from the norm in that it seeks to prescribe strategies India might adopt to alleviate some of the problems it confronts at all three levels—domestic, neighborhood, and regional.

Despite India's manifest domestic and neighborhood problems, Indians have for many years had a tendency to look beyond the neighborhood to the wider international system. They have done so in the belief that, in the words of Jawaharlal Nehru, "India will always make a difference in the world. . . . Fate has marked us for big things."[7] This Nehruvian world view was not only shaped by India's size and potential as a power, but also by the belief that India provided a moral "make weight" in the jaundiced post–Second World War, postcolonial world. This idealistic tendency contributed to a dislocation within Indian strategy—one in which India's view of its place in the global system did not necessarily correspond with the realities it confronted nearer home.

George K. Tanham's pioneering work focused on some of these aspects of Indian strategic thought.[8] Recently, Rahul Sagar and Kanti Bajpai, in separate works, have identified three broad strands to Indian strategic thought: realism (which also covers neorealism in the case of Sagar), liberalism, and idealism.[9] The general consensus among such commentators is that although the idealism of Nehru and others still exists, there has been a broad shift in favor of more realist views of India's place in the world.

We should note here the difference between strategic culture on the one hand and strategy on the other. Strategic culture is the "central strategic paradigm," to use Bajpai's expression.[10] Strategy may be shaped by strategic culture (indeed, it usually is), but it is also amenable to current circumstance. Our central interest in this work is strategy.

The focus on the subject of Indian strategy as distinct from strategic culture is relatively recent. It has mostly been confined to what might be called "grand strategy," rather than the assessment of how strategies at different levels of the international system might be formulated and harmonized.[11] A grand strategy for India, as expressed in *NonAlignment 2.0* by Sunil Khilnani et alia at New Delhi's Centre for Policy Research, for example, seems to carve out a path somewhere between the liberal and realist strands of thought as described by Bajpai and Sagar.

In *NonAlignment 2.0*, it is argued that further domestic economic reform and engagement with world markets should be the main means of generating wealth. This in turn implies a liberal international order. But the document also has realist overtones in that it regards economic growth as being an important tool for the acquisition of military power. In the words of the document: "We [Indians] cannot shut our eyes to the fact that *great power competition of a classical kind* will continue . . . we must [therefore] seek to achieve a situation where no other state is in a position to exercise undue influence over us [emphasis added]."[12]

Such a crossover between liberalism and realism might seem improbable, even contradictory, but the key to understanding it is to recognize the variability of behavior according to different stages of development and different levels of the international system at which the analysis takes place. According to this strategic approach, military spending should initially give way to social and infrastructure spending so India can become resilient and strong domestically. This is, in effect, the type of "grand strategy" for achieving balanced growth and eventually military power of the kind advocated in *NonAlignment 2.0*.

China provides a useful example of this need for an analytical approach that accommodates time and space. China is another megapopulation power that once had levels of poverty similar to India's. While China was weak, with large numbers of poor, leaders in Beijing sought to strengthen it through international economic engagement, investment, technology transfer, and using the wealth so acquired for social uplift. This dictated nonassertive international strategies so as not to "rock the strategic boat" and jeopardize the economic relations upon which growth depended. Such strategies can be characterized as liberal engagement with a liberal world order. But now stronger, China appears more frequently to be acting according to neorealist norms as would any significant power, at least when it comes to its own region, if not yet in terms of the wider global order. Presumably once it has global military as well as economic reach, if ever that time comes, it will behave in ways normally considered neorealist in the wider global context. This "grand strategy" is reminiscent of Deng Xiaoping's famous dictum: *Keep a cool head and maintain a low profile. Never take the lead—but aim to do something big.* In other words, China had to pause in its ambition while its people were uplifted.

This shifting analysis according to time and place does not overrule the neorealist analysis as such, but it does illustrate that neorealism has perhaps drawn too heavily on the context of the Cold War and superpower rivalry, without due consideration of the ways countries behave at a range of stages of their development and at a range of levels within the global structure, and of how circumstances at these different levels can shape overall behavior.

The argument in the present work shifts the focus from this type of very broad strategy as advocated by *NonAlignment 2.0* by emphasizing the need to improve governance in order to achieve better domestic and neighborhood outcomes. We argue that the focus on these lower-order issues is necessary to provide an adequate platform to achieve subregional stability in South Asia and thus allow India to maintain strategic autonomy more broadly. Strategic autonomy, however, is not seen just as a means of assisting economic growth, as it is in *NonAlignment 2.0*, but also as a means of allowing India to play a positive role in Asia's emerging strategic architecture—or to fulfill its role as a "swing state," to use Ashley J. Tellis's term.[13]

An understanding of the linkages between domestic, neighborhood, and regional levels of tension and dissonance is also relevant to the more general debate about regionalism, globalization, and rising powers.[14] In contributing to this debate, the book draws on a palette of factors driving and connecting these levels of dissonance. These include poor governance, the political problems of nascent democracies, economic imbalances, porous and poorly constructed borders, religious tension, the environmental crisis unfolding across South Asia, the effects of globalization, and interference from powers with global reach.

In the wider debate on the role of the region (or neighborhood) in relation to rising powers and the subsequent global order, it is important to make a number of distinctions. We first need to distinguish between analysis of regionalism itself and how it is developed on the one hand, and the discussion of the role of regions and regionalism in *mediating and delineating* power acquisition at the global level on the other. The former is concerned with what constitutes regionalism and how it can be developed. The latter determines the trajectory of a particular power's rise in the global system in relation to its position within its neighborhood and region. In this work, we seek to explore both these areas on the basis that, given the tight linkages between the various levels of the system, India's neighborhood strategies and performance contribute either positively or negatively to regional and global performance.

A third area of discussion tends to focus more on the nature of the international order itself—that is, the different levels within it and how they are defined. In this vein, Barry Buzan and Ole Waever consider the emergence of what they call a "super security complex" encompassing East Asia, Southeast Asia, and South Asia.[15] This level of discussion is highly relevant insofar as an understanding of the different levels of international activity, and what defines them, can tell us a great deal about the behavior of individual countries as they interact at those various levels. But the downward focus on India and its neighborhood in the present work, and what that tells us about the constraints acting on it within higher levels of the system due to the strategic "gravity" pulling it back to South Asia, causes us to be a little more skeptical about India's role in traditional strategic terms in the wider Asia-Pacific. That is not to say that Buzan's entire focus is on the strategic. In his later work, India's soft power and engagement in regional associations are also factored in. But we are more skeptical of India's role in strategic balancing, at least in the short to medium term, than Buzan.[16]

As India rises to power within the context of its difficult neighborhood, important questions arise. First, how are India and its neighbors bound together across their porous borders, and why is it that these links have tended to be negative? Second, how does India's position in South Asia affect its capacity to operate independently within its wider Asian and global mileux? Third, what strategies might New Delhi adopt in order better to stabilize India's internal security situation, integrate India within South Asia, and ensure that it becomes part of a region of growth and prosperity? And finally, how does India's likely trajectory to power, shaped as it is by its negative South Asian environment, impact on the developing, increasingly unstable Asian order?

India in its South Asian setting provides an excellent subject for examining these questions. India is widely seen as a rising power and potential world power. Yet it is also wrestling with a difficult neighborhood that puts it on the wrong side of the tracks, as it were, in which to grow up as a world power.

In approaching questions concerning rising powers, we should be mindful of the measures of power we adopt. Different measures will lead to different assessments of the trajectory of the nation in question. Classic determinants of power include size of population and territory, endowment of natural resources, size and capability of military forces, economic size and character, competence and industry of the inhabitants, political stability, and administrative and diplomatic capability. Joseph S. Nye and others have added the concept of "soft power" to this list.[17] Recently a number of scholars have pointed to the need not only to view power in the context of a country's neighborhood and region, but also to relate these levels of analysis to the global perspective thus introducing (or, more accurately, reintroducing) the concept of location to the list.[18]

For several reasons this issue of location is often underemphasized. As Benjamin Miller points out, international relations discourse has tended to be dominated by the question of big-power relations. The commentary has often ignored the role of neighborhoods in generating friction and war. Miller argues that lack of correspondence between what he calls "nation" and the borders of the countries in question is what makes some neighborhoods more prone to friction and war than others.[19] By implication, the effect on rising powers caught up in such neighborhoods is also overlooked. Crucially for our argument about India's rise to power, South Asia is one such neighborhood.

The focus on globalization in recent years also means that the role of location in power analysis tends to be underemphasized. In a globalized, technologically advanced setting, the nature of trade, finance, access to resources, and application of military power are no longer necessarily determined by location, or not significantly so—or so the argument runs. In the case of military power, modern weapons—including intercontinental ballistic missiles (ICBMs), nuclear-powered naval vessels, and even drones—can be global in reach. Distance and even "hard" borders can be overcome by the digital revolution in communications—cybercrime and cyberwarfare being two of many available examples.

The argument that globalization has trumped distance (and hence location) is true but relevant only up to a point. Intercontinental weapons do not necessarily have traction in every situation. Even the "pilot" of a drone is dependent on local intelligence and local hosting of facilities. Luckily, since the Second World War, all of the "dialogue of power" in the modern world has been conducted at the substrategic warfare levels. Major war is not practical at the level of the day-to-day exercise of power. Levers can be pulled against one's competitor well short of major conventional war. Given the costs of large-scale, conventional war and especially nuclear war, proxy war has evolved to achieve one's goals at the submajor conflict level. But proxy war is heavily dependent on having a cross-border or internal *force de frappe*, and so location is again brought into play.

In South Asia, where there are preexisting historical negativities, globalization has often acted to amplify and exacerbate negative, substate, cross-border phenomena. Such negative factors can include the spread of radicalizing and destabilizing political and religious ideas, transnational crime, international terrorism, environmental issues, and feelings of anomie with rapid economic and social change generated. Globalization also enables peer competitors of a regional power to interact within a particular region to support smaller neighbors of that power through trade, finance, and military relations. India's South Asian neighbors are thus strengthened by China against what they see as India's dominance. Such globalized but locally impacting problems complicate intraregional, state-on-state relations.

The globalization debate also causes us to consider the role of economic globalization both as a driver of growth and also possibly of inequality and distress. The role of economic globalization in India is contested. Some argue that it has on the whole been positive, and some that it has not solved the pressing problems of poverty and inequality.[20] While this debate is important, including in terms of its implications for India's capacity as a power, it is one already intensely canvassed. We concentrate in this book more on gaps in the debate. We believe that one is the question of how security and governance affect India's overall economic and political performance, both in terms of its own polity and in relation to its neighborhood and region. Although Ramachandran Guha and his colleagues raised these issues in the context of India's rise to power, they have not been thoroughly explored in relation to the way India is strategically enmeshed with South Asia.[21] So to the extent that the issue of economic reform is covered, the focus is on corruption and other security and governance issues and how they might have contributed to the failure of India's policy of distributing wealth and achieving its core goal of inclusive growth. We are also interested in the effects of trade liberalization, especially on relations between India and China and the concomitant effects on India's international relations and security.

The implications of location needs to be considered not just in terms of how it might be affected either positively or negatively by globalization, but also as a factor in itself. In these terms, the role of location in determining a country's trajectory to power and the character of that power is borne out by history. With the possible exception of the British Empire, which arose out of a maritime and trading domain "in a fit of absence of mind"[22] and depended on offshore balancing in relation to Europe, rising powers have needed first to consolidate their own neighborhoods and regions, as Varun Sahni and Rajesh Rajagopalan point out.[23] In relation to South Asia, India falls well short of that goal.

By refocusing on the role of location in helping to determine the trajectory of emerging powers, we are also forced to reconsider the study of geopolitics. In its classic form, "geopolitics is about the interaction among states and empires *in a particular geographical setting* [emphasis added]." Position "presents opportunities to, and imposes limitations on, the state."[24] Henry Kissinger, however, reconfigured the term to mean balance-of-power politics in the broad sense and as such changed the meaning in modern discourse to delink it from geography.[25]

In geopolitical terms, a country's location can confer both advantage and disadvantage.[26] In one sense, India is advantaged by the fact that it is the sole littoral power of potential in the Indian Ocean Region (IOR). The next largest littoral power in conventional terms is Australia, and it can only ever aspire to be a middle power. China, however, is vying for power among several significant powers in its Asia-Pacific region, including the United States, Russia, and Japan. This is not to say that these Pacific powers do not have a military presence in the IOR, but rather that to exercise it in conventional terms they suffer a significant disadvantage vis-à-vis India. This can best be illustrated by the fact that the steaming time for any of them to get there is roughly three times that of India.[27] Indeed, India has been somewhat dramatically likened by a Chinese analyst to a "giant aircraft carrier" pointing down at the vital energy sea-lanes of communication (SLOCs) of the Indian Ocean.[28]

But location can also confer disadvantage. The mere fact of proximity to hostile or suspicious neighbors means that an emerging power is grappling with different sets of problems than those it will encounter on the world stage. As Paul points out, "both state and societal-level interactions and insecurities [are in play]" at the neighborhood level.[29] These substate factors and actors are capable of acting either for the good of the neighborhood or in a fissiparous way. Europe has now had a long history of positive civil society relations. But in South Asia, substate actors often have negative effects. A good example is the terrorist organizations operating across the border from Pakistan to attack India and the negative effect they are having on Pakistan-India relations. The group Lashka-e-Toiba (LeT) has had a highly negative effect on India-Pakistan relations, especially in terms of the attacks on Mumbai of November, 26, 2008 (henceforth "26/11"). Moreover, given the substate status of such groups, they are more difficult to deal with. To deal with them would involve far-reaching domestic interventions going well beyond relatively simple state-on-state solutions. Reform on this scale is neither easy nor quick and is especially difficult for one state to impose on another. This requirement to impose radical societal reform extending across the entire South Asian subregion has been identified by Indian scholars such as Surjit Datta in their analysis of India's rise to power.[30] But as we shall see later in this book, such "leveraging," while certainly to be desired, is more easily said than done.

In South Asia, the necessity for neighborhood-wide change arises from the fact that the problem of enmeshed dissonance is particularly pronounced. South Asia has suffered on a number of levels: its colonial inheritance, including its inadequate postcolonial borders; its history of international interference; the fact that it is a melting pot of religions and cultures; and its "Kautiliyan" strategic architecture, whereby the Indian "giant," surrounded by relative "pygmies," is balanced by more distant powers such as China.[31] As Sumit Ganguly and others point out, according to the "stability-instability" paradox, nuclearization has failed to stabilize this situation. It may have restrained large-scale, conventional war, as argued by Devin T. Hagerty, but it has also provided cover for asymmetrical warfare.[32] Moreover, it has transformed a subregional situation that according to all measures ought to be unipolar into a bipolar one focusing on India and Pakistan.[33]

As pointed out by Arndt Michael, these interlocking problems within South Asia not only necessitate more robust regional cooperative mechanisms in order to deal with them, but also, paradoxically, make the construction of active regionalism, as opposed to the passive or "soft" regionalism kind, more difficult to achieve.[34] A potentially dominant subregional state such as India will perceive that it has no incentive to foster regionalism except of a soft nature that will not harm its perceived interests by allowing smaller countries to gang up on it. Nor will it want its competitor, Pakistan, to sow mischief (as New Delhi would see it) through the regional mechanism. This soft regionalism has certainly been the experience with the South Asian Association for Regional Cooperation (SAARC), founded in 1985.

But the question remains: Is the failure of regionalism within South Asia a by-product of preexisting antagonism, particularly between Pakistan and India, or does it reflect other failures within SAARC and its structure? This is an important question. If the failures of SAARC are mainly attributable to the India-Pakistan competition, then a breakthrough in bilateral relations would need to precede any meaningful advance in the capability of SAARC. If the problems of SAARC are inbuilt into its structures, on the other hand, then India could seek to modify those structures unilaterally, just as it imposed them unilaterally in the first place. In this sense, therefore, the two issues (how best to develop regionalism and the role of region in shaping emerging powers) are tightly linked.

Alternatively India could seek to transform South Asia irrespective of the role of Pakistan and see what might occur—a strategy made possible by the fact that not much harm and much potential good could arise. If such a strategy of "going around Pakistan" in South Asia could be made to work, then Pakistan may eventually have no choice but to latch on to the benefits accruing to its SAARC neighbors—in other words, to "bandwagon." Any such strategy could be conducted bilaterally or, where appropriate, multilaterally through SAARC and other associations.

Another way of seeking to go around Pakistan could involve India redefining its neighborhood either more broadly or in different geographic directions. This might be possible in the sense that region "is largely a subjective construct," depending on how one chooses to define it.[35] To an extent, India is already engaged in the exercise of redefining its neighborhood in terms of its "Look East" strategy and the related regional associations it has either constructed or participated in where they already exist. One such linking organization constructed by India is the Bay of Bengal Initiative for Multi-Sectoral Technical and Economic Cooperation (BIMSTEC). BIMSTEC provides a bridge between some South Asian and some Southeast Asian countries, while at the same time excluding Pakistan and China. If progressed more vigorously, it could also have the potential role of creating physical connectivity into Southeast Asia and thus facilitating Look East. But we argue that to do so it would need to include such major players as China and Indonesia, if not Pakistan. In addition, India is also now a member of regional groupings, such as the ASEAN Regional Forum (ARF) and the East Asia Summit (EAS).

India is also seeking to expand its influence and engagement in the IOR. It has played a leading role in developing regional groupings for the region, such as the Indian Ocean Rim Association for Regional Cooperation (recently renamed the Indian Ocean Rim Association, or IORA) and the Indian Ocean Naval Symposium (IONS). These organizations were established primarily for New Delhi's strategic purposes. One such purpose is to attempt to excise Pakistan from India's regional deliberations, at least in the case of IORA. Another is to ensure that organizations like IORA are structured in accordance with India's version of soft regionalism, which ensures that it can continue to dominate the IOR strategic discourse as the sole power of potential on the littoral.

The fact of South Asia's negative strategic enmeshment means that it has become the proving ground for a number of global competitions. The first of these was played out during the Cold War over the communist challenge to capitalism, when the former Soviet Union invaded Afghanistan. More recently, the competition has been over the nature of Islam and to a lesser extent Hinduism as their adherents confront the modern, globalized world. Other influences include the influx of Western, liberal economic ideas. Escalating competition within the neighborhood over water is spreading beyond South Asia and becoming a factor in Sino-Indian relations. The competition generated as the great Asian powers rise and consume more of the world's limited resources drawn from further afield is another important factor linking the different levels of the international system around South Asia. Chinese concerns about a rising potential peer competitor, India, how it might eventually link strategically with the United States, and how this might in turn threaten its key energy SLOCs crossing the Indian Ocean are also important factors driving linkages between different levels of the system.

These negative links between the countries of South Asia and their relationship to regional and global concerns have effectively acted to draw in outside powers. The dissonance within South Asia has also had the effect of keeping India "pinned down" in its neighborhood by thrusting on to it an essentially continental form of security.[36] These problems have, in turn, impacted on the pace and trajectory of India's rise as an Asian and global power, with implications for the Asian and global orders.

All this is occurring while a new order is developing in Asia caused by China's rise. Just what it will be is unclear. It may involve a peaceful rise for China, including further progress in developing regionalism through existing mechanisms such as the ARF and the EAS. It may involve the emergence of a "G2" (China plus the United States) or the formation of a "concert of powers," the latter being a difficult task in the Asian context, as Amitav Acharya points out.[37] More darkly, it may entail attempts to balance China's rise and even contain it so that we would have an emerging order that might look somewhat like the Cold War. As a major, emerging Asian power, India will have a critical role in helping to determine which of these outcomes might prevail. India's role will also be important by virtue of its geostrategic position vis-à-vis the energy-carrying SLOCs of the IOR and its developing relationship with the United States, which already has a strategic edge.

If India can stabilize and consolidate its domestic and neighborhood environments, it will be more capable of meeting its own goal of strategic autonomy. If, on the other hand, it continues to remain mired in the problems of South Asia, its growth and stability will be impaired and its strategic reliance on the United States, especially vis-à-vis China, will be greater. Its potential role in any Asian order will likely be more restrained.

To achieve a better outcome, it will need to adopt a step-by-step approach according to which attention is paid to domestic and neighborhood consolidation (the two being closely connected) as a priority over wider regional and global activity. Given the nature of the malaise confronting India and its neighbors and the fact that strategies will need to be built from the domestic domain upward, any successful efforts to address domestic and neighborhood issues will be a long-term project. This means that the Sino-US relationship will remain the crucial one for the foreseeable future in setting the Asian security agenda.

The book is broadly divided into two parts. The first, which is made up of the first four chapters, analyzes the interlocking set of problems India confronts domestically, in its neighborhood, and in its wider region. The final two chapters attempt to prescribe a set of strategies to address these problems.

Within this broad framework, chapter 1 deals with India's domestic problems. These are largely issues of governance—matters concerning corruption, crime, terrorism, policing, security, and the effect of these factors on economic development and India's strategy of "inclusive growth." Other problems considered are economic issues, such as the urgent need for better infrastructure and emerging environmental strain. Other important domestic issues such as environmental degredation and the economic effects of globalization are discussed in the next two chapters in the context of their international ramifications.

The second chapter examines how these various "pathologies" interact across the porous borders of South Asia, vitiating relations within the region and creating a region of enmeshed dissonance incapable of finding its developmental stride so all can rise on the same tide.

Chapter 3 considers global influences on the unstable situation in South Asia. These include the attraction of global powers to South Asia by the "bait" provided by dissonance; the closely related issue of the incursion of Wahhabi and Salafist (henceforth "Wahhabi"[38]) forms of Islam on South Asia's hitherto mainly syncretic, Sufi versions of that faith; the influence of global doctrines of economic liberalism; and the impact of global environmental issues such as climate change.

Chapter 4 canvasses the impacts of the developments explored within the previous chapters on India's wider domain, including the IOR and those parts of Asia to India's east. It examines the way India's membership of a troubled neighborhood has impacted on the disposition of defense and security resources to produce an essentially continental power, the way this has in turn affected India's aspirations for a major naval role in the IOR, and how it has shaped India's Look East policy and its approach to cooperative regional mechanisms.

The second part, which includes the final two chapters, advocates a strategy that is essentially a step-by-step approach to India's rise to power. We argue that while this approach is consonant with India's two broad strategies of "inclusive growth" domestically and seeking "strategic autonomy" in international relations, these strategies in themselves do not provide a complete blueprint of what India needs to do to achieve such goals.

These two final chapters draw on the analysis of the previous four chapters to argue that India must give priority to its pressing domestic and neighborhood problems in order more fully to approach its challenges in the regional and global spheres. That is not to say India will be constrained from engaging more broadly, but that it should arrange its priorities differently than it now does. Domestic reform is essential, both as a means of achieving greater resilience (or "target hardening") in India against cross-border problems in a difficult part of the world and of presenting India in a better light to its neighbors, international partners, and investors.

Chapter 5 draws on the previous analysis of India's domestic problems in order to suggest how India might address some of its governance problems. Suggestions include a radical reform of the policing, internal security, and justice systems, and the encouragement of a "virtuous circle" between the transparency agencies of government, civil society, a better-informed public, the media, digital government, and democracy.

The first part of chapter 6 extends this prescriptive framework into South Asia. It argues for a range of strategies, including the dual policy of patience with Pakistan while going around it into the rest of South Asia; greatly enhanced technical, trade, and economic assistance to the rest of South Asia; creation of far better transport, communication, and infrastructure linkages; and construction of far more robust transport and investment corridors through the eastern parts of South Asia, especially Bangladesh, into Southeast Asia and China, as a means of creating greater economic and social integration both within South Asia and between South Asia and Asia to its east, thereby strengthening the Look East policy. It argues that the Indian economy can afford a higher level of economic assistance to achieve these neighborhood goals than the minimal aid it already provides. It also suggests that one way of assisting India to raise the vast amounts of capital needed for infrastructure reform is to do exactly what the "Asian Tigers," such as China, the Republic of Korea, and Taiwan, did vis-à-vis the West—that is, to utilize Western capital and technology to build economies capable of both integrating with and competing with the West. But it also notes that in the current etiolated Western economic environment, India will need to resort to Chinese and other available East Asian capital and technology to do this, much as it may stick in New Delhi's craw to do so in respect to China.

The second part of chapter 6 considers what strategies India might adopt in the wider region beyond South Asia. It advocates the strengthening of the Look East policy, including by building on its domestic and neighborhood reforms to create greater soft-power credibility in Southeast and East Asia, seeking to construct genuine regionalism in the IOR as a means of preempting the worrying security dilemma developing there between India and the United States on one hand and China on the other, reforming the investment and diplomatic climates to make India a far more receptive partner of East Asian countries and thus unleash its vast soft-power potential, and abjuring for now a strategic role in the Asia-Pacific as being unrealistic and not helpful in terms of creating conditions for China's peaceful rise.

The object of this total package of domestic, neighborhood, and regional reforms would be to ensure that India can persist with its autonomous role, rise as an independent player in the Asia-Pacific, and thus contribute to an eventual multilateral balance similar to, if not the same as, a loose concert of powers—recognizing however, that a concert of powers is very difficult to achieve and maintain, especially in the current unstable Asian context. India would thus be capable of fulfilling the role envisaged for it by C. Raja Mohan and others as a multiethnic, democratic partner of the West in seeking to stabilize an unstable situation.[39]

NOTES

1. It is a somewhat invidious exercise to select scholars from a wide field such as this. The following is by no means an exhaustive list of the many and varied works touching on this subject. For a list of works relating specifically to India's interactions with South Asia, see Behuria, Pattanaik, and Gupta, "Does India Have a Neighbourhood Policy?," 229–46, 231–33. See also Muni, "Problem Areas in India's Neighbourhood Policy"; Sridharan, "International Relations Theory and South Asia"; Paul, "State Capacity and South Asia's Perennial Insecurity Problems"; Rajagopalan and Sahni, "India and the Great Powers"; Cortright and Matoo, "Carrots and Cooperation"; Kumar and Menon, *The Long View from Delhi*; Destradi, *Indian Foreign and Security Policy in South Asia*; Singh, *India in South Asia*; and Gordon, *India's Rise to Power in the Twentieth Century and Beyond*, especially part 2, "Limits to Power."
2. Or, in the words of Sridharan, "how [individual states] are organized and constructed, and by extension, how they are articulated within the regional and world system." Sridaharan, "International Relations Theory and South Asia," 11.
3. By "neighborhood," we refer here to South Asia. We use the term "region" for India's wider regional context, to include the Indian Ocean region, Southwest Asia, Southeast Asia, East Asia, and the Middle East. This contrasts with the more traditional nomenclature, which posits four levels: "domestic, regional [or neighborhood in our terminology], super-regional, and global." See ibid., 12. Buzan and Waever also posit four basic levels: domestic, the "security complex," the "super complex," and the global. See Buzan and Waever, *Regions and Powers.*
4. Ripsman and Paul, *Globalization and the National Security State*, 12–13.
5. This aspect of India's foreign policy was recently publicized by the widely noted document by Khilnani et al., *NonAlignment 2.0.* But well before that, it was a feature of Indian policy. See Government of India, Ministry of External Affairs, *Annual Report 2004–05*, i. The policy of strategic autonomy is discussed more fully in chapter 4.
6. This "core strategy" is discussed further in chapters 1 and 4. It has been pursued consistently but not always successfully from the time of Jawaharlal Nehru. See Government of India, Indian Planning Commission, *Approach Paper to the Twelfth Five Year Plan.*

7. Quoted in Nayar, "A World Role," 123.
8. Tanham, *India's Strategic Culture.*
9. See, for example, Sagar, "State of Mind," 801–16, and Bajpai, "India's Strategic Culture," 245.
10. Bajpai, "India's Strategic Culture," 245–303, 247–48.
11. See Khilnani et al., *NonAlignment 2.0*, and Kumar and Menon, *The Long View from Delhi.*
12. Khilnani et al., *NonAlignment 2.0*, 10.
13. Tellis was referring to a term originally used by the Central Intelligence Agency (CIA). See Tellis, *India as a New Global Power.*
14. See, for example, Paul, *International Relations Theory and Regional Transformation*; Tow, "Setting the Context," 1–28; and Miller, *States, Nations and Great Powers.*
15. Buzan and Waever, *Regions and Powers*, and Buzan, "Asia."
16. See, for example, Buzan, "Asia," 4.
17. Nye, *Soft Power.*
18. See, for example, Fawn, *Globalising the Regional, Regionalising the Global.*
19. Miller, *States, Nations, and the Great Powers.*
20. For a recent debate on these lines, see Sen and Drèze, *An Uncertain Glory*, and Bhagwati and Panagariya, *Why Growth Matters.*
21. London School of Economics, "India." See also Guha, "Democratic to a Fault?"
22. From Sir John Seeley, *Expansion of England*, as quoted in Brantlinger, *Rule of Darkness*, 81.
23. Rajagopalan and Sahni, "India and the Great Powers," 7.
24. Sempa, *Geopolitics*, 5.
25. See Gray and Sloan, *Geopolitics, Geography and Strategy*, 1–2.
26. Sempa, *Geopolitics.*
27. Anonymous, "The LM2500 Demonstration," 38, and Roy, "The Indian Navy from the Bridge," 74.
28. Erickson, "The Growth of China's Navy," 657.
29. Paul, "State Capacity and South Asia's Perennial Insecurity Problems," 9.
30. Datta, "The Asian Transition and India's Emerging Strategy," 25–26.
31. Kautiliya argued that neighbors are often enemies and such enemies often seek to balance their enemies with powerful friends in more distant places. See Kautiliya, *Arthashastra*, chapter 2, "Peace and Exertion," in book VI, "The Source of Sovereign States." Kautiliya and his ideas are discussed in more detail in chapter 2.
32. Ganguly, *Conflict Unending*, 110, 122–23. Devin T. Hagerty's position has evolved from his initial argument that nuclearization is stabilizing, to one in which it restrains large-scale conventional war but also can "enable" asymmetrical warfare. See Hagerty, "The Kargil War," 100–16. For an excellent summary of the optimist-pessimist debate on nuclear proliferation in South Asia, see Krepon, "The Perils of Proliferation in South Asia."
33. Sridharan, "International Relations Theory and South Asia," 12. Sridharan uses the term "multipolar" rather than "bipolar," but the implication remains the same,

namely that India's dominance has been challenged by Pakistan's acquisition of nuclear weapons.

34. Michael, *India's Foreign Policy and Regional Multilateralism.*
35. Camilleri, *Regionalism in the New Asia-Pacific Order*, 2. See also Sahni, "Regional Dynamics of Emerging Powers," 59.
36. The idea of "continental" versus "maritime" security is discussed more fully in chapter 4.
37. Acharya, "A Concert of Asia?" The idea of the concert of powers is discussed more fully in chapter 4.
38. Salafism and Wahhabism are similar in that they are both highly conservative and refer back to the Koran and Hadith as the sole source of reference. But they are a little different in their actual doctrine, and some Salafists resent Salafism being equated with Wahhabism, which is the "state doctrine" of Saudi Arabia. For convenience, we shall henceforth refer to those in this general mold of Islam as "Wahhabis."
39. Mohan, "India and the Balance of Power," 17–32.

CHAPTER 1

GOVERNANCE AND THE "HYBRID INHERITANCE"

India's governance problems partly derive from the fact that this vast, diverse collection of "nations" was shaped into a single political entity under an alien colonial disposition. Westminster ideas of democracy and governance have been overlaid on preexisting, deep-seated, and diverse ethnic, social, and economic structures. This tectonic change has occurred in a relatively compressed period of history.

Although India is similar to many postcolonial societies in respect of this overlay of systems, it is different by virtue of its size, diversity, complexity, and the ancient and refined nature of the series of societies now called India. This means that India is caught in a constant process of change as ancient predilections and traditions percolate up through the mantle of British colonial norms and these norms are in turn challenged from outside by the forces of globalization.

India is a giant country of 1.2 billion. It is more diverse than Europe, with thirteen major languages (each spoken by over 1 percent of the population), a major religious division between Hindus (81 percent) and Muslims (13.5 percent), and significant Sikh, Jain, Christian, animist, and other minorities. Hindus are themselves divided into hundreds of regional and caste-based traditions. Overlaid on this tapestry is a federated, Westminster democracy combined at the grass roots with locally derived institutions such as the village *panchayat* (governing council), *chowkidar* (watchman/policeman), and caste-based *jajmani* system (a patron-client system of mutual obligation and exchange between higher and lower castes). Even supposedly modern institutions such as the police service are heavily influenced by power relationships reflecting the underlying social structure.[1]

The borders bequeathed to India at independence in 1947 were in many ways arbitrary. They reflected a diverse collection of powers lumped together under the convenient rubric "British India." They also reflected the need to induct the populations of the so-called native states—British protectorates within overall borders of British India that were ruled in all matters except defense, communications, foreign affairs, and trade by local princes. These native states had developed at different rates, from the sophisticated and educated state of Travencore in the South, to the semifeudal principalities of Rajasthan, still ruled according to Hindu ideals of kingship reflected in texts such as the *Mahabharata* and Laws of Manu.

At the periphery of this "mainstream" India is to be found a collection of states in the Northeast containing Indo-Tibetan tribal populations (many of them converted to Christianity under the British), Assamese, Bengalis (both Hindu and Muslim), and animist tribal populations. These states also include Bihari and other migrants from the so-called Hindi heartland who came to work the tea plantations.

At the northwestern periphery of India are to be found Kashmiris from the Vale of Kashmir. They are predominantly Muslim and regard themselves as a culturally and racially distinct nation with a set of cultural norms known as the Kashmiriat. But even the modern state of Jammu and Kashmir contains significant Hindu and Ladakhi (Buddhist Tibetan) minorities.

Giant swathes of the central and eastern parts of India are occupied by tribal populations. Many of these people follow animist traditions that are significantly different from those of Hindus of the heartland. They have a close, quasi-religious relationship to the forested land on which they depend.

This diverse, complex society has been subject to a rapid process of modernization involving industrialization, urbanization, and democratization. Since economic liberalization commenced in 1991, economic growth rates have risen steadily and now range between 6 and 9 percent (although they have recently fallen to 5 percent). At independence in 1947, India was only 17.6 percent urban; today it is 28 percent urban.[2] The consultancy firm McKinsey Global Institute estimates that nearly 600 million people will live in cities by 2030 and that $1.2 trillion in investment will be needed to cater for them.[3] The size and rapid growth of these cities pose significant practical, environmental, and governance challenges.

An equally challenging problem has been the pace of democratization. The 1935 Government of India Act, under which India was governed until independence, gave only partial suffrage and mandated diarchy at the central and provincial levels. Leaving aside reservation of certain electorates for minorities, the Constitution of 1950 provided for universal suffrage. At the time of independence, India was only 12 percent literate, so the introduction of universal suffrage was in many ways a radical step. It is not surprising that the democracy that has developed does not yet meet all the standards expected of a so-called mature democracy.

While modernization and democratization have produced benefits, their effects on Indian political life have not always been as intended. As early as 1962,

Myron Weiner outlined some of these negative effects.[4] He noted that democracy creates expectations that the state is unable to fulfill in a timely manner and that this gap in turn creates a contradiction between the needs of a rational, planned economy and the perceived need to satisfy immediate political demands of specific groups of constituents. In these conditions of scarcity, constituents use different methods to try to "capture" the goods provided by the state, including corruption, violence, and the peddling of undue influence. Many since have commented on the ills of Indian democracy. Robin Jeffrey notes the vast unfolding of knowledge and information that democracy, education, and the free press have wrought. But he also points out that one implication is that India's ancient symbols, ethnicities, and religious and social divisions tend to bubble to the surface as a result and that modernization and prosperity do not necessarily provide an antidote.[5] Arundhati Roy, in her collection of essays *Listening to Grasshoppers*, takes the analysis of the discontents of democracy a step further. She argues that political parties "seem to have realized that a democratic mandate can legitimize their pillaging in a way that nothing else can."[6] In a view robustly contested by Ashutosh Varshney, Paul Brass claims that under democracy, communalism—particularly between Hindus and Muslims—is often used by those seeking influence for their own political ends.

Even the tools of democracy itself, such as the polling booth, are often co-opted by specific interest groups, particularly in rural areas. Caste and community politics have inserted themselves into all the interstices of Indian official and business life, as evidenced in today's caste politics in states such as Uttar Pradesh. In some states, a close relationship—known simply as "the nexus"—has emerged between the political class, the police, and criminals. In other words, politics is now as much about the division of the spoils as it is about achieving India's core policy of inclusive growth. The state is in possession of enormous assets of power and wealth—more so now in the modern climate of the pervasive state than it once was. Just who manages to capture that wealth and who misses out has become the stuff of politics. Pervasive corruption is one of a number of outcomes of this type of politics.

Although some assert that corruption oils the rusty cogs of bureaucracy and assists growth,[7] the flip side is that it also stymies development, especially for the poor. In a perceptive article, Raghbendra Jha and colleagues argue that while corrupt payments on the part of the poor generate considerable access to services and thus provide a sound apparent "return" on the rupee, such payments are also necessary because of the increasing numbers of intermediaries between the goods provided by the state and their recipients. In other words, corruption is necessary because of the impediment provided by corrupt bureaucrats and elected officials in the first place.[8] Also, corruption creates investment uncertainty and acts as a virtual tax on investment.[9] According to Bo Rothstein, "there is by now quite compelling empirical support for claiming that the quality of a country's political institutions determines its economic and social development."[10]

The core problem is that the state has no levers left to pull to achieve its policy objectives, no matter how worthwhile they may seem. By the time the rupee leaves the central exchequer and travels on its vast journey to the district and village levels, little is left. Rajiv Gandhi famously remarked that only 15 paisa in the rupee (15 percent) reach those for whom they are intended. And even if a percentage does make it to that level, there is no guarantee that the doctor or teacher it employs will be there in the clinic or classroom. A recent World Bank study found that only 40 percent of the food disseminated through the public distribution system reaches the poor.[11]

In a climate of pervasive corruption, to ask the state to heal itself is tantamount to asking it to pull itself up by its bootstraps. This problem of developing an antidote to state corruption is discussed in greater detail in chapter 5. For now the task is to chronicle the extent of the problem, its effects, and how it shapes India's place in its neighborhood and region.

But first a caveat. India's is a Western-derived legal system in which corruption is rendered illegal under the Constitution, and nobody is above the law (except serving presidents and governors). Even in such a system, however, "corruption" is a slippery, culturally loaded term that only serves us to a limited extent in exposing and explaining India's governance problems. The anthropologist's perspective on it has tended to be different from the legal view. According to legal perspectives, corruption represents criminal activity mainly, but not wholly, on the part of the servants of the state, designed to gain an illegal benefit. Anthropologists, however, seek to understand the nonlegal customs and social interpretations that may be found beneath the surface of actions considered legally corrupt.

In the Weberian state supposedly representing the democratic West, universalist perceptions of right prevail in which fairness involves equal treatment of all. But what if the prevailing political culture is one in which particularist notions of right prevail—for example, in which it is right to give favors to those whom you owe something, whether as filial loyalty or just a favor?[12]

Hindu notions of morality are enshrined, for example, in the idea of *dharma* (literally "to hold fast, to make secure").[13] According to Wendy Doniger, adherence to "law" (presumably human law) is only one of many attributes of *dharma*, others being listed as "duty, religion, religious merit, morality, social and ritual obligations, the law, and justice."[14] The implication is that particularist notions of right—for example, as they apply to the extended family and behavior within it, relations between castes, or rules governing the behavior of kings—may be as valid in determining behavior of a ruler as Western-derived perceptions of how society should function as a whole. The idea of supporting the existing social structure may be deemed more "moral" than supporting the so-called objective rule of law within the modern state. An example of this difference in perception comes readily to hand. Patrick French calculated that two-thirds of the members of parliament (MPs) in the Lok Sabha (India's lower house) who were age forty or under had "inherited" their seats from a family member.[15] While this would be taken as a shocking example of nepotism in the West, Indians perhaps hold a different view of it, which presumably is why they were elected in the first place.

According to A. L. Basham, kings were deemed to be both divinely appointed (and to an extent divine) and also to have a "contract" with the people to preserve the existing social order according to the sacred texts, protect the people, and lead in war.[16] Nor were pomp, luxury, and ceremony necessarily seen as bad according to traditional notions of power. People were to take pleasure in the fact that their ruler was splendid—an idea not out of keeping with imperial Britain. We see vestiges of this idea in Uttar Pradesh, where followers of the recently defeated chief minister, Mayawati (one name only), who comes from a low-caste background, took pleasure in the conspicuous consumption surrounding her, including the massive project of erecting statues to her throughout the "realm."

Ideas of power and how it is to be exercised may vary considerably from the Westminster tradition that justice is blind. In Hinduism, power may be interpreted in very personal, nonlegalistic ways. Often surrounded by corrupt officials, the Hindu king should short-circuit their influence by dealing *directly* with the people. According to Basham, "the best of Indian kings at all times have made the public audience or dabar an important instrument of government."[17] Underlying this idea is a much more direct and personal interpretation of power than the one idealized (if not always practiced) in the West, where the ruler is constrained by the rules governing the state, of which he or she is considered simply a part. Indira Gandhi understood this idea of the personal implicit in power very well. As prime minister, she used to hold *dabar* once a week, during which anyone from anywhere in India (then numbering 683 million people) could petition her.

Ideas of power and rightness can also reflect the structure of the society that lies within the overt, supposedly objective structures of the modern state. In more prosaic terms than those of the anthropologist, a corruption-fighting senior policeman can say of his experience of the Central Bureau of Investigation (CBI): "It was an unprecedented offence [on my part] in the annals of the CBI to proceed against the big VIPs in power . . . . Strong action against even the worst accused is foreign to [the] Indian ethos. It constitutes deviant behaviour on the part of a civil servant and is almost forbidden if the accused happens to be from higher echelons of society."[18]

Where corruption is pervasive, it is also likely to assume its own "culture," rules, and morality. This occurs because even in such societies things must work *to an extent*. Informal rules surrounding corruption were pervasive in Suharto's Indonesia and also operate in India today. Beatrice Anne Jauregui, who embedded herself with the police service in Uttar Pradesh over a period of several years, reported that there is "good" and "bad" money within corruption and that there are social rules to be followed based on caste, power, and influence in determining the structure of corruption. Even so-called encounter killings—extrajudicial killings of suspected gangsters or terrorists by police or armed forces—which are clearly against the law and "corrupt," are often considered justified by the perpetrators and the general populace so long as those killed are generally considered to be a blight on society.[19]

Corruption is also sometimes viewed as a means by which lower-caste people, otherwise excluded by custom, education, and law, can become upwardly mobile in India's supposedly rigid caste structure. Ashish Nandy controversially made such an assertion at the 2013 Jaipur writers' festival, triggering a harsh backlash from lower-caste groups who wrongly believed he was asserting that lower castes were more corrupt.[20] In a related point, folk notions of the role of the individual in negotiating the "loaded dice" of everyday living in India's still hierarchical and often unjust society advocate the art of *jugaad*, which can be roughly translated as the art of besting someone through trickery or worldliness.[21] Such notions have embedded within them a somewhat different view of personal morality than those idealized in the West.

To add to the concerns of the individual, the penalties of economic failure in India, which has a minimal social system beyond the extended family or network of connections, can be extreme. Often one person may be supporting an extended family of many people. To lose a job, not get a job, or not receive adequate compensation from a job carries an extreme penalty. Therefore one is more prepared to cut corners than one would be were one better supported.

What these factors together mean is that behavior that in the West would be considered to be blatant nepotism or corruption may in India be regarded as doing no more than fulfilling one's obligation to one's extended family, caste, more powerful protectors, or those to whom one owes some kind of obligation.

But, that said, we need a caveat on the caveat, as it were. We should be mindful of the fact that the state is itself caught up in a vast process of modernization and internationalization and that these forces involve increasing levels of interaction with more commonly held sets of standards. Moreover, the state and its subjects still have need of a process of development and uplift, no matter how that is to be achieved. In developmental and well-being terms, there is purpose in the mechanisms of the state working well. And in the Indian context, cultural interpretations of corruption cannot account for the growing discontent among the majority of people with India's pervasively corrupt state.

Most would admit that to address problems of development and achieve inclusive growth, the state needs "levers to pull" and higher standards of governance than those that currently exist. The Planning Commission notes in its

Eleventh Plan that access to essential services on the part of those below the poverty line is ultimate proof of "inclusive growth."[22] The problem is also illustrated by the Ministry of Home Affairs. In discussing the Maoist revolt that is gripping much of east-central India, the ministry asserts that the Maoists "operate in the vacuum created by functioning inadequacies [*sic*] of field level governance structures."[23] Even an anthropologist such as Akhil Gupta, who has done much to chronicle the anthropological elements of corruption, has this to say: "Probably more people die in India each year from humdrum causes inflicted by the failure of the developmentalist state to provision the poor with basic necessities [health, welfare, education, potable water, etc.] . . . than if there had been a major famine every ten years . . . and the anthropology of the state should ask why this kind of unspectacular suffering slips below the radar."[24]

A recent book by Armatya Sen and Jean Drèze challenges the view that Indian growth is addressing poverty and inequality.[25] Guha and his colleagues from the London School of Economics also express skepticism about India's status as a future superpower. They base this on concern that India will be held back by its failure adequately to address issues of poverty, corruption, diversity, and internal unrest and by the incomplete nature of economic reform.[26]

This complicated set of linkages between tradition and change provides background to the problems of governance India confronts. Whatever one's views on the provenance and role of corruption in India, however, there is broad consensus that the problem is holding India and its development back, that it is thwarting the key strategy of inclusive growth, and that this in turn leaves India vulnerable to a host of security issues. Since the problem of corruption appears to be at the heart of many other problems, we now turn to an examination of corruption in greater detail.

THE EXTENT OF CORRUPTION

At the heart of India's problem of corruption is the so-called nexus between corrupt politicians, law enforcement agencies, and criminals. It is this that makes the problem so difficult to overcome, since all of the potential agents of change, except perhaps the very senior levels of the judiciary, are involved. Because of this mutual back-scratching among key potential agents of change, there has previously been very little incentive for change and every impediment to it. (However, as we explore in chapter 5, that may now be changing with an upwelling of public opinion against corruption.)

The fight against corruption is also complicated by the fact that the stakes are enormous. As illustrated by the Koda case, described in greater detail below, millions—even billions—can be made by corrupt issuance of mining licenses. The alienation of land from the poor and subsequent corrupt issuance to developers, as allegedly occurred on a massive scale in the case of the Hooda government in Haryana, can also garner vast sums.[27] But the acquisition of significant funds is not confined to the powerful: Even a humble clerk in Madya Pradesh allegedly had assets of Rs 250 million on a salary of only Rs 40,000.[28] While those well placed can obtain intergenerational wealth from corruption, for the very poor it leads to failed government programs, starvation, chronic illness, and violence.

It is very difficult to measure corruption. Typically measures such as those of Transparency International (TI) are derived from surveys of business people within and outside the nation in question. According to TI, India's standing was 94 out of 176 in 2012–13.[29] Perceptions of corruption can also be ascertained from more specific surveys conducted within the concerned countries. A KPMG survey of businesses working with and in India found that 68 percent of them believed that India could achieve higher growth rates if corruption were reduced, with respondents believing that the real estate and telecommunications sectors were the most corrupt.[30]

TI has also conducted a series of surveys of households as they are affected by corruption. One such survey found that the percentage of Indians who actually paid a bribe over the last year was 54 percent, which put India as ninth worst globally and well above TI's survey of perceptions of corruption.[31] TI also conducted a survey in 2008 of 22,728 so-called below–poverty-line (BPL) households in terms of their access to basic services. The report found that "more than 40%" of BPL households paid a bribe during the year before the survey to access one of eleven nominated public services.[32] Alarmingly, the police service was ranked most corrupt of all government services in this survey. By extrapolation, these pitifully poor BPL households paid an estimated $54 million to the police in bribes on an India-wide basis.[33] But this would only be the tip of the iceberg of total bribes paid to police, most of which would have come from richer Indians. In the survey of BPL households, the ranking of corrupt services is as follows (beginning with most corrupt):

1. Police
2. Land Records/Registration
3. Housing
4. Water Supply
5. Mahatma Gandhi National Rural Employment Guarantee Scheme (MGNREGS)
6. Forest
7. Electricity
8. Health
9. Public Distribution System (PDS)

10. Banking
11. Education[34]

Jha et alia found that in rural areas, the amount of the average bribe paid by the poor for access to services had increased between 1999 and 2006 from Rs 120.33 per household to Rs 167.33 per household and that the percentage of poor households paying bribes rose over the same period from 77.7 percent to 82 percent.[35]

In another survey of global rankings of rule of law, India was also found to perform poorly. Although it ranks reasonably well in terms of transparency of government, it ranks poorly on corruption (eighty-third out of ninety-seven countries surveyed), order and security (ninety-sixth), regulatory enforcement (seventy-ninth), civil justice (seventy-eighth), and criminal justice (sixty-fourth).[36] The order and security ranking is surprisingly poor, suggesting that the country is almost nonfunctional in its day-to-day operations, which is clearly not the case.

As discussed below, these cases of corruption in the day-to-day running of the country at the grass-roots level are extremely serious in that they impact on the government's ability to achieve its developmental and economic objectives. What has most galvanized Indian government and society, however, is the problem of so-called megacorruption. A string of high-profile cases have lit the firmament of Indian civic life in recent years. They can be characterized both as a series of case studies and also in terms of what they illustrate about Indian public life. Some of the more prominent are described below, drawing on commonly available press and other sources, except where otherwise specified.

THE BOFORS BRIBERY SCANDAL

The Bofors scandal mainly took place in the 1980s. Although its effects linger on in the sclerotic Indian legal system, it has now sunk into history with the deaths of most of the major protagonists. But it is worth a brief mention because it was the first great scandal of the modern period with important political implications. Moreover, many features of the scandal were repeated in subsequent scandals: secret kickbacks; the involvement of senior politicians, bureaucrats, and shady middlemen; the central roles of money laundering and Swiss banks in hiding the money trail; the role of India's free press in unearthing the scandal; the apparent reluctance of the investigating authorities rigorously to pursue those in power; the political impact; and the judicial activism that provided a "circuit breaker."

The scandal centered on the contract India signed with the now-defunct Swedish arms manufacturer Bofors AB for $1.4 billion for howitzer field guns. The accusation that bribery had been involved in the purchase first surfaced in Sweden and was then taken up in the Indian press. The scandal simmered on through the 1980s and was a factor in the Congress Party's loss of power in the 1989 general election. Rajiv Gandhi was assassinated in 1991 and finally cleared of any wrongdoing in the scandal by the New Delhi High Court in 1994. Repeated efforts by the Central Bureau of Investigation to extradite the alleged middleman in the deal, Ottavio Quattrocchi, failed following a series of Keystone Cops–type blunders. Recently released documents suggest that both Win Chadda (an agent of Bofors) and Quattrocchi had been bribed to the tune of Rs 410 million (roughly $10 million). The funds allegedly passed to Chadda were laundered via Panama into Switzerland.[37] We do not know which senior bureaucrats and politicians subsequently received a portion of this illegal commission.

For years, the process of military modernization was held up as this scandal and other scandals within the military and Ministry of Defence meant that senior military officers, bureaucrats, and politicians were reluctant to sign off on defense deals lest the finger of suspicion be pointed at them. But this caution notwithstanding, Indian defense officials are still caught up in bribery scandals over acquisition of major defense items, such as the recent scandal over purchase of helicopters from the company AgustaWestland, which allegedly paid kickbacks disguised as software imports.[38]

THE 2G TELECOMMUNICATIONS SCAM

This fraudulent operation brings us up to the present and involved the sale in 2008 of so-called 2G spectrum licenses by the Department of Telecommunications (DOT). The deal was subsequently audited by the Indian government's Office of the Comptroller and Auditor General (CAG), which found that the licenses could have been undersold by $39 billion. (The CBI assessment of losses was considerably lower, at about $8 billion, and a joint parliamentary committee also "rubbished" the CAG sum as being too high.[39]) The auditor, Vinod Rai, criticized what he referred to as the "brazenness" of government decision making as "appalling."[40] Many of the involved companies were ineligible to bid under the rules set by the DOT. No auction was held, but awards were made on a "first past the post" system. Forty-five of the eighty-five companies involved did not have telecommunications as their primary business. Prices used were based on prices determined in 2001, and $2.8 billion was raised. In 2010, an auction of 3G spectrum realized $15 billion, suggesting the scale of the losses suffered in the bigger auction of 2008. Peddling of influence between the concerned companies and the DOT was allegedly conducted through a middle person, corporate lobbyist Niira Radia, whose sister is being investigated for opening five accounts in the British Virgin Islands, allegedly to launder the illicit funds of the beneficiaries of the scam.[41] Other alleged destinations of the "black money" included the United Kingdom, the Isle of Man, Cyprus, Mauritius, Russia, and Jersey. At least thirty-two offshore companies were involved in the laundering process, and the money from these destinations was allegedly laundered back into India in a classic loop structure.[42] The Dravida Munnetra Kazhagam (DMK) politician Kanimozha (one name) was also allegedly involved. She allegedly laundered her money via *benami* transactions and check payments, which are difficult to trace, through Mauritius.[43] (Under *benami*, which is illegal, somebody holds property on somebody else's behalf to avoid tax. Often agricultural property is involved because profits arising from it are untaxed.) The minister of telecommunications at the time the scam unfolded, the DMK politician A. Raja, was subsequently dismissed and is now under arrest and criminal investigation. Other ministers, such as Dayanidhi Maran, who held the telecommunications portfolio between 2004 and 2007, are also under investigation. The CBI, after dragging its heels on the investigation, had to be forced by the Supreme Court to speed up the process. Parliament was paralyzed for the best part of a year as the scandal was forced to a head.

The 2G scam is interesting by virtue of its scale; high public profile; effect on political perceptions, particularly of the Congress Party; the role of judicial activism, mainly through the Supreme Court; the role of money laundering into exotic locations; and because it was the then relatively low-profile public instrumentality, the CAG, that brought the matter to public notice.

THE KODA CORRUPTION SCANDAL

Madhu Koda, son of an *adiwasi* (tribal) laborer in Bihar, amassed a fortune that allegedly amounted to Rs 40 billion (roughly $1 billion) in a few short years as minister for mines and minerals and then as chief minister in the state of Jharkhand, which had been carved out of Bihar in 2000. Koda's "portfolio" included a mine in Africa, a hotel in Thailand, and a bullion company in Mumbai. Koda's illegal activities depended on confidantes who drew money through bribes out of the criminal "coal mafia" and other mines of Jharkhand on his behalf and then laundered the money. He fostered a network of associates, including children (who were employed to count the vast quantities of cash creamed off in bribes), money launderers, and trusted associates to hold his properties as "ghosts." The Koda money trail stretched from Jharkhand to Delhi and Mumbai via bus and train (which did not require baggage searches) and thence to Dubai.[44]

His downfall came about when an associate was caught by Customs officials trying to smuggle a suitcase of cash from Mumbai to Dubai. As a result of political pressure by Koda the man was initially released, but the Customs officials were so incensed that they informed the Enforcement Directorate (ED—India's financial crime investigation and enforcement body, equivalent to the Financial Crimes Enforcement Network in the United States). Once the matter received initial publicity in this way, it was hard for Koda to escape further scrutiny. But tellingly, when the Income Tax Department attempted to transfer the tax official investigating the matter after only seven months in his position, the Jharkhand High Court intervened to prevent this happening. Koda is now in jail.

The Koda saga illustrates many of the themes that we will be subsequently exploring, including the massive quantities involved in megacorruption, the criminal-political-police nexus (Koda had been protected by the police in his home state and worked through the coal mafia), the involvement of low-profile government instrumentalities, court activism, India's vigorous free press in bringing matters to justice where the police are corrupt or inept, the use of the transfer system by those attempting to thwart justice, and the widespread use of *hawala* (traditional money transfer) networks. It illustrates that corruption in India can occur at the very pinnacle of the political system.

THE ADARSH HOUSING SCAM

The Adarsh Housing Society scam involved the erection of a thirty-one-story block of flats on the Mumbai foreshore, an area containing some of the most expensive real estate in the world. The flats were originally intended for war heroes and war widows of the Kargil campaign (1999), in which almost a thousand soldiers died. The building was originally intended to be only six stories but was enlarged illegally so that it eventually came to breach environmental height provisions. Many of the flats were sold to high-ranking bureaucrats, politicians, and military officers or their relatives rather than the veterans of the Kargil campaign or their dependents. In a subsequent military inquiry, officers up to the rank of general were found to have been involved and the chief minister of Maharashtra was forced to resign and later charged with a criminal offense.

The scandal was exposed by an investigative journalist from *The Times of India*. After it was exposed, the CBI was slow to issue a first information report (FIR),[45] and the Bombay (Mumbai) High Court had to force it to do so—yet another example of the role of judicial activism in fighting corruption.

While not perhaps the most serious example of corruption, the Adarsh scandal illustrates that even the military, hitherto considered relatively clean, is now suffering from the corrosive problem of corruption. There are several similar cases where the military has sold military land in corrupt deals between military officers and developers.[46] The deal also illustrates the high profile of land deals in corruption in India and the importance of the free press in exposing corruption.

THE COMMONWEALTH GAMES SCANDAL

Collectively known in India as the CWG scandal, this consisted of a series of corrupt deals and incompetent decisions that together cost the government over Rs

10 billion (about $250 million) in lost revenue. A subsequent investigation by the CAG assessed that contractors made Rs 2.6 billion in excess of what they should have received and that delays cost the government a further Rs 9 billion.[47] At one point, the Central Vigilance Commission (CVC) was investigating twenty-two separate deals alleged to be corrupt. Eventually even the Commonwealth Games Committee's chair, Congress politician Suresh Kalmadi, was under investigation for corruption. Kalmadi has, however, continued to serve on India's Olympic Committee—a scandalous state of affairs that forced the International Olympic Committee to suspend the Indian Olympic Committee.

The scandal was important because of its international dimension, the apparent shambles of the run-up to the games, and the international shame it brought on an India that was hankering after a global position and future hosting of the Olympic Games. In dealing with the press during the scandal, bureaucrats showed themselves to be particularly insensitive, arrogant, and incompetent. In the aftermath, payments—many for contracts legitimately fulfilled—were frozen, which further worsened the international perception of India as a business destination.

THE ISRO ANTRIX-DEVAS SCANDAL

In this scandal, the commercial arm of the Indian Space Research Organisation (ISRO), Antrix, struck a deal with a media company with US and other international links, Devas Multimedia, to allocate 90 percent of the use of two communications satellites full-time over twelve years solely for that company.[48] According to *The Hindu*, Devas is a "Bangalore-based start-up, founded in 2004 . . . headed by Dr. M. G. Chandrasekhar, former Scientific Secretary at ISRO."[49] A subsequent audit by the CAG found that the deal did not even cover the costs of building, launching, and maintaining the satellites. In effect, the government would have lost Rs 1.9 million through the deal.[50] The audit also raised concerns that Antrix used 7 percent of its profits on a yearly basis to "shower" gold coins on various clients, including officials in the Department of Space, responsible for ISRO.[51]

This scandal is important because ISRO is a highly prestigious arm of the government of India, because the deal was kept secret for so long, and because a journal, *Business Line* (in *The Hindu*'s stable), was involved in uncovering it. Also, the CAG was again involved. There was an apparent conflict of interest in that a former senior employee of ISRO was at the receiving end of the deal. The deal illustrates the blatant lack of transparency and use of secrecy provisions by elements of the government of India and by implication shows the possibility of severe compromise of India's communications and defense needs by commercial interests. Had the deal gone ahead (it has now been canceled), it would have resulted in a blatant example of successful "rent-seeking" behavior.

THE COALGATE SCANDAL

The so-called Coalgate scandal covers the period from 2003 to 2008. During this period, the Congress-led United Progressive Alliance (UPA) and its predecessor, the Bharatia Janata Party (BJP)–led National Democratic Alliance (NDA), were in office. The essence of the problem is the lack of transparency in the allocation of coal-mining blocks to private and state companies. The scandal eventually involved a CBI investigation of three hundred companies. In the CBI's preliminary findings available at the time of writing, it had identified nine of these companies as potentially corrupt and issued them FIRs. The CBI concluded that "some public servants had vested interests in the award of contract for the development of mines or joint ventures with private parties. It was also suspected that large number [*sic*] of private companies had unduly benefited in the process."[52]

One interesting side issue arising out of Coalgate reflects on the role of the CBI. The Supreme Court found that the government, through the attorney general, had prior knowledge of the CBI report into Coalgate and tried to influence it. This is one of many examples in which the CBI has come under government influence, some others of which are explored below. It was an important factor in subsequent moves to reform and distance the CBI from the government of the day, which are described more fully in chapter 5.

CORRUPTION AND SOCIAL PROTECTION PROGRAMS

India's social protection programs are vital to its core strategy of inclusive growth. The basis for the strategy is that India cannot develop as a stable nation unless it also includes the large number of very poor people in the development process. The strategy has become even more important to India's development since economic liberalization began in 1991. Social uplift through a variety of government interventions came to be seen as a means of mitigating some of the ills associated with greater globalization that economic liberalization entailed. Although poverty alleviation is important in this process, inclusive growth is about more than just poverty alleviation. It also seeks to incorporate India's poor into the economy as better-functioning individuals capable of contributing to the process of growth itself. This latter goal is particularly important if India is fully to pick up the labor-intensive manufacturing mantle that China will progressively shed as its labor force ages and becomes more expensive. Consequently, the policy of inclusive growth goes beyond poverty alleviation to take in areas such as education, health, and infrastructure development. As a strategy it will be discussed more fully in subsequent chapters. For now it is important to note that it is a core part of India's overall developmental strategy. It is also being seriously compromised by India's massive governance problems.

According to the World Bank, India devotes two percent of its gross domestic product (GDP) per annum to its social protection programs.[53] These include the massive release of subsidized food and other essential commodities through the PDS and the $12 billion MGNREGS.[54] Jha and his colleagues point out that amounts of per-capita welfare expenditure grew by 77 percent between 1999 and 2006, "consistent with the policies of the central government."[55] Unfortunately, however, these higher levels of welfare also generate more corruption.[56]

In India's largest state, Uttar Pradesh, 40 to 70 percent of food scheduled for distribution by the PDS is said by an anonymous senior official reporting to the BBC to be stolen. The amounts involved reportedly add up to $42.6 billion over ten years. According to the BBC report, "the micro-economy around the stolen supplies was estimated to be worth $7.45bn (£4.8bn) in the year 2004–2005 . . . and if you calculate for the last 10 years, it adds up to more than $42.6bn (£27.5bn)."[57] A recent report on the PDS by the World Bank slammed the program, finding that "only 41 percent of the grains released by the government reach households, according to 2004–2005 NSS [National Sample Survey data], with some states doing much worse. In 2001 the Planning Commission has estimated this leakage of BPL [households] grains at 58 percent nationally."[58] According to the World Bank, the problem is that the administration of the program falls largely on the states, and the poorer states—which naturally receive more—are also less able to administer the scheme without "leakage."[59]

The flow of funding into such programs will increase with the introduction of an expanded food-security plan that will subsidize two thirds of the population under a commitment from the UPA government during the last national election. The Food Security Bill, which recently passed through parliament, will cost an estimated $24 billion a year. Such an impost has enormous implications for governance.

A government of India evaluation of an early food-for-work program, Sampoorna Grameena Rozgra Yojana, found that 65 percent of participants were paid well under the minimum wage stipulated for it by the government, thus suggesting significant corruption.[60] Mindful of this and similar depredations, the UPA government built a series of checks and balances into MGNREGS when it was initiated in 2005. There are three such checks: decentralized planning involving planning at the level of the *panchayat*, proactive disclosure involving publication of records at planning offices and digitally, and social audits, involving cross-checking between government data and reality on the ground, including using the agency of civil society.[61]

The auditing of MGNREGS has shown some serious anomalies, which are frequently reported in the press. In one case, a district court judge was found to have a MGNREGS job card, which he claimed to know nothing about.[62] According to a report in *Outlook India* based on audits by the CAG, "the estimated loss to the exchequer [from MGNREGS] in Uttar Pradesh and Madhya Pradesh is Rs 200 crore each [Rs 2 billion]; in Chhattisgarh, Rs 50 crore [Rs 500 million]; and in Rajasthan, Rs 700 crore [Rs 7 billion]. Figures are not available for Bihar, but the embezzled funds may well run into several hundred crore here too. Nationwide, the leakages surely add up to a mind-boggling figure."[63]

A *New York Times* article, which overall takes a positive slant on the social auditing process, nevertheless quoted V. Vasanth Kumar, the minister for rural development in Andhra Pradesh, who noted that "social audits statewide have found $20 million worth of fraud over the past five years, and 4,600 officials have faced administrative or criminal charges."[64] Jha and colleagues found that even with direct cash payments, poor participants still needed to bribe officials in order to obtain their job cards. Thirty percent of participants in Uttar Pradesh were required to pay such bribes, which involved making over a portion of the awarded cash to the concerned officials in exchange for less work done.[65]

The World Bank, however, praises the program for its innovations, including social auditing and decentralization, and finds that it has performed better than earlier programs.[66] This finding is in part borne out by one of the few, if not the only, study of MGNREGS data at the household level. By the Australian South Asia Research Centre at the Australian National University, the study found a mixed picture, with some positive elements. The study concluded, inter alia, that "while it is broadly true that the selection of workers for [MG]NREGS favours illiterate workers and those from deprived backgrounds, female workers appear to have a lower chance of being selected .... Once employed in [MG]NREGS, the duration of such employment is affected by social background or educational status."[67]

For now, it is sufficient to note that the traditional propensity of such giant redistributive programs to fail to deliver at the grass-roots level as intended acts to constrain the capacity of all governments to achieve their goals of inclusive growth. What might be done about it and, indeed, is being done in some cases will be further considered in chapter 5.

HAWALA AND THE "NEXUS OF THE NEXUS"

As illustrated in a number of cases cited above, money laundering is an important link in the process of corruption and poor governance in India. It is the means by which massive corruption can be effectively hidden. *Hawala* is in turn vitally important to money laundering.[68] It is central to the nexus—the linkage between corrupt politics, law enforcement, and criminality. It also goes to the heart of the internal-security issue because, as noted by the Asia/Pacific Group on Money Laundering (APG), *hawala* is heavily linked to the financing of terrorist groups.[69]

India probably produces more "black money" than any other jurisdiction in the world. A study by the Federation of Indian Chambers of Commerce and Industry found that India "lost" Rs 260 billion to so-called grey markets through counterfeiting of goods, intended either to steal brands or avoid tax. An example is the illegal production of cigarettes in Bihar, which is an offshoot of the *bidi* (an indigenous type of cigarette) industry in that state.[70] According to a recent study by Global Financial Integrity (GFI), Indians moved the staggering sum of $462 billion overseas illicitly between 1948 and 2008, not including smuggling, underinvoicing, and gaps in available statistics, which could take the total to well over $500 billion.[71] According to the study, these illicit outflows constitute 72 percent of the black economy. In other words, only 28 percent of illicit money is kept in India. However, of the illicit external transfers, a significant amount would eventually be repatriated for investment in India—again by means of *hawala* and other illegal transfers. According to GFI, the illicit economy in total constitutes 50 percent of GDP.[72] The report also finds that the illicit economy acts as a proxy for governance. This illicit transfer of wealth is driven not only by criminal activity, but also by licit businesses seeking to avoid taxes and corrupt government activity.[73]

The *hawala* business in India operates in various ways, all of them opaque and difficult to assess in terms of their contribution to the quantum of the problem. But business underinvoicing in exports would likely remain the major way in which funds are illicitly transferred overseas. As demonstrated in the Jain case (see below), gold, silver, and gem dealers also figure prominently in the illicit transfer of funds. Sometimes, as with the Koda case, money is simply moved as cash, and Customs officials are bribed to enable this to happen. Indians also move funds by providing services within India in exchange for currency paid overseas or simply by currency "swaps." Indeed, *hawala* itself in its original form is based on currency swaps, which is what makes it so difficult to detect.[74]

A considerable proportion of *hawala* involves licit funds. The US Bureau for International Narcotics and Law Enforcement Affairs found that in 2009, *hawala* transfers for incoming, legally derived remittances amounted to $13–17 billion, leaving aside the fact that a considerable proportion of *hawala* dealings probably relate to criminality and tax evasion rather than remittances.[75] This finding also illustrates the enormous scale of the *hawala* trade.

Despite the central position of money laundering in maintaining the nexus, Indian laws on money laundering and their enforcement remain problematic. In a 2009 amendment to the Prevention of Money Laundering Act, the list of predicate offenses was greatly expanded, and the time was brought forward at which the Enforcement Directorate could intervene. But there are still weaknesses in the legislation. For example, the definition of a predicate offense only cuts in if the amount involved is over $60,000, except where there are "cross-border implications."[76] Offenders can only be fined the equivalent of $10,000 for contravening the act, which is a paltry amount given the scale of laundering in India.[77]

As a result of the 2009 amendments, the number of offenses investigated rose dramatically in 2009, but the number of trials remains extremely low. For example, in 2009–10, 739 cases were investigated, but only nine persons were arrested and only four prosecuted (convictions are not recorded).[78] Hopefully, this low rate of trials reflects the glacial pace of Indian legal processes, and statistics will improve the longer the 2009 amendments remain in operation.

One way of illustrating both the scale and central role of *hawala* in the criminal-political-law enforcement nexus is to trace the careers of major *hawala* dealers. The examples we use are those of the Jain brothers and Hasan Ali Khan. The former stood at the fulcrum between corrupt politics and criminal disposition of resources in the 1990s, while the latter allegedly operated up until his arrest in 2011.

The Jain Hawala *Case*

The CBI's investigation of money laundering in relation to the insurgency in Kashmir in 1991 led them to the Jains.[79] On searching S. K. Jain's premises, they came across a diary that not only linked S. K. Jain with J. K. Jain, but also contained the names of 115 people, including prominent politicians, bureaucrats, and businesspeople. Against these names were various amounts, which the CBI investigating team assumed were amounts of money that had been laundered on behalf of the named individuals. The amounts totaled Rs 650 million (over $16 million). It transpired that this money trail initially led to *hawala* dealers in the United Kingdom. Since private banking was not then an offense in the United Kingdom, however, the trail initially went cold. Eventually CBI investigators worked out that the funds were sent from the United Kingdom to Dubai, and from there Indian gangsters translated the money into gold and smuggled it back into India in the classic loop structure. A Mumbai *hawala* kingpin, "Amir Bhai," had allegedly been involved in laundering Rs 530 million of the original Rs 650 million identified in the diary. "Amir Bhai" was an alleged pseudonym for Tamil gem dealer H. Ameerdeen.[80]

Further investigation by the CBI on urging from the Supreme Court also linked the Jain brothers to a number of Indian public-sector undertakings, mainly in the power and steel industries. It appears from the investigation of S. K. Jain that the money in question constituted payments to the individuals involved for corrupt personal favors. Jain also divulged under questioning that one of the people thus paid off was the late P. V. Narasimha Rao, then prime minister. He also alleged that Rajiv Gandhi had been paid Rs 105 million as a kickback for the modernization of a steel plant. The Italian contact of the Gandhis, Quattrocchi (of Bofors scandal fame), had allegedly introduced Jain to Amir Bhai. Further questioning of Jain revealed that a total of Rs 900 million (about $22 million) had been involved in four major kickbacks covered in the diaries.

The CBI investigator in the case, B. R. Lall, maintains he was directed by the director of the CBI, Rama Rao (who was appointed by Narashima Rao), to delete the name of the prime minister.[81] Lall prevaricated, wishing to retain all the names found in the investigation so as not to compromise the case against the Jains as a whole. Eventually, he was removed from the case, according to him because he had refused to remove the prime minister's and senior cabinet members' names. Lall maintains that the director then "scuttled" the case by pressing charge sheets against minor players with inadequate evidence—namely the diary—while refusing to investigate the assets and known means of those important men mentioned in the diary, which would have constituted admissible evidence.[82] Lall says he wrote to Rama Rao after his dismissal from the case accusing him of deliberately scuttling the case.[83]

Lall then makes an interesting observation on the Indian view of loyalty. The context is that Rama Rao had been appointed director of the CBI by Prime Minister Narashima Rao, and Rama Rao had in turn appointed Lall. According to Lall, Rama Rao then accused Lall of disloyalty because he, Lall, had been appointed via this chain by Narashima Rao. Lall comments: "Unfortunately the [Indian] mythology . . . holds a very shady concept of loyalty. Loyalty to a person is idealized over loyalty to truth or God or even the nation. In Ramayan [sic], Vibhishan stood for truth, as against absolute loyalty to his brother Ravan, but he is [therefore] known as a spy inside the house, despite the fact that he sided with Satya [truth], represented by God himself."[84]

Hasan Ali Khan

The case of an alleged *huwala* dealer, Hasan Ali Khan, who is currently in the spotlight, appears to illustrate the working of the nexus, the role of Swiss banks and other locations of convenience, the vast amounts now involved, and the activist role of the judiciary.

By way of background, the Swiss Bankers' Association has claimed that India has more illicit funds in Swiss banks than any other country—$1.45 trillion. Eighty thousand Indians are alleged to travel to Switzerland each year, with twenty-five thousand traveling "frequently."[85] Meanwhile, the Liechtenstein Global Trust Bank (now known as LGT Bank)—the bank infiltrated by a German who subsequently sold information to German intelligence—was found to contain substantial holdings by eighteen Indians. The Indian tax authorities initially refused to publish these names because of India's double taxation agreement with Germany, which maintained the privacy of all individuals involved in the sharing of information either way.

In the case of the alleged money launderer, Hasan Ali Khan, the matter is equally opaque. Khan owns fast cars, several expensive properties, and a stable of racehorses, and allegedly had $8 billion in assets in the United Bank of Switzerland (UBS). He has never filed any tax return or declared any assets.

As a result of probing by the ED and a complex family feud within the family of Khan's partner, the Calcutta-based Marwari businessman Kashinath Tapuriah, a letter was uncovered that appeared to indicate Khan held $8 billion in UBS. The ED subsequently made tax claims of approximately $11 billion on Khan and his wife. However, the account with UBS allegedly containing $8 billion, along with four other Khan accounts, were eventually found to contain only relatively small amounts. UBS denies Khan held significant funds. His critics argue this denial is usual by Swiss banks, which do not identify their clients by name.

Khan has been pursued by India's tax authorities for years but with no results. The Supreme Court took the view that this was not simply a civil taxation case constrained by taxation privacy laws, but a cover-up of massive criminality in India itself. The court directed the government to investigate the matter more widely as a *criminal* case rather than a purely civil taxation case. When told that nothing had been done over a considerable period, the presiding judge famously asked, "What the hell is going on in this country?"[86]

It is difficult to determine the origin of Khan's massive wealth, where it has gone, or even whether it existed. One theory is that Khan was acting as a front man for Saudi arms dealer Adnan Khashoggi, who had become persona non grata in Switzerland's banks (difficult but evidently not impossible). According to some reports, at least some of his wealth had been derived from his own criminal activities. He was an alleged fraudster, including of banks, and he is alleged to have stolen some of the jewelry of the former Nizam of Hyderabad. But it is inconceivable that his alleged massive resources originated from his criminal activities alone. The more likely explanation is either that he had no such funds or that he was involved in a massive money-laundering operation on behalf of other people. One such named person is Tapuriah, who, along with his wife, allegedly holds Rs 210 million of the Khan funds. Others claim Khan has links with the noted gangster Dawood Ibrahim, but there is no evidence that this is the case. He is also allegedly linked to several Congress politicians via his association with Tapuriah.[87] *The Economic Times* reports that he also earned kickbacks on a Boeing–Air India deal in the 1980s.[88]

Another theory is that he never had such wealth at all but that he forged a letter from UBS stating he had $8 billion in order to further his scams—the letter that was subsequently to show up in the context of the Tapuriah family feud. And in fact, another alleged scamster, whom the *Sydney Morning Herald* refers to as Ahsan Ali Syed, also operated on the basis of a letter from a Swiss bank saying he possessed an account with $8 billion, the exact amount allegedly possessed by Khan. Like Khan, Ahsan Ali Syed hails from Hyderabad.[89] However, the fact that the ED has sued Khan for $11 billion in back taxes casts this theory in a strange light, unless the ED is simply using the threat of back taxes to force him to concede to other charges of criminality.

Whether or not Khan's wealth is real and whether or not he is a major money launderer, his goings-on have gripped the public imagination in India. He is widely perceived to be indicative of the workings of the nexus and the vast amounts of money allegedly involved. Money laundering and the seeming supine government response to it have emerged as major political issues. Along with allegations of corruption, these developments promise to change the political landscape of India. These public concerns and government's response to the problem will be discussed in a later chapter.

CRIME AND POLITICS

If one accepts the reality of the nexus, then one must also accept the reality that democratic politics in India has become significantly criminalized and corrupted.

There are two closely related issues: that of politicians such as the aforementioned Koda seeking their main chance for enrichment and the fact that many Indian MPs have pending criminal cases against them.

Although we have broadly covered the acquisition of illicit wealth in politics, there are several generic studies to illuminate this problem. Research by the Association for Democratic Reform (ADR) and National Election Watch found that "the percentage rise in assets of re-contesting MPs in the 2009 Lok Sabha elections was 289% over the intervening five years. In the recent assembly elections, ADR's comparisons based on assets of 337 re-contesting candidates from four states and one Union territory indicated an average increase of 71% to 195%."[90]

The second problem concerns criminality in general within the political class. According to ADR's website, 29.1 percent of MPs have pending criminal charges.[91] Another study based on similar data found that between the 2004 and 2009 elections, the overall number of criminally charged MPs rose by 17.2 percent, and those facing serious charges rose by 30.9 percent.[92]

Regarding all these data, we need to note that they relate to criminal charges and not convictions. Conviction for more serious offenses would effectively debar an MP from serving under the Representation of the People Act of 1951. However, under the act, "conviction" does not apply until all appeals are exhausted—a process that under the Indian system often takes decades. Moreover, it is quite common in the Indian system for charges to be brought against parliamentarians on grounds that would in other jurisdictions be regarded as political. A recent example is the way the Mayawati government in Uttar Pradesh (UP) prosecuted the Congress UP leader Rita Bahuguna Joshi for alleged offensive remarks against the chief minister. She was arrested on three separate charges, including under the Atrocities Act! Until these charges are heard, which could be years, she will presumably have these cases pending against her. Nevertheless, there is no doubt that a significant number of MPs are facing genuine charges associated with their criminality, a point underlined by the fact that 14 percent of those Lok Sabha MPs with charges against them are charged with serious crimes.[93]

There is also a connection between organized crime and electoral politics. In Gujarat, for example, the recently deceased leader of a gang of Meher community members based in Porbunder, Santokben Jadeja (also known as "the Godmother"), entered electoral politics and became first a *panchayat* member and then a member of the (state) legislative assembly (MLA) to protect her criminal domain after her husband was murdered. The Jadeja gang started out smuggling liquor and gold into Gujarat, a dry state. But the gang's interests have now expanded to include mines and transport companies. According to an article about her in *Outlook India*, "to the police brass and her detractors, Santokben symbolises the criminal-politician-businessman nexus in Gujarat. Says Nirmala Gotru, the young district SP: 'To maintain their economic superiority the criminals enter politics and all these gangs are an expression of this phenomenon.'"[94]

Where criminals have not actually entered politics, often they will provide entire blocks of votes for professional politicians but expect a quid pro quo in the form of political protection—protection that flows from the political domain into the police and other law enforcement agencies such as Customs, as in the case of Koda mentioned above. Services provided by crime groups for politicians can include delivering votes, providing "rent a crowd" groups to intimidate opponents, capturing voting booths during elections, providing electoral funding, and even attacking opponents physically. The former Chennai deputy commissioner of police, C. K. Gandhirajan, details continuous, high-level political involvement with the gangs in Chennai and wider Tamil politics.[95]

So far, we have chronicled a somewhat depressing scene, one in which politicians, criminals, and police are engaged in an unholy alliance to get rich quickly. But what does this say about wider Indian society and the levels of criminality and violence suffered by ordinary people? This is an important point, because the level of violence against individual citizens is a significant, if crude, measure of the effectiveness of law enforcement and governance in India more generally.

CRIME AND VIOLENCE IN INDIA

Those of us who follow security issues in India are regularly assaulted by accounts of seeming high levels of violence, such as multiple deaths from terrorist attacks, rioting between religious communities, Maoist attacks involving high numbers of police casualties, burning of women in so-called dowry deaths, gang rapes by perpetrators who are often treated with impunity by the police, or encounter killings.

But on the other hand, those who travel through India are often struck by the way in which optimism and goodwill prevail amid extreme poverty. Syncretic values still seem to persist, and different religious groups and communities live in harmony and close proximity. Nor do booming economic data indicate that violence, dissonance, and unrest in India are sufficient to dampen the economy in any significant way.

But these are subjective views, and the question still remains: How violent, corrupt, and dysfunctional is India in comparative terms? The data are hard to extract for India, let alone other, possibly more violent regions and subregions such as Africa and parts of Central and South America.

The Global Peace Index is flawed as an absolute measure of violence. It includes factors such as "democracy" and excludes important areas such as "domestic violence." Nevertheless, the large South Asian countries rank relatively low (poorly): Pakistan 127th, Sri Lanka 125th (although that was during the civil war), India 107th, and Bangladesh a surprisingly good 86th.[96]

Up to 2007, the US State Department continued to collect comparative data on deaths caused by "terrorism." Besides definitional problems with the term, these data did not cover the full spectrum of violence. The 2007 report recorded 2,300 lives lost from "terrorism" in India (no comprehensive data were available in the 2008 report).[97] According to data provided by the South Asia Terrorism Portal (SATP), India lost 22,789 people to extremist violence between September 2001 and November 2009.[98] Even allowing for a flexible view of terrorism that includes all forms of extremist violence and taking account of India's population of 1.2 billion, this appears at first sight to be a significant problem.

Other data, however, paint a less alarming picture of the situation in India. The official figure for the murder rate in India (which presumably also reflects deaths in terrorism and political violence) has somewhat *fallen* since independence—from 3.7 per 100,000 in 1951 to 3.4 per 100,000 in 2007.[99] In terms of general crime rates, the officially recorded statistics are also reasonably positive. They report a declining crime rate for Indian Penal Code crimes (generally at the more serious end of the spectrum) in relation to the population growth rate over the decade prior to 2007.[100] Others put India's murder rate at 3.8 per 100,000, still well below that of the United States at 5.5 per 100,000, but well above many Western European countries.[101]

A thorough survey by the India Armed Violence Assessment project conducted with the Small Arms Survey (based in Geneva) points out that the murder rate data based on crime reporting are significantly lower than data based on health reporting as provided by the World Health Organization. They say the crime statistics murder rate is given at 2.8 per 100,000, compared with 5.5 per 100,000 for health-related statistics. The report points out, however, that this discrepancy is not unusual for other countries too and that the health data are somewhat more opaque than the crime data.[102] Tellingly, the report also notes that deaths from murder were fourteen times greater than deaths from terrorism in 2009.[103]

China is the most valid point of comparison with India given its vast population. It has a murder rate of 2.4 per 100,000 (compared with an Indian range of 2.8–3.8 depending on which statistics are used).[104] But China is a more homogeneous country, is more tightly controlled by its undemocratic political system, and has a lower percentage of young people.

It would seem, then, that in per capita terms, India is not especially violent by the standards of the world's developing countries and even the United States. While political violence, including terrorism, is concentrated in some cities and subregions, it does not, on the whole, stifle the daily lives and economic transactions of the majority of people. According to anecdotal reports, South India is less violent than the North, a point, however, belied by the statistics, possibly because the South is more competent at collecting them than the North.[105]

Although India is in statistical terms not an especially violent place, there are nevertheless worrying signs that in some parts of the country a destructive cycle of violence could intensify, possibly leading to a classic downward spiral of terrorism (or other forms of violence), excessive state response, and further violence triggered by this response. Such was the pattern that led to the multigenerational civil war in Sri Lanka. It would be particularly worrying if such trends were to emerge in key economic centers such as Mumbai, Hyderabad, and Bengaluru. Another key area in terms of India's economic performance is the Maoist-affected area, which contains most of India's important mineral and energy provinces. Violent separatist movements in Kashmir and India's Northeast also have worrying strategic implications in respect of Pakistan and China.

There is also evidence that India's general crime (as distinct from murder) problem is seriously underreported. Worse, this underreporting apparently occurs in part due to a loss of faith in policing in India. It is impossible to know the extent of underreporting of crime in any country, but there are ways we can explore the data to give an indication of the dimension of the problem. Crime victim surveys are a useful tool in this regard but are not sufficiently developed in the Indian context to enable us to draw countrywide conclusions. One survey of four major cities in Tamil Nadu (a state with more effective policing than most) found that "many crimes occurring in India are not reported and that police [crime] figures are only the tip of the iceberg."[106] A victimization survey of Rajasthan conducted by the Massachusetts Institute of Technology on behalf of the Rajasthan Police reportedly found that only 29 percent of crimes were ever reported and that, of those that were, only 72 percent received a FIR.[107] But we need also to note that the more serious the crime (such as murder), the more likely it is to be reported and therefore incorporated into the statistics.

Serious underreporting is also likely in relation to illicit drugs crime. It is worth exploring this problem in a little detail, because serious illicit drugs crime is usually associated with high levels of organized crime, corruption, narco-terrorism, and addiction.

The Indian Narcotics Control Bureau (NCB) reports a virtually flat pattern of opiates seizures at about one metric ton of heroin annually and two metric tons of opium, suggesting India's trafficking in and use of this class of drugs are not rising markedly or that interdiction has fallen markedly.[108] The US Department of State gives a different picture, however, with combined heroin/opium seizures as follows, in kilograms: 2004, 488; 2005, 259; 2006, 1,033; 2007, 2,658; 2008, 2,489; 2009, 1,663; and 2010, 1,832.[109] This presents a rapidly rising set of statistics for the mid-2000s, followed by a plateau in later years. In a survey of India, the United Nations Office on Drugs and Crime found that "in 2004 the number of *chronic substance-dependent individuals* were as follows: 10 million (alcohol), 2.3 million (cannabis) and 0.5 million (opiates) [emphasis added]." The report pointed out that this was twice the global (and Asian) average prevalence.[110]

A national statistic of half a million chronic opioid users is indicative of consumption of large quantities of illicit drugs, even allowing for the presumed lower levels of purity in India. This is in turn indicative of high levels of criminality. Several years ago a report from a Punjab university found that 70 percent of young men in Punjab had some kind of addiction.[111] While this figure seems high, Punjab is a major conduit for heroin smuggling from Afghanistan via Pakistan into India, and, as we know, addiction problems often occur along the trafficking routes for illicit drugs. Other reports also tell of widespread addiction in the state.[112]

The US State Department in its 2007 report also designated India as a major hub for illicit drugs. It was concerned by the possibility of diversion of India's substantial licit opiate production and noted the sudden surge in discoveries in illicit growing in 2007.[113] The NCB notes of that year: "It was decided to conduct an intensive survey of the probable areas [of illicit cultivation] involving NCB, state authorities and other central authorities." Eight thousand hectares of illicit poppy were destroyed in that year, compared with 218 hectares in 2006 and 623 hectares in 2008.[114] Illicit harvesting of at least eight thousand hectares (the amount discovered and destroyed) suggests major criminal involvement in the purchase, consolidation, and processing of opium gum. This area constitutes nearly one-third of the estimated *total* illicit cultivation in Burma in the same year.[115] The concerns of the State Department were reflected by findings of the Australian Crime Commission. Australia reported an increasing quantity of heroin originating from Southwest Asia (mainly from Afghanistan), with India supplying "the largest number of detections [as a global source of origin] over 500 grams" in the 2007–8 reporting year.[116]

India thus appears to be emerging as a major source of heroin transshipment from the Golden Crescent and a major user of opioids. This heightened involvement with illicit drugs is disturbing in that growing addiction, corruption, and high-level criminality are usually associated with this level of use and trafficking.

From the above we can conclude more generally that although India is not an especially violent or crime-ridden society, a number of problem areas are emerging. Terrorist and insurgency-related violence does not extend across the country by any means but is focused in some sensitive areas in both strategic and economic terms. Illicit-drugs crime is showing some worrying trends, and this is disturbing in light of the capacity of such crime to undermine the health of the population and the law enforcement processes. Crime in India is seriously underreported, and this in part reflects the lack of trust in the police, which brings us to examine the issue of policing and its relationship with security.

POLICING AND GOVERNANCE IN INDIAN SECURITY

As with any large country, India's security mechanisms are required to meet multiple needs. In each one of these roles, and at each level of activity (national, state, or local), security authorities and governance mechanisms can be part of either the problem or the solution. Often they act in different ways and are driven by different political imperatives at different levels.

In relation to the policing element of security, Indian police are more often seen as part of the problem rather than the solution. They are generally held in poor repute, and their status in Indian society is low. Their poor performance has now reached a critical level in the context of a society starting to expect more of its government as represented by police, who are often at the front line when it comes to the government's interactions with its citizens.

In December 2012, a young woman in Delhi was raped in horrible circumstances and eventually died from her internal injuries in a hospital in Singapore. She was an upwardly mobile young woman from a poor background seeking to better her lot through education. There was an upwelling of anger, at first in New Delhi and then cascading throughout India. The degree of this anger took the authorities by surprise. The event was widely reported internationally.

A high degree of acrimony was directed at the police. The young woman had been left with critical injuries beside the road for some time before the police or emergency services reacted. The event represented a tipping point at which public anger and resentment against a long history of arrogant, incompetent, corrupt, and misogynist policing in India could no longer be contained. The middle classes in particular are frustrated that the increasingly wealthy and complex Indian state is being held hostage to inadequate, colonial-derived policing that is jeopardizing the lifestyles to which they aspire.[117] Women too are incensed at the way they are regularly abused by police when they seek to report the many depredations against them. Police reform is urgent, but the challenge for Union and state governments is to know how to reform the rambling, antiquated, under resourced system.

In terms of the more general picture of policing in India, five factors ensure that the performance of Indian police remains generally poor. First, India's sprawling polity means that New Delhi is distant from events on the ground in far-flung provinces. The realities of day-to-day governance and of the Constitution dictate that state governments generally hold sway in law and order matters. India has approximately six hundred thousand villages, and it is impossible to provide police protection to all of them or to scrutinize the behavior of the police where they happen to be present. In most of these villages, the presence of authority is little better than the locally employed *chowkidar*. Even in many cities with their vast slums, the police presence is either distant or degraded. These few police with little resources are required to maintain order over a vast, heterogeneous population.

Second, India has a long history of using police in a repressive role dating well back into the colonial era. In this process, the doctrine of separation of powers takes a back seat. As pointed out by the Commonwealth Human Rights Initiative, continued adherence to India's 1861 Police Act is an important element of the accountability problem in policing.[118] The 1861 Act was originally based on another repressive instrument, the Irish Police Act. Although the Indian act has been subject to multiple amendments, the colonial philosophy is still at the foundation of Indian policing. Basically, the act does not support separation of powers in the way that would be understood in other Westminster-based legal structures. There are no external processes of complaints or review in many jurisdictions, despite a series of attempts from outside to impose them. In the colonial disposition, political intelligence was gathered and consolidated by police under the auspices of the Home Department every day. Today the "special branch" role is still very much in evidence, even though in most Western democracies such roles are considered dangerously political for the police. This pervasive political-intelligence role opens up the possibility of police being misused to support the incumbent government. Both the nature of the Police Act and system of transfers at the behest of state governments place the police even more firmly under the political thumb. This misuse of the right of transfer is also applicable throughout the other enforcement agencies, such as the CBI and the ED. According to Human Rights Watch, "officers are frequently told to drop investigations against people with political connections and sometimes told to harass or file false charges against political opponents. Refusal means transfer to remote areas, and with it the loss of prestige and the hardship of removing children from good city schools."[119]

Political influence over senior police is also increased by the fact that promotion is often bought. The going rate for appointment as a subinspector in Manipur is said by the Asian Human Rights Commission to be between Rs 1.4 million ($35,000) and Rs 1.8 million ($45,000).[120] These are vast sums in Indian terms. They demand an equally vast income from bribes, thus perpetuating the vicious circle. Even the Supreme Court has expressed frustration at the politicization of the CBI. In the context of Coalgate, the court admonished the CBI for taking direction from the government in its investigations, saying, "Our first exercise will be to liberate CBI from political interference."[121]

Third, as a direct reflection of the British need to maintain the public order, the Indian police services are still divided into an investigatory role and an armed constabulary role (the Provincial Armed Constabulary, or PAC). These PAC units are highly militarized and constitute just under half of the police force if federal paramilitary units are included. In their role as maintainers of public order, they are sometimes required to fire on the populace to prevent a mob getting out of hand. Such killings were common under the British and are still all too frequent. This is hardly conducive to best-practice community policing. These paramilitary traditions within the police are reinforced by the fact that the Union government paramilitary forces are increasingly called in to assist states struggling with public-order issues. They have been interposed in this way in order to protect the military from overexposure and consequent possible politicization. The most prominent of these central groups is the Rapid Response Force (RRF). This force was established so that it could be dispatched quickly to states that cannot maintain civil order. The 165,000-strong Central Reserve Police Force (CRPF) is intended for longer-term assistance to states suffering law-and-order problems and provides the backbone of the anti-Maoist effort in a number of states.

Fourth, the inherited colonial structure of policing has dictated another norm inimical to best-practice community policing: the separation of the officer class from the constabulary in terms of the selection process and promotional chain. The Indian Police Service (IPS) is an august and useful institution similar to the Indian Administrative Service (IAS)—the successor of the Indian Colonial Service, or so-called steel frame of colonial times. The IPS involves a highly competitive selection process at the central level. Some appointees are used as officers in the various echelons of the Union government police services, and some are sent to the state police. At state level, the IPS is mirrored by a state-selected officer class.

The existence of this officer class proved beneficial for a vast police service with a primary role of keeping the peace. But it has also forced community policing into a lowest common denominator. Under this system, most police, who are constables and senior constables, are poorly educated, trained, paid, accommodated, and equipped and have little prospect for promotion. Because of the constabulary system, Indian police are generally considered to be of low status in the overall hierarchy of the nation. This low status is reflected in the influence and command politicians are able to exercise over them, thus reinforcing the ambiguities of the separation of powers mentioned above. Such people cannot provide for genuine community policing.

In order for an unbroken line of promotion to be introduced, it would require far better recruitment, education, and training outcomes than those currently available to the Indian constabulary service. Given there are over two million state police,[122] this would be a costly and time-consuming enterprise. But as discussed in chapter 5, it would be possible.

Finally, policing in India is seriously under resourced. According to Ministry of Home Affairs data, India has only one policeman or policewoman for 516 citizens.[123] The ratio is far worse than that in some states. It is also considerably worsened by the fact that of these police, 50,000 are on VIP protection duty and 431,000 are from the states' PAC units.[124]

Efforts to reform the police have not significantly progressed despite the expressions of frustration from leading institutions. The Indian Police Commission met eight times between 1988 and 1991. Its recommendations were wide ranging—from the establishment of proper, independent complaints mechanisms, to the replacement of the repressive and anachronistic 1861 Police Act and to ensuring the independence of policing from the influence of the government executive.[125] In 2006, a frustrated Indian Supreme Court brought down seven requirements (six applicable to the states and one to the Union) reflecting the recommendations of the Police Commission. Most have never been implemented. One important factor apparently preventing reform is the political nexus between police and senior politicians in some states. Obviously, such states will be reluctant to introduce reforms attacking cozy relationships that are of mutual benefit. So far, eleven of twenty-six states have implemented some kind of reform, but often such reforms fall short of providing accountability and transparency.[126]

POLICING AND COUNTERTERRORISM

As well as being at the front line in fighting crime, India's police are also crucial in countering terrorism. According to former minister of home affairs, P. Chidambaram, "if intelligence-gathering is the corner stone of fighting insurgency or insurrection or terror, the foot soldier [police man or woman] cannot work in isolation. He must be enabled to gather intelligence from the people . . . . It is therefore important that State Governments adopt Community Policing."[127]

In terms of developing a more sustainable approach to internal security (and consequently the closely related area of external security), the police and judiciary have crucial roles to play. Police are the eyes and ears of the system. They are a massive force. If properly trained and networked, they can acquire intelligence at the grass roots and pass it upward to the strategic level. They are the ones in a position to preempt attack and provide a first response once it occurs. (We shall not quickly forget the images of police in Mumbai attempting to do battle with Kalashnikov-armed terrorists with antiquated, bolt-action Lee-Enfield rifles). A police service capable of providing these services should be more oriented to community policing than the paramilitary structure dictated by the 1861 Police Act.

Much of the above is common sense and covered elsewhere. What is sometimes overlooked, however, is that the ability to conduct successful *investigations* is a prime tool of counterterrorism and that police are the key investigators in counterterrorism. Successful investigations can break up terrorist cells and organizations and provide far-reaching intelligence leads.

For example, B. Raman pointed out in 2009 that there had been no major attacks in India in the year since 26/11. In part he attributed this to the successful investigation of the Indian Mujahideen (IM) series of attacks that took place on major Indian cities throughout 2008 and the consequent significant erosion of the IM cells.[128] The opening up of the investigations into the IM through an encounter with three IM activists in New Delhi in September 2008 and the subsequent arrest of one revealed a whole chain of cases in India that had hitherto escaped detection.[129]

But despite this success, there is evidence that India's capacity to investigate terrorism and crime is still inadequate. Even crime-scene management in important cities such as Mumbai and New Delhi is often poor, as evidenced by the lack of control in Mumbai in the aftermath of 26/11.[130] (However, it must also be said that crime-scene management after any massive terrorist attack such as 26/11 is bound to be difficult.) In other instances, investigations have not always had early successes and have sometimes been characterized by poor practices and worse. For example, the investigations of the bombings in Hyderabad in 2007 resulted in a number of false arrests and accusations of use of torture by police—accusations subsequently upheld in a report of the Andhra Pradesh Minorities Commission.[131] The investigation of the bombing of the Samjhauta Express train in 2006 was incompetent. Despite a number of initial false arrests of Muslims, it now appears Hindu radicals were involved. The attacks on the Mumbai rail system in July 2006 resulted in serious differences between agencies as to which terrorist group was responsible, with the Maharashtra Anti-Terrorism Squad arresting Students Islamic Movement of India (SIMI) members and the Crime Branch of the Mumbai Police arresting IM members. Eventually the Crime Branch was forced by the courts to release its arrestees.[132] Even the investigation of the 26/11 attacks was mired in controversy. A suppressed official report of the Maharashtra government reportedly points to poor policing practices in the response to the attacks.[133]

Reporting from the court system also appears to support the view that investigations are generally poor in India. The conviction rate for Indian Penal Code crimes in India in 2007 was 42.3 percent.[134] This compares with a conviction rate of 80.7 percent in the United Kingdom.[135] It is worth noting that conviction rates are a different data set than "clear-up" rates, which would be far lower than 42.3 percent, given the fact that in 2007, 14.5 million were awaiting trial on IPC crimes alone, suggesting that on an annualized basis the clear-up rates are extremely low.[136]

As one would expect given the problems with policing described above, basic policing and human rights norms often come unstuck under the pressure of counterterrorism needs and in light of some of the more draconian legislation. Frequently, suspects have been rounded up and detained over lengthy periods with no charges being brought. Sometimes these episodes are accompanied by extensive police leaks or reports that appear to establish the "guilt" of the person even before a trial has been conducted.[137] Following the train blasts of July 2006 in Mumbai in which 209 people died, 300 Muslims were arbitrarily rounded up and questioned, generating considerable fear and bitterness.[138] Although the technique requires the prior consent of a magistrate, suspects are frequently interrogated under the influence of sodium pentothal. Its use can lead to poor outcomes, as noted in an article in the *Indian Journal of Medical Ethics*.[139] According to their own report, police in Kashmir have presided over 332 deaths in custody during the Islamic insurgency in that state, and 111 people have gone missing.[140] It is highly likely that the real figures would be far higher.

Incompetent and corrupt policing of this nature exacerbates Hindu-Muslim tension and helps foster homegrown terrorism. The Sachar Committee Report (2006) found that in India as a whole, Muslims are underrepresented in the police, constituting only 6–7 percent of constables, whereas they constitute 13.4 percent of the population.[141] The situation is even worse for the IPS, where the Sachar Committee reportedly found only 4 percent is Muslim.[142] Bias in police numbers in favor of Hindus, lack of separation of powers, a grossly overburdened legal system, and draconian counterterrorism legislation have all contributed to a perception in minority communities that they are seriously disadvantaged.

Sometimes the political collusion by police and police bias can have more long-lasting consequences—consequences that have ricocheted down through Indian history. The evidence of police bias at the behest of incumbent politicians abound. At the time of the assassination of Indira Gandhi in 1984, local Congress (I) authorities and the police were accused of doing nothing to protect Sikhs in New Delhi from attack or in subsequently prosecuting alleged attackers.[143]

Similar allegations—to be dealt with in detail in the next chapter—were leveled against the BJP Gujarat state government in relation to the anti-Muslim riots of 2002. All too often politicians have taken a leading role in manipulating the police for negative rather than positive purposes, or at least they have turned a blind eye to police inactivity in the face of disorder.[144]

Conversely, there are also cases in which strong, neutral political leadership has mitigated any supposed bias within the police. Although the report of the Justice B. N. Srikrishna Commission found government (at the time the religious chauvinist organization Shiv Sena) and police were implicated in the Mumbai riots of 1992–93, in recent years strong action by the government of Maharashtra has resulted in several potentially inflammable communal situations being contained. Despite two terrorist attacks on the communal tinderbox of Malagoan, careful handling by the Maharashtra government and police managed to defeat the obvious purpose of such attacks—to trigger communal rioting and consequent polarization of communities towards extremists.[145]

Senior police in India express considerable frustration with a legal system that can take years to bring cases to judgment and that is increasingly subject to the "purchasing of justice" by the deployment of slick lawyers capable of finding loopholes on technical grounds.[146] The backlog of legal cases at the time of writing is fifteen years, and a report by the court system predicts it will blow out to an incredible 150 million cases by 2040.[147] In these circumstances police are increasingly taking matters into their own hands. In less serious cases they are giving alleged criminals a thrashing and letting them go. In more serious ones they are killing them in so-called encounters. In one of the most serious of these, three senior police have been arrested in Gujarat, but this is alleged to be only one of a number of such encounter cases in that state.[148] Even a frustrated public is increasingly resorting to so-called lynch law. A video of a man in Bihar being beaten nearly to death by a mob shocked even the president, who remarked that something needed to be done to prevent ordinary citizens taking the law into their own hands but also commented drily that "the realm of judicial administration is not without its own share of inadequacies and blemishes."[149] While such methods might be seen to give temporary relief from criminality, they unfortunately also lead to grave injustices and further alienate disaffected minorities, who are often the targets of police or mob bashings, torture, and encounter killings.

Nor can general crime be delinked from counterterrorism, especially in the South Asian context. In South Asia, there is a particularly close relationship between crime, corruption, and terrorism. Criminal gangs such as Dawood Ibrahim's D Company have widespread networks for smuggling purposes involving agents of corruption in the police and customs. Court cases show that these were heavily utilized in the Mumbai bombings of 1993. In 2010, members of a criminal gang reportedly working on behalf of D Company were arrested for issuances of false passports.[150] Given D Company's links with terrorists, the security implications of these activities are profound. According to the US Congressional Research Service (CRS), "lending his [Ibrahim's] criminal expertise and networks to such terrorist groups, he is capable of smuggling terrorists across national borders, trafficking in weapons and drugs, controlling extortion and protection rackets, and laundering ill-gotten proceeds, including through the abuse of traditional value transfer methods, like hawala."[151]

These shortcomings within the policing and judicial frameworks have a negative effect on counterterrorism by eroding the investigatory, first-response, and intelligence functions of the police and alienating minority communities. Unfortunately these negative trends act further to erode the capacity of an already inadequate and poorly coordinated security community.

INDIA'S SECURITY AND INTELLIGENCE COMMUNITY

In common with many developing countries, India's internal security architecture has evolved in an ad hoc way by means of evolution from its colonial base. Because of this ad hoc process and India's federal structure, the current security architecture is characterized, in the words of former home minister Chidambaram, by the fact that "there is no single authority to which these organizations report and there is no single or unified command which can issue directions to these agencies and bodies."[152] It is also plagued by "turfdom," fragmentation, and careerism, not to mention pervasive corruption and political interference.

The apex of India's security architecture is the prime minister and Cabinet and various offices attached to them. The Cabinet Committee on Security (CCS) consists of ex officio ministers (the prime minister, the minister of home affairs, the minister of defense, the minister of external affairs, and the minister of finance). The CCS is supported by a National Security Council (NSC), which has representatives of the above ministries plus the national security adviser (NSA), who answers to the prime minister, and a range of other ex officio members. The NSC is served by a secretariat of officials. The NSA is also responsible for the organization that conducts military scientific research, the National Technical Research Organisation, and the Joint Intelligence Committee, which brings together the heads of the various intelligence agencies. The Cabinet Secretariat is responsible for the external intelligence agency, which is known as the Research and Analysis Wing, or more widely by the acronym RAW. The Aviation Research Centre (India's aerial reconnaissance and signals intelligence agency) also falls within the purview of RAW. The Ministry of Finance hosts the ED. The Defence Intelligence Agency is located within the Ministry of Defence (MOD) and the respective arms of the defense forces host their own intelligence agencies.

The Ministry of Home Affairs (MHA) hosts the major domestic security intelligence agency, the Intelligence Bureau (IB). The IB developed out of the daily police reporting of the police district special branches to the central government in colonial India. The MHA also hosts the various central government police and paramilitary services, such as the IPS, the Central Paramilitary Forces (which in turn hosts the National Security Guard[153]), various border paramilitary forces such as the Border Security Force (BSF), the CRPF, the CBI, and the recently formed National Investigation Agency (NIA). The Multi-Agency Centre (MAC), an intelligence "fusion center" within the IB, was first mooted in the aftermath of the intelligence failure associated with Kargil in 1999 and refurbished in the aftermath of the 26/11 attacks.[154]

The major intelligence connectivity between the center and states comes through the state offices of the IB, which are located both centrally and in the various state capitals. The fact that the center can insert its various agencies into the states at their request also helps maintain links. Another link is provided by the newly created Subsidiary Multi-Agency Centres (SMACs), which are linked to the MAC within the IB and to the state police special branches through the SMACs. Except in the cases of president's rule, intelligence relating to national security, investigations relating to the central government's jurisdiction such as fraud in a central government agency, or investigations under the legislation of the NIA, intelligence links between the tactical and strategic levels all exist at the invitation and good will of the states.[155]

As with other federal structures, the artificial division within intelligence between state and central authorities constitutes a major impediment to the flow of intelligence between the grass roots and the central agencies. This natural tendency of federations is greatly exacerbated in India because of the vast size of the country. Moreover, intelligence agencies everywhere are extremely poor at sharing intelligence, and India is no exception. They are restricted in doing so by different "intelligence cultures," "stove-piping" (pushing information upward without the sharing of it), lack of trust, and the natural desire to protect sensitive sources. Unfortunately police are particularly prone not to share intelligence for all the above reasons and because of a culture that can often be skeptical of the intelligence function and suspicious of outsiders.

CONCLUSION: THE SECURITY AND ECONOMIC CONSEQUENCES OF CORRUPTION AND POOR GOVERNANCE

Given the close nexus between crime, corruption, and terrorism in South Asia described above, it would be impossible to make India safe from terrorism and insurgency without also greatly improving the performance of the police and related agencies in investigating major crime and corruption. Policing, however, is predominantly a state government function and mainly still undertaken in India according to the authoritarian mold bequeathed by the perceived needs of the colonizing power. Judging from the quotation of the minister of home affairs given above, it is apparent that the Union government is well aware of the problems with policing in India. It also understands the need to improve policing is integral to the counterterrorism effort. Indeed, stimulated by the poor response evident to the attacks of 26/11, the government under former home minister Chidambaram commenced a major process of reform of India's counterterrorism and security mechanisms. If implemented in full, these reforms would go a good way to meeting some of the major concerns about internal security in India. But as we shall see in chapter 5, they are still likely to have some serious limitations.

Traditional defense has also been compromised by poor governance. Military modernization has been delayed by corruption surrounding major defense acquisitions. Military land and assets have been wrongly sold off. Weapons have been sold into the hands of criminals and possibly terrorists.

No lesser body than the Indian Planning Commission has pointed out that the poor performance of the legal and security sectors is actually dragging India and its development down. In its words, "a more orderly society is the bedrock of planned development."[156] Their concern is that the considerable spending of various governments for the uplift of the poor, which is a largely bipartisan policy within the Indian polity, cannot be realized given the massive corruption preventing government programs reaching those for whom they are intended. Development is also being seriously curtailed by the law-and-order problems throughout India's extensive minerals and energy provinces located in central India. The Maoist revolt is not just a problem of violence but, as admitted by the Department of Home Affairs (see above), it is also a manifestation of the patent failure of the government's development efforts. As explored in subsequent chapters, international trade, investment, and political connections are also being vitiated by perceptions of violence, corruption, and poor governance in India. Potential partners remain skeptical of India's capacity as an economic and security partner.

And as we shall see in the next chapter, all of these problems feed into the toxic neighborhood sets of relationships—relationships that in turn affect India's rise to power and the nature of the power it will become.

NOTES

1. For an excellent firsthand account of this, see Jauregui, "Shadows of the State, Subalterns of the State."
2. Government of India, Census of India 2011.

3. McKinsey Global Institute, *India's Urban Awakening*, 8–9.
4. Weiner, *The Politics of Scarcity.*
5. Jeffrey, *What's Happening to India?*
6. Roy, *Listening to Grasshoppers*, xxiv.
7. See, for example, Huntington, *Political Order in Changing Societies*, cited in Méon and Sekkat, "Does Corruption Grease or Sand the Wheels of Growth?," 70.
8. Jha, Nagarajan, and Pradhan, "The Role of Bribes in Rural Governance."
9. Méon and Sekkat, "Does Corruption Grease or Sand the Wheels of Growth?," 69–97.
10. Rothstein, "Anti-Corruption," 229.
11. "India Aid Programme Beset by Corruption."
12. For example, see the discussion by Rothstein, "Anti-Corruption," 238.
13. Doniger, *The Hindus*, 201.
14. Ibid.
15. French, "The Princely State of India."
16. Basham, *The Wonder That Was India*, 82–94.
17. Ibid., 91.
18. Lall, *Who Owns CBI?*
19. Jauregui, "Shadows of the State, Subalterns of the State," passim.
20. Sethi, "No Room for Nuance in This Fragile Republic."
21. This pervasive concept is discussed in Jauregui, "Shadows of the State, Subalterns of the State," 36–41.
22. Government of India, Indian Planning Commission, *Approach Paper to the Twelfth Five Year Plan.*
23. Government of India, Ministry of Home Affairs, *Annual Report for 2008–09*, 15–16.
24. Gupta, "Narratives of Corruption," 5–34, 29.
25. Sen and Drèze, *An Uncertain Glory.*
26. London School of Economics, "India." See also Guha, "Democratic to a Fault?"
27. "Behind Reality Rush in Haryana, a Guilt-Edged Licence Raj."
28. "This MP Clerk's Salary Is Rs 40,000, Assets Rs 25 Crore."
29. "India Ranked 94th in Corruption Perception Index Ratings Says Transparency International."
30. KPMG, "Survey on Bribery and Corruption."
31. "India Ninth-Most Corrupt Country."
32. Centre for Media Studies, *India Corruption Study*, 4. But note that in the executive summary of the same report it is noted that "a third" of households paid a bribe over the year.
33. Ibid., 10.
34. Ibid., 4.
35. Jha, Nagarajan, and Pradhan, "The Role of Bribes in Rural Governance."
36. World Justice Project, "Rule of Law Index."
37. "Revealed: Quattrocchi, Chadda Bribed in Bofors Deal."
38. "Software Deal Used a Cover for Helicopter Bribes."

39. The CAG report may be seen at the CAG website at www.cag.gov.in/. The CAG reports are in the form of PDF files from links from this website. For the CBI estimate, see "2G Scam: Witnesses to Be Examined from June 29." For the JPC report, see "JPC Clean Chit to PM."
40. "CAG Vinod Rai."
41. "2G Scam: ED to Attach Rs 2340 cr of Unitech Properties."
42. "ED, CBI to Visit UK, Isle of Man for Alleged Money Trail." See also "2G Scam: 32 Accounts with Dodgy Transfers under Lens."
43. "Cheque Payments in Kalaignar Money Transfer Nailed Kanimozhi."
44. "Decoding Koda."
45. Under the Indian legal system, a first information report is the first step of the investigation and prosecution process. It outlines the details of the case.
46. For a comprehensive list, see "Land Scam General."
47. As reported in "Rs 1k cr CWG Loss Could Have Been Education Bonanza."
48. This hitherto secret contract was made available in *The Hindu* in a facsimile version of the original at www.hinduonnet.com/thehindu/nic/devasone.pdf, accessed March 28, 2011. The document is no longer available.
49. "What Is Devas Multimedia?"
50. "Antrix Led to Revenue Loss of 1.2 Crore."
51. "Antrix Showered Gold coins on DOS, ISRO Officials."
52. Quoted in "Irregularities Found in Coal Blocks Allocation."
53. World Bank, "India's Poor Yet to Reap Full Benefits of Its Anti-Poverty Programs."
54. It is difficult to give a precise cost for MGNREGS since the offtake under the program varies each year.
55. Raghbendra Jha et al., "The Role of Bribes in Rural Governance," 16.
56. Ibid., 13.
57. "India's Immense 'Food Theft' Scandal."
58. World Bank, "India's Poor Yet to Reap Full Benefits of Its Anti-Poverty Programs."
59. Ibid.
60. As in Aiyer and Saniji, "Transparency and Accountability in NREGA," 5.
61. Ibid., 6–7.
62. "Judge, Family Have NREGS Job Card."
63. "A Sieve of a Scheme?"
64. "Indian State Empowers Poor to Fight Corruption."
65. Jha, Nagarajan, and Pradhan, "The Role of Bribes in Rural Governance," 16.
66. World Bank, "India's Poor Yet to Reap Full Benefits of Its Anti-Poverty Programs."
67. Jha, Gaiha, and Pandey, "Determinants of Employment in India's National Rural Employment Guarantee Scheme,"18.
68. But it is also important to recognize that the two are not synonymous. *Hawala*, also known as the *hundi* system, has roots that go back to time immemorial and serves a vital banking function in village South Asia, where there are often no formally constituted banks.

69. See the concerns of Indian officials expressed in Asia/Pacific Group on Money Laundering, *APG Mutual Evaluation Report on India, March 2005*, 14–15, paragraph 18, and Lal, "South Asian Organised Crime and Terrorist Networks," 293–304, 295, and passim.
70. "India Lost 26,000 cr to Grey Markets Says a Study."
71. Kar, *The Drivers and Dynamics of Illicit Financial Flows from India*, iii.
72. Ibid., vii.
73. Ibid., ix.
74. Person X will go to *hawala* dealer A in one location (say, Mumbai), wishing to send money to person B in another location (say, Dubai). Person X will give the money to *hawala* dealer A, who will take a commission and instruct *hawala* dealer B in Dubai to pass that amount of money to person Y. Dealer B will in turn deduct his commission and pay person Y the amount less the two commissions already deducted. No funds will actually pass between X and Y on this occasion. Instead the dealers will each keep secret books recording the transaction and settle only periodically, perhaps once a year, through the mail by check or some other means of transfer.
75. "Take Steps to Curb Terror Funding, America Tells India."
76. Asia/Pacific Group on Money Laundering (Financial Action Task Force), *Mutual Evaluation Report: Anti-Money Laundering and Combating the Financing of Terrorism*, 43.
77. Ibid., 44.
78. Ibid., 42, table.
79. The following account is based mainly on that of B. R. Lall, a former joint director of the CBI, who led the investigation of the Jain *hawala* case. See Lall, *Who Owns CBI?*, 22–74.
80. See interview with Ameerdeen, "I Am Not the Hawala Kingpin, I Was Just Branded One."
81. Lall, *Who Owns CBI?*, 34.
82. Ibid., 50–54.
83. Ibid., 53.
84. Ibid., 57.
85. V. Venkateswara Rao, "Black, Bold and Bountiful."
86. "What the Hell Is Going On."
87. "Top Uttar Pradesh Bureaucrat Removed for Alleged Links with Hasan Ali" and "Renuka, Tyler Deny Links with Hasan Ali Khan."
88. "Hasan Ali Earned Commission in Boeing-AI Deal."
89. "The $100 M Global Scam."
90. "MLAs' Fortunes Grow More Than All Other Investments."
91. Association for Democratic Reform, "Reference Material."
92. National Law Institute University, Bhopal, "Criminalisation of Politics in India."
93. "Over 30% of MPs, MLAs Face Criminal Charges."
94. "Santokben, Godmother."
95. Gandhirajan, *Organized Crime*, 182–87.

96. "Vision of Humanity," Global Peace Index.
97. United States Government, Department of State, *Country Reports on Terrorism 2007.*
98. South Asia Terrorism Portal, www.satp.org/satporgtp/countries/india/database/indiafatalities.htm.
99. Data extrapolated from Government of India, Ministry of Home Affairs, National Crime Records Bureau, *Crime in India*, table titled "Snapshots (1953–2007)," unpaginated.
100. Ibid.
101. Pasupuleti et al., "Crime, Criminals, Treatment and Punishment," 131–47, 134.
102. *India Armed Violence Assessment*, Issues Brief no. 1, 2, table.
103. Ibid., 1.
104. See "China's Murder Rate Decreases as Arrests Jump."
105. *India Armed Violence Assessment*, Issues Brief no. 1, 2.
106. Chockalingham, "Criminal Victimization in Four Major Cities in Southern India," 125.
107. The survey covered sixteen thousand households and eleven districts. See Singh and Keniston, "Telling It like It Is."
108. Government of India, Ministry of Home Affairs, Narcotics Control Bureau, *Annual Report 2009*, annex A, 65, with an update for 2009 provided by the bureau for the author.
109. United States Government, Department of State. 2012 INCSR, Report on India.
110. United Nations Office on Drugs and Crime, "Executive Summary," 27.
111. "Major Drugs Haul in India's Punjab."
112. Doherty, "Sinking into Deep Despair of a Drug Epidemic."
113. "India Is a Major Drugs Hub."
114. Government of India, Ministry of Home Affairs, *Annual Report 2008*, 31–32. The NCB denies Maoists were involved in this illicit growing (interview with a senior NCB official in November 2009).
115. United Nations Office on Drugs and Crime, *World Drug Report 2008*, 25.
116. Australian Government, Australian Crime Commission, *Illicit Drug Report 2007–08*, 51–53.
117. See, for example, Sen, "The Delhi Rape Crisis."
118. Patil, *Feudal Force*, 10.
119. Human Rights Watch, "Broken System."
120. Asian Human Rights Commission, "Stop Talking and Start Acting."
121. "From Hawala Scam to Coalgate."
122. Government of India, Ministry of Home Affairs, Bureau of Police Research and Development, "Data on Police Organisations in India, 2012." There are 1.7 million sanctioned civil police and a total of 2.124 million state police.
123. "3 Cops to Protect Each VIP, Just 1 Policeman for 761 Citizens."
124. Ibid.
125. For a selection of the recommendations see Patil, *Feudal Force*, 35, box.

126. "Indian Police Reform Gains Ground."
127. Chidambaram, "A New Architecture for India's Security."
128. B. Raman, "India and Jihadi Terrorism during 2009."
129. Many previous attacks, going right back to the attack on the American Centre in Kolkata in 2002, had an entanglement with personnel who subsequently became involved with what came to call itself the IM. See "Burning Gujarat." Page nine of the document written by the OCTOPUS Unit of the Andhra Pradesh Police, on completion of the charge sheet completed for the Hyderabad High Court concerning the IM accused in the twin blasts of 2007, also identifies the seminal role of the Gujarat riots in radicalizing the IM.
130. See for example "26/11 Probe: Poor Crime Scene Management Say Experts."
131. A pdf version is provided on the website Twocircles.net at www.twocircles.net/2009apr08/ravi_chander_report_reveals_torture_and_illegal_detention_ap_police.html, accessed January 6, 2010.
132. "Mumbai Cops Goof Up."
133. Pinglay, "Police Slated over Mumbai Attacks."
134. Government of India, Ministry of Home Affairs, National Crime Records Bureau, *Crime in India 2007*, chapter 4 (unpaginated), table 4B. In 2007, only 13 percent of cases scheduled for trial were actually heard.
135. United Kingdom Government, Department of Public Prosecutions, "Conviction Rate Increases."
136. Government of India, Ministry of Home Affairs, National Crime Records Bureau, *Crime in India 2007*, chapter 12 (unpaginated). The other category of crime is Special and Local Law (SLL) crime. This category of crime is generally representative of a lower level of offense than IPC crime.
137. See, for example, "Masjid Blast."
138. Bagchi, "Tension among Mumbai's Muslims."
139. Jesani, "Medical Professionals and Interrogation."
140. See "332 Deaths in Custody during Islamic Insurgency, Kashmir Police Say."
141. Government of India, Prime Minister's High Level Committee, *Social, Economic, Educational Status of the Muslim Community of India*, 101–2.
142. As reported in "With Few Muslims in Civil Services, Sponsors Chip In."
143. Khurana, "India's 1984 Anti-Sikh Riots."
144. In making such claims, we do not seek to enter into the debate between the academics Paul Brass and Ashutosh Varshney over whether communal rioting in India is staged for political ends (broadly Brass's view) or whether it is contained and mitigated by intercommunal mechanisms of civil society (broadly Varshney's view). We are simply claiming that how authorities provide leadership in early stages of communal tension can make a significant difference to the outcome. For Varshney's review of Brass's book, see "Aligarh Is Not India." For Brass's response to Varshney's review, see "Response to Ashutosh Varshney." Brass's book, which touched off the debate, is *The Production of Hindu-Muslim Violence in Contemporary India*. For Varshney's view on communal conflict, see *Ethnic Conflict and Civic Life*.

145. Malagoan is a mill town of 700,000 that is 75 percent Muslim and has a terrible reputation for communal rioting. Despite two attacks, concerted government and police action was able to prevent the situation from erupting, and not one life was lost other than in the initial attacks.
146. Interviews by the author with senior police members of the IPS, New Delhi, October and November 2009.
147. "India to Have 15 Crore Pending Cases by 2040, Report Says."
148. "A Journalist Who Cracked the Gujarat Fake Encounter Case."
149. "Arrests Follow India Mob Attack."
150. "ATS Arrests Man Who Arranged Fake Passports for D-Company."
151. United States Government, Congressional Research Service, *International Terrorism and Transnational Crime*, 16.
152. Chidambaram, "A New Architecture for India's Security."
153. Founded in 1986 in the aftermath of Operation Blue Star.
154. An intelligence fusion center is a place, usually within a host organization, in which intelligence from a variety of organizations that may have different protective protocols or legislation that limit sharing can be brought together. Often actual representatives of the organizations concerned sit within the fusion center, from where they can access the respective databases of their organizations and present the findings in a way that does not jeopardize any sensitive material. Usually the intelligence is fused in the form of strategic reports on individual cases rather than in a general way, as would be the case in "data warehousing."
155. President's rule: Under Section 356 of the Constitution the central government may dismiss a state government and govern the state directly if the state is deemed to exhibit a failure of the constitutional machinery. If, after six months, no workable majority has emerged, fresh elections must be held.
156. Government of India, Indian Planning Commission, "Mid-Term Appraisal of the Tenth Five Year Plan (2002–2007)," part II, chapter 17, 496.

CHAPTER 2

Enmeshed Dissonance in South Asia

India's failure to come to grips with its internal difficulties has both contributed to neighborhood disharmony and been fueled by it in a complex, two-way process. It is the purpose of this chapter to explore the nature of these linkages between India and its South Asian neighbors. But first, it is necessary to put the region's troubled present into the context of the past.

This history has transformed problems ripe for collective solutions (for example, "problems of the commons") into ones that further divide South Asia. Geographical circumstances—mainly to do with the flow of rivers, the creation of borders across economic regions, and the size of India in relation to its neighbors—also play a significant role in creating cross-border suspicion and tension in the region.

Independent South Asia inherited a difficult set of borders that were drawn up with scant regard for ethnic, religious, or economic factors (see map 2.1). Pakistan emerged on independence in 1947 containing a mosaic of ethnicities, with the most serious fault line between predominantly Bengali East Pakistan and Punjabi-dominated West Pakistan. This fault line eventually led to the war of 1971, when India provided crucial support to the Bangladeshi independence movement, for which it was never forgiven by Pakistan.

The princely state of Kashmir was contiguous to both India and Pakistan and has been in contention ever since. Kashmir had a Hindu ruler, Maharaja Hari Singh, but a population that was 70 percent Muslim. As was his right under transfer-of-powers legislation, Hari Singh declared Kashmir would join neither India nor Pakistan. When Pakistan sponsored an invasion of tribal "liberators," he felt constrained to accede to India in return for military support, which turned back the invaders. Subsequently there was a short border war between India and Pakistan, which resulted in a truce brokered by the fledgling United Nations and

MAP 2.1 Map of South Asia

a cessation of hostilities along what remains approximately the Line of Control (LOC) today. Under the ceasefire agreement, Pakistan was to withdraw its forces from the princely state, and India would then permit a UN-supervised plebiscite on whether Kashmir should join Pakistan or India. Pakistan did not withdraw, and India has never held the plebiscite on the grounds that Pakistan has not withdrawn.

In 1989, this stalemated situation erupted into a full-fledged insurgency in Indian Kashmir, which was sponsored and supported from across the LOC in

Pakistani Kashmir. Pakistan's military intelligence organization, the Inter-Services Intelligence Directorate (ISI), set up training camps, fostered insurgent groups, and filtered them over the LOC into Indian Kashmir. Pakistan hopes thereby that someday Kashmir might become India's "East Pakistan."

Other borders also remain contested. The Afghanistan-Pakistan border was defined by Mortimer Durand, the foreign secretary of colonial India, in 1893 and is today known as the Durand Line. It cuts through the middle of the Pashtun and Baluch ethnic groups. In the 1950s and 1960s, there were demands for a separate Pashtunistan, but since then the issue has been largely quiescent. The Baluch have been engaged in a sporadic separatist movement dating back to the 1970s. Afghanistan, which controlled Peshawar during periods of the nineteenth century as its winter capital, also continues to dispute the Durand Line as a false border imposed by British power.

Many of India's northeastern states have Indo-Tibetan majorities that are ethnically and religiously different from the populations of the Indian heartland and are seeking independence or autonomy. One of the most persistent of the many independence movements in the Northeast is the United Liberation Front of Assom (ULFA) in Assam. Started by disaffected students in 1979, the movement seeks independence for Assam and to stem the flow of "outsiders" into the state—meaning Bangladeshis. Ironically, for significant periods the ULFA leadership sought sanctuary in Bangladesh, complicating the task of Indian security forces and Indo-Bangladesh relations.

As well as numerous insurgencies and separatist movements located in border regions, a giant swath of east-central India, constituting over one-third of India's more than six hundred districts, is affected by the Maoist (or Naxalite) revolt. In these districts the largely tribal populations have been alienated from the land with which they often have a semi religious affinity. Corrupt forestry contractors and officials have eaten away at the forests on which they depend. All too often compensation for land from which they have been displaced by mining or dams has gone into the pockets of corrupt officials.

As noted in the previous chapter, terrorism is also relatively common throughout India. Of India's 170 million Muslims, a very small minority, often working with the support of groups in Pakistan, has engaged in acts of terrorism. While the numbers are small in percentage terms, the impact of these attacks, targeting particularly high-value economic and religious targets, has been high. All of these problems greatly add to the challenge of maintaining good governance and security over the vast, diverse country.

Most importantly, the very process of dividing British India along religious lines precipitated a state of antagonism between India and Pakistan. The actual process of partition resulted in an estimated one million deaths and enduring bitterness. But the fact of designating states on the basis of religion, when they had not previously been so designated, also introduced a new dynamic to the region. Pakistan, which derives its very being from Islam, has had a continuing incentive to use religion politically to define itself and unite its disparate ethnic groups. This has resulted in a process under which the state has become progressively more religiously oriented. India, while defined in its constitution as a secular state, has also wrestled with the role of its Hindu identity, especially since Hindus constitute 81 percent of the population. Tension about the degree to which the Hindu identity should be incorporated into the state has been fanned by the political process and sometimes used by the BJP to gain political traction. An example is the so-called *Rath Yatra* (literally a chariot festival but in this case a "grand tour" around north India) conducted by L. K. Adwani, contributing to the destruction of the Babri Masjid (mosque) at Ayodhya in 1992 and the serious rioting that followed.

Added to these problems, decolonization caused the great industrial cities of Bombay and Calcutta (Mumbai and Kolkata today) to lose significant segments of their agricultural supplier hinterlands. The railway systems developed by the British to feed both local demand and their mercantilist needs cut across the newly defined borders. Given the antagonism between India and Pakistan, they were consequently closed down. This adversely affected both the supplier regions such as the Sindh cotton fields, which supplied Bombay, and the jute-growing areas of what was then East Pakistan, which supplied the jute mills of Calcutta. This loss of supply caused major disruption and badly damaged the emerging economies of the region.

Other economic anomalies were also produced by decolonization, such as loss of control over vital rivers that flow through India into Bangladesh and Pakistan. India erected the Farakka Barrage in 1975. It diverted water flowing into Bangladesh via the Ganges into the Hooghly to flush out the port of Calcutta. The barrage was contested by Bangladesh and has been in contention ever since, worsening relations between the two. Pakistan also claims to have similar problems due to India's upper riparian role in relation to that country—an issue discussed in greater detail below.

When it comes to India's location, the fact that it is a "giant among pygmies" is both an asset and a disadvantage. It is an asset in the sense that India has the economic benefits of scale and the security benefits that it can easily deal with conventional threats (although not, of course, nuclear or asymmetrical ones). But it is also a negative in the sense that India's relative size brings into play the Kautiliyan dictum discussed briefly in the introduction. Kautiliya (also widely known in South Asia as "Chanakya") argued at the end of the fourth century BCE that in such circumstances, the smaller states will naturally seek ballast and support from a powerful but more distant and therefore less threatening state in order to balance the effect of having to deal with a larger neighbor. Closely related—indeed part of the same thought—was the aphorism "the enemy of my enemy is my friend."[1]

Although by "states" Kautiliya probably had in mind the collection of small South Asian entities of his day, the dictum fits modern South Asia to a classic degree. The smaller states that surround giant India, each sharing a border with it, will naturally look for support from more distant large powers such as China. The situation is further complicated by the fact that India shares a border with all of its smaller South Asian neighbors except the Maldives, whereas the small neighbors do not share borders with each other.[2] India thus tends to be on the receiving end of individual and collective feelings of insecurity on the part of other South Asian countries.

Partly because of these negative physical, political, and economic influences arising from partition, South Asia has failed to reflect the successes of East and Southeast Asia, either in terms of alleviating poverty or building a sense of cooperative community with a capacity to mitigate the dissonances of the region. The antagonism between India and Pakistan has negatively affected the whole region and vitiated any capacity that SAARC (founded 1985) may have had to provide a cooperative framework. Given India's travails in South Asia and its concerns that smaller powers might use regional cooperation to gang up on it, both S. D. Muni and Arndt Michael argue that India has acted to ensure that SAARC remains a "soft" regional institution.[3] As pointed out by Michael, India tends to favor what he calls "*Panchsheel* multilateralism."[4] And "Panchsheel multilateralism . . . exhibits a shallow degree of institutionalization and the lowest degree of commitment and interdependence of interstate cooperation."[5] India, as the largest South Asian power, virtually has a power of veto over SAARC (no India, no SAARC), and so it has managed to force this form of soft multilateralism on its neighbors.

India can do this because it is by far the biggest country in South Asia. But it is a strategy that contrasts markedly with the role of Indonesia in ASEAN. Part of the success of ASEAN (keeping in mind it is certainly more successful than SAARC) is due to the fact that Indonesia appears to have deliberately put itself on an equal footing in ASEAN with all other states, including tiny ones such as Singapore and Brunei. This has never occurred in the case of either South Asia or the IOR.

A partial manifestation of SAARC's failure (along with lack of regional economic complementarity) is the region's low intraregional trade, which twenty years after SAARC was founded was only five percent of the region's total trade (in other words, the aggregate value of trade of all SAARC countries).[6]

Another partial consequence of the failure of SAARC is that South Asia remains one of the poorest and most troubled regions of the globe. With a population of over 1.5 billion, it has well over 400 million people living in poverty.[7] The 2010 *United Nations Millennium Development Goals Report* notes that the proportion of undernourished people in South Asia is again growing and is now on a par with that of 1990.[8] Pakistan is especially at risk. Struggling with violent jihadist terrorism, it has an estimated population of 190 million that is projected to grow by 85 million over the next twenty years.[9] It suffers from chronic environmental problems, poor literacy rates, and a stagnated demographic transformation. In its 2010 report on failed states, the Fund for Peace ranked Pakistan as eleventh in terms of fragile and failing states.[10] The US National Intelligence Council, in its latest *Global Trends* document, notes: "South Asia faces a series of internal and external shocks during the next 15–20 years. Low growth, rising food prices, and energy shortages will pose stiff challenges to governance in Pakistan and Afghanistan . . . [whose] youth bulges are large. . . . Inequality, lack of infrastructure, and education deficiencies are key weaknesses in India."[11]

The failure of SAARC also means that South Asia has failed to develop cooperative mechanisms against the multitude of transnational problems that plague the subregion.[12] These include riparian and other environmental problems, illegal migration and people trafficking, transnational crime, terrorism, money laundering, and weapons and explosives smuggling. This failure feeds into a vicious circle in which problems such as terrorism—in turn facilitated by corruption, smuggling of weapons and explosives, and *hawala*—fuel mutual hostility and suspicion among the countries of the region.

Other factors have also intervened in recent years to "turbo-charge" these postcolonial problems. As will be discussed in depth in the next chapter, globalization and the so-called war on terrorism have hardened positions within religious communities and eroded the traditional syncretic values enjoyed in South Asia. But globalization and associated changes have also had negative effects as transmitters of trouble within South Asia itself. So-called 24/7 reporting, enabled by light video cameras, smart phones, and other technologies, provides a crucial transfer mechanism for trouble and tension, both upward and downward. (But equally, 24/7 reporting also provides a mechanism for greater transparency.)

As illustrated by a number of case studies, these factors have assisted the process whereby events of essentially local impact can be raised to national and international significance. Such cases include the destruction of the Babri Masjid in 1992 by Hindu zealots and subsequent terrorist bombings in Mumbai in 1993, the riots in Gujarat of 2002, the 26/11 terrorist attacks of 2008, the economic and other factors associated with illicit migration between East Pakistan / Bangladesh and India, riparian issues as they impact on the India-Pakistan and India-Bangladesh relationships, and the growing problem of cross-border crime, which often acts to facilitate terrorism and other problems.

In these studies, we do not deal in detail with the situation in Kashmir. Although extremely important as *the* most serious negative feature in India-Pakistan relations, the subject is vast and complex and could not be fully treated in a study such as this. It has, moreover, been covered in many excellent, specific studies both of the situation itself and of its effect on India-Pakistan relations.

But before we commence our case studies, a brief note is in order concerning the role of politics throughout the region in acting to uplift and amplify issues that would otherwise be local in origin and impact.

DOMESTIC POLITICS AND CROSS-BORDER TENSION

The democratic process in South Asia is fragile. Most countries of the subregion have struggled to find a balance between traditional and community norms on the one hand and Western ideals of democracy and human rights on the other. Most are heterogeneous in their composition and are challenged by significant levels of poverty.

In Pakistan, the military has been in power for almost half of the time since independence was achieved in 1947. During that time even parties claiming to be on the left of the political spectrum such as the Pakistan People's Party have used the competition with India to maintain entrenched elites and avoid reform of Pakistan's quasi-feudal system of landholding. The military has also used the competition with India and claims to Kashmir to maintain its privileged position. The fact that Pakistan owes its raison d'être to its character as an Islamic state has privileged Islamic-leaning parties. They have also benefited from holding the balance of power. Thus a state conceived by its founding father, Mohammed Ali Jinnah, as secular has become more religious in both law and outlook. In these circumstances no party can give way to India over Kashmir and hope to remain influential. For example, in October 2004, then president Pervez Musharraf's "October surprise" offer, which appeared to abandon Pakistan's demand for a plebiscite for the entirety of Jammu and Kashmir, was met with widespread hostility in Pakistan.[13] As pointed out by Stephen P. Cohen, Pakistan's problems with identity impact profoundly on its relationship with India.[14] These internal conditions in Pakistan have all impacted negatively on India-Pakistan relations, as discussed more fully below.

In Bangladesh the military has also on occasion intervened in the democratic process. When the military has not been in power, government has fluctuated between the more pro-India Awami League and the more nationalist Bengali National Party, which has frequently been in alliance with religiously oriented parties and which is more antagonistic to India. All parties have consequently been wary of forging solid links with India lest they be accused of selling out to the powerful neighbor. Recently India was again dragged into Bangladeshi domestic politics over the issue of the trial of the alleged war criminals from the time of the battle for independence from Pakistan. Large gatherings of pro–Awami League youth have been calling for the death sentence for guilty war criminals, a call seemingly supported by leading Indian politicians.[15]

A similar state of affairs persists in Nepal, which has been struggling since the end of the Maoist revolt in 2006 to develop a constitution capable of accommodating the interests of the people of the Terrai, who see themselves as having been marginalized by the interests of the Kathmandu Valley and Hills peoples. Another issue dogging Nepal is what to do about the approximately seventeen thousand former Maoist fighters who were demobilized in 2006. A deal was struck to induct at least some of them into the army. But the army does not want them, or at least not too many of them. The Constituent Assembly, which has been charged with developing a new constitution, has been stalemated. In this turgid political competition, India has frequently been accused of interfering—as happened when the Maoist-dominated government of the day tried to dismiss the army chief over the issue of induction of the Maoist fighters before his term had expired. In response, New Delhi has chosen somewhat to stand back from its traditional relationship with Nepal, but meanwhile China has been garnering influence in the strategically vital country.

Bhutan, another small Himalayan country caught between its giant neighbors India and China, has a traditionally close relationship with India inherited from the colonial period. The Indian military is heavily represented, particularly in the strategically vital West of the mountain kingdom. Bhutan became a multiparty, constitutional monarchy in 2008 and is relatively stable. It seeks to measure its progress not so much in GDP but "gross domestic happiness." Despite this, there have been some tensions with the Nepali community, some members of which have been forced out as refugees. As we shall see in chapter 6, China does not have diplomatic relations with Bhutan, but of late Thimphu has been moving to open out limited relations with Beijing, much to New Delhi's concern.[16]

Sri Lanka's minority Tamil population has been engaged in a separatist revolt since at least 1983—a revolt only ended by total victory on the part of the government in May 2009. From the first, this civil war has played into Indian domestic politics through its effect on India's Tamil majority state of Tamil Nadu and because of the role Tamil politics has in turn played in coalition building in India. After her loss of government following the Emergency (1975–77), Indira Gandhi became dependent on the South as an electoral base. This in turn became a factor in her support for the Tamil cause in the Sri Lankan Civil War. Later Congress found itself dependent upon coalition building and allied itself variously with the All India Anna Dravida Kazhagam (AIADMK) and DMK—its recent partner being the DMK. These two parties became locked in competition over support for the Sri Lankan Tamil cause in the aftermath of the denouement of the civil war, thus ratcheting up criticism of Sri Lanka in the state. Continuing arguments over arrests of Tamil fishermen and mistreatment of Tamil Sri Lankans have fed into the unrest. Such was the anger against Sri Lanka in Tamil Nadu that Sri Lankan pilgrims in buses there were recently stoned.[17] The DMK president, Muthuvel Karunanidhi, urged New Delhi to cancel Sri Lankan president Mahinda Rajapaksa's state visit in February 2013. Consequently, the government in New Delhi felt constrained to carry forward criticism of Rajapaksa's government on human rights grounds and supported censoring of Sri Lanka in the UN Human Rights Council in 2013, despite its predilection to leave such issues alone in view of India's competition with China over influence in Sri Lanka (see chapters 3 and 4).

And, as we will see in the more detailed discussion below, even India, the most robust of the South Asian democracies, has struggled with the role Hinduism should play in the constitutionally secular Indian state, with repercussions on communal life within India and cross-border relations with Pakistan.

Where domestically driven dissidence has been in evidence throughout South Asia, ruling parties have often found it convenient to blame these troubles on the ubiquitous "foreign hand." Indira Gandhi was notorious for blaming communal problems in India on it, meaning the Pakistani ISI and US CIA. More recently, and perhaps somewhat fantastically in the case of the Islamist extremist groups, Pakistan has blamed India and Afghanistan for supporting the Lashkar-i-Jhangvi, the Baloch Liberation Army, and the Tehrik-i-Taliban Pakistan.[18] What may be no more than a political convenience at home, however, can have the highly negative effect of whipping up paranoia and cross-border hatred. The BJP's Narendra Modi allegedly damaged the ongoing discussions on Sir Creek with Pakistan by bringing up the issue in the context of the Gujarat state elections and demanding that the UPA government refrain from giving any ground on the issue to Pakistan.[19]

It is evident from the above that the day-to-day conduct of politics throughout South Asia has played a central role in fostering cross-border antagonism. This negative role is intensified by other drivers we discuss below, including environmental factors, cross-border terrorism, cross-border crime, and economic imbalances. As the influence of the great parties that won independence, such as the Congress Party in India and Awami League in Bangladesh, has faded, politics has become more fraught, localized, and hotly contested. And this has made the kind of leadership capable of cutting through local concerns in favor of regional solutions even more elusive.

INDIA'S EXPERIENCE WITH TERRORISM AND ITS CROSS-BORDER IMPLICATIONS

A number of cases covered below touch upon the violence emanating from a small minority of India's 170 million Muslims. For want of a better term, we refer to this as "violent jihad" to distinguish it from jihad, which of course is not necessarily violent. Most of this activity can also be described as "terrorism."

A leading analyst of violent jihadist terrorism in India, B. Raman, argues it is caused by three events: the demolition of the Babri Masjid in December 1992; the rioting thereafter in Mumbai, in which many more Muslims died than Hindus; and the anti-Muslim riots in Gujarat in 2002, which also resulted in many more Muslim deaths.[20] It is also worth noting that other Indian analysts, such as Praveen Swami, date violent jihad even earlier than 1992.[21]

According to Raman, these events, which are covered below as case studies, "contributed to the radicalisation of two Muslim organisations which had existed before the demolition of the Babri Masjid [SIMI and al Umma] and to the birth of a new organisation after the anti-Muslim massacre in Gujarat [IM]."[22] But more than this, both the events themselves and the resulting radicalization of some Indian Muslims caused by them had wide-ranging repercussions among India's neighbors and resulted in a feedback loop of cross-border dissonance that continues to this day, vitiating India's regional standing and greatly complicating the task of achieving a more settled South Asia. This has in turn become a factor in links between some of those neighbors and India's competitors in the wider international system, especially China.

THE DESTRUCTION OF THE BABRI MASJID

The destruction of the Babri Masjid in December 1992 was the culmination of a long political process dating back at least to the 1920s. It had important political repercussions, which continue to this day. The mosque itself, supposedly built by the Mughal emperor Babur (the first of that dynasty) in the sixteenth century, is said to have been erected on the site of a substantial Hindu temple. Although there is archaeological evidence of an important structure on the site, the issue of whether this structure marked the birthplace of the god Ram must remain open, despite the decision of the Allahabad High Court, which simply stated that Hindus "believe" this to be Ram's birthplace.[23] Ram is a god who was widely popularized in the Bhakti Movement, which swept northward from South India during the Mughal period, perhaps as a popular response to forced conversions to Islam.[24] The story of Ram and the destruction of the temple on his birthplace have multiple meanings, in which the religious, cultural, and political aspects are tightly interwoven. These meanings in turn relate closely to the question of what constitutes India and the related question, who may call himself or herself a Hindu.

As early as 1923, Vinayak Damodar Savarkar had argued in favor of the cultural continuity of those born in India—a continuity based around the concept of *Hindutva*, or Hinduness. According to an often-quoted passage from Savarkar, "a Hindu means a person who regards this land . . . from the Indus to the seas as his fatherland . . . as well as his Holyland."[25] As Varshney points out, "the definition is thus territorial (land between the Indus and the Seas), genealogical ('fatherland'),

and religious ('Holyland'). Hindus, Sikhs, Jains and Buddhists can be part of this definition, for they meet all three criteria. All of these religions were born in India. Christians, Jews, Parsis, and Muslims can meet only two, for India is not their holy land."[26]

Those Muslims, Christians, and Parsis who accept cultural affinity with Hindus, however, could also be considered "Indian." One consequence of this is that the BJP chose a Muslim, Abdul Kalam, who is culturally syncretic in the Sufi tradition, as president. (Ironically, many Muslims of Wahhabi or Salafist leanings accused Kalam of not being a "true Muslim.") Those Muslims, however, who continue to look to Mecca as their holy land could not be considered loyal Indians—or at least according to the Hindu-leaning school of politics.

The founder of the Rashtriya Swayamsevak Sangh (RSS), Keshav Baliram Hedgewar, a Brahmin from Maharashtra, was a member of the Hindu Mahasabha, founded by Savarkar. He was deeply influenced by Savarkar's thought. Savarkar's idea about the cultural affinity of true Indians and Hindus was thus passed down through the RSS to the present day BJP, many of whose important personalities were *swayamsevaks* (volunteers) in the RSS.

The agenda of the Hindu Right was by the 1990s therefore twofold: to assume political office by emphasizing the differences between Hindus and Muslims/Christians and the fact that they threaten the majority Hindus through their "disloyalty" on the one hand and, on the other, to instill among Hindus the idea of cultural/religious uniformity, such that they are capable of being used as a uniform political tool.

The latter agenda was greatly complicated by the fact that Hinduism is a fragmented, polyglot faith, divided regionally, by caste, and by tradition into literally thousands of "little traditions."[27] Effectively to use religion as a means to gain political traction, the BJP therefore needed to achieve a higher degree of unity among Hindus and to show it was not simply a Brahminical religion. The god Ram suited this purpose exceptionally well. Ram is a popular god, especially in the North, the BJP's main area of influence at that time. He represents an egalitarian form of Hinduism about which all can agree. The attack on the Babri Masjid, supposedly built on Ram's birthplace, therefore brought together a number of key strategies: to show Muslims as alien invaders who sought to destroy Hinduism, to raise the profile of Ram, and to gain political leverage over the Congress Party.

Following the destruction of the mosque on December 6, 1992, there occurred around India a number of communal (Hindu-Muslim) riots. These were especially serious and costly in Mumbai, where a regional, Hindu chauvinist party, the Shiv Sena ("Shivaji's Army," named after the great eighteenth-century Maratha leader and patriot Shivaji Bhosale), formed the government in the state of Maharashtra. The Shiv Sena triggered vicious rioting. An estimated nine hundred people were killed, far more of them Muslim than Hindu, due partly to police bias, as found by the subsequent Srikrishna Commission Report.[28]

The devastation, loss of life and destruction of communal trust the demolition of the Babri Masjid generated within India also reverberated in highly negative terms around India's neighborhood. In Pakistan and Bangladesh, scores of Hindu, Sikh, and Jain temples were attacked and destroyed. In both countries the Air India office was ransacked, resulting in loss of life in the case of Bangladesh. In Bangladesh, where the Hindu population was then about 10 percent, many Hindus were attacked and some killed, as described in Tasmina Nasreen's novel *Lajja* (Shame), published in 1993. As the office of the United Nations High Commissioner for Refugees (UNHCR) reported, "Muslims attacked and burnt down Hindu temples and shops across Bangladesh."[29] These attacks still occasionally continue: As recently as 2013, Hindus and their temples were attacked in Bangladesh by Islamists angry at the passing of the death sentence on a leader involved with massacres during the Independence struggle.[30] And *The Pioneer* reported of Pakistan: "During the enhanced Islamisation of Pakistani society, the demolition of the Babri Masjid at Ayodhya was a distinct watershed. Hindu temples were looted and razed *en masse* with bulldozers, women were brutalised, priests were beaten up, and the community was terrorised. Now temples mostly survive as small shrines within homes."[31]

As might be expected, the depredations against Hindus in Bangladesh and Pakistan following the destruction of the Babri Masjid also had echoes back into India, particularly in the popular discourse of the Hindu Right. For example, in 1995, the Vishwa Hindu Parishad (World Hindu Council), the intellectual and doctrinal arm of the Sangh Parivar (Hindu Family), was calling on the UN to protect the rights of Hindus in Pakistan, Bangladesh, and Kashmir.[32]

The destruction of the Babri Masjid also had important indirect effects in terms of regional relations. As Raman noted, the process of domestically inspired terrorism perpetrated by Muslim extremist groups such as the SIMI and later the IM actually commenced after the destruction of the mosque, presumably inspired by the desire for revenge.[33] These events increasingly became tied in with extremism in Pakistan, especially on the part of some of the groups set up specifically to prosecute Pakistan's proxy war in Kashmir. The most notorious of these were the LeT and Jaish-e-Mohammed (JeM).

By far the most important of the terrorist attacks perpetrated in the backwash of Ayodhya was the bombings in Mumbai undertaken by the Bombay gangster Dawood Ibrahim and his D Company. These occurred in March 1993 and resulted in 257 deaths and the wounding of 700—to this day the most serious losses ever suffered in a terrorist attack in India.

Ibrahim is the son of a police constable from Ratnagiri, a coastal city to the south of Mumbai. He rose in the Mumbai underworld of the 1970s and 1980s through thuggery to gain control of property, prostitution, and racketeering. He graduated to major heroin trafficking, currency smuggling, and film financing and piracy in Bollywood.[34] By 1986, he had reportedly decamped to Dubai because of the danger of prosecution in Mumbai.

Following the destruction of the Babri Masjid and subsequent rioting triggered by the Shiv Sena in Mumbai, Ibrahim was incensed by what he saw as the unfair attack on Muslims. This precipitated a classic attack-revenge cycle—the serial terrorist attacks in March 1993. Subsequent trials of over 129 Ibrahim associates (100 of whom were convicted), which stretched out over the next decade and a half, illustrate the extent to which criminality and corruption among the network of officials and associates of D Company played a key role in the perpetration of this event. But more troubling still, the explosive used was the military explosive RDX (for "Research Development Explosive"). The large amount obtained signified likely involvement of the Pakistani authorities, especially the ISI. According to the Indian authorities, Ibrahim subsequently took refuge in Pakistan and is on Indian extradition lists to this day.[35] The United States has also placed Ibrahim on its list of wanted terrorists. The D Company involvement in the bombings and Ibrahim's alleged subsequent escape to Pakistan remains a continuing impediment to better relations between India and Pakistan, especially given the enormous loss of life in the 1993 bombing and Ibrahim's alleged continuing involvement in support of major criminal and terrorist activities.[36]

As already noted, in South Asia there is a particularly close relationship between crime, corruption, and terrorism. The fact that criminal groups such as D Company also engage in *hawala*, document fraud, and firearms and explosives smuggling makes them even more dangerous in terms of their support of terrorism.[37] Moreover, these problems are general throughout South Asia, which only goes to complicate India's situation. For example, India suffers from the fact that a major arms shipment route from South East Asia to South Asia passes through the Bangladeshi ports of Cox's Bazaar and Chittagong. The largest-ever interdiction involved a shipment of ten truckloads of arms through Chittagong, allegedly destined for the ULFA and allegedly involving corrupt senior Bangladeshi ministers and intelligence officers.[38] India's porous border with Nepal also often features as a source of smuggled weapons and explosives subsequently used in terrorist attacks and other crimes.[39] While the countries of the region have had difficulty cooperating, the region's criminals, such as Ibrahim, often operate regardless of national, religious, or regional divisions, being driven mainly by profit and, in the case of Ibrahim, apparently religious sentiment.[40]

The Babri Masjid destruction was an important factor in triggering a spate of terrorist attacks and militancy by groups linked to Pakistani groups such as the LeT. The tit-for-tat extremism generated between Hindus and Muslims, along with the fact that the subregion's borders have proven particularly open to terrorists and criminals, has caused an increase in the negative rhetoric between the two communities and triggered a vitriolic response at the political level. These developments continue to affect relations between India and Pakistan to this day. Among Indian Muslims, the party Majlis-e-Ittehadul Muslimeen and a member of the Legislative Assembly, Akbaruddin Owaisi, have been involved in a vicious stream of vitriol, only to be answered in kind by Vishwa Hindu Parishad leader Praveen Togadia.[41] The politicization of such rhetoric is relatively new for Muslims in India, who have generally preferred to keep a low profile. As such it is a profoundly negative development.

THE GUJARAT RIOTS

Another event that has resulted in increased terrorist activity in India was the riots in Gujarat of February 2002. The trajectory of these terrible riots is now well known and will not be discussed in detail here. Nor will we discuss in depth the interesting academic discussion around these and similar disturbances and their place in the understanding of Indian political and social life.[42] The main discussion will, rather, focus on their national and international implications.

Briefly, the riots occurred following the killing of fifty-eight *kar sevaks* (Hindu volunteers) at Godhra in Gujarat on February 27, 2002, allegedly by a Muslim mob. Following that event, riots against Muslims broke out around Gujarat, but they were particularly severe in Ahmedabad. In all, about two thousand people were said to have been killed, mostly Muslims. The governing party of Gujarat at the time was the BJP, led by Narendra Modi. The BJP is still in power in Gujarat, and it has chosen Modi to be its prime ministerial candidate in the 2014 national elections.

The allegations against the Gujarat government, police, and courts have several dimensions. During the riots, the police allegedly stood by and even assisted the rioters. Following the outrages, which included horrendous scenes of rape, torture, and burning of victims alive, none of the rioters was initially brought to trial, necessitating the eventual intercession by the Union government. It was only in November 2011 that a special court appointed by the Union government finally convicted thirty-one people for burning Muslims alive during the riots.

One level of complaint does not involve government conspiracy as such, but rather the allegation that the police simply reflected wider community anger over the Godhra killings and therefore failed to control the anti-Muslim backlash that followed.[43] As already noted, the Sachar Committee Report found that in India as a whole, Muslims are underrepresented in the police forces. But there have also been more troubling accusations of actual police connivance in supporting the riots at the behest of a biased political class in Gujarat. Although reports of police and political connivance are contested, the special investigations team established by the Supreme Court to inquire into the riots demanded the arrest of at least one senior policeman for complicity in the riots.[44] The team also conducted investigations that resulted in the conviction of sixty-three, with some trials still continuing. The allegations against Modi have, however, now been dismissed by the team.

The international response to the riots was relatively muted. Most countries took the line that they were an internal Indian problem. But the response among Muslims within India and throughout the region was far more troubled, even anguished.[45] Reports of the riots had a wide impact on Muslim sensibilities through the advent of 24/7 television news reporting of the riots themselves, recordings of the atrocities on video, and their subsequent circulation among Muslims both in India and abroad, including on Islamic websites such as indianmuslimobserver.com. Indeed, there is considerable evidence that the riots were a catalyst for recruitment and revenge attacks by violent jihadist groups in the following years, just as the destruction of the Babri Masjid had been a decade earlier.[46]

For example, IM operatives allegedly repeatedly showed footage of the riots to motivate young recruits to seek revenge.[47] The 2006 serial train blasts in Mumbai also evidently targeted Gujaratis, who regularly traveled the western line. Footage was also used by groups such as Ahl al-Hadith, which is in turn closely associated with the LeT and Markaz (a charitable and educational group drawing heavily on Persian Gulf returnees). Ahl al-Hadith is also active in the Gulf States where it provides an important recruiting base for the LeT and other militant groups. According to a report of the Maharashtra Anti-Terrorism Squad, Gulf money was also used to fund the tellingly titled Gujarat Muslim Revenge Force, which, again according to the Anti-Terrorism Squad, perpetrated the bombings in Mumbai of 2003—clearly targeting the Zaveri Bazar, in which many wealthy Gujaratis worked.[48] This role of the Gulf generally and Gulf returnees in particular in spreading Wahhabi versions of Islam throughout South Asia and providing finance for terrorism groups will be discussed more fully in the next chapter.[49]

Following the Gujarat riots, a damaging tendency for Muslim communities in western India (and also to an extent elsewhere such as in Uttar Pradesh) to become ghettoized was speeded up. *Mohullas* (neighborhoods) that had previously been mixed were split up. Streets were barricaded. In many instances Muslims were forced from neighborhoods in which they had lived for generations into specifically "Muslim" ones. Some of those thus expelled were kept in camps in shocking conditions, and no effort was made to move them back to their locations of origin.[50] Eventually, the riots and the reaction they provoked were to be used as propaganda for the perpetration of the second-most serious terrorism attack India has suffered, that of November 26, 2008.

THE 26/11 ATTACKS

The attack of 26/11 in Mumbai can be viewed both as an ongoing, negative factor in India-Pakistan relations and also as an aspect of the globalization of local South Asian concerns. The event will be discussed in the former context now and in its global context in the next chapter.

Briefly, the facts of the attacks, as currently known from investigations through phone intercepts, the interrogation and trial of the sole terrorist survivor, Ajmal Kasab, the trial of David Headley, and the interrogation of Syed Zabiuddin Ansari (alias Abu Jundal), are as follows.

The attacks were organized by the Lashkar-e-Toiba (now under the cover of a charity called Markez-ud-Dawa) under the general direction of a man called Zakir ur Rehman Lakhvi, a co-founder of the LeT along with Hafiz Saeed. He and six other alleged organizers of the attacks were subsequently arrested by Pakistani authorities, who refused to hand either them, or the head of the LeT, Saeed, over to India. Indian authorities also allege the close involvement of either the ISI, or recently retired ISI personnel, in supporting the attacks. India asked the Pakistani authorities to arrest a total of twelve suspects, including Saeed, but only seven have been arrested. Since the attacks, Saeed has been operating freely in Pakistan. Whether he was responsible for overseeing the Mumbai attacks or knew about them in advance is unclear, but he has frequently preached hate against "the Crusaders, the Jews, and the Hindus" in a way that would get someone arrested for hate speech in many countries.[51]

In his trial in the United States, LeT operative and former undercover US drug agent Headley asserted that a Maj. Sameer Ali, who was allegedly from the ISI, was in the LeT control room at the time of the 26/11 attacks, an assertion supported by Ansari, also under interrogation in India. Another alleged ISI operative, a Sajid Mir, was also accused of being involved in the training of the attackers by the same sources.[52]

The attacks, which killed 164 (including 28 foreigners) and wounded 308, involved ten gunmen who came by boat from Karachi. They mounted attacks on the Taj Hotel, the Oberoi Trident Hotel, the Chabad House Jewish Centre (Nariman House), the central rail terminus, and various other sites. After several days of fighting, the attackers were finally all killed except Kasab, who was wounded at the rail terminus and captured. He was subsequently sentenced to death and hanged, having given valuable information about the attacks, including the involvement of the LeT.

But perhaps the most convincing evidence of official Pakistani involvement comes from the sophisticated communication system used by the attackers and their LeT handlers. Subscriber identity module (SIM) cards for the ten attackers came from the LeT in Jammu and Kashmir, where it is under the close scrutiny of the ISI.[53] But more telling in terms of possible official involvement was voice-over-internet protocols (VOIP) for communications paid from Italy, some using Austrian country codes, and routed through an American company in New Jersey, CallPhonex. The cell phone of one of the killed terrorists also contained the e-mail of a certain Colonel Sadatullah at the Special Communications Office (SCO), a Pakistani government agency staffed by members of the Army Signals Corps. (The e-mail address is, or rather was, pmit@sco.gov.au.) The terrorists also used satellite tracking devices to navigate from Karachi to Mumbai. In the rush, the attackers, who thought they were about to be interdicted, forgot to throw the tracking devices overboard as instructed.

Whether any involvement by government or military officers was "official" or was perpetrated by "freelancers" within government agencies is more difficult to say. But the fact remains that the chief perpetrator of the attacks, the LeT, has been operating openly in Pakistan since it was formed in 1990.[54] Indeed, the LeT was actually set up with the connivance of the ISI. Today, in the guise of the Markez-ud-Darwa, it is allowed to keep training camps in Pakistani Kashmir, has been in close association with al-Qaeda, and as mentioned above its leaders, such as Saeed, speak openly of the need to kill Christians and Jews in language reminiscent of al-Qaeda.

What should have been police-to-police cooperation between Pakistan and India over the attacks has degenerated into a politically destabilizing process of tit-for-tat accusations. The rapprochement between Pakistan and India opened out after the attacks on the Mumbai rail system of July 2006 collapsed in the backwash of the 2008 attacks. Under this process, Pakistani and Indian officials had already met twice to try to establish some counterterrorism cooperation and protocols. Not only was this process overturned by the attacks, but also relations actually worsened amid Indian claims that it was getting no cooperation on its list of twelve Pakistanis allegedly involved in the attacks. New Delhi was also upset by the slow pace of the prosecution of the seven arrested in Pakistan in connection with the attacks. It was only some four years after the attacks that a Pakistani delegation was finally able to go to Mumbai to gather evidence in relation to these trials. But recently the prosecutor in the trials was attacked and killed by extremists, which will again set back proceedings.

Worse, the attacks brought the two nations to the brink of war—an event that will be discussed in greater detail in chapter 3.

THE INDIAN MUJAHIDEEN

The IM is said to be an offshoot of the SIMI and to consist of lower-level operatives forced to change their designation and go underground as a result of the concerted counterterrorism activities against the SIMI. As with the SIMI, IM cadres are reportedly motivated by the Gujarat riots of 2002.[55] The IM's attacks have been generally smaller in scale and of lesser complexity than SIMI attacks, being more indigenous in character. They occurred between 2007 and 2011 and included a series of attacks in rapid succession in 2008 on Jaipur, Bangalaru, Varanasi, and Pune. There were also more complex and destructive serial attacks in Ahmedabad, Delhi, and Mumbai. Some IM operatives seem to have links into Bangladesh, including through the Bangladeshi arm of Harkat-ul-Jihad al-Islami (HuJI), a group that spans Pakistan and Bangladesh. According to the Indian news portal *Rediff*, these links are facilitated by the fact the operatives can benefit from the porous border to take refuge in Bangladesh when under pressure in India. They can cross the border with the assistance of "brokers" for as little as Rs 200 and cross back to commit terrorist attacks.[56] A Bangladeshi student group, Islami Chhatra Sangh, reportedly assisted members of the IM in a jailbreak, with a view to assisting them to go to Bangladesh.[57] But generally the foreign connections of the IM have been more muted than those of the SIMI, which was closely connected to and supported by the LeT of Pakistan. The IB reportedly maintains that the IM was initially connected to the ISI but severed those links in the aftermath of 26/11, which drew major attention onto the ISI.[58]

TERRORISM AND THE HINDU RIGHT

Terrorism perpetrated by Hindu activists has had a relatively long history in India dating back at least to the assassination of Mahatma Gandhi in 1948 by Nathuram Godse. In the modern period, it seems to have intensified in reaction to the widespread, violent jihadist activities mentioned above. It is also evident as an offshoot of violent elements within the broader *sangh parivar* ("family" or group of Hindu associations) such as the Bajran Dal (the youth wing of the World Hindu Council). In itself, it is interesting in that it provides an excellent illustration of the kind of negative feedback loop we have been discussing concerning the propensity for domestic events to reverberate across South Asia's borders, especially between India and Pakistan. A good example of this arose when the home minister, Shushil Kumar Shinde, referred to "Hindu terror" and claimed that the BJP and RSS were running terrorist training camps in India, sparking a brush fire of negative commentary in India, especially from the BJP and its avatars. However, these comments were also picked up by the LeT leader, Saeed, who said that Indian organizations were "involved in all kinds of terrorism in Pakistan."[59] To date so-called Hindu terrorists have allegedly been involved in attacks on mosques, on the Samjhauta Express, and on the mill town of Malagaon, among others.

THE NATURE OF INDIA'S TERRORISM PROBLEM

Violent jihadist terrorism in India is generally conducted in a highly strategic context, in terms of both the viability of the Indian nation and the international war on terrorism. For example, since the destruction of the Babri Masjid in 1992, there has been heavy targeting of the commercial and industrial hub of India, Mumbai, with over ten major attacks, each involving multiple deaths.[60] Other targets included the vibrant information-technology (IT) centers of Bengaluru and Hyderabad. The capital, New Delhi, has also been attacked. Religious sites in the most holy of Indian cities, Varanasi, have been hit. The city known as a communal tinderbox, Malagoan, has also been targeted.

This apparently strategic targeting appears to be aimed at either damaging India's economic renaissance or stirring up religious hatred between Hindus and Muslims and thus undermining the viability of India's secular polity and derailing the India-Pakistan rapprochement—a task finally accomplished with the attacks of 26/11. This rapprochement had disadvantaged the militants fighting in Kashmir because it had resulted in a lower level of support from the Pakistani authorities. Further, the violent jihadists in Pakistan assess that should India and Pakistan be pushed into conflict by a terrorist attack, as nearly occurred both in 2001 and 2008, it would significantly undermine the United States–led war on terrorism, including the campaign in Afghanistan.

To a significant extent, terrorist attacks in India have been sponsored and supported from across the border in Pakistan. Bangladesh, with its highly porous border, has also been used as a terrorist haven but on a lesser scale than Pakistan. In the case of Pakistan, this support includes overall planning by perpetrator groups such as the LeT and the JeM, provision of explosives and arms, and training of cadres, especially in the camps of Pakistani Kashmir.

Although there is evidence of high levels of cross-border support for terrorism in India from Pakistan, terrorist attacks in India are also motivated by a significant homegrown component involving a small number of India's 170 million Muslims. In many attacks, Indian Muslims, including members of the SIMI, participate alongside members of extremist groups infiltrated, or otherwise supported, from Pakistan or Bangladesh. In some cases, such perpetrators are recruited from within India and in others from among Indian guest workers in the Gulf, where the LeT and Ahl al-Hadith have a significant presence. In the case of the IM, the group appears to have been largely homegrown.

These homegrown elements appear to be motivated by localized grievances of two closely related kinds. First, there is the poor socioeconomic status of Muslims in general, recently chronicled in considerable detail by an official Government of India report.[61] This report found that Muslims were worse off than the general population and even worse off than the Dalits (formerly known as "Untouchables"). This relative position was found to have worsened since independence in 1947. This is partly due to the fact that while the Indian Constitution provides special consideration for socially backward groups such as the Dalits, as a secular country no provision is made in India for minority religions such as Islam. The matter is further complicated by the fact that since Islam came to India in the twelfth century, those tending to convert were often from the lower Hindu castes. Many have remained in low-grade occupations representative of such castes, such as butchers, leather workers, and washermen, but have been unable to access the benefits that their low-caste Hindu brethren have enjoyed.

But the relatively low socioeconomic status of Muslims is not the major motivator of terrorism in India of this nature, at least not in the sense of terrorists being drawn from this background. It is patently the case that many of the terrorists, and especially their leaders, are not especially badly off by Indian standards. Indeed, they often have tertiary education, particularly in the science-based degrees, IT, and the professions.[62] This fact does not prevent such people from being motivated by the difficult conditions of their poorer brethren.

Another factor is that Muslims have been used as a "political football" by forces on the Hindu Right. Elements within the Hindu Right have tended to ramp up Hindu-Muslim tension in order to gain political traction against the secular Congress Party and its allies. As already noted, the 1993 Mumbai serial bombings were indirectly caused by the destruction of the Babri Masjid in December 1992 and a direct result of the widespread rioting that followed. Similarly, again as noted, a number of the terrorist attacks in Mumbai that followed the anti-Muslim rioting in Gujarat in 2002 appear to have been directed against the Gujarati community of Mumbai, seemingly in revenge for the Gujarat riots.

The sense of grievance is also driven by the perception that the Muslim community is treated unfairly by law enforcement authorities. The failure of local courts in Gujarat following the 2002 riots to make any convictions against perpetrators, necessitating the eventual intervention of federal authorities, sharpened this perception. Draconian counterterrorism legislation has also played a role in precipitating a classic downward spiral into terrorism, violent state response, and further terrorism. Police bias, the arbitrary rounding-up of Muslims following terrorist attacks, and torture and brutality have also played their part.

Between 1985 and 1995, the Terrorism and Disruptive Activities Act (TADA) was the major piece of counterterrorism legislation but was widely abused. It contained a very loose definition of terrorism, which allowed state and central governments to undertake mass arrests, ranging from trade unionists to agitating Dalits. According to Human Rights Watch, although the act enabled the authorities to hold detainees without trial for months, less than one percent of TADA arrestees were convicted.[63] In 2002, the Prevention of Terrorism Act (POTA) was introduced to replace TADA. POTA allowed detainment without charge for 180 days, and special POTA courts were established to try those arrested under the act. These courts worked under less stringent rules of evidence than the normal Indian courts, including the provision that a confession constituted an admission of guilt. In part because torture was sometimes used and in part because the usual rules of evidence were relaxed, POTA courts made many unjustified decisions. For example, a Delhi academic of Kashmiri origin was sentenced to death for allegedly assisting the attack on the parliament in December 2001. Subsequently, the Supreme Court acquitted him. Also, as with TADA, POTA was widely abused by state governments seeking to harass political opponents.[64] The act therefore became unpopular, especially among minority communities. It was repealed by the Singh government in 2004 but has been retained in a number of states. It was effectively replaced by an upgraded act of earlier origin, the Unlawful Activities Prevention Act (UAPA). Although somewhat better than TADA and POTA, UAPA still has problems. According to Amnesty International, elements of the superseded POTA have been incorporated into UAPA, such as an inadequate definition of terrorism.[65] Worse still, the National Security Act enables governments to hold those declared to be a national security threat in preventive detention for up to a year. This act is applicable in particularly troubled regions such as Kashmir. The Armed Forces (Special Powers) Act also enables the military to act with virtual impunity in terms of human rights violations in areas in which it is in operation, such as Jammu and Kashmir and some states in the Northeast.

Despite the fact that to a significant degree India's terrorism problem is homegrown, it is not necessarily always perceived that way either by the authorities or public in India. The undeniable fact of cross-border involvement in support of terrorism in India, mainly from Pakistan but also to an extent from Bangladesh, lends credibility to the view often expressed in India that most, if not all, India's problems derive from Pakistan. This perception, especially following the attacks of 26/11, has done significant damage to India-Pakistan relations. The fact that Islamabad has refused to extradite those accused and continues to allow groups like the LeT to operate with impunity only gives credence to these views. Unless Pakistan moves significantly to rein in such groups and cooperate more fully with India, it is difficult to see relations between the two countries moving forward. If, on the other hand, there is another serious attack hosted from Pakistan, the danger of a rapid deterioration in relations between the two, leading possibly to war, cannot be discounted.

CROSS-BORDER CRIME AND ITS IMPLICATIONS IN SOUTH ASIA

South Asia in general suffers from many of the problems and low standards in policing described in relation to India in chapter 1. Throughout the subregion, policing is still widely based on the British colonial model, which was an authoritarian, paramilitary one designed to suppress subject communities. There is no proper separation of powers. Most police are poorly paid, educated, and trained constables and senior constables, as in India. This is inimical to best-practice community policing. It also seriously undermines the capacity of police to investigate crime and provide adequate intelligence from the grass roots.[66]

South Asia as a whole also exhibits the close links between criminality, terrorism, and insurgency evident in India. Such links are often used to assist terrorist acts across borders. As we have seen, D Company is active across South Asia and the Gulf. Extremist groups across South Asia maintain a close nexus with sympathetic criminal groups, which provide funding, people, weapons, and money-laundering facilities. Groups such as the Haqqani network, which is based in Pakistan, and the Pakistani Taliban are often funded through criminal activities, especially illicit drug smuggling, illegal timber trading, and tobacco fraud and smuggling.[67] *Hawala* is widely used by both criminal networks and terrorists to move funds. Separatists and terrorists alike tap into the cross-border trade in stolen explosives and illegal weapons.[68]

Due to the traditional high tariff levels in South Asia, extensive smuggling networks crossed the region and were important vectors of transnational crime. With lower tariffs on consumer goods, commodities no longer feature so heavily in the smugglers' repertoire. Instead, the groups concentrate on human trafficking for exploitation in the sex industry and sweatshops or smuggling of arms, explosives, and illicit drugs. Other important transnational crimes include intellectual property piracy and money laundering. Cybercrime is a rapidly growing problem throughout the subregion.

While falling tariffs have diminished the role of smugglers, they have not yet been lowered to the extent that the incentive to smuggle has been entirely removed. According to one estimate commissioned by the World Bank in 2004, "informal" trade within South Asia is still between $0.5 billion and $3 billion annually.[69] The same report found that this illegal trade consisted of smuggling via Afghanistan through the UN-facilitated Afghan Trade and Transit Agreement (ATTA) trade corridors and thence on to Pakistan, by means of direct shipment from India with false bills of lading (purchasable for as little as $50) or via more minor routes across the India-Pakistan border.[70] Another commentator puts the informal trade between Afghanistan and Pakistan as high as $10 billion, which compares with an official trade of only $2 billion.[71] According to a reporter from the Pakistani newspaper *Dawn*, this volume of smuggled goods outweighs demand in Peshawar (the principal initial destination in Pakistan) and is presumably intended for elsewhere in South Asia.[72]

Corrupt and poorly paid border guards have contributed to the porosity of borders across South Asia. These porous borders in turn contribute to cross-border crime. A recent study by the BSF noted that its border posts were highly vulnerable on the Kashmir border, the Punjab border, and especially the border between West Bengal and Bangladesh. According to the report, these areas were subject to weapons and narcotics trafficking, human trafficking, counterfeit currency smuggling, and smuggling of cattle (on the Bangladesh border). The NIA alleges that counterfeiting is state-sponsored by Pakistan, with the intention of causing economic instability in India. The agency further alleges that fake Indian rupees, which are made from paper used for Pakistan's official currency, are smuggled into India from Nepal and Bangladesh.[73] Of the 987 border posts on the Bangladesh border, 112 were deemed vulnerable. The BSF plans to erect 286 new border posts in an attempt to address the problem.[74]

ILLICIT DRUG SMUGGLING

South Asia has for many years been at the crossroads of the international illicit drug market. In the 1980s and 1990s, Pakistan grew opium, manufactured heroin, and provided an outlet for Afghan heroin. It was also an important source of cannabis resin. Drugs were trafficked by the "scattergun" technique, often by West African organized-crime groups.[75] As with many trafficking locations, Pakistan developed a significant domestic addiction problem. Pakistan's role as a conduit for drugs diminished with a successful crackdown on West Africans and others involved in the trade. Recently, however, there has been an upswing in the amounts of illicit drugs, particularly heroin and opium, being trafficked across Pakistan and into India, adding significantly to India's growing problem of heroin addiction, as described in the previous chapter.[76] West African groups are prominent traffickers of heroin from Indian cities such as Mumbai and dealers in heroin within India, but indigenous groups are also heavily involved. Tribal groups located on the Indo-Burmese border in India's Northeast bring drugs across the border from Burma.[77] Precursor chemicals such as acetic anhydride for the production of heroin and pseudoephedrine for the production of amphetamine-type stimulants are sent from India to Southeast and Southwest Asia.

Since the early 1990s, Afghanistan has emerged as the largest grower of illicit opium in the world. Traditionally opiates were trafficked out of Afghanistan in the form of opium gum or morphine base. Most went through Iran, from where they were taken to Turkey to be made into heroin. The northern route through the Central Asian republics has also become important during the post-Soviet era.

Today an increasing volume of heroin is produced in Afghanistan itself. However, the NATO surge, in combination with crop substitution by the Afghan government and the United Nations Office on Drugs and Crime, has reduced overall production in recent years. At the height of production in 2007, Afghanistan was producing 8,200 metric tons—or 92 per cent of the world's opium.[78]

Afghanistan is often cited as a center of so-called narco-terrorism. During the period of direct Taliban rule (1996–2001), the Taliban taxed the production of opium and also hosted terrorist groups such as al-Qaeda. In this sense, drugs had an indirect role in supporting terrorism. Following the fall of the Taliban in 2001, the organization (now designated a terrorist group by many) became more directly involved in the trafficking of drugs, raising an estimated $70 million to $400 million per annum.[79] Key criminal figures such as Haji Bashir Noorzai, who was arrested in the United States in 2005, provided linkages between the Taliban and overseas trafficking routes.[80]

ILLEGAL MIGRATION, PEOPLE SMUGGLING, AND PEOPLE TRAFFICKING

People trafficking involves the movement of large numbers of women and girls from poorer areas to work in the sex industry in large cities such as Mumbai. Men, women, and children are also sometimes trafficked to work as semi–slave labor in factories, domestic service, and quarries. Nepal and Bangladesh are major source countries for trafficked persons in South Asia. In Nepal, official connivance reportedly exacerbates the problem.[81] Organized criminal groups are also involved, at both the sending and receiving ends of the trade.

Bangladesh has been a major source of illegal migrants into India, where there are an estimated ten to twenty million Bangladeshis living illegally.[82] This situation is only likely to worsen as Bangladesh struggles to accommodate the estimated ten to fifteen million of its population currently living on and farming low-lying areas subject to ever-increasing inundation from climate change.

Since at least the beginning of the twentieth century, people have been forced to migrate from the poor, relatively dry Meymensingh province of what is now Bangladesh into the lush plains and dangerous but fertile *char* lands (land created by shifting rivers) of Assam in India.[83] Today Bangladeshis are still being forced across the border by economic circumstances, assisted by the fact that the border, which is pockmarked with enclaves and irregularities, is highly porous, a situation made even more complex by the region's shifting rivers and *char* lands.[84] Anand Kumar claims that the Bangladeshi authorities support illegal migration as a way of gaining additional "lebensraum" for Bangladesh and that it has been assisted by weak regimes in India. He also claims that Bangladeshi migration poses a terrorism risk among a small number of the migrants and that the problem should be further "securitised" by India.[85]

A thriving brokerage trade assists people across the border for illegal migration and smuggling purposes. Low-paid border guards on both sides turn a blind eye to these activities in response to small but regular payments. In one case in 2012, a border crosser, unable to pay up, was beaten mercilessly by Indian Border Security Force guards. This crime was video-recorded and distributed widely, to the shock of fellow Bangladeshis.[86]

While many illegal border crossers drift into Assam and other neighboring provinces such as West Bengal, some end up in faraway Mumbai and Delhi. They have upset the ethnic and religious balance in Assam and are often resented by the local people. This resentment has sometimes spilled over into attacks on people of Bangladeshi origin. The influx of Bangladeshis has also fueled the separatist movement in Assam and elsewhere in the Northeast.

The situation in Assam is especially acute. In 2012, almost a hundred people were killed and four hundred thousand displaced in clashes between the Bodo ethnic group and Muslim Bengalis, mainly from Bangladesh. Five years ago, seventy were left dead in ethnic violence, and in 1983 an estimated two thousand Bengali Muslims were killed. Following the 2012 clashes, ethnic Northeasterners elsewhere in India received threats from Muslims and many fled to their homes in the Northeast for protection.[87]

The issue of Bangladeshi illegal migration has been taken up by the central wing of the BJP and other elements on the so-called Hindu Right, which either have genuine concerns about the national character of India or wish to exploit such tensions in order to extend the influence of the party beyond the Hindi heartland. The BJP also accuses Congress of leaving weak border controls in place in order to allow for the influx of Muslim Bangladeshis and garner vote banks in Assam for the Congress Party.[88]

Because of these local and national political ramifications, the migrations, which are essentially generated by local issues of governance and the environment in Bangladesh and facilitated by poor border control on both sides, have developed as a troubling, negative factor in India-Bangladesh relations. Securitization of such problems—that is, when they are considered to constitute an existential threat to the receiving state—has contributed significantly to the international ramifications of the problems themselves.[89]

ARMS AND EXPLOSIVES SMUGGLING

The smuggling of arms and explosives is widespread throughout the region. In terms of firearms trafficking, major routes involve the flow of arms from Southeast Asia into South Asia via the Bangladeshi ports of Chittagong and Cox's Bazaar.

Explosives and weapons are also widely smuggled across the porous India-Nepal border, including by Kashmiri insurgents. Although India has tightened control over the border between India and Pakistan in recent years, explosives and weapons are also still smuggled across this border for terrorist and criminal purposes. Sometimes Bangladesh is also used because the Pakistan-India border has become increasingly militarized. Weapons and explosives are also infiltrated by sea, a task made easier by the thousands of small craft that ply the coasts of South Asia. As already noted, both the RDX for the 1993 Mumbai bombings and the attackers of 26/11 came by sea from Pakistan.

MONEY LAUNDERING

Money laundering, especially via the traditional channel of *hawala*, is pervasive throughout South Asia. *Hawala* provides the major conduit for tax evasion and the laundering of criminal and terrorist funds. There is a major *hawala* "triangle" between Mumbai, Karachi, and Dubai. The Dubai link is also a staging post for the sending of illicit money back into India in a recycling loop. The issue is complicated by the fact that traditional banking still plays a legitimate role in the hundreds of thousands of villages of South Asia. India has tightened its anti-money-laundering provisions, as described in chapter 1, but it still arguably falls short of Financial Action Task Force requirements.[90] A 2009 study by the Asia/Pacific Group on Money Laundering conducted by the World Bank found that although Pakistan had criminalized money laundering and the financing of terrorism, it still suffers from significant levels of money laundering for both criminal and terrorism purposes.[91] Since then, the Financial Action Task Force reports that much has improved but that there are still some problems with the implementation of the action plan set down for Pakistan.[92]

CYBERCRIME AND INTELLECTUAL PROPERTY CRIME

Given India's love affair with information technology, vigorous pursuit of outsourcing, and rapid development of call centers, one would expect cybercrime and intellectual property crime to be major emerging problems. A 2010 report by the University of Brighton claims that cases of spam, hacking, and online fraud escalated fiftyfold in India between 2004 and 2007 but points out that the problem in India is still not as great as it is in China, Russia, and Brazil.[93] However, a more recent report claims that India is now the source of more international spam than any other country.[94] A *New York Times* report claims that India is *the* major source of the wave of cold calls offering fraudulent computer-virus repairs that has flooded English-speaking countries.[95] As elsewhere, this type of crime tends to be based on individual activity or relatively small groups, but it is worth noting that major organized crime groups, including D Company, are now involved in intellectual property crime in Mumbai.[96] In another disturbing trend, the counterfeiting of medicines—or worse, the sale of products having no therapeutic value or that are actually harmful—is now a growing problem in India and has serious international repercussions, including among India's South Asian neighbors.

SAARC AND COOPERATION AGAINST TRANSNATIONAL CRIME AND TERRORISM

As South Asia's economies continue to liberalize and develop, they will likely become even more exposed to cross-border crime. Yet the mechanisms to deal with transnational crime cooperatively within the region, such as those of SAARC, have manifestly failed. SAARC nations have implemented a SAARC Regional Convention on Suppression of Terrorism and an Additional Protocol to the SAARC Regional Convention on Terrorism. These documents emphasize cooperation against organized crime and terrorism among relevant agencies, especially in information exchange, completion of all law harmonizations, and the criminalization of terrorism, as mandated by UN Resolution 1373 of 2001. SAARC also has a Regional Convention on Narcotic Drugs and Psychotropic Substances and has finalized a text of the SAARC Convention on Mutual Legal Assistance in Criminal Matters.[97]

The actual state of cross-border cooperation against terrorism and crime within the SAARC region, however, is a far cry from the declared policy. India and Pakistan have no extradition or MLAT arrangements, and a SAARC policing arrangement (SAARCPOL) establishing the equivalent of EUROPOL or ASEANAPOL has yet to be formally established. Although information exchange appears in the exhortatory policy, it does not occur to any significant degree. Again, Pakistan-India and, to a lesser extent, India-Bangladesh problems and suspicions lie behind these failures. Nor are the region's poorly resourced and trained police services capable effectively of dealing with modern criminality, riddled as they are by deep-seated corruption. SAARC has no extensive programs in place to inculcate better cooperation among these inadequate police services.

The resulting cross-border crime and terrorism has a number of negative effects on the region. It provides significant enablers for terrorism and cross-border dissonance through international money laundering, cross-border smuggling of weapons and explosives facilitated by official corruption, and illicit transfers of people, including terrorists for purposes of communications, training, and perpetrating terrorist acts. It also adds significantly to mutual hostility and suspicion as countries blame their neighbors for their illicit drug, cross-border crime, and terrorism problems. It impacts negatively on domestic and regional politics, which have become criminalized and corrupted in a number of regional countries, including India, Pakistan, Nepal, and Bangladesh. And finally, unless addressed, it will act to restrain much needed cross-border trade and investment as trust is diminished at the commercial level.

ENVIRONMENTAL PROBLEMS AND SOUTH ASIAN DISSONANCE

Environmental problems provide good examples of the way global factors can interact with local factors and vice versa. Although problems such as climate change can impact locally, not all environmental problems are globally driven. But whether initially globally driven or not, they can still impact across the spectrum of security levels. In this chapter we discuss their impacts within South Asia, while in the next we will consider the impact of global environmental problems.

Thomas Homer-Dixon and Jessica Blitt have explored the way such problems can be transferred from localities to districts, nations, and neighborhoods, thus completing the loop of negativity. For example, a deteriorating local environment can cause local political instability, civil strife, out-migration, civil war, and other state-level governance problems that can make an affected state a bad neighbor.[98] Alternatively, poor governance can cause environmental degradation and all of the subsequent effects at state and interstate levels, as demonstrated in the chapter on Pakistan in the same publication.[99]

In South Asia, such drivers of poverty, displacement, and unrest are evident wherever one looks. We have already discussed illegal migration from Bangladesh into India and the tension it has caused. While it is difficult to attribute this entirely to environmental factors, since many illegal migrants might simply be economic refugees, we note that overpopulation in some areas of Bangladesh has certainly been a factor. Shanthie Mariet D'Souza and Bibhu Prasad Routray argue in a recent paper that many of the problems in Assam result from pressure of population and consequent scarcity of land, a point made in earlier work by the author.[100] Moreover, with climate change and rising sea levels, the problem is likely to become more acute, as discussed in the next chapter.

Across South Asia, problems of governance, tension over riparian issues, and traditional animosity have combined in a veritable witches' brew of trouble. As a subregion, much of South Asia faces an impending water crisis, driven by the needs of agriculture and industry and rapid population growth in some countries such as Pakistan. A study by the consultancy firm McKinsay et alia estimated that by 2030 India would have a water deficit of 50 percent on demand unless remedial action is taken.[101] The report continues: "As a result, most of India's river basins could face severe deficit by 2030 unless concerted action is taken, with some of the most populous—including the Ganga, the Krishna, and the Indian portion of the Indus—facing the biggest absolute gap."[102] The report also noted that by

2030, unless remedial action is taken, competition for scarce water would increase between major users such as India and China.[103]

Many commentators, including an official of the Punjab [Pakistan] Irrigation Department, Mohammad Javed, point to the role of poor governance over water resources as a factor in the severe diminution of ground water.[104] The problem is, however, widely perceived by affected farmers to be the result of the upper riparian power, India, using more than its fair share of the river waters.[105] The degree to which this accusation is true is unclear. But what *is* clear is that the two sets of problems (the riparian and water governance problems) have become entangled in the discourse and have placed additional stress on an already difficult relationship.[106]

Fish stocks throughout South Asia are also under pressure, with the livelihoods of traditional fishermen being threatened by large, modern trawlers.[107] They have been forced to fish further afield, often in foreign waters, resulting in arrests, deaths, and bilateral tension. In the case of Tamil Indian fishermen, the situation is complicated by the fact that the Sri Lankan authorities suspect them of having ferried aid and assistance, including weapons, to Sri Lankan Tamils. Hundreds were killed during the civil war. Even since the end of the war, fishermen have been fired on and killed by the Sri Lankan navy, and over a hundred have been taken into custody. All this has occurred despite a joint working group being set up by the two governments to try to deal with the problem.[108] These events have reverberated through Sri Lanka–India bilateral relations via the antipathy they have generated in Tamil Nadu, which is important electorally for the Congress-led UPA government.

Equally, the antipathy between India and Pakistan has exacerbated the problem of fishermen straying into each other's waters. Subsequent arrests have fed into the mutual hostility, providing a classic example of the cross-border vicious feedback loop. The situation is exacerbated by the disputed boundary at Sir Creek, which makes it sometimes unclear where the actual maritime border is located. Following the attacks of 26/11, which as we have seen involved the seizure of an Indian fishing vessel, India confronts a challenging task of policing its maritime domain, especially since India alone has two hundred thousand traditional fishing craft to monitor. Any crewmen of Pakistani vessels that therefore happen to stray into Indian waters are often treated harshly, further exacerbating tension between the two countries.

Another environmental problem faced by all nations of South Asia—but particularly India and Pakistan—is the growth of megacities such as Delhi, Mumbai, and Karachi. These cities are often poorly serviced and planned and contain vast slums where infrastructure is virtually nonexistent. While not all of these are necessarily dysfunctional places in which to live, some are breeding grounds of social dislocation and discontent, with their host cities and nations struggling to provide jobs, potable water, education, and other essential services. As noted above, the consultancy firm McKinsey estimated that India would need to spend $1.2 trillion by 2030 to cater for the high levels of urbanization it will experience.[109]

Such places could emerge as locations of discontented, unemployed young people who would fuel the problems of the region and provide recruits for terrorist and other violent movements. Karachi is a bellwether in terms of such urban decay. As Huma Yusuf points out, it has for many years suffered chronic political and gang violence, the two often being related. Seven thousand have died violently on its streets since 2008. Political and ethnic groupings battle for control, including through violent means. The city is also increasingly providing a venue for violent jihadist activities.[110] A number of senior al-Qaeda members have been captured there, such as Khalid Sheikh Mohammed, and the city provided the backdrop for the kidnapping and subsequent beheading of journalist Daniel Pearl in 2002. When elements of the Taliban and other extremists were forced out of South Waziristan and the Swat Valley by the Pakistani army, many were said to have decamped to Karachi to melt into the crowded city of twenty million.[111]

CONCLUSION

Many of the ills experienced by India and described in the previous chapter are also present throughout South Asia. Policing across the subregion exhibits many of the postcolonial imprints and problems of policing in India. Crime and terrorism have put down roots across the region, and the soft regionalism of SAARC is ill-equipped to deal with such problems. Unless better mechanisms can be put in place, these cross-border problems will only increase as trade liberalizes and grows. Local problems, driven by environmental degradation, scarcity of water, and rapid growth of population, have led to movement of people within and between the countries of South Asia and have often increased tension between subregional countries. These sets of problems are tied together in a Gordian knot that is difficult if not impossible to untangle. The nascent, often unstable democracies of the region add to such tension rather than helping to ameliorate it. Political and regional leadership seems unable to come to grips with these problems.

Together these problems mean that South Asia has failed to realize its potential as a region. It has troubling dimensions of poverty and confronts enormous challenges. Across the top of this difficult situation is overlaid a further set of global challenges, which will be described in the next chapter.

NOTES

1. "The king who is situated anywhere immediately on the circumference of the conqueror's territory is termed the enemy. The king who is likewise situated close

to the enemy, but separated from the conqueror only by the enemy, is termed the friend (of the conqueror)." Kautilya, *Arthasastra*, 296. For a modern discussion of the negative effects of size disparity, see also Miller, *States*.

2. Bangladesh shares a border with Burma, but the latter is usually not regarded as falling within South Asia. Pakistan also shares a border with Afghanistan, which is sometimes regarded as part of South Asia. Were India in possession of an undivided Kashmir, it would also share a very short section of border with Afghanistan. India shares the border of an exclusive economic zone with Maldives but not an actual maritime border.
3. For Muni, see the quotation in Michael, *India's Foreign Policy and Regional Multilateralism*, 63. For Michael's position, see the same publication, 107.
4. Panchsheel multilateralism refers to the system established by India and China in 1954 emphasizing noninterference and mutual respect in all international relations. It later became a leading doctrine of the Non-Aligned Movement.
5. Michael, *India's Foreign Policy and Regional Multilateralism*, 17.
6. Rajan, "Renewing SAARC."
7. World Bank, *Economic Growth in South Asia*, 4.
8. Reported in "Hunger Back to 1990 Levels in South Asia."
9. British Council, *Pakistan*, iv. The British Council puts Pakistan's present population at 170 million, but in fact the true population of Pakistan is not known, and an estimate of 190 million would probably be nearer the mark.
10. Fund for Peace, "Failed State Index 2010."
11. United States Government, National Intelligence Council, *Global Trends 2030*, ix.
12. For a general account of this problem, see Gordon, "Regionalism and Cross-Border Cooperation against Crime and Terrorism in the Asia-Pacific Region," 75–102.
13. "Musharraf's Kashmir Solution Hypothetical: Aziz."
14. Cohen, *Shooting for a Century*.
15. "Protesters at Shahbagh in Bangladesh Backed by India."
16. Arora and Sinha, "Bhutan Switches Focus to China."
17. "Relations between India and Sri Lanka Sour."
18. "Foreign Hand behind Balochistan Unrest, NA Committee Told."
19. "PMO Hits Out at Modi's Bid to Rake Up Sir Creek on Poll-Eve."
20. Raman, "Evolution of Militancy in Indian Muslim Community."
21. Swami, "The Well-Tempered Jihad," 303–22.
22. Raman, "Evolution of Militancy in Indian Muslim Community."
23. For the judgment, see eLegalix, Allahabad High Court Judgment Information System.
24. In the South, the movement focused on devotion to the gods Vishnu and Shiva and provided a popular, nonpriestly path to the knowledge of God. In the North, however, the movement focused on popular northern gods, Ram and Krishna, who were said to be reincarnations of Vishnu.
25. Quoted in Johnson and Johnson, *Through Indian Eyes*, 216.

26. Varshney, *Ethnic Conflict and Civic Life*, 65–66.
27. The term "little tradition," to be juxtaposed with "great tradition," was coined by the anthropologist Robert Redfield in his book *Peasant Society and Culture*.
28. For the full report, see Skrikrishna Commission Report, Sabrang Communications.
29. United Nations High Commissioner for Refugees, Minorities at Risk Project.
30. "Hindu Temples, Homes Attacked across Bangladesh."
31. "Fleeing Hindus Seek Shelter."
32. United Nations High Commissioner for Refugees, Minorities at Risk Project.
33. Raman, "Evolution of Militancy in Indian Muslim Community."
34. For an account of Ibrahim's rise and subsequent involvement in terrorism, see United States Government, Congressional Research Service, "International Terrorism and Transnational Crime," 14–15. See also RAND Corp., *Film Piracy, Organized Crime, and Terrorism*.
35. Unnithan, "Why We Can't Get Him."
36. For an interesting perspective on D Company and how it fits in to Pakistan's economic and foreign policy objectives, see Clarke, *Crime-Terror Nexus in South Asia*.
37. See the concerns of Indian officials expressed in Asia/Pacific Group on Money Laundering (Financial Task Force), "APG Mutual Evaluation Report on India, March 2005," 14–15, paragraph 13, and Lal, "South Asian Organised Crime and Terrorist Networks," 293–304, 295, and passim.
38. "Chittagong Arms Were for ULFA."
39. For an in-depth examination of weapons smuggling from both Nepal and Bangladesh, see Tripathi, "The Easy Way to Arms and Violence."
40. Prior to the 1993 attacks, D Company was a syncretic gang, involving Muslims, Hindus, and members of other communities.
41. "After Owaisi, It's Togadia's Turn to Make Hate Speech."
42. The broad parameters of the Varshney-Brass debate were outlined in the previous chapter. Rather than taking a position in that debate, we are simply claiming here that the type of leadership provided by authorities in the early stages of communal tension can make a significant difference to the outcome.
43. The Ahmedabad police commissioner at the time, Prashant Chandra Pande, is on record as having said to an interviewer from a Web magazine that "where the whole society has opted for a certain colour in [*sic*] a particular issue, it's very difficult to expect the policemen to be totally isolated and unaffected." Quoted in "Gujarat Riots Point to Need for Police Reform."
44. A deputy superintendent of police was arrested as a result of those investigations. See "Senior Police Officer Arrested in Gujarat Riots Case."
45. Dubey, "The World's Reaction to Gujarat."
46. For example, the Mumbai suburb of Ghatkopar, where many wealthy Gujaratis reside, was twice targeted by bombers. The eight attacks on the Mumbai rail system in July 2006 all occurred on the western line, along which Gujaratis tend to live. Even the attackers of 26/11 in Mumbai cited revenge for Gujarat while

mounting their attacks. Photos of the riots and of victims are still widely circulated on the internet. See "Burning Gujarat."

47. Chauhan, "Atif Showed Gujarat Riot Visuals to Provoke Youngsters," and Andhra Pradesh Government, Andhra Pradesh Police, OCTOPUS unit charge sheet.
48. "Saudi-Based NRIs Funded Mumbai Blasts."
49. On LeT financing from the Gulf, see Jamestown Foundation, "Lashkar-e-Taiba's Financial Network Targets India from the Gulf States."
50. United Nations Committee on Economic, Social and Cultural Rights, "The Marginalised Status of Muslims in Gujarat," 2, quoting inter alia Amnesty International.
51. Swami, "The Terror Commander in the White Kufi Hat."
52. "Major Sameer Visited 26/11 Control Room, Confirms Zabuiddin," and "Rana, Headley Implicate Pak, ISI in Mumbai Attack during ISI Chief's Visit to US."
53. "Jundal Reveals Source behind Procuring 10 Indian SIM Cards for 26/11 Gunmen."
54. For a fuller account of the operations of the LeT, see Tankel, *Storming the World Stage*.
55. The charge sheet and supporting documents written by the OCTOPUS Unit of the Andhra Pradesh Police for the Hyderabad High Court concerning the IM accused in the twin blasts of 2007 also identify the seminal role of the Gujarat riots in radicalizing the IM.
56. "The Terror Transporters of India."
57. "Cops Claim Bangladeshi Student Body Guided Sabarmati Tunnel Diggers."
58. "Why the Indian Mujahideen Is Keeping a Low Profile."
59. "Hafiz Saeed Seeks to Exploit Shinde's 'Hindu Terror' Remarks, BJP Launches All-Out Attacks."
60. IM serial attacks of 2011: 26 killed. November 2008: 157 killed. July 2006: 207 killed. August 2003: 52 killed. July 2003: 2 killed, 34 injured in bus blast at Ghatkopar. March 2003: 11 killed in commuter train attack. January 2003: 30 injured in market attack. December 2002: 23 injured in McDonald's restaurant. December 2002: 2 killed and 24 injured in bus blast at Ghatkopar. March 1993: 260 killed in serial blasts.
61. Government of India, Prime Minister's High Level Committee, *Social, Economic and Educational Status of the Muslim Community of India*.
62. It is an open question why this is so. My own view is that professions such as IT and engineering are often framed in less nuanced, more black-and-white terms than arts-related subjects and subjects such as law. This type of approach can sometimes lead to less compromise. But of course that can only ever be a theory.
63. Human Rights Watch, "Anti-Terrorism Legislation."
64. For example, the leader of the opposition of Tamil Nadu was arrested under POTA for advocacy on behalf of the Tamil Tigers.
65. Amnesty International, public statement, March 3, 2008.
66. For a critique of policing in South Asia, see Patil, *Feudal Force*, 10.

67. Mufti, "Funding the Pakistan Taliban."
68. United States Government, Congressional Research Service, *International Terrorism and Transnational Crime*, 16; Asia/Pacific Group on Money Laundering (APG), *APG Mutual Evaluation Report on India, March 2005*, 14–15, paragraph 13; and Lal, "South Asian Organised Crime and Terrorist Networks," 293–304, 295, and passim.
69. Khan, "Can Illegal Trade between Pakistan and India Be Eliminated?"
70. Ibid.
71. Yusufzai, "Across Afghan Border, a Smugglers' Market."
72. Quoted in ibid.
73. "Smuggling Fake Currency from Pakistan to India Is a Terrorist Act."
74. "BSF Maps Vulnerable Spots along Border with Pak, Bangladesh."
75. This involved recruitment of many couriers, or "mules," who did not know the details of those recruiting them. It was expected by recruiters that some mules would be arrested, but this did not jeopardize the operation or massive profits as a whole—hence the term "scattergun."
76. See Gordon, "India's Growing Problem with Illicit Drugs."
77. "Manipur Drug Trafficking Case to Be Handed Over to CBI."
78. United Nations Office on Drugs and Crime, *World Drug Report 2009*, 34, table 1.
79. Schmitt, "Many Sorces Feed Taliban's War Chest."
80. A PDF version of Noorzai's grand jury indictment, United States Government, US District Court, Southern District of New York.
81. United States Government, Department of State, *The Trafficking in Persons Report 2009*, 217–18.
82. Joseph, "Securitization of Illegal Migration of Bangladeshis to India," ii. See also Asfar, "Population Movement in the Fluid, Fragile and Contentious Borderlands between Bangladesh and India," 4, which puts the figure at twelve to twenty million.
83. Gordon, "Resources and Instability in South Asia," 72–74, and Goswami, "Bangladeshi Illegal Migration into Assam."
84. Asfar, "Population Movement in the Fluid, Fragile and Contentious Borderlands between Bangladesh and India," 1–4.
85. Kumar, "Illegal Bangladeshi Migration to India," 106–19.
86. "Bangladesh Anger over India Torture Video."
87. See Sailo, "The Great 'Exodus.'"
88. For an expression of this view by the BJP, see Kumar, "Illegal Bangladeshi Immigration."
89. Joseph, "Securitization of Illegal Migration of Bangladeshis to India," ii. However, Anand Kumar argues that there has been insufficient securitization, resulting in a lax attitude to the problem in India. See Kumar, "Illegal Bangladeshi Migration to India."
90. "Take Steps to Curb Terror Funding, America Tells India."

91. World Bank, "Anti-Money Laundering and Combating the Financing of Terrorism."
92. Financial Action Task Force, "FATF Statement re AML Strategic Deficiencies."
93. Rush et al., *Crime Online.*
94. "'Spam Capital' India Arrests Six in Phishing Probe."
95. "Multinational Crackdown on Computer Con Artists."
96. RAND Corp., *Film Piracy*, passim.
97. SAARC Fifteenth Summit, Declaration.
98. See, for example, Homer-Dixon and Blitt, *Ecoviolence.*
99. Ibid., 147–200.
100. D'Souza and Routray, *Violence in Assam*, and Gordon, "Resources and Instability in South Asia."
101. Water Resources Group, *Charting Our Water Future*, 15, exhibit 4.
102. Ibid., 16.
103. Ibid., 15.
104. Ghosh, "What Are India and Pakistan Really Fighting About?"
105. Bunscombe and Wariach, "India Is Stealing the Water of Life, Says Pakistan."
106. Sinha, "India and Pakistan," 961–67.
107. See Greenpeace, *Safeguard or Squander.*
108. Ramachandran, "India Fishing for Trouble in Sri Lanka."
109. McKinsey Global Institute, *India's Urban Awakening.*
110. Yusuf, "Conflict Dynamics in Karachi."
111. "Taliban Spread Terror as New Gang in Town."

CHAPTER 3

SOUTH ASIAN DISSONANCE, GLOBAL FACTORS, AND GLOBAL POWER COMPETITION

The impact of global developments on South Asia has been evident for centuries. The British, with the new ideas they brought and economic changes they wrought, may in a sense be seen as an agent of globalization. The growing influence of Salafist and Wahhabi versions of Islam in the late eighteenth and early nineteenth centuries, which challenged the syncretic, Sufi norms then widely in evidence in South Asia, can in turn be regarded as a reaction to the modernity creeping in as a result of the coming of Europeans.

Our concern is, however, to chronicle the impact of globalization as understood in the modern context—that is, as driven by the revolution in communications, travel, and trade that followed the Second World War and particularly as characterized by the digital age.

The other element we will consider in this chapter is the impact of global power competition on South Asia and the way it has exacerbated tension across the subregion. During the Cold War, this competition was intense and resulted in so-called blowback suffered as a result of the Soviet invasion of Afghanistan and subsequent Western intervention aimed at ousting the Soviets.[1] The Wahhabi and Salafist ideologies that came with Saudi and other Gulf money to support the mujahideen and the blowback resulting from the Afghan campaign eventually became mutually reinforcing.

Strategic competition between global powers has been able to take root in South Asia in part because of the climate of interstate tension described in the previous chapters and in part due to the conditions to be described in the present one. These conditions effectively provide a "hook" upon which wider troubles and tensions can take hold within the subregion. Several case studies, each dealing with recent events, will be discussed to illustrate this phenomenon.

Today competition among significant global powers is still to an extent being played out within South Asia. But it is now evident in the incipient, and sometimes actual, rivalry between China and the West and between China and the United States in particular. And as India itself emerges as a significant global player and competes with China in South Asia, this competition also takes on some of the elements of great-power competition. This recent rivalry is not nearly as intense as the Cold War version, however. Nor has it solidified into fixed patterns of behavior. It is consequently amenable to the way diplomacy and strategy are conducted. But it is also more complex than was the Cold War rivalry and thus subject to miscalculation.

In our consideration of global factors and competition among globally significant powers as they affect strategic relations at the regional level, we seek to broaden the emphasis of Miller and others. They are primarily concerned with the capacity of enduring, regionally generated friction, like that discussed in chapter 2, to escalate upward and affect global relations.[2] In this view, for example, the Indo-Pakistani competition over Kashmir could impact on the capacity of the United States to defeat the type of militant Islamic terrorism directed against it by groups such as al-Qaeda that have become embedded in the region. In determining the reasons for chronic conflict in South Asia, Miller looks to what he calls the "state-nation incongruence" as the primary cause.[3] By this he means the failure of sovereign borders to correspond with the "nation" or "nations" within them—nations being used in the sense of a group of people who define themselves separately. While such incongruence is certainly present in South Asia, the movement is a two-way one in the sense that global factors also act *downward* to exacerbate (and sometimes help contain) regional tensions, as will be illustrated in this chapter.

There is also a body of literature that argues that many of the discontents that trouble developing countries are products of the ill effects of the globalization of capital and trade and the destruction of the "global commons," particularly by its overexploitation by developed countries. Those subscribing to this view argue that globalization has weakened the role of already weak states.[4] And of course, in terms of the environmental debate, at least some of the environmental problems affecting modern South Asia are said to be the result of assaults on the global commons, particularly through climate change induced by carbon-dioxide emissions.[5]

Although globalization certainly has had a role in South Asia's malaise, that role is complex and falls on both the positive and negative sides of the ledger. Moreover, in analyzing South Asia's difficulties, it is problematic to know just what role is played by global versus local events. This difficulty is most pronounced in the case of the India-Pakistan problem, which has dogged South Asian security since 1947. It is difficult to assess, for example, to what extent the problem is attributable to the basic premise upon which the two states were founded and to factors such as Miller's "state-nation incongruence" and to what extent it is attributable to the way international events, such as the Cold War, the war on terrorism, and globalization, have intervened since.

To complicate matters further, at times globalization acts as a vector in drawing outside powers in and at times outside powers are drawn in by preexisting subregional tensions. Outside powers are also encouraged to play a role in South Asian security by the operations of the Kautilyan dictum discussed in previous chapters. And further, as will be discussed in the latter part of this chapter and in the subsequent one, such external presence is actually driving a classic security dilemma between China and India in South Asia and the adjacent IOR.

While the debate over cause and effect is theoretically important, the core of the argument of this book is not so much that tension is caused by global events, but rather that such tension, whatever its genesis, gives entrée to non–South Asian actors into the South Asian power equation that would not otherwise be there and that, concomitantly, this entrée negatively affects India's rise to power.

There are three major ways in which the global context impacts on power equations among the countries of South Asia. First, South Asia has been, and to an extent still is, a proving ground for competition among the world's leading powers. This competition in turn feeds into preexisting, intraregional tensions and exacerbates them.

Second, global ideas and forces concerning democracy and human rights, religion, economic management, and the environment impact on South Asia both for good or ill. Insofar as the effects are negative, such factors can further add to regional economic distress, unrest, and cross-border tension.

And third, South Asia has also become an important venue for the playing-out of the global struggle between what might broadly be termed the secular West and inheritors of that mantle such as India on the one hand, and the ideological-political-religious framework known as "militant Islam" on the other. This tension has in turn enhanced differences between India and Pakistan and greatly complicated their resolution.

These three areas are often interrelated, and it is a complex task to disentangle them. Conceptually the two most enmeshed are global power competition and the struggle over Islam. This is because Islam was at the very root of the response to the Soviet invasion of Afghanistan—which was itself both a manifestation of the then superpower competition and to a lesser extent a Soviet response to fears about an Islamic backlash in what was then Soviet Central Asia. Later, superpower competition also became enmeshed with the struggle over ideological Islam because of the harboring of al-Qaeda by Taliban-ruled Afghanistan and the subsequent invasion of Afghanistan by the United States and its allies after 9/11.

Again, as in the Soviet era, militant Islam was at the vanguard of the struggle to oust the United States.

MILITANT ISLAM AND GLOBALIZATION

Islam in South Asia has in recent years been shaped by two forces, each entwined with the other in terms of its effect. First, the Wahhabi doctrines as practiced in the Saudi Kingdom and elsewhere in the Gulf spread into South Asia in the context of the globalization of communications and ideas, the oil booms and the money they provided for proselytization and education, and the global spread of labor, particularly from South Asia into the Gulf. And second, a series of regional interventions by major, non-Islamic powers—first Soviet Russia and then the United States–NATO combine—inspired a conservative Islamist response, which ultimately led to the phenomenon of blowback.[6] Ideas and money from the Gulf both inspired the resistance to outside incursions and shaped the character of blowback itself.

In this section we deal first with the spread of Wahhabi and Salafist Islamist thinking as part of the general phenomenon of globalization and spread of ideas and wealth from the Gulf into South Asia. We then proceed to examine the effect of this phenomenon as it relates to the superpower incursions. We conduct this analysis on the basis that Afghanistan is strategically related to South Asia, particularly through the shared Pashtun lands between Afghanistan and Pakistan, but also by virtue of a long historical tradition.

The influx of more puritanical versions of Islam from the Middle East—and especially Saudi Arabia—into South Asia is not a recent phenomenon. The Wahhabi and Salafist revival movements and ideas in South Asia date back at least to the late eighteenth century, when they started to percolate into a Mughal India that was dominated by syncretic and Sufi forms of Islam that allowed the Muslim-minority Mughals to rule a populous and diverse subcontinent.

As the Mughals came under increasing pressure from the British, however, these compromises upon which Mughal rule had rested began to unravel. The reformist Wahhabi doctrine, especially as introduced by Shah Waliullah, was used to counter the evangelical and "modernizing" tendencies of the British in India.[7] Other examples may also be found of the use of Wahhabi and Salafist versions of Islam as a response to colonial incursion. In the 1830s there was a "jihadist" revolt against the growing influence of Sikhs and British in the Northwest. In the twentieth century, it can be argued that Abu A'la Maududi, founder of the Jamaat-e-Islami in South Asia, and Hassan al-Banna, founder of the Islamic Brotherhood in Egypt, were both responding to the modernizing colonial enterprise. As Dalrymple has remarked, "the histories of Islamic fundamentalism and European imperialism have very often been closely, and dangerously, intertwined."[8]

Although perhaps oversimplifying a complex situation, it can be said that three broad trends emerged from the forces acting on Islam in the nineteenth and twentieth centuries. The first of these was a stream that is today represented by sects within Sunni Islam such as Ahl al-Hadith in India, Pakistan, and Bangladesh and that may be seen as the intellectual heir to Shah Waliullah in the eighteenth century. Next is the Deobandi approach, which was in the Hanafi school of jurisprudence adopted by the Mughals but was nevertheless a puritanical reformist movement in response to the perceived modernization then being imposed by the encroaching British. And finally, the Barelvi school, also within the Hanafi legal tradition, represented a reaction to the rise of Wahhabi and Salafist versions of Islam. It was thus more consonant with the "traditional" Sufi base of Islam in South Asia.

This multifaceted response to colonialism warns that the equation in South Asia is not a simple one that consists of Islam on the one hand and other forces (such as revivalist Hinduism and modernism) on the other. Rather, it represents a complex overlay of tensions that is as meaningful in terms of Muslim-on-Muslim competition and violence as it is in terms of Muslims versus the rest. For example, one of the more violent movements in Pakistan consists of Sunni attacks on Shi'ites, a trend that has been further complicated by the relationship between Pakistan and Iran. In Indian Kashmir, the long-running insurgency has run into the sands of rivalry between the traditional, Barelvi-oriented, "Kashmiryat" on the one hand and sects such as Ahl al-Hadith on the other. And in Bangladesh there has long been a fault line between Wahhabi revivalism and the "traditional," syncretic Islam colored by the Bengali culture that was so instrumental in triggering the East Pakistan revolt in the first place.

In Pakistan this tension between the different Islamic sects was further exacerbated by the fact that both the Wahhabi and Deobandi streams were eventually to become embedded in Pakistani confessional politics. In this ongoing competition, the Wahhabi-leaning groups are today strong in both North and South Punjab, as represented, for example, by the terrorist group LeT (and its front Jamaat-ud-Dawa) and the violent anti-Shi'ite group Lashkar-e-Jhangvi. The Deobandis are strong in Khyber Pakhtunkhwa; the Taliban and terrorist group JeM are adherents.[9] Barelvi, or Sufi, traditions continue to be represented throughout but particularly in rural areas and in Sindh.

Aside from these historical influences, in more recent times Tahir Kamran identifies four factors that have assisted the rise of Wahhabi Islamist ideas in Pakistan. These are the Afghan jihad of the 1980s and associated blowback; the Iranian Revolution of 1979, which fostered the Shi'ite cause in Pakistan and caused a violent Sunni backlash, which continues today; the programs of President Muhammad Zia-ul-Haq and particularly his introduction of the Zakat and Ushr ordinance of 1980, which gave a sound financial base to religious groups; and the role of Saudi money and returned Gulf emigrants in fostering Ahl al-Hadith and similar ideologies.[10] Particularly important was the jihad against the Soviets in Afghanistan—obviously a venue where outside power competition and global factors coalesced.

The Afghan mujahideen, who were seeking to oust the Soviet Union from Afghanistan, were funded by the United States and Saudi Arabia. In the US case, the funds came through the CIA and in the Saudi case through the Saudi intelligence agency, Al Mukhabarat Al A'amah, with Prince Turki al-Faisal as its director-general. The CIA also provided large numbers of "nontraceable" weapons, mainly diverted from Egypt, which possessed a significant stock of Soviet-era weapons, including the Kalashnikov much loved by the mujahideen. As for the Saudis, Prince Turki took special care to ensure that funds were channeled to groups that favored the Saudi, Wahhabi approach to Islam.[11] Such groups subsequently gained considerably in strength.

With the ousting of the Soviets in late 1989, some within the mujahideen movement turned on their Western supporters and also commenced fighting violent jihad in Indian Kashmir, which was part of the blowback. The Soviet invasion and its aftermath also wrought a profound change in Pakistan, giving a boost to the now pervasive "Kalashnikov culture."[12] President Zia-al-Huq was given space as dictator to introduce aspects of Sharia Law, including the Hadood Ordinance, which was heavily criticized by human rights groups in the West. Crucially, he also increased the Islamic content in the training and conduct of the officer corps of the army. As the "most allied ally" of the United States and an essential factor in supporting the Afghan mujahideen, Pakistan was also enabled to complete the process of acquiring nuclear weapons under A. Q. Khan and with the direct assistance of China.[13] It was given F-16 fighter aircraft, which it was able to modify as an early delivery vehicle for such weapons. The influx of some three million Afghan refugees not only unsettled Pakistan, but also unleashed a breeding ground for future movements of violent jihad, including the Taliban, some elements of which, such as the Haqqani network, are still backed by the ISI. Mostly poor, the refugees sought to educate their boys in the proliferating madrassas, some of which (especially of the Deobandi persuasion) became recruiting grounds for the future Taliban leadership.[14] As the main conduit for support for the mujahideen and subsequently the Taliban, the ISI was able to position itself as one of the most powerful and secretive institutions in Pakistan.

Cashed-up oil states such as Saudi Arabia not only gave money to the mujahideen, but also provided funding for mosques and madrassas. This in turn buttressed those on the conservative, religious Right within Pakistani confessional politics. Their balancing status within Pakistani politics also assisted a growing interest in puritanical versions of Islam, as the religious parties sought to further their political positions by constantly raising the religious stakes. Consequently the Pakistan of Jinnah, who had envisioned the country as a pluralist home for Muslims, Christians, and Hindus, emerged as a relatively rigid, religiously oriented state under a hybrid of Sharia and common law.[15]

This challenge to traditional South Asian Sufism came to extend well beyond Pakistan into Bangladesh and India. As Kaplan comments in the context of Bangladesh, "a new class of society is emerging that is 'globally Islamic' rather than 'specifically Bengali.'"[16] New Delhi was so concerned it passed the Foreign Contribution Regulation Act (FCRA) in 1976, intended to limit the flow of foreign money into India. Even as recently as 2001, the Indian Union minister of state for the Ministry of Home Affairs claimed that $1 billion flowed into India each year for religious education, including for madrassas.[17] (This is such a large amount that it is difficult to credit.)

It is now widely argued that these funds and effects of blowback provide significant ballast to violent jihad. A Wikileaks cable emanating from Islamabad revealed that as recently as 2011, as much as $100 million per annum was flowing into southern Punjab alone from Saudi Arabia and the United Arab Emirates (UAE). The cable pointed out that much of this money was being channeled into extremist groups such as the LeT (or its proxy, Jamaat-ud-Dawa), the al-Khidmat Foundation, and the JeM. It was then used to channel boys (and sometimes girls) of poor, large families into Ahl al-Hadith or Deobandi madrassas. These were in turn allegedly purpose-designed recruiting grounds for violent jihadi activity. Such activities were fostered by the deteriorating conditions in South Punjab as the population expanded and landlessness increased.[18]

This argument about the connectivity between Gulf money and the rise of extremist Islam has also been used in the context of the separatist movement in Indian Kashmir. According to this argument, ex-mujahideen, who might otherwise have been a thorn in the side of the Pakistani state, were channeled against Indian Kashmir by the ISI.[19] It is further argued that the background in Indian Kashmir against which these extremists operated was reshaped away from the so-called Kashmiriyat by the influx of Gulf money.[20] For example, the newsmagazine *India Today* claimed that the equivalent of billions of dollars is flowing into the Kashmir Valley from Saudi Arabia, including through *hawala*, in order to circumvent the FCRA. Further, it is claimed that this money has eroded the traditional Kashmiriyat values and inculcated Wahhabi and Salafist doctrines, including those of Ahl al-Hadith. The article claims there are now seven hundred Ahl al-Hadith mosques across the valley, along with associated madrassas.[21] *The Times of India* argues that the Wahhabi incursion, including with Saudi money, has now triggered a Barelvi backlash in the valley and sectarian strife.[22] Interested parties—whether agents of India, Pakistan, or separatist groups—are attempting further to split the Muslims of the valley by torching Sufi religious shrines.[23]

Despite such evidence, it is still difficult to separate the role of blowback from the general globalization picking up pace before and since the Soviet withdrawal from Afghanistan. For example, globalization of the labor market has witnessed increased flows of South Asian guest workers into the Persian Gulf. By 2004, there were an estimated 1.9 million Pakistanis working in the Gulf.[24] In 2011, the *Asian Wall Street Journal* reported: "Arab manpower once comprised the bulk of this imported work force [of Gulf nations]. Now, some 11 million of the GCC's [Gulf Cooperation Council's] guest workers hail from countries east of the Persian Gulf, mainly India and Pakistan." The *Journal* further reported that these included 4.9 million Indians, 2.0 million Pakistanis, and 0.9 million Bangladeshis. According to the *Journal*, large numbers of South Asians reportedly started to enter the Gulf in the 1990s, where they were preferred over Arab workers because they were cheaper and did not put down roots.[25]

Of course, only a small percentage of these workers were radicalized as a result of their experience. But in terms of that minority, the role of the Gulf has been threefold: as a location for radicalization, as a source of funding to commit violence (as distinct from the funding mentioned above to progress Islamic education), and as a place of refuge from which it is difficult to be extradited. Within the process of radicalization, Ahl al-Hadith has been an important vehicle, especially for those from Pakistani Punjab and South India.

In terms of terrorism in India, Indian authorities claim to have established a money trail and identified terrorist networks into the Gulf.[26] The Maharashtra Anti-Terrorism Squad (ATS) alleges that an amount of Rs 12 million was sent from Saudi Arabia by nonresident Indians (NRIs) and used to fund the multiple blasts of July 7, 2006, in which over two hundred died.[27] The serial blasts of July 13, 2011, were also allegedly funded through *hawala* by criminals from Dubai via a Delhi-based *hawala* dealer, as were the August 2012 serial blasts at Pune.[28] And there are many other instances of Gulf connections, in terms of recruitment, refuge, and funding, relating to terrorism in India. Indeed, significant numbers of the membership of the two most active homegrown terrorist groups in India—the SIMI and its later incarnation, the IM—had Gulf experience. As suggested in the previous chapter, many were working in technical and IT areas. They were also often recruited through their links with the LeT and Ahl al-Hadith. According to the noted commentator on terrorism in India, Praveen Swami, "investigators in India have developed significant new insights into the almost invisible threads linking together three apparently distinct jihadist enterprises: the urban bombing campaign that has claimed hundreds of lives across India since 2005; the November 2008 assault on Mumbai; and a wider jihadist apparatus stretching across the Indian Ocean from the Persian Gulf to Bangladesh."[29] Swami goes on to point out that by 2009, the LeT was a multicountry-based, networked organization that was difficult to deal with in any one country.[30] In other words, like al-Qaeda, it had become a "globalized" concern.

For many years Gulf countries have played a significant role in providing havens for those wanted for terrorism attacks in India. Most notoriously, Dawood Ibrahim, planner of the 1993 Mumbai serial bombings, has made Dubai his headquarters. Recently India achieved a significant breakthrough in extraditing an alleged key organizer of the 26/11 attacks, Zabiuddin Ansari (alias Abu Jundal), from Saudi Arabia, the first-ever such extradition of an alleged terrorist. At the time of writing, India is also seeking to extradite Fasih Mahmood, an engineer who is an alleged participant in two terrorist attacks in 2010 and alleged member of the IM.

The coming of the internet, which made extremist, violent jihadist ideas readily available on Islamic sites in South Asia, also played a significant role in the process of undermining syncretic forms of Islam. Today social network sites such as Facebook, Twitter, and YouTube carry extremist messages.[31] Lashkar-e-Taiba puts considerable store on the internet, and it reportedly even has a team of experts dedicated to managing its various sites.[32] Even moderate, well-known Islamic sites in India have used events such as the destruction of the Babri Masjid and Gujarat riots of 2002 to galvanize opinion and radicalize young Muslims.[33] Although they do not advocate violence, Deobandi sites such as that of the seminary Darul Uloom provide classic Sunni, conservative interpretations of the Sharia and Koran, including through prolific use of fatwas.[34] Then there is a whole range of more sinister sites encouraging terrorism and hatred, such as Jamaat-ud-Dawa's official website and Facebook page. Although seemingly anodyne, with quotes from Hafiz Saeed showing his allegedly peace-loving nature, the commentary on these sites, when one digs down, is redolent with hatred, including vehement anti-Semitism and anti-Hinduism.[35] More darkly still, there is ample evidence within India and the region that potential violent jihadists have been inspired by internet sites such as al-Qaeda's online magazine *Inspire*.[36]

As explored in the previous chapter, however, the fact that much of the jihadist violence experienced in India was either directly or indirectly related to the rise of the politics of the Hindu Right confuses the already complex chain of causality evident in the rise of violent jihadist terrorism in India and elsewhere in South Asia. While the rise of Hindu politics in India had its own domestic and colonial roots going back to the 1920s and even earlier, there is also a sense in which the increasing salience of Hindu politics is itself driven partly by forms of globalization. The inexorable rise of the Indian diaspora has played an important role, both in funding and in terms of the process of radicalization. And the internet has in turn played a key role in cementing together disparate diaspora communities, as illustrated, for example, in McComas Taylor's analysis of the tension between the diaspora in the United States and the non-Indian academic community. According to him, "shared outrage is a form of social glue that binds a group together. In the case of the Indian diaspora, it enables devotees to perform a new type of Hindu identity: a globalised, assertive, 'muscular' Hinduism."[37]

EFFECTS ON GLOBAL POWER COMPETITION AND SOUTH ASIA

As the United States increasingly falls out with its erstwhile ally Pakistan and moves closer to India, an incipient leading-power competition is again emerging in South Asia similar to the sets of relationships that pertained during the Cold War. In this potential competition, China is bonded with its longtime friend Pakistan, while India and the United States move closer. To an extent, however, this emerging "quadrilateral" is an unnatural creation in terms of the role of Islam in Pakistan, at least insofar as it relates to secular China and Beijing's troubles in Xinjiang. But in saying that, we also note that in the past there appears to have been little if any relationship between an intensifying role for Islam in Pakistan and the strength of the bond with China. For example, during those times when the Pakistani relationship with the United States has been at a nadir, such as after the Soviet Union quit Afghanistan in 1989 when the United States appeared to abandon Pakistan, Islamabad intensified the role of Islam in Pakistan's social, political, and diplomatic policies on the one hand and sought closer relations with China on the other. The binding force in both instances was Pakistan's anti-Indian and anti-Western tendencies.

The complexity surrounding the four-way relationship between India, Pakistan, the United States, and China is evident in two developments: deepening terrorism in India and the progression of the war in Afghanistan. In regard to the former, we will explore some of the issues by revisiting the attacks on Mumbai of November 26, 2008. In the previous chapter, 26/11 was discussed in relation to India-Pakistan relations; in the present one it will be viewed from the wider, global perspective. Following that, we will explore the international ramifications of the war in Afghanistan and the likely denouement of the war.

26/11 AND ITS AFTERMATH

The attacks of 26/11 were both a local (South Asian) event and a global event in terms of the playing out of the war on terrorism. In the South Asian context, they in part emanated from the desire of the LeT to avenge the 2002 riots in Gujarat. They also fulfilled the perceived need of the LeT to damage India by moving beyond the initial area of attack in Kashmir, which had been fully supported by the Pakistani state, to wider "strategic" attacks on India designed to damage India's commercial and industrial hubs, sow religious hatred between Muslims and Hindus, and derail the rapprochement between India and Pakistan then in place.

In the wider global context, the attacks were related to the war on terrorism. By that time, the LeT had increasingly developed the traits of an international terrorist group in support of the so-called jihad against the West. This was evidenced by the nature of the attacks, which targeted up-market hotels where Westerners were likely to be found and the Jewish Centre at Nariman House. Indeed, at one level these two objectives—that of "liberating" Kashmir and conducting international "jihad"—actually coalesced, in the sense that the violent militants came to consider that it was strategically necessary to separate the Pakistani state from the West and reverse Islamabad's growing rapprochement with New Delhi, thus derailing the war on terrorism, which was dependent on basic stability in South Asia.

China's apparent role in all this should have been at arm's length, insofar as Beijing had no interest in seeing Pakistan driven further into the arms of the violent jihadists. However, China did, in fact, play an indirect role in subsequent events, as will become apparent.

The concern here is to examine India's options and behavior in the aftermath of 26/11, keeping in mind that the attacks had a major impact on the Indian state, constituted a severe humiliation for the Congress-led UPA government due to the incompetent handling of the attacks themselves and the political attacks by the BJP they engendered, and represented a direct attack from Pakistani soil, possibly sponsored by elements of the Pakistani state as described in the previous chapter.

In deciding what to do about the attacks, New Delhi was constrained by the perceived failure of Operation Parakram in 2001–2 in the aftermath of the attack on the Indian parliament by the LeT and the JeM. Under this operation, India's mobilization of half a million men for a period of ten months had cost over $4 billion. While the mobilization achieved part of its purpose in eventually prompting Pakistan to withdraw at least some of its support from the armed Kashmiri groups by 2003, New Delhi also found itself severely constrained in the use of mobilization as a diplomatic and military tool by the fact that both India and Pakistan were now nuclear powers. Further, although India pledged "no first use" during the crisis, Pakistan considered it could make no such pledge as the smaller power in conventional terms. Finally, the mobilization itself was a clumsy procedure that took over three weeks, thus proving to be an inadequate tool for a rapid response to a terrorist attack—one capable of preempting diplomatic pressure for restraint. In short, in implementing Operation Parakram, India found itself stuck in a difficult one-way street strategically. New Delhi had no desire to be caught in such a costly dilemma again.

Given the perceived failure of Operation Parakram, the then BJP-led government sought to develop an alternative line of action in the event that another such attack should occur. This was a so-called surgical strike by limited forces. Designated Operation Cold Start, the plan was finalized by the Indian military by 2004. Such a strike would be strictly limited to an attack on a specific location such as a terrorist training site in Pakistani Kashmir or to a limited armored thrust from Punjab or Rajasthan. It could be quickly mounted—perhaps within seventy-five hours—thus avoiding the problem of international diplomatic pressure. And it would supposedly come in under the threshold of the level of violence that would provoke a nuclear response or even a major Pakistani conventional response.

Despite India's intention to calibrate Cold Start to a level that would avoid a major Pakistani response, New Delhi remained doubtful about the nature of that response. At the time of the 26/11 attacks, the then Indian Army chief, General Kapoor, said, "Surgical strikes are definitely [militarily] feasible but whether you wish to take that decision or not is a separate issue."[38] General Kapoor's statement was presumably intended to highlight the fact that, according to "the law of unknown consequences," there was no guarantee any limited strike might not escalate dangerously. It was therefore surrounded by uncertainty, and in the end the decision to use it would be a political rather than a military one. The US embassy in New Delhi also argued that there was no guarantee that Cold Start might not escalate dangerously. Nor, the embassy argued, would India necessarily have the capacity to carry it out effectively.[39] New Delhi's attitude to any limited military response in reply to 26/11 may also have been colored by Beijing's generally supportive attitude to Pakistan following 26/11, as described below.

In any event, the hesitancy from New Delhi (for whatever reason) to invoke a limited military response following the 26/11 attacks enabled Washington to bring its considerable influence to bear to prevent an Indian military response. The US action was twofold: first, to bring assistance to bear, principally through collaboration with the FBI, to ensure that a civil case for prosecution of the 26/11 attackers could be made, and, second, to urge restraint on India at the highest level and use its good offices as an intermediary between the two antagonists. As revealed by *The Hindu* in another Wikileaks cable, the US secretary of state, Condoleezza Rice, cut short a European visit to fly to South Asia and visit both capitals as tensions escalated over a hoax phone call to President Asif Ali Zardari threatening an Indian invasion. The United States was able to determine the incident was, in fact, a hoax, and elicit a guarantee from India that it was not intending to invade.[40]

The attacks of 26/11 thus placed Washington on the horns of a dilemma: Dependent on Pakistan for the conduct of the war on terrorism, it was nevertheless in the position of having to rein in both India and Pakistan and placate India by attempting to force Pakistan to take resolute action against the perpetrators.

To do so, it ramped up all its considerable soft power and diplomatic resources to the highest level.

But where did China, the other major player in South Asia, stand? Indirectly Beijing was already involved through the assistance it had given over the years to Pakistan's missile and nuclear programs, which contributed considerably to the Pakistani nuclear umbrella under which it was able to engage in such activities.[41] But in the direct sense, China would seemingly have nothing to gain from the rising tension and a great deal to lose. A destabilized Pakistan, which might well fall into the hands of Islamic extremists, could upset the whole of the Chinese province of Xinjiang. It could also indirectly contribute to wider instability in the vital oil and gas regions of Central Asia and the Gulf. One would think, therefore, that Beijing would have been privately urging restraint on Pakistan.

In fact, the chairman of the Pakistani joint chiefs of staff, Gen. Tariq Majid, met with the Chinese vice premier and defense minister in Beijing during the height of the postattack tension, when China pledged continuing support. Senior Chinese officials also visited Pakistan in the aftermath of the attacks to lend their support. According to G. Parthasarathy, a former Indian high commissioner to Pakistan writing in the *Business Line* (a publication of the Hindu Group), "Foreign Ministry-run China Institute for Strategic Studies [CISS] warned 'China can firmly support Pakistan in the event of war. . . . While Pakistan can benefit from its military cooperation with China while fighting India, the People's Republic of China may have the option of resorting to a strategic military action in Southern Tibet [Arunachal Pradesh] to thoroughly liberate the people there.'"[42]

Since this view of the CISS remained uncorrected by senior Chinese leaders, New Delhi would likely have concluded that, far from attempting to damp down the situation in South Asia, Beijing was engaged in a strategy of intimidating India so it would not retaliate against Pakistan. This would have raised uncomfortable memories in New Delhi of the 1965 war with Pakistan, when China issued an ultimatum demanding India dismantle border posts within its considered territory in order to exert pressure on India. As reported by the then defense minister R. D. Pradhan in his diary, the ultimatum caused grave concern within the Indian leadership.[43]

Later, in the aftermath of the killing of Osama bin Laden, China was reportedly the only power that publicly expressed support for Pakistan, even though bin Laden was located near the heart of the Pakistani military establishment at Abbottabad.[44] Despite the fact that a number of the ten thousand Chinese citizens working in Pakistan have themselves been killed or kidnapped by Islamic extremists, despite the strong evidence of the ongoing connection between the Pakistani military and some extremist groups, and despite China's evident vulnerability to Islamic extremist tendencies spreading from Pakistan and Afghanistan to Xinjiang, China still took this supportive line. As Harsh V. Pant points out, Chinese support for Pakistan appears to be virtually "rusted on" and to be impervious to any negative impacts on China of the conduct of the "war on terrorism in South Asia and Pakistan's role in it."[45]

From New Delhi's viewpoint, therefore, 26/11 and its aftermath illustrated the limitations imposed on India within South Asia by outside interference, particularly by China but also to an extent the United States. Such restraint was not consonant with the role of a putative superpower within what it would have considered to be its own backyard. Moreover, the ability of such powers to use intraregional antagonism as a hook to gain strategic traction in the subregion, particularly in relation to the India-Pakistan tension, was also a powerful factor in how the events of 26/11 were eventually to play out.

THE AFGHAN WAR AND GLOBAL COMPETITION IN SOUTH ASIA

The border regions between Pakistan and Afghanistan have always been unstable, virtually no-go areas. The important Pashtun ethnic group straddles the Afghan border into Pakistan. Up to the early nineteenth century, Afghanistan controlled Peshawar, which was its winter capital. For over a century the Durand Line has been a nominal, as much as an actual, border. The hands-off administrative conditions that apply in Pakistan's Federally Administered Tribal Areas (FATA) also mean that the border is even more porous than would otherwise be the case. Today Pakistan fears India may use its growing influence in Afghanistan as a means to open a second front against it. Islamabad may also have lingering interests in using Afghanistan as a means of acquiring strategic depth against India. Taken together, these factors ensure that Afghanistan is strategically and historically closely enmeshed with South Asia.

At its narrowest point, Pakistan is only about four hundred kilometers across. This leaves it highly vulnerable to being cut asunder during times of war with India. This strategic vulnerability is exacerbated by the fact that vital transport routes between north and south, and especially between the critical agricultural area of Punjab and the port of Karachi, are squeezed through the narrow Indus corridor. Pakistan therefore desires space to expand into Afghanistan in such circumstances. Equally, if not more so, it fears that should India gain influence in Afghanistan, it may be able to catch Pakistan in a pincer movement at its narrowest point. To mitigate the effects of any move by India to cut Pakistan in two, Pakistan's military has sought to gain a foothold in Afghanistan to counteract the Indian presence and possibly provide strategic depth. This was part of the reason for the Pakistan-sponsored takeover by the Taliban in 1996. It remains a factor in Pakistan's continuing desire to retain an interest in influencing the Afghan settlement today, for example by sponsoring certain elements within Afghan militant circles such as the mainstream Taliban (given haven in Quetta) and the Haqqani network, lodged in North Waziristan and supported by the ISI.

In recent years India has sought to counter these Pakistani moves by building an independent and robust relationship with the Hamid Karzai government in Afghanistan. India is also concerned to ensure stability in Afghanistan to prevent a repetition of the post-Soviet invasion situation, when mujahideen who had been involved in the anti-Soviet war were unleashed on Kashmir. A Taliban-controlled Afghanistan would also challenge India by providing a haven for those seeking to attack it, just as it did in the context of the hijacking of Indian Airlines flight 814 in 1999.

Until 2011, the strategy mainly involved application of soft power in the form of aid, technical assistance, and investment. But in October of that year, India opened out what New Delhi referred to as a "strategic partnership" with the Karzai government. In 2012, when US defense secretary Leon Panetta visited New Delhi, he expressed strong support for the Indian role.[46] Despite some skepticism concerning India's capability to provide strategic ballast to Afghanistan, India's record on exercising soft power in Afghanistan is reasonably sound. According to the Indian Ministry of External Affairs (MEA), India has already invested $1 billion of a $2 billion commitment, including on roads, power transmission lines, and a hydroelectric project. India has also funded a thousand Afghan students to be educated in India. Indian nongovernmental organizations (NGOs) have a good reputation in Afghanistan, particularly for their work with women. The *New York Times* reports that India has investments of $10.8 billion lined up for Afghanistan, including a steel mill to be developed by the Steel Authority of India Ltd., which, it might be added, is itself struggling to complete its own projects in a cost-effective manner in India.[47]

As to the strategic relationship, when taxed MEA officials explain that all that is really involved is some low-level training of the Afghan National Police (ANP) and other security officials, along with agreements on aid programs and lines of credit. They add that India does not intend to pick up the major NATO commitment to train the Afghan National Army (ANA) upon NATO's departure. They further explain that the term "strategic" was an unfortunate one to apply to the agreement, which was intended to convey a more general "road map" for the developing relationship.[48] The text of the actual agreement has been removed from the MEA's website. But according to reports, the agreement did and does involve training of the ANA as well as the ANP, along with equipping those forces. Already, as reported in *India Today*, India is training ANA attack helicopter pilots.[49]

Another facet of India's strategy for Afghanistan is to link that country into a regional solution—one that provides a strong base for the continuing existence of a moderate government not dependent on support from Pakistan. To that end, India has convened a meeting of relevant regional powers in New Delhi, including Turkey, China, and Pakistan. India is also developing with Iran, Russia, and the Central Asian republics the North-South Transport Corridor. This is intended to link Mumbai with Bandar Abbas in Iran, then provide access by land to the Caspian Sea and thence to Moscow. An important side corridor will branch off from this route into Afghanistan. India is engaged in rail and port developments and in coordinating the negotiation of various customs protocols. The route is even being seen as an eventual quicker and cheaper way from India to Europe. But from the strategic perspective, the side route into Afghanistan is especially important since it potentially gives India a viable transport link that does not involve passing through Pakistan.

India's aims in Afghanistan are, however, limited in scope and likely effectiveness by the uncertainty surrounding the situation in Iran and Afghanistan. On the one hand, Washington has strongly opposed India's economic relationship with Iran, which is a long-standing one. But on the other, America's strategic objectives in Afghanistan, which would appear to favor a greater role for India and other regional supporters (even Iran), seem to run counter to its nuclear objectives in Iran, since Iran is a key factor in allowing access to Afghanistan that does not pass through Pakistan. But this amounts simply to another complication in an already complicated region.

Certainly, the strategic partnership agreement between India and Afghanistan is perceived in Pakistan to represent "strategic" Indian engagement in the conventional military usage of that term. Pakistan was reportedly "furious" about the move. Islamabad is of the view that India's three consulates (located at Mazar-i-Sharif, Kandahar, and Jalalabad) are spy facilities and is concerned that any deepening military-to-military relationship could constitute a significant strategic challenge, for reasons mentioned above.[50] It is likely, therefore, that any further Indian activity in Afghanistan following the NATO withdrawal could prompt Islamabad to more forthrightly support the Taliban and like-minded groups such as the Haqqani network in their efforts to destabilize the successor to the Karzai government. In doing so, Islamabad would have the distinct strategic advantage of preexisting relationships with the groups and geographic contiguity. A report by the RAND Corporation, however, tends to discount the threat of Pakistani retaliation in the following terms: "Islamabad's actual retaliatory options are not likely to be very effective in influencing US or Indian policies. Pakistan's cooperation on counterterrorism is already only half-hearted at best; it takes action only against groups that are seen to pose a domestic threat while supporting such entities as the Haqqani network and Lashkar-e-Taiba (LeT)."[51]

While that assessment is likely true in relation to Pakistan's influence over the United States and India, it does not address the issue of the likely effect of

Pakistan's involvement on the balance of power in Afghanistan once NATO has substantially left. For all its gathering capability, India is no NATO. Moreover, it is not contiguous to Afghanistan (whereas Pakistan is), it does not have the kind of relationship with key Islamist groups that Islamabad enjoys, and it could be involved with a deeply corrupt and increasingly unpopular post-Karzai government, depending on how the 2014 elections develop. In the words of the International Crisis Group, "in the current environment, prospects for clean elections and a smooth transition [in 2014] are slim."[52] To all appearances, while currently weak, Pakistan after NATO will possess many useful cards in its deck, which is exactly why the Pakistani military and ISI are working so hard to hang onto their assets among the militants, at considerable cost to the relationship with the United States.

Nor would these be the only elements at play in post-NATO Afghanistan. Already the Kabul government has been garnishing its "China option." President Karzai traveled to Beijing in June 2012 in relation to the meeting of the Shanghai Cooperation Organization (SCO)—at which Afghanistan was accorded observer status. This was yet another indication that China intended to open out a new strategic relationship with Kabul. Beijing is fearful that the impending NATO withdrawal would mean that Afghanistan could be destabilized, with highly negative consequences for Central Asia—a region of vital importance in terms of Beijing's resources requirements.

Ironically, it is China, not the United States, that is well positioned to reap any longer-term economic benefits of the NATO efforts to stabilize and "de-Talibanize" Afghanistan. This strategic advantage arises from the fact of China's greater available investment assets, greater geographic proximity (China actually shares a short border with Afghanistan and is developing land access with Xinjiang through the Wakan Salient), and policy of noninterference in states in which it is investing and providing aid.[53] While NATO and the United States have invested blood and treasure in Afghanistan, China is better positioned to benefit.

India is therefore likely to find itself in strategic and especially economic competition with China in a post-NATO Afghanistan, with every indication that China has already stolen a march on it, at least in the economic sphere. China has invested in a massive copper mine, which is still being delayed by security concerns, however. China is also interested in the oil production potential of Afghanistan. A Pentagon report estimates that Afghanistan has a trillion dollars' worth of minerals to be exploited. In addition, China has reached agreement with Afghanistan to train the ANP.

Ultimately, Afghanistan may be stabilized to the extent that a more moderate government than the previous Taliban government ousted in 2001 prevails. But according to the International Crisis Group and many other seasoned commentators such as William Maley, the process is likely to be slow, uncertain, and costly.[54] Even Afghanistan's much-vaunted mineral wealth could turn out to have its darker side in terms of fostering corruption and warlordism, as an article in the *New York Times* points out.[55] Pakistan is not as weak as it appears in relation to the Afghan endgame. On the other hand, India might be overambitious in seeking a strategic role in Afghanistan. China is also well placed to play a significant role in the unfolding of events. China's role in Afghanistan should also be seen as part of its Pakistan strategy, insofar as it may prove that at least in physical terms, Afghanistan offers a more viable route into southern Pakistan and the mouth of the Straits of Hormuz than the route across the Khanjerab Pass, which is geologically unstable and a challenging environment for major energy and transport infrastructure. To the extent India is looking westward as well as eastward, that gaze is unlikely to encompass Churchill's "broad uplands" of peace—or at least not for many years to come. Significantly, the struggle for forms of Islam and the way that struggle has coalesced with major power incursions into South Asia—whether it be the nations of the former Soviet Union, the United States, or China—have played a significant role in separating regional interests and making South Asia a difficult environment for India to rise to power.

GLOBAL POWER POLITICS AND THE END OF THE SRI LANKAN CIVIL WAR

The case of Sri Lanka and the denouement of its civil war in May 2009 provides another example of the way in which leading power competition and tension can still reverberate throughout South Asia. In this case the island, which is located athwart the highly strategic SLOCs supplying oil to East Asia, was able to shoulder off growing doubts on the Rajapaksa government's commitment to human rights by tapping into funding and weapons from China, weapons from Pakistan, and oil from Iran. According to Kaplan, "partly because of Chinese strategic concerns, Sri Lanka was able to win a war while rejecting the West."[56]

By the end of the war, Sri Lanka faced mounting debts and financial difficulties as a result of the militarization that had occurred under Rajapaksa in his government's final push to achieve complete victory over the Tamil Tigers. Sri Lanka was holding out for an IMF loan, but Washington was insisting that the government forces impose a humanitarian pause in the fighting so that an estimated fifty thousand trapped civilians, who had been used as human shields by the Tamil Tigers, could be brought to safety. The United States also cut supplies of spares for Sri Lanka's radars, C-130s, and Bushmaster naval cannons. According to Kaplan, "the Sri Lankans felt the Americans were slamming the door in their face just as they were dealing efficiently with a nihilistic insurgency."[57]

Following the end of the war, human rights concerns about Sri Lanka grew. The government refused to honor Amendment 13 of the Constitution, an amendment allegedly "imposed" at the time of the Indian intervention under Rajiv Gandhi that called for devolution for the Tamil-majority areas. The government has since denounced the amendment. Meanwhile, the Tamil areas were kept under military rule, and no effort was made to find a realistic political solution that would satisfy the Tamils. Instead, the government declared its policy to be one of full economic and political incorporation of the Tamil areas.

Allegations of human rights abuses mounted. General Sarath Fonseca, who split from the government and opposed it in the national elections that followed the war, was jailed. The attorney general was sacked, allegedly for corruption but more likely because she had opposed legislation designed to give the government an even tighter hold over the Tamil-majority provinces. A British television channel aired footage suggesting serious human rights violations and executions took place at the end of the war. These were followed up in 2013 with footage suggesting that Tamil Tiger chief Velupillai Prabakaran's twelve-year-old son had been executed by the Sri Lankan army.[58] The *Financial Times* reported that thirty-nine journalists had been killed or gone missing over the last seven years and that the NGO Reporters Without Borders ranked Sri Lanka only 163 out of 179 countries assessed in terms of freedom of the press.[59] Sri Lanka was admonished on its human rights record for the second time in the UN in 2013, although there were accusations that the resolution had been watered down on the insistence of India and Australia.[60]

The dilemma confronting India was acute. In India's case, New Delhi would have preferred that the human rights issue had not been raised at all. Locked into a competition with China over influence in the strategically vital island, India could ill afford to alienate the Rajapaksa government in circumstances in which China was applying liberal aid and investment with its usual policy of "no questions asked" on human rights. On the other hand, New Delhi was dependent on electoral support from the Tamil party, the DMK, which had threatened to withdraw such support because of India's weak-kneed policy on Sri Lankan human rights.

Meanwhile, China, with no discernible concerns about human rights and vast supplies of foreign exchange, was riding high. China had spent $1.5 billion on the development of Hambantota Port. The port is located astride the crucial mid-ocean oil-bearing SLOCs that service East Asia and China. Two to three hundred megavessels pass Hambantota daily. In August 2012, Beijing announced a grant of $100 million to the Sri Lankan military. In June 2012, it pledged $50 billion in spending on civil and military projects over ten to fifteen years.[61]

So even though there is no actual cold war in the Indian Ocean region, already we see there a phenomenon very similar to that which occurred during the Cold War, when the strategic competition became heated and both sides turned a blind eye to major human rights abuses, whether it was the Soviet Union in the case of the regime of Mengistu Haile Mariam in Ethiopia or the US support for the dictatorship of Zia-ul-Haq in Pakistan.

ECONOMIC GLOBALIZATION AND "INCLUSIVE GROWTH"

The individual countries of South Asia have become increasingly linked to the wider global domain by trade and investment. But this has not necessarily resulted in better and closer intraregional ties. Intra–South Asian trade is still only 5 to 6 percent of the total of South Asian trade, a rate that has been stubbornly entrenched for many years. This malaise exists despite a number of most-favored-nation agreements and the lowering of intra-SAARC tariffs under the South Asia Free Trade Agreement (SAFTA), signed in 2006.

According to a Bangladeshi official, the problem is due to nontariff barriers, with many SAARC countries putting major traded items on the "sensitive" list. The exception is India, which has removed all but twenty-five.[62] Another factor, however, may well be that trade complementarities are not all that great among members of SAARC, which is a problem difficult to fix with the best will in the world, a commodity often lacking among SAARC members.

Nor do SAARC countries fare all that well in terms of global trade. Overall tariffs are still relatively high and impediments to doing business relatively severe, especially in the regional giant, India, as the table below indicates.

Despite these problems within SAARC and within individual trading regimes, a number of regional countries have raised their international trading

TABLE 3.1 Difficulty of Doing Business and Trade Tariff Restrictions in South Asia, 2006–7

	Difficulty of doing business: Rank out of 178 (2006–7)	**Trade tariff restrictions, MFN applied tariff, all goods, 2006–7**
Afghanistan	159	—
India	120	15.05
Bhutan	119	—
Nepal	111	—
Bangladesh	107	14.4
South Asia average	106.6	13.02
Sri Lanka	101	7.21
Pakistan	76	12.28
Maldives	60	—

Data source: Ara and Raheman, *The Competitiveness and Future Challenges of Bangladesh in International Trade,* 11–12, based on the World Bank's *World Trade Indicators, 2008.*

profiles as a result of economic liberalization. India, by far the largest regional economy, commanded about only 0.4 percent of global trade prior to its economic liberalization process, which commenced in 1991. By 2010, India's share had risen to 2.2 percent. Trade as a percentage of total GDP rose from 15 percent in 1990 to 35 percent by 2005.[63] However, South Asia as a whole and India in particular still rank relatively low in world trade and have chosen not to emulate the foreign direct investment (FDI)–led model for exports used so successfully in East Asia.[64] Despite the widespread debate about FDI in India and the political sensitivity of the issue, which saw the Congress-minority government policy of 51 percent FDI in retailing overturned in 2012 (but since reinstated), FDI in India is only a fairly modest $31.6 billion, compared with $124 billion for China.[65]

To put this level of FDI in context, India is at a developmental stage in which it badly needs a vast injection of capital into its infrastructure if it is to assume the labor-intensive mantle likely to be divested by China as its population ages. The report cited in chapter 2 by the consultancy firm McKinsey estimated that India would need to spend $1.2 trillion by 2030 to cater for the high levels of urbanization it will experience.[66] Another report estimates that India will need to spend $200 billion per annum in the 2012–17 plan period to achieve its infrastructure goals to allow for a growth rate of 9 percent.[67] The devastating consequences of India's antiquated and poorly managed infrastructure were reinforced by two consecutive losses of power over the grid in twenty-one states in July 2012, which was a major blight on India's image as a destination for international investment.

China, on the other hand, has already invested heavily in infrastructure and reached a position in which it can generate a considerable amount of capital itself. One must therefore ask why India has not performed better in terms of providing a more favorable climate for foreign investment, business, and trade. The answers to this question will go some way to explaining how India sees its place in the economic world and what this means for its overall security.

Indian policymakers perceive themselves to be restrained in their entry into world markets in several respects. The first and most obvious is the political restraint arising from the fact that all Indian governments since 1989 have been minority governments. This restraint is especially important for the Congress-led partnership, the UPA, which is partly dependent on left-leaning parties. But even in the case of the BJP, which is widely seen as a party on the political right, there was a powerful element of economic nationalism within the party prior to its achieving government, as expressed by the Swadeshi Jagran Manch, an economic nationalist pressure group within the BJP.[68] Once in government, the BJP was more restrained in its program of economic reform than would have been expected of a party on the traditional right. And in fact, the major steps to open the hitherto autarkic Indian economy were carried out by a Congress-led minority government in 1991.

This element of restraint even within so-called rightist parties points to a second condition of Indian politics—a bipartisan view of the need to achieve "inclusive growth." The strategy of inclusive growth will be discussed in detail in the following chapter, but for now we need to note its effect on India's conduct of its foreign trading relations.

A major effect of the inclusive growth strategy has been on the conduct of negotiations in international trading forums such as the World Trade Organization (WTO). Initially, India formed part of—and indeed might be said to have led—a powerful group within the WTO negotiation framework that argued for concessional access for all developing countries. This group also included China following its accession to the WTO in 2001. Several arguments were brought to bear in framing this position.

Agricultural subsidies in the developed world, especially the United States and European Union, were said to have artificially depressed agricultural prices in developing countries and to have added to the pressure on poor farmers. The existence of large cohorts of very poor people, and the need to uplift them, was seen as a reason for allowing differential sets of tariffs favoring developing countries, especially applying to agriculture but also more broadly. Trade in services was seen as important to developing countries, and complaints were levied concerning their continued limitation under WTO rules, which were seen as favoring developed countries seeking to protect themselves from outsourcing and cheap labor.

India was deeply involved in pushing these positions, especially in relation to agriculture. Such was India's role that it was widely seen in the West as the principal reason for the failure of the 2011 world trade negotiations at Doha. The United States was especially critical of the BRICS (Brazil, Russia, India, China and South Africa). According to the *Wall Street Journal*, "Washington is asking the major emerging economies like China, India and Brazil to make more generous offers that reflect their tremendous growth in exports over the past decade."[69]

In 2011, the Indian commerce and industry minister, Anand Sharma, noted in relation to the Doha round of talks, "The critical interests to be served are those of protecting the food and livelihood security of [Indian] farmers."[70] Behind this statement lies not just India's desire to protect its perceived interests in the WTO, but also an attempt to address the political imperative of pleasing the agricultural community. This sector still employs over 50 percent of Indians and is home to over 60 percent. It is allegedly suffering due to globalization, resulting, it is claimed, in the burgeoning problem of farmer suicide.[71] (Other studies, however, suggest more complex reasons for farmer suicides, at least in Tamil Nadu, where lack of water, high costs, and high interest rates have also allegedly taken their toll.[72])

As developing countries, India and China share the comparative benefits provided under the WTO regime (such as they are). This shared benefit has led to a history of joint and coordinated activity between India and China in the WTO and other international trading forums.

Indeed, it has become an accepted view that India and China share a good deal in common as very large, developing countries when it comes to dealing with globalization of trade and investment.[73] Each is said to have a common interest in protecting its large cohorts of very poor people from the alleged ill effects of globalization and from the perceived domination of developed countries. Similarly, each is said to have a common interest in joining together on climate change to win a better outcome for developing countries. Indian official rhetoric on world trade still reflects the view that it is the West, and particularly the United States, that both dominates trade and controls the international agenda on trade. According to this view, it is the West that caused the latest Doha round to stall.[74]

But recently India and China have tended to drift apart on trade, as China increasingly becomes a leading force in the world economy. China is now mostly viewed by Indian business as a potential threat rather than an ally against developed countries. The situation is exacerbated by the fact that the WTO structures are stalled and still reflect a version of the international economy now rapidly passing.

Originally the commonalities between India and China were underwritten by a rapidly expanding trade relationship, as evidenced by table 3.2. What is also evident from the table, however, is that India's trade deficit with China burgeoned in absolute terms as total trade grew. India appeared incapable of making up any ground in this trade, so, ipso facto, the higher the total trade, the higher the absolute deficit. Worse in the context of a labor-rich country such as India, the structure of trade is overwhelmingly in favor of imports of

TABLE 3.2 Sino-Indian Trade 2006–7 to 2011–12 (in Millions of US Dollars)

Year	India exports to China	India imports from China	Total	Indian deficit	Deficit as percentage of total
2011–12	18,077	57,518	75,595	39,441	52
2010–11	15,483	43,798	59,281	28,315	48
2009–10	11,618	30,824	42,442	19,202	45
2008–9	9,354	32,497	41,851	23,143	55
2007–8	10,871	27,146	38,017	16,275	43
2006–7	8,322	17,475	25,797	9,153	35

Data Sources: For 2006–7 to 2010–11, Indian Ministry of Commerce and Industry, as at www.commerce.nic.in/eidls/icnt.asp, accessed July 16, 2012. For 2011–12, as at http://www.infodriveindia.com/export-import/trade-statistics/trading-partners.aspx#india_top_import_trading_partners, accessed November 14, 2013.

manufactured goods from China and exports of commodities such as low-grade iron ore, diamonds, and cotton from India. On its part, India attributes this poor performance in part to unfair trading practices on the part of China. According to Srikanth Kondapalli, "China always has an advantage over us. . . . China has opened its market very selectively. Neither our software industry nor the pharmaceutical firms have been able to market their products well in China."[75]

As a consequence, India has introduced a whole new set of nontariff barriers (NTBs) aimed specifically at China, particularly in the form of claims under the antidumping provisions of the WTO. In June 2012, India determined to lower the time frame for antidumping investigations from an average of twelve months to nine. Although on a much smaller scale, China has sought to match these with antidumping claims against India. Mark Wu interprets this escalation of antidumping on the part of India and China as being directed at *developed* countries and to be caused by the weakness of the legal definition of dumping. He therefore advocates that the West seek to tighten the definition of dumping to make it more difficult to apply to specific cases.[76] According to Wu's own data, however, the tool of antidumping now seems to be directed much more against fellow developing countries than the West. This is particularly true for India, which has directed a significant array of antidumping provisions at fellow Asian countries, especially China. The latter still levies the majority of its antidumping cases against developed countries but with the category "Asia," in which India would be prominent, gaining ground.[77]

Nor are such NTBs the only barriers presented by India against China. In terms of FDI, which is badly needed in India in the very area in which China could have most to contribute, infrastructure, India has frequently barred Chinese investment on the grounds of national security. Such bans have covered telecommunications, aviation, space-related technology, port development, shipping, energy, and investment in sensitive border areas. These restraints in part relate to fear of Chinese economic domination. But they also represent genuine security concerns, drawing on India's fear about China's alleged poor track record in cybersecurity, the predominance of state-owned Chinese companies, the ongoing border dispute with China, and China's growing footprint in South Asia and the Indian Ocean region.

As well as limiting Chinese investment on security grounds and escalating antidumping retaliation against China, India set up a new office, the primary purpose of which appears to be to stem Chinese economic incursion. New Delhi issued a démarche to China on trade, citing the need for better market access for India's more competitive agricultural products, such as fruit, vegetables, and Basmati rice.[78] India's decision to cease cotton exports—most of which were destined for China (a decision later reversed)—on the grounds of a poor crop in India had the effect of further undermining the trade relationship.

Thus in terms of the effects of economic globalization on Sino-Indian relations, fluidity appears to be the new norm. A situation that initially indicated a strong common purpose between the two has now evolved into one in which China is in many respects seen as a threat as well as an opportunity. This is not a temporary shift but represents real structural changes in the international economy—changes not yet reflected in the international politics of trade, in part because trade negotiations have effectively been frozen in time due to the fact they are stalemated. But this shift, while not yet actualized in the academic literature, is likely already affecting the nature of Sino-Indian relations by removing at least one of the buffers long perceived to be causing a more neutral rather than contested relationship between the two—that is, their common positions in international trade negotiations.

CROSS-BORDER ENVIRONMENTAL FACTORS

Although there is clear evidence of local-level-induced environmental stress in both India and China, there is greater uncertainty about the level of stress already caused by problems within the so-called global commons and across international borders, especially those related to climate change. In India, there is some evidence of a falling-off in the crucial monsoon. According to *The Economist*, "specialists who met in February [2012] in Pune . . . reported a 4.5% decline in monsoon rain in the three decades to 2009."[79] But it is probably too soon to attribute such events definitively to climate change. In China, the effects of climate change on agricultural production are even more ambiguous because a portion of Chinese agriculture located in the colder north may benefit.

Both China and India are, however, vulnerable in future to the effects of climate change in terms of the destructive effects of extreme weather events and water stress. The New Delhi conurbation, already numbering twenty-two million and still growing, is located in a semidesert and is dependent for water in the dry season on dams and glacial melt. It needs to share this scarce water with India's food-bowl state of Haryana. The waters are also claimed by Punjab, a claim that contributed to the Khalistan separatist movement.[80] In Mumbai there have already been water riots in 2007 resulting in a death when the monsoon was delayed by several weeks. Another riot in 2012, when slum dwellers tried to stop a water tanker, resulted in seven deaths. Given the extreme crowding and narrow streets of the metropolis, water tankers are unable to enter quickly enough to provide sufficient drinking water for the population.

In China the situation is also dire. China is engaged in a giant, costly, and ecologically uncertain project to divert water to the water-starved North and Northeast from the water-rich South—the so-called South-North Water Transfer Scheme. Three components to the scheme are under either implementation or consideration, only one of them involving the Yarlung Tsangpo (which becomes the Brahmaputra in India and Jamuna in Bangladesh). In part due to confusion over similar names of the involved rivers, India and Bangladesh have become concerned that this water may eventually be diverted from the Yarlung Tsangpo. And indeed, the Chinese Sinohydro Company has actually lobbied for the construction of a giant, 38,000-megawatt hydroelectric project. There are also allegations that water is to be diverted to the North, involving a dam in the Great Bend of the Yarlung Tsangpo, just north of the disputed Indian state of Arunachal Pradesh that would be twice the size of the Three Gorges Dam. Bramha Chellaney, in a major study on water stress in Asia, attributes China's claim to Arunachal Pradesh at least in part to the desire to harness the large amount of water generated in the state, which experiences one of the heaviest annual monsoon dumps in the world.[81] The issue is complicated by the fact that China steadfastly refuses to enter into any multilateral or bilateral water-sharing agreements with downstream riparians. Its agreement with India relates only to data sharing on the Yarlung Zangpo / Brahmaputra during the flood season.[82] Recently China appears to have leaned toward turning the Great Bend area into a tourist attraction, somewhat easing the tension over the dam.[83]

To further complicate matters, Beijing is already building several dams on the upstream reaches of the Yarlung Tsangpo, which they claim are run-of-river hydroelectric dams—that is, dams that do not conserve river water for irrigation or human consumption but use its energy for hydroelectric generation. Although India claims that China has failed to consult on these dams as required under an agreement to share hydrological data, it has no basic objection to such dams. But Beijing has not helped by refusing to answer New Delhi's queries on the dams for three years.[84]

Whatever the realities, the issue of diversion of the Yarlung Tsangpo has already entered the public discourse in India. Civil society groups such as the Jan Chetna Manch (Organization for People's Awareness) are mounting public demonstrations against the alleged Chinese plans.[85] Should climate and population-induced water stress in India and China increase, as appears likely, there is little doubt that the issue of water will emerge as a major cause of misunderstanding and tension between the two Asian giants. Moreover, just as India's potential to control oil flows over the Indian Ocean is seen as a strategic lever against it in China (see chapter 4), so too is China's ability to control water in Tibet seen as a potential strategic lever against India.[86]

At Copenhagen in 2009, India and China developed joint positions on climate change, calling for heavy compensation from developed countries for any decision to limit emissions. Several months after the end of the conference, India and China synchronized their agreement to accede to the 107-country, nonbinding accord to limit climate change to two degrees Celsius and to provide a $100 billion assistance package to developing countries.[87]

But despite these common positions, there are some differences between India and China on climate change, in terms of both the realities they confront and of the policies they are consequently likely to adopt. China's consumption of energy per capita is still low by the standards of developed countries but is over three times that of India's, at 2,456 units per capita for China and 731 for India. China's process of rural electrification is far more advanced than India's, with about 40 percent of the Indian population still not covered by the grid. China has also progressed down the route of renewable energy more rapidly than India, but the latter is also investing strongly in renewables. Nevertheless, on energy and climate change, the total picture between India and China looks more similar than dissimilar, and the two are likely to continue to share common positions in international forums. If climate change starts to cause a reaction in terms of glacial melt and water scarcity, however, and given China's command over the Himalayan Plateau, tension between the two over water may well be generated in future.

Another problem for India is the expected indirect effects of climate change through the impact on its South Asian neighbors. Both Pakistan and Bangladesh are probably even more vulnerable to the effects of climate change than India. Well-being in both the near neighbors will have a vital impact on stability in India.

Pakistan's rapidly growing population—already an estimated 170–190 million—is heavily dependent for its dry-season water on the glacial melt, which enters the Indus River system from the Himalaya and Karakorum mountain ranges. Pakistan's exceptionally severe floods in 2010 have been attributed by some to the extreme weather events associated with global warming, which was said to have trapped the depression that caused the devastation.[88] The effects of the severe weather pattern in terms of flooding were also exacerbated by the fact the Indus has slowed down as a result of irrigation water being extracted, leading to excessive levels of silt and consequent raising of the river bed surface, thus showing how local environmental problems can combine negatively with problems of the global commons.[89] As these problems in Pakistan start to cut in, so too will the nation's social and political problems likely increase. A destabilized Pakistan will likely be one that is less able to make the necessary changes needed to "normalize" relations with India. Affected populations in riverine areas might also increasingly blame India for dry-season water scarcity.

Bangladesh is equally, if not more, at risk. According to a World Bank assessment, two-thirds of Bangladesh is less than five meters above sea level, with 14.6 million people in coastal areas vulnerable to inundation due to increased cyclonic surges—a number that will rise to 18.5 million by 2050 under moderate climate-change scenarios.[90] All of Bangladesh's great rivers enter from India and some also pass through China. India and Bangladesh have made significant progress in resolving riparian issues through the water agreement of 1996, which distributed the waters of the Ganges and its tributaries. Even this agreement is periodically contested by Bangladesh, however, especially when Bangladesh Nationalist Party governments hold power. Moreover, a recently negotiated treaty over the sharing of the Teesta waters came unstuck due to local politics in Bengal, when Mamata Banerjee, who has fallen out with her erstwhile Congress allies and is seeking to develop northern Bengal (through which the Teesta flows), opposed the treaty for local political reasons—again an example of how local pressures can impact internationally. These pressures, along with diminution of dry-season flows due to diminishing glacial melt and overuse by upstream riparian powers China and India, will place greater pressure on the population illegally to cross borders into India. And as illustrated in chapter 2, we have seen that already illegal immigration has upset the ethnic and religious balance in India and caused local and national instability.

CONCLUSION

The impact of globalization and outside-power intervention on South Asia needs to be viewed against the backdrop of preexisting tensions and dysfunction within the region. Both intra–South Asian and global factors are clearly in play in determining regional dissonance, but it is often difficult to disentangle them.

The erosion of South Asia's syncretic values is by no means a recent phenomenon, but it has nevertheless been "turbocharged" by the conflict in Afghanistan—which itself has a global dimension in terms of global-power competition. The influence of the Wahhabi doctrine from the oil-rich Gulf has also affected the nature of Islam in South Asia and especially Pakistan. This already complex scenario is further complicated by the role of Islam in seeking to oust various global powers from Afghanistan. The transformation of Islam in this way in South Asia has sharpened differences between India and Pakistan. This has, in turn, played into differences between India and China, given that China and Pakistan have a long-standing relationship that is strategic in nature. Added to this, the war on terrorism being waged by the United States within South Asia has also involved US interests in a complex balancing act between cultivating India as a possible hedge against the rise of China on the one hand and ensuring that Pakistan remains at least a neutral force, if not a positive benefit, in the war on terrorism on the other.

The effects of economic globalization on the security and politics of South Asia are also complex, not least because economic globalization has been a force for both good and ill. Globalization has affected regions and subregions differently by fostering winners and losers. Overall Pakistan would appear to have been a loser, while different regions of India, such as some of the southern states, Maharashtra, and Gujarat, have been winners. In terms of Sino-Indian relations, the situation is also complicated. The two megapopulation powers initially took similar positions in world trade forums, but this initial convergence now appears to be eroding as India increasingly confronts economic challenges from a China that has managed to industrialize far more effectively and that now consequently poses some of the economic challenges to India formerly posed by the West.

The same degree of separation between the positions of India and China has not yet occurred in terms of the challenge of climate change, however. The two powers still adopt basically similar positions in world forums. But environmental challenges have produced—and are likely to produce in future—other sets of challenges, both local and international. Already there is growing competition within nations of the region and between them over the sharing of scarce water. China and India are likely to feature more heavily in this competition as their populations suffer more and more from water scarcity. Already this tension over water has become a factor in the preexisting tension over the border, especially in the eastern sector. And climate change itself is likely to exacerbate existing problems of food, water, and sustainability, such that regional tensions over issues such as illegal migration and water sharing are likely further to mount. Both India and China are on a potential collision course concerning the uses of the waters that originate on the Tibet plateau.

Of course, all these challenges within the various polities are also affected by—and in turn affect—what might be called the metareality of global power relations between South Asian powers and those powers outside South Asia, such as the United States and China. It is to relationships with those outside powers that we now turn, in terms of both how those relations are affected by the internal South Asian dynamics we have been discussing and of the wider global powerplay of which South Asia is a part.

NOTES

1. The term was first used by the CIA to describe "the unintended consequences of policies kept secret from the American people." See Johnson, *Blowback*, 8.
2. There is now a relatively wide literature as described in the introduction. See also Miller, "States, Nations, and the Regional Security Order of South Asia," 73–97.
3. Ibid., 74.
4. For example, Kaushik Basu argues that globalization negatively affects state efforts to alleviate poverty and inequality by setting up, in effect, international competition in tax. See "India's Dilemmas," 58–59. See also Stiglitz, *Globalization and Its Discontents*, and the opposing view in Bagwati, *In Defense of Globalization*, and Nayar, "Economic Globalization and State Capacity in South Asia," 98–121.
5. World Bank, *Managing Climate Risk*. It must be said, however, that most of these global environmental problems (as distinct from localized environmental

problems discussed in the previous chapter) still lie in the future rather than the present.

6. See especially Coll, *Ghost Wars*.
7. Hussain Haqqani, "The Ideologies of South Asian Jihadi Groups"; Jalal, *Partisans of Allah*; Kamran, "Salafi Extremism in the Punjab and Its Transnational Impact," 31–43, 32; and Dalrymple, *The Last Mughal*, especially chapter 2.
8. Dalrymple, *The Last Mughal*, 84.
9. Although differences between these two puritanical versions of Islam may seem arcane, at times they are vehemently opposed. For example, the LeT (Salafist) will no longer mount joint operations with the JeM (Deobandi in the Hanafi legal tradition).
10. Kamran, "Salafi Extremism in the Punjab and Its Transnational Impact," 36–37.
11. Coll, *Ghost Wars*, passim, and Yousaf and Adkin, *The Bear Trap*.
12. Chaterjee, "Kalashnikov Culture in Pakistan."
13. Federation of American Scientists, "Pakistan Nuclear Weapons."
14. United States Government, Congressional Research, *Islamic Religious Schools, Madrasas*, 5.
15. Jinnah himself was a Shi'ite. He was a Westernized lawyer who supported a pluralist, inclusive Pakistan.
16. Kaplan, *Monsoon*, 144.
17. Nair, "The State and Madrasas in India."
18. "2008: Extremist Recruitment on the Rise in South Punjab Madrassahs."
19. See, for example, Joshi, *Lost Rebellion*.
20. The Kashmiriyat was a supposed syncretic Kashmiri culture that embraced Sufi Islam and elements of Hinduism, allowable because of a supposed overarching culture within the Vale of Kashmir. Some, such as Karan Arakotaram, argue it was a twentieth-century construct. See "The Rise of the Kashmiriyat."
21. Jolly, "The Wahhabi Invasion."
22. "Centre Wades into Barelvi-Wahabi Duel?"
23. "Another Shrine Charred in J and K."
24. Arif, "Recruitment of Pakistani Workers in the Gulf."
25. "Transfer of Jobs to Asian Workers Feeds Discontent." Based in turn on World Bank data.
26. Roul, "Lashkar-e-Taiba's Financial Network Targets India from Gulf States."
27. "Saudi-Based NRIs Funded Mumbai Blasts."
28. South Asia Terrorism Portal, www.satporgtp/countries/india/database/maharashtra_incidents.htr, accessed June 13, 2012, and "IM Men Got 10 Lakh for Pune Blast."
29. Swami, "The Indian Mujahidin and Lashkar-i-Tayyiba's Transnational Networks."
30. Ibid. See also Tankel, *Storming the World Stage*.
31. Ahmed, *Enquiry and Analysis Series Report 816*.
32. "Lashkar-e-Taiba Has Dedicated Internet Team."
33. See, for example, "Gujarat Riots in Pictures."

34. See Darul Uloom Deoband website.
35. Found at www.jamatdawa.org/ and www.facebook.com/JUDOfficial, respectively, on June 6, 2012. However, the material cited has since been removed from the site.
36. In 2012, alleged violent jihadists were arrested in Bengalaru. They had supposedly been inspired by this site. See "On Line Terror Plot."
37. Taylor, "Mythology Wars," 149–68, 163.
38. "Surgical Strikes Are Feasible Militarily."
39. A full text of the cable appeared in "US Embassy Cables."
40. "MEA Added to Confusion over 2008 Hoax Call to Zardari."
41. Federation of American Scientists, "Pakistan's Nuclear Weapons." See also Pant, "The Pakistan Thorn in China-India-US Relations," 83–95, 83, 86.
42. "India Faces Growing Chinese Hostility after 26/11."
43. Pradhan, *1965 War*, chapter 13.
44. Pant, "The Pakistan Thorn in China-India-US Relations," 86.
45. Ibid., passim. This point is, however, disputed by Michael Beckley, who describes what he sees as narrowing interests between Pakistan and China. See his "China and Pakistan."
46. Timmons, "Can India 'Fix' Afghanistan?" See also Hanauer and Chalk, *India's and Pakistan's Strategies in Afghanistan*, x–xi.
47. Timmons, "Can India 'Fix' Afghanistan?"
48. Conversations with senior MEA officials visiting Australia, 2012.
49. Joshi, "US, India and Af-Pak Endgame."
50. "Afghanistan Favors India and Denigrates Pakistan."
51. Hanauer and Chalk, *India's and Pakistan's Strategies in Afghanistan*, xii.
52. International Crisis Group, *Afghanistan*, 3.
53. "V. K. [Singh] Scents a Chinese Tunnel."
54. International Crisis Group, *Afghanistan*, and Maley, "Afghanistan in 2011," 88–99.
55. "Potential for a Mining Boom Splits Factions in Afghanistan."
56. Kaplan, *Monsoon*, 208.
57. Ibid., 207.
58. "The Killing of a Young Boy."
59. "Sri Lankan Reporter Shot in Colombo."
60. "Canberra, India 'Water Down' UN Resolution on Sri Lankan Human Rights."
61. "Inside China."
62. "SAARC Secys [*sic*] Meet in July to Review Measures, Policies."
63. World Bank, "India: Foreign Trade Policy."
64. Ara and Raheman, *The Competitiveness and Future Challenges of Bangladesh in International Trade*, 4 (chart 2), 9 (chart 7).
65. "India Seen as an Attractive Destination for Foreign Direct Investment."
66. McKinsey Global Institute, *India's Urban Awakening*.
67. Ahmed, *India's Infrastructure Needs*, 2.
68. Gordon, "Globalisation and Economic Reform in India," 78.
69. "India Does Not See Doha Round Concluding before 2013."

70. "Doha Round Must Consolidate Progress Made So Far."
71. Chaudhary, "India's Farming Crisis."
72. "Agricultural Distress Main Reason for Farmers' Suicide, Says Study."
73. Palit, *China-India Economics*; Whalley and Shekhar, "The Rapidly Deepening India-China Economic Relationship"; and Merrington, "Beyond the Protracted Contest," 186–91.
74. "India Does Not See Doha Round Concluding before 2013."
75. "Govt Looks for Ways to Cover Trade Gap with China."
76. Wu, "Antidumping in Asia's Emerging Giants."
77. Ibid., 184, tables 12 and 13.
78. Gordon, "India's Political Economy."
79. "Monsoon or Later."
80. When Haryana was carved out of Punjab in 1966, it received all the waters of the Jamuna and also a share of the Beas and Ravi. Punjab claimed it was unjustly treated, since it lost all of the Jamuna and a portion of the other two rivers.
81. Chellaney, *Water*, 2.
82. Tripathi, "Hydropower in Asia," 219–35.
83. Bisht, "Diversion of the Yarlung Tsangpo." See also "China's Tourism Plan Quells Brahmaputra Dam Fears."
84. "After Keeping India in Dark on Dam, China Promises No Harm."
85. As at www.youtube.com/watch?v=99md7vIW5Xk, accessed September 26, 2012.
86. Malik, *China and India*, 135.
87. "Climate Goal Is Supported by China and India."
88. Others maintain that the event was caused by a blockage in the jet stream, which may or may not have been due to climate change. See Marshall, "Frozen Jet Stream Leads to Floods, Famine and Disease," 14–15.
89. See Lahiri-Dutt, "Indus Floods, 2010."
90. World Bank, "Bangladesh and Maldives Respond to Climate Change Impacts."

CHAPTER 4

WIDER REGIONAL IMPLICATIONS

India's problems of dissonance and poor governance, the way these problems interact negatively with its troubled neighbors, and the scope this gives for outside powers to "interfere" in South Asia together mean that India remains in essence a continental power. According to Iskander Rehman, "an array of land-driven concerns has . . . since Independence, had a way of dragging India back to shore, thwarting its sporadic thalassocratic [maritime] ambitions."[1]

That is not to say India is not gradually accruing power-projection capabilities beyond South Asia as its economy grows or that it is not spending more on its navy.[2] But it will not be capable of reaching its potential as a power until it can rise above the domestic and neighborhood problems that trouble it and force upon it a basically continental thrust to its security.

In this chapter we will describe the characteristics of India as a continental power and the consequent limits on its ability to act in the wider region, defined as East Asia, Southeast Asia, Southwest Asia, the Middle East, and the Indian Ocean Region (IOR). In doing so, we will argue that India is more powerful as an Indian Ocean power than as a power in the wider Asian region. This is due principally to its location at the Indian Ocean littoral, where it remains the sole power of "potential" and where it is positioned athwart the SLOCs that bring vital energy supplies to the energy-hungry powers of East Asia. These strategic benefits in turn enable India to operate in Asia with more influence than would otherwise be the case.

Furthermore, India's landward problems, and especially the China-Pakistan strategic linkage, have made it cautious in pursuing cooperative mechanisms in South Asia and the IOR. India feels "surrounded" by China's growing activities throughout this region and its reaction has been to attempt to keep both China and Pakistan out of key regional cooperative institutions or, where it cannot keep them out, to ensure that regionalism involves soft regionalism rather than genuine cooperative association. The IOR in particular has thus been left in an etiolated state that jeopardizes its role as a global connector of trade—indeed, "the great connector." Nonconventional security issues continue to be poorly addressed, and a security dilemma of classic proportions continues to build in the IOR between India, China, and the United States.

INDIA AS A CONTINENTAL POWER

A number of commentators argue that both India and China have started to cast off the shackles formerly constraining them as continental powers.[3] Before discussing the details of these arguments, we need to develop an understanding of what it means to be a "continental" power as opposed to a "maritime" one.

In addressing this issue, most analysts stress that it is insufficient that a maritime power is reflected in predominant naval modes of strength alone. True maritime powers, such as Great Britain during its imperial phase and the United States today, are also said to incorporate global economic strength and global trading interests—a point originally made by Alfred Thayer Mahan.[4]

H. J. Mackinder argued that continental powers, on the other hand, are strong in forces that can be bought to bear on land and have extensive hinterlands ripe for domination. They are geopolitically positioned to favor that mode of power projection, as was the Russian Empire of the time he wrote (1904), which stood astride the Eurasian land mass.[5]

But such powers may be deemed continental not just because their geopolitical location favors that mode of power over the maritime, but also because their modes of power delivery remain focused on their immediate neighborhood (which happens to be continental) by virtue of the fact that they are vulnerable in that neighborhood. This vulnerability causes them to focus on their landward environment rather than accrual of power in the maritime domain. As Christopher R. Bullock notes, referring to the work of Bernard Cole, "an essential prerequisite for a maritime-oriented strategy is that the country be insulated against the threat of overland invasion."[6] A power forced to focus on internal stability will have difficulty emerging as a true maritime power. Large powers such as China with long, vulnerable land borders will also be inclined to continental modes of thinking, notwithstanding the intrinsic strength this expansive territorial domain provides. As noted by Bullock, referring to the work of Charles E. Hawkins, "China's size and location have been crucial determinants in the way its political and military leadership think about strategy."[7] India is even more shaped by its long and porous land borders, size, and internal instability. Although the most recent invasions from Europe came by sea, the earlier great invasions all came by land from the northwest.

Despite the factors that incline India toward a continental posture, it aspires to be a naval power. But given current restraints and threats, acquisition of naval power must take a back seat to other aspects of policy such as border security, aerial defense and attack capabilities, land armies and armored corps, internal security, poverty alleviation, and development generally. Thus India's plans to become a significant naval power tend to remain aspirational. On the other hand, India enjoys a significant long-term geostrategic advantage as a maritime power in the IOR by virtue of its highly strategic location athwart the major SLOCs of the Indian Ocean, especially the energy links into East Asia, an advantage not enjoyed by China, which is located at the end of the long SLOCs that traverse the Indian Ocean and Western Pacific.

Finally, notwithstanding our discussion to the contrary in the introduction, the nomenclature "continental" and "maritime" *to an extent* needs updating to accommodate modern technology, especially as it relates to ballistic missiles and space. Mastery of the dimension of space may in the future enable emerging powers, at least to an extent, to leapfrog the incremental stages of normal sea-power development. China's successful destruction of one of its own satellites in 2007 had a galvanizing effect not just as a technology demonstration, but because control of space has become so central to power projection. If China could control space, it could potentially leave a maritime power such as the United States "blind" in the oceans and also vulnerable to antiship ballistic missile attacks. Although still well behind China in this regard, India too is developing its capabilities in space, a factor that could in time act as a significant force multiplier for its Indian Ocean naval role.[8]

That said, India is still essentially a continental power and is likely to remain one for some time. To recapitulate our previous discussion, the continental character of Indian power derives from a number of factors. They include its difficult internal and border-security environments; its large number of people living in poverty; its strategy of inclusive growth, which diverts resources from classic force-projection capabilities; the problems of corruption and poor governance; the existence of a negative feedback loop between the domestic ills and problems in the equally troubled South Asian neighborhood; emerging environmental and resource problems; and China's continuing ability to "fish in South Asia's troubled waters."

Not only have these factors contributed to an overall continental security posture, but they have also shaped the character of Indian security in other ways, as we further discuss, below.

DEFENSE AND SECURITY SPENDING

India's allocations for the totality of its security as a percentage of GDP are difficult to quantify. The most common figure used by analysts is defense spending as in the budget papers expressed as a percentage of GDP. In these terms, Indian defense spending has remained consistently and comparatively low, at under 3 percent of GDP. This figure, however, neither reflects the totality of defense spending nor overall security spending. Defense spending should also include military pensions—which constitute a substantial amount of roughly 10 to 20 percent of the official total, depending on when the measure is made. It should also include expenses allocated to running the Ministry of Defence. Some would also include some elements of spending within the Departments of Space and Atomic Energy (to cover the nuclear weapons and military space programs), but they are difficult to separate from overall spending within those portfolios, and so we will not be including them. To quantify security as distinct from defense spending, we also need to add significant amounts from state governments to cover police and significant costs under the Ministry of Home Affairs portfolio within the Union government.

A further consideration is that in terms of the priorities of the Union government, the critical relationship is the one between total Union government spending and security spending rather than between security spending and GDP. This is because government is at its most transparent, and in a sense vulnerable, when it comes to allocating *available* funds within the budget process, a point only increased in salience now the fiscal deficit is 5.3 percent at time of writing.[9] In terms of official defense (as distinct from security) spending as a percentage of the Union budget, the percentages may be seen from Table 4.1, below.

It can be seen from this table that defense spending as a percentage of total Union government spending has deviated very little, from a low of 12.9 percent in 2007–8 and 2008–9 to a high of 15.9 percent in 2005–6. By way of comparison, the United States, a power with a genuine power-projection capability and worldwide military commitments, spends approximately 23 percent of its central government budget on the military. Of course, it should be noted that the United States and India are both federations, and so the above percentages do not reflect percentages of overall government spending but only central government spending.

It can also be seen that despite the fact that the BJP projects itself as being somewhat more nationalistically inclined than other mainstream parties, there is no obvious relationship between shifting patterns of defense expenditure and the political complexion of the government in office, suggesting that India's relatively low expenditure on defense is basically bipartisan.

Although spending on conventional defense has been relatively low, when we include security as a whole, which includes items we now call "homeland security" in the context of the attacks on the United States of September 11, 2001 (9/11), the picture is a little different.

In table 4.2 we have set down the level of the overall security resource devoted to homeland security in relation to defense. In those terms, the impost of homeland security vis-à-vis defense has been fairly steady at roughly 44 percent. Given

TABLE 4.1 Defense Spending as a Percentage of Total Union Government Spending, 1993–94 to 2011–12

Year	Percent of total Union budget	Government
1993–94	15.4	Congress
1994–95	14.5	"
1995–96	15	"
1996–97	14.7	Janata Dal
1997–98	15.2	"
1998–99	14.3	BJP (NDA coalition)
1999–2000	15.8	"
2000–1	15.2	"
2001–2	14.9	"
2002–3	13.5	"
2003–4	12.7	"
2004–5	15.2	Congress (UPA coalition)
2005–6	15.9	"
2006–7	14.7	"
2007–8	12.9	"
2008–9	12.9	"
2009–10	13.3 (Revised Estimates)	"
2010–11	13.5 (Budget Estimates)	"
2011–12	13.3 (Budget Estimates)	"

Source: Gordon, "Nation, Neighbourhood and Region," 208, table 1 (reprinted by permission).

defense spending has itself been fairly steady, as a percentage of both GDP and of government spending, ipso facto the overall burden of security on the Indian economy is still relatively low and is not increasing markedly. In this sense, India cannot be designated a "security state."

When it comes to an analysis of India's overall defense posture as between continental and force-projection security and defense spending, however, the issue is heavily weighted in favor of a continental posture. This is particularly evident when we examine allocations within the Ministry of Defence portfolio (see table 4.3).

Although the share of the navy is growing gradually, a number of factors suggest this should not be taken as indicative of a substantial shift in India's defense posture in favor of maritime interests.[10]

First, the rise recorded for the 2011–12 and 2012–13 fiscal years is higher in relation to the previous long-standing trajectory of growth in which only about one percentage point was added to naval expenditure per decade over the last three

TABLE 4.2 India's Defense and Security Expenditure: Total Spent on Conventional Defense (in *Crore*), Compared with Spending on Various Aspects of Homeland Security and Homeland Security as a Percentage of Defense

Year	Total military	Homeland security other than police*	State and Union police	Total homeland security	Homeland security as a percentage of defense
2000–1	49,622	433	21,343	21,776	44
2001–2	54,265	449	23,641	24,090	44
2002–3	55,662	465	25,058	25,523	46
2003–4	60,066	709	26,852	27,561	46
2004–5	75,856	772	29,875	30,647	40
2005–6	80,549	845	33,506	34,351	43
2006–7	85,510	868	37,465	38,333	45
2007–8	91,681	893	39,743	40,636	44
2008–9	114,223	953	51,399	52,352	46
2009–10	141,781	1,272	64,510 (R)	65,782	46
2010–11	151,582 (Revised Estimate)	1,422	68,033 (B)	69,455	46
2011–12	164,415 (Budget Estimate)	NA	NA	NA	NA
2012–13	153,423 (Budget Estimate)	NA	NA	NA	NA

*Comprises Intelligence Bureau, Civil Defence, Home Guard, Special Protection Group, and Jails (but excludes some relatively expensive items such as border roads, border fencing, police training, crime statistics, coastal protection plans, etc.). Available in revised estimates only.

Data Sources: India budget papers as at http://indiabudget.nic.in (various years), especially Expenditure Budget Volume II; Indian Economic Survey for various years for combined state-union police expenditure; Ministry of Defence Annual Reports as at http://mod.nic.in/aboutus/welcome.html; Indian Economic Survey Statistical Table 2.2 (various) as at http://indiabudget.nic.in/es2011-12/estat1.pdf. Note: Total defense spending is from Economic Survey Statistical Table 2.2 up to 2011–12 and thence compiled from the budget papers.

decades. Second, the recent sharp rise is likely to be caused in part by temporary phenomena such as the requirement for large tranches of naval payments—for example, for the former Soviet aircraft carrier *Gorshkov*, to be inducted some time in 2013—or for the construction of the *Scorpène*-class submarines. To meet these

TABLE 4.3 Allocations between the Army, Navy, and Air Force (in *Crore*), with Percentages of Each of Total Spent on the Three Services in Parentheses

Year	Army	Navy	Air Force	Total Army/ Navy/AF*
1985–86	4,872 (63)	1,000 (13)	1,860 (24)	7,732
1990–91	9,383 (62)	2,100 (14)	3,693 (24)	15,176
2000–1	27,879 (61)	7,385 (16)	10,611 (23)	45,875
2001–2	31,097 (61)	8,369 (15)	11,784 (22)	51,250
2002–3	32,128 (61)	8,155 (15)	12,385 (24)	52,668
2003–4	33,200 (59)	10,109 (18)	13,187 (23)	56,496
2004–5	35,252 (49)	13,529 (19)	23,036 (32)	71,817
2005–6	39,458 (52)	13,967 (19)	21,704 (29)	75,129
2006–7	39,578 (49)	16,198 (20)	24,274 (30)	80,050
2007–8	45,803 (54)	15,885 (19)	23,594 (28)	85,282
2008–9	57,677 (55)	17,248 (17)	29,271 (28)	104,196
2009–10	75,228 (58)	22,694 (17)	32,791 (25)	130,713
2010–11	78,240 (55)	27,119 (19)	38,177 (27)	143,536
2011–12	86,817 (R) (54)	29,606 (R) (18)	43,872 (R) (27)	160,295 (R)
2012–13 (BE)	96,565 (B) (53)	37,314 (B) (20)	48,220 (B) (26)	182,099 (B)

*Totals for the army, navy, and air force will be lower than total military spending, but the figure gives a more accurate idea of the division between the services. (Percentages may not always add up to 100 percent due to rounding.)

Data sources: Gordon, *India's Rise to Power*, 127 (table 1.9), 129 (table 1.11), for pre-2000 data. Army, navy, and air force expenditure from Government of India, Ministry of Defence, Annual Reports.

needs, the navy got a massive 72 percent of the capital modernization budget in 2012–13, at nearly $5 billion. Third, the comparative rise for the navy may also in part relate to the stalled nature of the modernization programs being conducted by the army and to a lesser extent the air force. Such stalling in the acquisitions program has tended artificially to raise the capital share of the navy, which has had a more consistent, less "jerky" acquisitions history. Given impending modernization needs in the army and air force, such as for purchase of the Rafale fighter, new attack helicopters, and the light howitzer, it is most unlikely that this hike in capital spending for the navy will be sustainable.[11] Indeed, according to Laxman K. Behera, "the marginal increase in the Air Force's modernization budget and the decrease in the Army's do not seem to be in sync with their modernization requirements."[12] This point is further reinforced by Deba R. Mohanty, who argues that "unless the MOD catches up with at least replenishment requirements [for the Army], the Army is likely to lag behind in overall modernization."[13] And finally, we need to note that the budget for the navy incorporates that of the coast guard, which, although small at 7.42 percent of total naval spending (actuals for 2010–11), has been growing. In fact, the coast guard will expand from 110 surface vessels to 200 and from 50 aircraft to 100 as a result of the concerns around coastal defense generated by 26/11. And the coast guard cannot, of course, be equated in any way with power projection. Indeed, its increasing salience relates directly to those forces dragging India back toward a continental posture.

Further, at the time of writing, the 2012–13 defense budget is clearly proving overambitious given India's parlous economic circumstances. The fiscal deficit is set to widen to as much as 6 percent, and Finance Minister P. Chidambaram is reviewing expenditure with an eye to cuts.[14] Signs are that defense will not be spared from these cuts.[15] Cuts could include delays in the navy's capital program, especially given concerns about delays and poor quality of the refitting of the *Gorshkov*. And at present it is unclear how the actuals of expenditure between the three services will work out.

But even were naval expenditure proportionally to rise on a sustained basis to, say, over 17–20 percent of the defense allocation, we also need to consider that in percentage terms it would still fall short of that of the United States, which spends 27 percent of its budget on the navy and marines. Since naval power is *the* classic means of conventional-force projection, this level of spending in percentage terms would appear to represent a power with an ambition to have such capabilities, even if they were on a more limited scale than the global scale achieved by the United States.

Furthermore, India's nonnaval expenditure is overwhelmingly focused on defending India in a continental posture rather than on mounting expeditionary forces. For example, the Indian Army's seven military commands are focused on border and internal security and are headquartered at Agra, Lucknow, Kolkata, Udhampur (Jammu and Kashmir), Pune, Jaipur, and Chandimandir. India's is predominantly a land-based army, with an emphasis on heavy artillery and tanks: It possesses over three thousand main battle tanks, reflecting the apparent need to fight tank battles along and around the borders with Pakistan. India has also considered it necessary to raise four additional mountain divisions, totaling ninety thousand troops at a cost of $13 billion, to counter China. It is replacing outdated Soviet-era aircraft with its frontline Su-30 Mk I aircraft and constructing associated infrastructure in Assam, also intended to confront and deter China in terms of the latter's claim to Arunachal Pradesh. It is engaged in an expensive and time-consuming process of upgrading its Himalayan road system—a process dogged by corruption and inefficiency and not reflected in military spending. And it has recently decided to extend its rail system into Arunachal Pradesh in order to counter Chinese rail building on the Tibet side of the border. Again, this expenditure will be essentially military but will not be reflected as military spending in the budget.

Although India aspires to a substantial expeditionary capability as expressed in its 2009 version of its naval doctrine, it does not yet possess one at the brigade level. From the point of view of the navy, assets are being planned toward this end, for example, the intended indigenous construction of four landing platform docks (LPDs).[16] (One LPD has already been acquired in the form of the ex-US Navy vessel *Trenton*, acquired in 2007.) But given other pressing priorities in all three services, India is well short of acquiring the type of multiservice capability needed for substantial force projection.

Given the situation in and around India discussed in the previous chapters, this difficult local and neighborhood environment is unlikely to become more benign in the near future. India's internal security problems are also likely to prove stubborn. Maoist insurgencies in central India are likely to be protracted. Their resolution in part depends on achieving better governance and developmental outcomes in affected regions. This is a long-term enterprise dogged by the overall poor state of governance outlined in chapter 1. Ethnic and religious violence in the Northeast is also likely to continue to be a serious problem, especially give the continuing influx of Bangladeshi Muslims into the already delicately balanced ethnic makeup of the region, perhaps exacerbated by escalating environmental problems. No early end is in sight to the problems in Kashmir, which involve a presence of about three hundred thousand Indian troops, along with police and paramilitary forces. Nepal will likely remain unstable, and its border with India porous. The border with Bangladesh will also likely remain porous for some time. In terms of domestic political problems, corruption will likely be slowly dealt with but will remain a troubling aspect of Indian politics for many years (see the following chapter), while coalition governments, with all the uncertainty they entail, are likely to remain the dominant political form.

These domestic and South Asian difficulties not only shape allocations of defense spending, but also the national mindset for making strategy. In this mindset, the navy is the most outward-looking element, which is, of course, typical of navies in general. But the postures of both the air force and army have mostly been defensive, as demanded by their difficult operating environments within South Asia. The focus of government itself has of necessity been on local and regional crises, such as the impact of terrorism and insurgency, the ongoing tension along the borders with Pakistan and China, and the need to maintain security in Kashmir, the Northeast, and the Maoist-affected areas of central India.

DEFENSE AND SECURITY VERSUS INCLUSIVE GROWTH

Most Indian government spending is still devoted to the inclusive growth approach favored by the Planning Commission.[17] For example, expenditure on social services as a proportion of GDP has increased from 5.6 percent in 2006–7 to 7.3

percent in 2010–11.[18] The flagship of these social sector programs, MNREGS, costs about $12 billion per annum. This social spending will increase further in percentage terms once India proceeds with its extensive new food subsidy plans, which seek to provide subsidies for two-thirds of the population. The massive demand for expenditure on infrastructure and commitments for universal education and health care will add greatly to these demands.

The inclusive growth strategy is so central to India's grand strategy that it was specifically covered (although not by that name) in the second paragraph of the introduction to the now often-quoted *NonAlignment 2.0* document: "The fundamental source of India's power in the world is going to be the power of its example. If India can maintain high growth rates, *leverage that growth to enhance the capabilities of all its citizens*, and maintain robust democratic traditions and institutions, there are few limits to India's global role and influence. The foundation of India's success will, therefore, depend on its developmental model [emphasis added]."[19]

Although India is likely to keep its continental form for many years, the navy will likely accrue significant power as India's overall economy grows and, with it, the defense budget and navy budget. We need also to reinforce the point that India has some distinct geostrategic advantages when it comes to its Indian Ocean location, despite its situation in the difficult South Asian neighborhood. These advantages effectively leverage it as a naval power.

The Indian Ocean and India's Geostrategic Aspirations

India has always tended to see the Indian Ocean as both an opportunity and a threat. It inherited from the British the idea that the Indian Ocean could provide a kind of protective barrier, provided India remained strong in the maritime domain, as was Britain during the period of the colonial occupation. On the other hand, it was a tenet of the nationalist movement that India had been invaded by the European powers from the sea, and so there was also a sense of vulnerability from that quarter. According to James R. Holmes, Toshi Yoshihara, and Andrew C. Winner, "the ability of the Royal Navy to apply constant military pressure from the sea—controlling Indian sea communications, and thus India's economic life—only amplified the efficacy of British strategy in the subcontinent."[20] That is, not only was India "lost" through the maritime "blindness" so lamented by K. M. Panikkar,[21] but it also had its economy profoundly shaped and exploited as a result of British control of the vital sea lanes on which its trade depended.

Today this history shapes India's perceptions of the role of the Indian Ocean in its security. Despite the fact that the calls on the Indian budget remain stronger in terms of maintenance of inclusive growth and the imperatives of continental defense, there is also a growing awareness in New Delhi of the need to foster a powerful navy capable of protecting India's massive maritime domain and vital energy SLOCs. India's sense of vulnerability vis-à-vis the Indian Ocean is also exacerbated by the nation's acute shortage of domestic sources of energy, especially oil, and its dependence on its own oil SLOCs for the bulk of its energy.

India is poor in most sources of energy. Although it has large coal reserves, they are distant from locations of industry, are of poor quality, and their extraction and transport is poorly managed under the government-owned Coal India Ltd. Liquid fuels are in especially short supply, and India imports 65 percent of its oil requirement. India would need to increase primary energy supplies by three to four times to sustain a growth rate of 8–9 percent over the next twenty-five years.[22] The high import levels arising from India's paucity of indigenous supplies places a significant burden on India's balance of payments. Due to ever-rising global demand in relation to supply and ongoing strategic shocks such as Libya and Iran, this situation is only likely to worsen.

These factors mean India is heavily dependent on sources of energy in the Persian Gulf. This, in turn, shapes its policies toward that region, the West, and its own Muslim population of 170 million. Another reason the Gulf is important is that India has 4.9 million guest workers there. They earn a significant proportion of India's $55 billion global remittances inflows.[23] India's naval strategy lists energy security and SLOC security across the Indian Ocean as major factors in the perceived need to maintain a capable blue-water navy.[24]

These interests together mean that India is at times torn between supporting its own interests and the demands of the United States. For example, India's refusal to join the "coalition of the willing" in the Iraq War in 2003 was in part due to its concern about the effect on its own Muslim population (and in part also to its concerns about the wisdom of the enterprise). Its reluctance to accede to US demands that it not trade in oil with Iran arises from its dependence on Gulf oil and its long-standing relationship with Tehran.[25] Finally, India's hunger for energy also dictates an increasing, but so far contained, competition with China in Central Asia, East Africa, and the East China Sea.

Although India's dependence on Gulf oil sometimes dictates policy divergence from the United States, ironically the prospect of the United States drawing away from dependency on Gulf oil as it becomes more self-sufficient fills Indian policymakers with concern, just as it does policymakers in Beijing and Tokyo, since all three countries have been "free-riding" on the massively costly US presence in the Gulf.

Energy security and India's need to retain good relations with the Islamic world because of its own large Muslim population are therefore important in determining its foreign relations posture and will remain so. Its energy links with the Gulf dictate tight economic relationships. These have in turn acted to maintain New Delhi's focus on the Gulf, Southwest Asia, Central Asia, and East Africa, and the trade routes that connect them with India. As we observed in chapter 3,

India also has strong security concerns in the Gulf and has recently had some success in winning extraditions of alleged terrorists from Saudi Arabia and Dubai.

The Indian Ocean is not just seen as a source of potential threat, however. There is growing recognition in Indian policy circles that India's location centrally in the Indian Ocean gives it a number of distinct strategic advantages, especially in relation to the rising powers of East Asia and particularly China. This perception is also now starting to percolate into India's naval ambitions.

The strategic advantage accorded India by its Indian Ocean location derives from two factors. In the Western Pacific, four significant powers—China, Japan, Russia, and the United States—vie for influence and to an extent balance each other. In the Indian Ocean, India is the only power with significant potential. The next most powerful littoral navy belongs to Australia, a power that can only ever aspire to middle-power status. Of course, the US Navy still represents the most powerful navy in the Indian Ocean and will likely maintain that position for many years. But over time India is likely to grow in power vis-à-vis the United States, especially should Washington's Gulf interests decline as US energy independence increases. Moreover, despite the policy differences mentioned above and India's desire for strategic autonomy, the two are increasingly strategically engaged and have an essentially symbiotic relationship, which will be described in greater detail below.

India enjoys an additional strategic advantage in the Indian Ocean. As already noted, littoral powers such as India typically retain a three-to-one steaming advantage over external powers such as the United States and China. As David Scott notes, with a coastline of about 7,500 kilometers (including its major island territories), India "alone [of the Indian ocean powers] projects 'into' the Indian Ocean, her long triangle wedge-shaped landmass extending some 1500 miles [2,400 kilometers] into the Indian Ocean."[26] Moreover, significant portions of the coastline face both east and west.[27]

India's geostrategic advantage in the Indian Ocean is greatly increased by the fact that it inherited from British India the Andaman and Nicobar Islands and maritime territories that went along with them. These territories take Indian maritime waters to within ninety nautical miles of Aceh in Indonesia and give it reach toward the western entrance of the strategically important Strait of Malacca. In recent years India has made some effort to upgrade its military resources in the Andaman and Nicobar Islands. A joint command was opened at Port Blair in 2001. In 2012, India's easternmost facility, the naval/air base INS Baaz (Hawk) was opened on Great Nicobar Island overlooking the strategically important Six Degree Channel separating Indonesia and India and close to the Strait of Malacca. Press reporting at the time identified the need to monitor China as an important factor in the move.[28] Plans are in progress to locate a carrier battle group, guided-missile destroyers, and the future fleet of nuclear submarines on the east coast at

Visakhapatnam.[29] An important factor in this shift in assets to the East has been to monitor and possibly control future access of China into the Indian Ocean through the Strait of Malacca.

India's potentially dominant strategic position in the IOR and its belief in its role as a future leading power have largely dictated its approach to regionalism in the Indian Ocean. As the only littoral power of significant potential, it has sought to ensure its dominance by supporting weak forms of regionalism in the IOR. It has also endeavored to keep Pakistan and major external users, especially China, out of regional forums where possible. As will be discussed in detail in chapter 6, this has certainly been the case with the Indian Ocean regional organization, the Indian Ocean Rim Association (IORA). This kind of behavior is typical of significant powers in the global domain or regionally dominant powers because they consider they can solve their problems bilaterally. They also fear that regional forums with significant powers might be used to "gang up" on them. In the case of the IOR, however, more effective regionalism is badly needed to address pressing nonconventional security issues such as piracy, illicit drug smuggling, people smuggling and trafficking, climate change, and search and rescue. A forum capable of addressing at least some of China's concerns about possible interruption of its key oil SLOCs would also assist in alleviating the serious security dilemma developing between India and China, which promises adversely to affect the entire region of not addressed. This latter problem leads us into a discussion of the Sino-Indian relationship in the context of the IOR.

The Indian Ocean Region and Sino-Indian Competition

The geopolitical assets of India described above together put it into a strategic "box seat" in the Indian Ocean. Security in the Indian Ocean is central to the passage of oil and liquefied natural gas (LNG) into the energy-hungry powers of East Asia, especially China, Japan, and South Korea. China in particular is concerned because of its long-standing strategic rivalry with India. According to one Chinese commentator, "India is just like a giant and never-sinking aircraft carrier and the most important strategic point guarding the Indian Ocean."[30] Kaplan argues that, given the structure of the Indian Ocean and its choke points, China is to all intents and purposes a "landlocked" country when it comes to its energy imports.[31] John Lee points out that "around 80 percent of China's oil imports already come from the Middle East and Africa, with all but 10 percent . . . on foreign owned tankers headed to China passing through U.S. patrolled laneways of the Indian Ocean." He continues: "The fear of interdiction of China-bound oil tankers by the U.S. Navy is acute and real."[32] China's concern about the interdiction of its oil is exacerbated by the growing strategic engagement between the United States and India. Beijing fears that New Delhi and Washington might act in collusion to blockade the flow of oil over the Indian Ocean to China during times of acute strategic stress or even war. This is what is driving China's acquisition of interests in the Indian Ocean, which is in turn precipitating concern in New Delhi that it is in danger of being "surrounded," thus fueling a security dilemma in the Indian Ocean of classic proportions.

Another concern in Beijing is that as India develops its own nuclear ambitions, which currently include a planned fleet of four nuclear-powered submarines, each with twelve nuclear ballistic missiles, the Indian Ocean could again become a stalking ground for nuclear-powered ballistic-missile submarines and nuclear-powered hunter-killer submarines, just as it was in the Cold War, when the United States was able to use the Indian Ocean to target Soviet Central Asia. While the range of the current Indian submarine-launched ballistic missile, the K-15, is only seven hundred kilometers, India is developing the K-4 missile, which would have a range similar to that of the Agni III (approximately thirty-five hundred kilometers) and which could target parts of China from the Indian Ocean. Indian submarines will only be able to carry four of these missiles instead of twelve K-15s, however.[33]

Chinese interests in the Indian Ocean now include port development in Gwadar in Pakistan, Hambantota in Sri Lanka, Chittagong in Bangladesh, and Sittwe, Kyaukpyu, Bassein, Mergui, and Yangon in Burma.[34] Some have also asserted that China has developed a signals intelligence and telemetry site on Burma's Great Coco Island.[35] China also has burgeoning economic and defense links throughout South Asia, except Bhutan, which remains for the time being close to India.

In Bangladesh, Chinese trade has been larger than Indian trade for some years. China still exports substantial amounts of fabric to supply the rapidly growing garment industry in Bangladesh—which itself has considerable Chinese investment. Although trade is heavily weighted in China's favor, Beijing has sought to mitigate this by offering duty-free access to some five thousand Bangladeshi products as a "goodwill gesture." China has picked up funding for the second bridge over the Meghna River, a project that proved too costly for India.[36] It also has a defense cooperation agreement with Bangladesh, signed in 2002. Under this agreement, it has supplied main battle tanks, naval vessels, radars, and fighter aircraft.

In the political vacuum now troubling Nepal, China has been able to capitalize on Nepalese suspicion of India, described in greater detail in chapter 2, to garner significant links with the strategically important country. China is building several new road links into Nepal, including through Mustang, which was the location of the CIA efforts at destabilization in Tibet that continued till the Sino-US rapprochement of 1971–72. Nepal has also heeded Chinese blandishments not to accept Tibetan refugees, and many are now being stopped at the border. It has cracked down on Tibetan political activities, again at the behest of China. Formerly dependent on India for its vital trading links, the landlocked country is now receiving many of its goods from China, facilitated by the railway into Tibet extended toward Nepal. India is deeply concerned by these developments, since growing Chinese influence potentially brings its presence to beyond the strategic barrier provided by the Himalayas. China's growing influence with Sri Lanka is discussed separately, as is its long-standing relationship with Pakistan.

In sum, these growing interests of China across South Asia and the IOR have created anxiety in New Delhi. Some commentators have pointed to the acquisition by China of a "string of pearls" of Chinese "bases." According to Chellaney, "China's strategy [is] to assemble a 'string of pearls'—ports, staging posts and hubs for expanding its interests and presence from East Africa to the Pacific."[37]

The Chinese defense minister, in an interview with *The Hindu* in 2012, strongly denied China had any interests in bases in the Indian Ocean.[38] Most commentators accept China has no actual "bases" in the Indian Ocean, including on Great Coco Island.[39] Indian strategists are not so much concerned about the current situation, however, but what might develop from these interests in future. Kaplan, while noting the skepticism in some quarters about China's intention to acquire actual bases, also comments: "The real lesson here is the subtlety of the world we are entering, of which the Indian Ocean provides a salient demonstration. Instead of the hardened military bases of the Cold War and earlier epochs, there will be dual-use civilian-military facilities where basing arrangements will be implicit rather than explicit, and completely dependent on the health of the bilateral relationship in question."[40] C. Raja Mohan's view is that while there may be no Chinese or Indian bases now, the jury is out on whether they will acquire them in future. And in any case, the central issue is that "whether or not China and India will eventually acquire military bases, it is quite obvious that the new outward maritime orientation is a structural shift in their [postcolonial] worldviews."[41]

Malik puts it more forthrightly: "China has a penchant for doing things in small steps and piecemeal: quietly, patiently, and eventually bringing the jigsaw pieces together 'when the conditions are ripe.' Then the fog suddenly clears, the 'string of pearls' emerges, and takes everyone by surprise."[42] This view highlights the uncertainty about China's intentions, an uncertainty that in turn underwrites India's hedging strategy of seeking a powerful naval presence in the Indian Ocean, one capable of monitoring China's activities and also potentially denying China access, and of developing its relationship with the United States.

One location of particular concern to India is the port of Gwadar in Pakistan. Gwadar is ideally placed to cover the Arabian Sea—an area vitally important to India vis-à-vis Pakistan. For example, in the 1971 India-Pakistan War, India was able to bottle up Pakistani maritime communications with then East Pakistan in the port of Karachi. Establishing a maritime blockade of Pakistan would be more difficult given a greater spread of Pakistani ports and possible Chinese involvement. Second, Gwadar occupies a key location in terms of the transportation of oil and gas through the Arabian Sea. It is only four hundred kilometers from the Straits of Hormuz, the choke point through which much of Asia's oil and gas is carried. It will be the location of new refineries, which will process oil to be transported from Iran through the planned Iran-Pakistan oil pipeline. Third, the importance of the Chinese involvement in Gwadar is greatly enhanced by the long-standing strategic relationship between Pakistan and China, which is in turn a manifestation of the strategic differences between India and China.

Recently the Singapore Ports Authority (SPA), which had a forty-year contract to run the port, walked away from the project because of the fact that Pakistan had failed in its commitment to complete roads linking the port to the hinterland, resulting in the port being a commercial failure. China will now take over the running of the port and complete the roadwork, much to the concern of India. This wariness on the part of India has become linked to the fact that China is developing its transport links with Pakistan across the Karakorum Highway over the 4,700-meter Khunjerab Pass, with the route ultimately to link up with Gwadar. Chinese military engineers are currently engaged in widening the Karakorum Highway to forty meters and constructing a rail connection to the head of the pass on the Chinese side. India has complained about Chinese military personnel (mainly engineers) already in Baltistan, which New Delhi regards as integral to an undivided Jammu and Kashmir, and which it in turn claims. New Delhi fears that these links and the growing Chinese presence could in turn jeopardize its position in Kashmir and Ladakh.[43]

Whether it will prove technically feasible to construct a railway into Pakistan, and on to Gwadar, is a moot point. A prefeasibility study has already been undertaken and a memorandum of understanding to conduct a feasibility study into the railway has just been signed. But any railway is many years away. Even more daunting would be the construction of the often-proposed oil or gas pipeline from Gwadar over the pass. The geological instability of the entire Baltistan region was demonstrated by the massive earthquake of 2005, which among other substantial damage caused a dam to form over the Indus that blocked the highway for many months. The devastating floods of 2010 also severely damaged the highway. Costs of pumping oil over the pass would be exorbitant. A more realistic concern would be the development of land links to Pakistan via Afghanistan through the Wakan Salient. This is less challenging country—although still difficult.

China's growing naval activity in the Indian Ocean region includes a 2003 People's Liberation Army Navy (PLAN) joint naval exercise with Pakistan; bilateral exercises with the French, British, Australian, Canadian, Philippines, and US navies in the IOR; the 2008 deployment of a task force to the Gulf of Aden for antipiracy duties; continuing participation of two warships in the Shared Awareness and Deconfliction body; and the possible "incursion" of a Chinese spy trawler off the Nicobar Islands.[44]

Added to this, China is busy developing its power-projection capabilities through its aircraft carrier ambitions, the first of which recently received its first landing of a military jet. According to the Stimson Center, China could eventually have four such carriers—two of them nuclear-powered—to host the Su-33, a naval variant of the Su-27. "This would enable the PLAN to deploy multiple CVBGs [carrier battle groups] to more than one theatre simultaneously, providing China with precisely the kind of power projection that can and will be sent to the Indian Ocean to protect Chinese interests."[45]

The sense of competition between India and China in the Indian Ocean goes well beyond the northern littoral. In terms of access to energy, other raw materials, and markets, Africa has also emerged as a venue for competition, albeit of a more commercial than strategic nature. Both China and India are seeking to diversify their oil sourcing from the Middle East to Africa. China currently sources 30 percent of its imported oil from Africa, while India is seeking to raise its percentage of energy imports from Africa from 16 percent today to 20–21 percent in 2020.[46] According to Kaplan, "competition with China is pushing India to deepen its engagement with the African continent."[47] India is assisted by the fact that it has also had a long historical engagement with Africa dating to the colonial period, when large numbers of Indians provided the commercial class of East Africa. Although the Indian population was expelled from Uganda under Idi Amin, in Kenya up to 75 percent of retailing is still owned by Indian Kenyans.

But despite these historical links, India will find it hard to compete with China in Africa. China's trade with Africa has risen from under $5 billion in 1995 to over $130 billion in 2010. Sub-Saharan Africa reportedly accounts for 15 percent of Chinese outward investment between 2005 and 2010.[48] India has on its part announced $5 billion of development deals over a three-year period.[49] India's summit of African nations in 2008 attracted only fourteen African leaders, whereas China's of two years earlier attracted forty-eight. India has neither the capital nor expertise of China, and it cannot match China's ubiquitous export regime in manufactures. All over Africa, China is engaged in investing in infrastructure and extractive industries, and Chinese goods are flooding African markets. Some Indians argue, however, that India does have some advantages, mainly in the form of its proximity, democracy, membership in the Commonwealth, and engagement in communications, governance, and UN peacekeeping.[50]

India also has some special advantages over China in some parts of the Indian Ocean, particularly the offshore islands and archipelagos of Mauritius and Seychelles. In Mauritius, the fact that the majority is of Indian origin has favored the relationship, as has a unique taxation agreement that means that much of the money flowing into India does so though Mauritius, which benefits from its liberal tax regulations. (But conversely this has also been a thorn in the side of the relationship from time to time.) Indian ships have also patrolled Seychelles waters against piracy, and India has a listening post and radar facility in northern Madagascar.

India previously had good relations with the Mohamed Nasheed government in the Maldives. This saw it installing several radars on atolls and conducting a joint venture to run the airport. With the overthrow of Nasheed by Mohammed Waheed in a bloodless coup in February 2012, however, India has lost ground to China. Waheed threw out the Indian company GMR, which, along with a Malaysian company, had a twenty-five-year contract to run the airport. He is also more disposed to favor China, which now supplies the majority of tourists to the tourism-dependent archipelago. All this caused India to threaten to withdraw its aid. But as illustrated by New Delhi's apparent backdown when Nasheed sought, and was for a period given, refuge in the Indian High Commission, there is little India can do about the problem. Meanwhile, the airport contract, and the influence that goes with it, is likely to be awarded to a Chinese company.

Elsewhere in the Indian Ocean, China is likely to be the lead investor on the northern Kenyan island of Lamu, which will be developed as a major oil- and gas-processing center to ship energy from landlocked South Sudan and the emerging gas provinces off the East African coast. China is flirting with Seychelles on the possibility of building a military facility on the island chain. President Hu Jintao visited in 2007. In 2011, a forty-member military delegation came—an enormous number considering it was visiting a minute atoll chain. China has given two maritime surveillance aircraft and trained members of the Seychelles defense forces, matching India in this area virtually tit-for-tat.[51]

INDIA'S MARITIME RESPONSE

India's concerns about the Chinese presence in the Indian Ocean have often been repeated at the official level. For example, the Indian Navy first wrote a naval doctrine in 2004. A public version was released the following year. It states: "India stands out alone as being devoid of a credible nuclear triad, especially when a powerful adversary like China has massive capability in 14 submarine launched ballistic missiles (SLBMs)."[52] (This "massive capability" is located on a single submarine.) This is an ambitious document that identifies the navy—always the poor cousin of Indian strategy—as the torchbearer of India's global strategic ambitions. It treats the Indian Ocean as India's backyard. According to Harsh V. Pant, this is a traditional approach for Indian naval planners.[53] It calls for a blue-water capability and "sea control" in designated areas of the Bay of Bengal and Arabian Sea. It refers to India's "policing" role in the Indian Ocean and declares India needs the navy to protect far-flung populations of Indian origin. It calls for a full-fledged SLBM capability as the main plank of India's strategic nuclear capacity. And it suggests India should maintain at least two carrier battle groups.

Although more diplomatic in not specifically mentioning China in these terms, the 2007–11 version says essentially the same thing.[54] It places considerable emphasis on the development of maritime surveillance and knowledge of the "maritime domain." India's space program is cited as an important element in this ambition. The strategy emphasizes the development of India's sealift and amphibious assault capabilities so it can exercise power on a territorial basis if need be. It also claims "there is a critical need to wean the littoral states away from increasingly pervasive influence of states hostile to India's interests"—which can only mean China—and to "shape" probable battle spaces, these being the Arabian Sea and Bay of Bengal.[55] According to David Scott, India's naval ambitions are being developed with "the strategic 'end' . . . to be the pre-eminent maritime power in the Indian Ocean" in the Mahanian sense of acquiring capability to exercise denial and sea control.[56]

These stated aims for the navy are ambitious and involve a massive injection of capital. According to a Deloitte study conducted in 2010, by 2022 the navy will have more than 160 ships, including three aircraft carriers, sixty major combatants (including submarines), and four hundred aircraft.[57] Some commentators have also pointed out that the 2012–13 budget accords 19 percent of the defense budget to the navy—a significant rise—and concluded that this represents a major shift in favor of a maritime strategy.[58]

As discussed above, there are real doubts whether this apparent shift in favor of the navy is sustainable in terms of future requirements of the other services. Moreover, there is also evidence of bottlenecks in India's program of naval construction arising in particular from failure in the past sufficiently to invest in modernization of the naval dockyards and associated infrastructure.[59] From table 4.4, it can be seen that consequently India is likely to suffer a lag in its program by 2022.

It will be especially deficient in conventional submarines. The *Scorpène* construction program is being delayed by lack of yard space due to failure to invest in infrastructure. Judging from the experience with the *Scorpène*, the building and phasing in of any new foreign submarine acquisitions promises to be a long, difficult, and costly process. By 2022, India's remaining nine *Kilo*-class Russian vessels will be ancient, if not already phased out—noting that one, which was recently refitted in Russia, was destroyed in a serious explosion involving munitions in 2013. Moreover, India's program to develop three carrier battle groups will have likely slipped to two. Even these two will be expensive to run and of doubtful strategic utility, given the increasing vulnerability of aircraft carriers to antiship ballistic missiles (ASBMs) such as the Chinese DF-21D.[60] This raises the questions, how valuable will the carriers be for India's overall strategy, and is there a cheaper, more efficacious solution in terms of India's defensive and force projection needs?[61]

TABLE 4.4 Present and Planned Assets in the Indian Navy

Type	Actual	Planned	Number by 2022
Surface			
Aircraft carriers	1 (INS *Viraat*—was scheduled for retirement in 2009): **Total: 1**	1 ex-Russian, *Admiral Gorshkov*, delivered 2013, not complete till 2017; 2 indigenously built, first scheduled 2015 but slipping badly—now scheduled for 2017.	Possibly 3, probably 2
Destroyers	3 *Delhi*-class; 5 *Rajput*-class: **Total: 8**	3 stealth destroyers, contract issued, to be built indigenously, with option for a further 4.	11
Frigates	2 *Shivalik*-class (stealth); 3 *Talwar*-class; 3 *Brahmaputra*-class; 3 *Godaveri*-class; 2 *Giri*-class: **Total: 13**	1 under construction; some say a total of 8 to be built. The *Godaveri*- and *Giri*- class frigates are old and will likely be phased out by 2022.	Possibly 20, likely about 14
		3 from Russia (*Krivak III* guided-missile with *Brahmos*) 2 for delivery 2012; 1 delivery 2013.	
Corvettes	4 *Kukri*-class; 4 *Kora*-class: **Total 8**		8
Offshore Patrol Vessels	6		?
Antisubmarine Patrol	4	4 ASW corvettes under domestic construction for delivery 2012–13.	4
Minesweeper	9		
LPD	Former USS *Trenton* acquired 2006: **Total 1**	Tenders issued internationally for 4.	1–5
LST	5		?
LST(m)	4		?
LCU	39	8 under domestic contract (not yet commenced).	?
Missile Boats	12		?

Training	3		3
Survey/Research	9		[illegible]
Supply and replenishment	3		3
Submarines (conventional)	4 Type 209; 9 *Kilo*-class: **Total 13**	6 *Scorpène*-class under construction for 2015–20 phase in; 6 stealth conventional submarines to be acquired, no dates. The final 3 *Scorpènes* may not be built due to lack of yard space. Assume *Kilo*-class will be phased out. One *Kilo* destroyed by fire in 2013.	Probably 10 but possibly only 6
Submarines (nuclear)			
Hunter-killer	1 *Akula II*-class (10-year lease with option to buy) **Total: 1**	1 *Akula II*-class, awaiting delivery.	2
SLBM		1 launched, awaiting commission; 3 more planned, based on Russian *Charlie III*-class.	1 and possibly up to 3
Aircraft			
Carrier-borne A/C	17 Sea Harrier; 16 MiG-29K	46 MiG-29K, purchased, delivery commenced 2012; assume Sea Harriers will be phased out.	46
Maritime patrol	5 Tu-142 (Bear), refurbished but not all operational; 15 Dornier 288-101; 12 UAV	12 P-8I (Neptune), ordered for delivery 2013—possibly 24 to be acquired in total; assume Bears will be phased out.	24

Data sources: Various as compiled by the author and in Aviotech, *Indian Naval Acquisitions I*.

But if the navy has an ambitious, forward view of policy in the IOR, there are also more sophisticated voices in New Delhi. Kaplan notes: "It became clear to me that although they [Indian defense planners] have plans for India's projection of power throughout the Indian Ocean world, they are also deeply worried about the feebleness of India's own borders, to say nothing of India's internal strife. The voices I heard [from defense officials in New Delhi] mixed a determined ambition with a prudent sense of tragedy."[62] These voices temper the power equation with the inclusive-growth doctrine. Or, to paraphrase the national security adviser Shiv Shanker Menon, India is working toward peaceful borders, including in the IOR, and only peaceful borders would allow it to meet the internal challenges of poverty, disease, and illiteracy. Such words could virtually be lifted from the pages of *NonAlignment 2.0*.[63]

One remaining advantage India possesses because of its Indian Ocean domain has yet to be discussed. India may be the only power of potential at the Indian Ocean littoral, but it is not the only *significant* power. The other significant power operating in the Indian Ocean, the United States, is likely to move strategically closer to India, thus "turbo-charging" India's natural Indian Ocean advantages, especially in regard to China.

The Indian Ocean and Indo-US Relations

Ever since the renaissance in Indo-US relations of the post-1991 period, the Indian Ocean has been central to Washington's interest in pursuing the relationship. The two Gulf wars (the Gulf War in 1990–91 and the Iraq War in 2003) demonstrated to the United States the importance of an alternative route into the Gulf. Luckily for the United States, Operations Desert Shield and Desert Storm during the first Gulf war were conducted in the immediate aftermath of the Cold War. This meant that enormous quantities of matériel and large numbers of troops were already prepositioned in Europe and no longer required to confront the Soviet bloc. They were thus readily available for rapid transfer to the Gulf.

Nevertheless, US Pacific Command (USPACOM), with its headquarters in Hawaii, was responsible for the vast stretch of ocean taking in the Pacific and Indian Oceans, with that portion of the Indian Ocean between Pakistan and the Gulf covered by Central Command. This route, and associated bases and facilities in the Indian Ocean, were important to US Gulf strategy in a number of respects, which remain a constant today.

The route provided backup should transit facilities or vital sea lanes such as the Suez Canal ever be denied through Europe or the Gulf and Middle East regions, as occurred in the Yom Kippur War (1973). It provided the means by which US forces and equipment located in the western continental United States and in the Pacific itself could be deployed into the Gulf. Dedicated Indian Ocean bases such as Diego Garcia had been used as vital locations for prepositioned, rapidly deployable forces and for B-52 bombers ranging over the Gulf / Southwest Asia region. Finally, various points around the northwestern segment of the Indian Ocean and Gulf were used as launch points for ship-based ballistic missiles and aircraft targeting the Gulf and Southwest Asia.

The abiding strategic interests of outside powers were, of course, viewed somewhat differently by the littoral powers, especially India. Prior to the Gulf War and the subsequent fall of the already rickety Soviet Union, India was generally seen in the West to have had a pro-Soviet tilt. This became particularly pronounced after the US Seventh Fleet steamed into the Bay of Bengal during the India-Pakistan War of 1971.

The Gulf War and the Soviet Union's fall gave a sharp jolt to this status quo. India had sourced about 70 percent of its weapons and matériel from the Soviet Union. Its military doctrine was also heavily dependent on the Soviet model of fighting massive land wars. The losses suffered by Iraq—another power using Soviet equipment and doctrine—shocked India. According to the *Times of India*, "non-western nations will have to learn several searing lessons from operation Desert Storm. The first is the wholly ineffectual role of the Soviet Union in this conflict."[64] New Delhi quickly reached the conclusion that India's Soviet-derived military model of large land armies was anachronistic. The US military's AirLand Battle doctrine, the revolution in military affairs (RMA), and military modernization were now the order of the day. Second, with the loss of Soviet power, India realized it would have to deal with the United States in the Indian Ocean whether it liked it or not.

The shift in Indian thinking vis-à-vis the United States did not come quickly or easily, however. It could even be argued that this debate is by no means resolved in India, as witnessed by the domestic political difficulties experienced by the government of Manmohan Singh in signing an Indo-US nuclear agreement and the ambivalent attitude to the US evident in the recent *NonAlignment 2.0* document.[65]

For the United States, the end of the Cold War meant that Pakistan was no longer a frontline state in relation to Afghanistan (although ironically it was to reemerge in that role after 9/11, thus further earning the title of "most allied ally"). It also meant that India was no longer seen in Washington as a "fellow traveler" of the Soviet Union.

The Gulf War victory in 1991 cost the United States $14 billion. This enormous expense (in then prevailing prices) was fortunately for Washington eased by contributions from the Gulf allies and Japan—known as "burden sharing." But Washington, anxious to reap a "peace dividend" from the end of the Cold War, was also keen to exercise burden sharing not just in a financial way, but also in terms of contributions by countries such as India to regional security—in this case the security of the Indian Ocean. Therefore, far from being concerned about India's rise as an Indian Ocean power, the United States switched tack and became an active supporter of that process. Significantly, USPACOM, with its two-ocean responsibility, was a driver of the new relationship.[66]

Driven by these and other imperatives, Washington quickly set aside its reservations arising from India's nuclear detonations of 1998. By the time of the visit by President Bill Clinton to South Asia in 2000, the United States had made it clear that it believed India, not Pakistan, was the power of the future in the Indian Ocean. As Mohan Malik sums it up, "since 2000, Washington's India policy has moved from containment to empowerment."[67] Even the 9/11 attacks and subsequent rapprochement between Washington and Pakistan did not seriously derail the emerging Indian-US relationship.

Such was the logic pushing the two together that by 2005 the United States was calling for a "broad strategic relationship" with India. Not only was USPACOM associated with taking the new relationship forward in the post–Cold War environment, but also the defense and security relationship is now far-reaching.

This desire on the part of the United States for a *strategic* relationship is a major factor behind the Indian–US nuclear agreement. The reason why the nuclear agreement is important is that it would be difficult for the United States to support and build Indian power in some key technologies—for example, ballistic missile technology, anti-ballistic missiles, and space—without first bringing India into "to the nuclear tent." The "end user" agreements signed following the conclusion of the nuclear agreement are but a logical outcome of this process. As Stephen Cohen and Sunil Dasgupta point out, however, the strategic content of the relationship needs to be progressed with sensitivity, as part of a subtle exercise. According to them, "these programs [of technology transfer] should be structured so as to facilitate the reform of Indian defence structures and processes. India is too important a state to be regarded simply as a cash cow when it comes to arms sales and technology transfer."[68]

The strategic content of the relationship is explicit in the type of technologies being transferred to India, both through the United States and indirectly through Israel with US permission. These include the Israeli Phalcon airborne early-warning-and-control system, based heavily on American technology (and denied to China on that basis), and an anti–ballistic missile (ABM) system probably based on the Israeli Arrow 2, in turn developed with American technology and jointly with Boeing. While Arrow 2 is an anti–tactical ballistic missile system, Arrow 3 will have a capability against medium-range ballistic missiles. Some are also suggesting that India seek jointly to develop with Israel a version of the Iron Dome system, capable of intercepting short-range missiles.[69] India will also probably acquire the Israeli Spike antitank missile ahead of the American Javelin, on concerns the United States will not agree to adequate technology transfer. India launched an Israeli Tecsar spy satellite in 2008 (designed to spy on Iran), and a quid pro quo could be assistance with India's own military satellite program. In 2012, India signed a contract for Rs 12 billion–worth of Israeli drones.[70] And in terms of direct purchases from the United States, India has acquired sophisticated targeting radars and a large naval vessel. The sale of the Orion P-3C maritime reconnaissance aircraft is also in progress, as is the sale of ten C-17 Globemaster III heavy-lift aircraft, which will give India strategic airlift reach throughout what it refers to as its "area of interest." Another six are scheduled to be located in the Northeast, for potential use against China.[71] Defense sales with the United States already concluded over the last decade are worth $8 billion, and much more is in the pipeline.

Within this deepening military-to-military relationship, the exchange of military doctrine and training is just as important as technology, in keeping with the point made above by Cohen and Dasgupta. Since the New Framework Agreement was signed by India and the United States in 2005, the military aspects of the relationship have become more comprehensive. According to the US Department of Defense, "the United States and India are natural partners, destined to be closer because of shared interests and values and our mutual desire for a stable and secure world."[72] The bilateral Defense Policy Group, which governs the agreement, has prioritized maritime security, humanitarian/disaster relief, and counterterrorism (CT) within the framework. But in fact, the bulk of activities by far has related to maritime security in the Indian Ocean, and for good reason. Even the CT cooperation is slanted toward maritime security.[73]

The ambitious program of exercises takes Indian military practitioners to the heart of US doctrine, including in the area of joint (in the sense of interservice) operations, or "jointery" as it is known in the jargon, an area in which India has a great deal to learn from the United States. The key to all of this exercising is the highly complex future task of conducting joint operations. Although the focus appears to be on transnational threats such as piracy, the tabletop exercises on jointery—for instance in Alaska in 2010—appear to go well beyond that. The two navies conduct four exercises annually: the flagship Exercise Malabar (generally at the strategic level), Exercise Habu Nag (amphibious operations), Exercise Spitting Cobra (explosive ordnance), and SALVEX (salvage). The navies have also jointly participated in actual operations on four occasions: provision by the Indian Navy of security for US ships transiting the Strait of Malacca after 9/11, tsunami relief in 2004–5, noncombatant evacuation from Lebanon in 2006, and counterpiracy operations in the Gulf of Aden since 2008.[74]

The China Factor in Indo-US Relations

If Washington was originally motivated in seeking Indian support by the perceived need of burden sharing in relation to its role in the Middle East, today the United States is increasingly driven toward India by the rise of China. The

US goal in cultivating relations with India, however, is not so much to create an ally against China (although that would be deemed a useful outcome if it could be achieved), but rather to create of India another powerful force in global affairs and thus unsettle China's rise and allow for a more multipolar security environment—one capable of balancing China's rise if needed. This seemingly semantic point actually has considerable import in view of the fact that a number of analysts have dismissed closer Indo-US relations on the ground that, in the words of Hugh White, India would never have an "alliance" with the United States since it is a significant power with its own agenda.[75] While this is probably technically correct, it does not preclude tightening strategic relations in the future. The US strategy is thus a hedge against a difficult rise of China, rather than a "balance in being" against China's rise. The concomitant of this strategy is that India should be supported in its aspirations to become a significant power, including through sensitive military technology transfer. According to a statement made in India by Secretary of State Condoleezza Rice in 2005, the United States has "a vision for a decisively broader strategic relationship, to help India achieve its goals as one of the world's great multi-ethnic democracies. This vision embraces cooperation on a global strategy for peace, on defense, on energy, and on economic growth."[76]

China's rapid economic and strategic rise is a challenge to both powers. But the nature of that challenge differs, and the approaches to China are somewhat different. India currently seeks stability in relations with China pending finding solutions to its pressing problems of growth and development. Washington, while also wanting stability, is determined to continue the US balancing role in Asia, currently in the form of the "pivot" or "rebalance." What that actually means is still under negotiation, but New Delhi certainly does not want to be part of any pivot that unduly upsets China and destroys the status quo. Consequently, although Washington and New Delhi have powerful incentives to work together on China, they do not always see eye to eye.

The matter is further complicated by the fact that the Sino-US relationship is currently the seminal one in the Asia-Pacific in terms of setting the security agenda. It will thus also to an extent set the context for Sino-Indian relations. Should the Sino-US relationship prove difficult, China's rise as an Asian power is also likely to be more difficult, and relations with India are likely also to suffer. Thus Sino-Indian relations need to be assessed not just in their bilateral context, but also as they are overlaid by the triangular relationship between India, China, and the United States, a situation further complicated by China's long-standing relationship with Pakistan. Although the Sino-US relationship is the seminal one in terms of nearer-term security in Asia, Sino-Indian relations will be key to the longer-term peace of the wider region—the two being the obvious regional superpowers of the twenty-first century.

Despite the apparent strategic congruity between India and the United States vis-à-vis China, the nature of the "threat" posed by China in the case of India and of the United States is different. The United States is one of the most intrinsically secure countries on earth. It is protected by two oceans, is bordered by friendly powers to north and south, and possesses the world's most effective nuclear arsenal. So the challenge posed by China for the United States is a challenge to Washington's "world role" and its economic well-being rather than to its existence.

For India, Sino-Indian relations are existential, in that the two have a 3,500-kilometer border, a good deal of which is challenged. Just as India sits in the box seat in terms of Indian Ocean strategic security, so too China sits in the box seat in relation to Tibet. It dominates the high ground and the easier territory to approach the frontier, where India confronts the extremely steep, unstable, Himalayan southern slopes.

Moreover, although the border claims appear to constitute but a small portion of India's total territory and only just over one million of India's population of 1.21 billion, the Chinese claim to Arunachal Pradesh has profound strategic implications. Were such a claim to be realized, Chinese strategic power would be brought beyond that vital barrier, the Himalayas, down to the vulnerable Brahmaputra River valley, in the heart of India's unstable northeastern states. India is a heterogeneous country with a number of separatist movements existing within weak borders. It would be further weakened in terms of China's capacity to "fish in the troubled waters" of South Asia by any Chinese presence below the Himalayas. And finally, India's vital water supplies could be profoundly threatened, just as China's vital energy flows could be threatened by India in the context of the Indian Ocean.

Nor is the border dispute the only negative element in Sino-Indian relations. China's relationships with other South Asian powers also come into play. China's relationship with Pakistan, for example, could be likened to the relationship between the former Soviet Union and Cuba, in that Cuba was on America's doorstep, just as Pakistan is contiguous to India.

Against this background that strategically favors China, China's position on the border appears to have hardened since 2005. In particular, China apparently switched its approach to negotiations on the border—negotiations that have now been in train for over thirty years without much progress. The parameters set in 2005 for the "Guiding Principles" for future negotiations included the phrase "in reaching the boundary settlement, the two sides shall safeguard due interests of their settled populations in the border areas [Article VII]."[77] India interpreted these words to mean that China's claim to Arunachal Pradesh, with its population of 1.1 million, would not be pursued. However, by the time of the visit of Chinese president Hu to New Delhi in 2006, it was clear that China had reneged on this position, if indeed it had ever adopted it. By 2009, the Chinese position had further hardened. China challenged an ADB loan for India, a small portion of which was to go to Arunachal. Beijing refused to grant visas to visiting officials from Arunachal. The Chinese embassy began pointedly to staple visas into passports of people from Indian Kashmir visiting China, implying renewal of support for Pakistan's claim for Kashmir. China challenged a visit of Prime Minister Singh to Arunachal and was especially troubled by a visit of the Dalai Lama to Tawang, the birthplace of the revered sixth Dalai Lama.

Malik argues that an internal study on India undertaken in 2005 at the behest of the Chinese leadership's Foreign Affairs Group recommended that Beijing maintain pressure on India at all levels—military, diplomatic, and economic—with the purpose of containing its rise to power and especially of constraining its emerging strategic relationship with the United States. Prior to 2005, he argues, China had perceived India in a far more benign light, but this perception changed in view of India's economic advancement and growing relationship with the United States.[78]

Given these circumstances, the surprise is not so much that Indo-US relations have solidified, but rather that, at least according to mainstream Indian declarations, they are still not all that close. Indeed, India's quasi-official, and even official, security strategy (such as it is) has time and again reiterated the need for India to remain equidistant between the other leading powers. The logic behind this is twofold: India as a future leading power believes it need defer to no other power, and India also requires time and space to engage in inclusive growth, as previously discussed. This requires a stable foreign policy that focuses on achieving India's global economic objectives and maintaining its interests without creating undue international perturbations, such as a closer strategic relationship with the United States might suggest.

While it has been the *NonAlignment 2.0* document that has attracted publicity in this regard, it is not difficult to see the seeds of such a policy going right back to Nehru and the original policy of nonalignment, which was seen as a necessary corrective to the old, war-inducing alliances of Europe and the colonizing West.[79] More recently, postdating the Cold War but predating the publication of *NonAlignment 2.0*, the Ministry of External Affairs has been wont to reiterate, in its annual reports and elsewhere, India's strategy of "strategic autonomy." For example, take this excerpt from the report of 2004–05: "The guiding principles of India's foreign policy have been founded on Panchsheel, pragmatism and pursuit of national interest. . . . [Foreign policy] must be an integral part of the larger effort of building the nations' [sic] capabilities through economic development, strengthening social fabric and wellbeing of the people and protecting India's sovereignty and territorial integrity."[80] The MEA document, moreover, declared this policy to be bipartisan. Leaving aside the reference to *Panchsheel*, these words could be taken almost directly from *NonAlignment 2.0*. They have very little to do with power balancing and alliances and everything to do with protecting inclusive growth, internal stability, and strategic autonomy.

Given this seemingly entrenched policy, how are matters likely to unfold as China rises to power? Is the rhetoric likely to change? Are the facts on the ground already starting to change? What is India's actual policy as distinct from its often-declared policy? These questions cannot be answered without first dealing with a number of related questions. Just how is China likely to rise as a power? Will it be essentially benign (while asserting its economic and diplomatic interests as would any leading power), or will it be revisionist in the sense of using its power to readjust current security relationships to its preferences? If the latter, it would involve readjustment of Chinese border claims, including with India, to its advantage and leaning on smaller, weaker regional nations to ensure that its broader interests—both strategic and economic—are met. Further, how are these changes likely to be interpreted in New Delhi, where there are many voices and an essentially ambivalent policy on China?

The diversity of views on China in India is shaped both by ground realities and by the nature of those holding such views. In terms of reality on the ground, there are both positives and negatives driving the relationship. Positives include some common positions in international forums such as on climate change. But at the moment the negatives appear to both outweigh the positives and to be growing, especially given rapidly escalating trade imbalances, as discussed in chapter 3.

By 2009, elements within the Indian polity were increasingly of the view that the best way to handle China was to stand up to it.[81] The Singh and Dalai Lama visits to Arunachal Pradesh went ahead. As already detailed, India's military positioning along the border is in the process of being upgraded. In discussions in Bangalore in that year and at the periphery of the East Asia Summit in Bangkok, the Chinese and Indian leadership were able at least to an extent to defuse the situation and reestablish a kind of watchful modus vivendi. We must therefore conclude that to the extent India has a China policy, the following can be said: Policy has hardened in recent years, especially in view of the apparent shift in China's thinking between 2006 and 2009. Many influential officials and commentators are increasingly of the view that the only way to deal with China is to "stand up to it." But that said, New Delhi's policy is still basically to hedge, for fear of making of China that which India fears most—an out-and-out enemy.

By 2013, the Indian position was further shaped by a significant Chinese incursion into Ladakh in April and May. Although this was seemingly innocuous, involving only a few tents and thirty men, the location involved potential Chinese control over a much larger area and was nineteen kilometers inside the area India claimed. It also had considerable strategic value to India as both a military marshaling site and also a site that overlooked the Siachin Glacier, contested by India and Pakistan.[82] China only withdrew once India threatened to cancel the forthcoming visit of Chinese premier Li Keqiang. But the incident left India even more uncertain as to China's motivation. Was the incursion a part of the softening-up process associated with scheduled prime ministerial visit, was it indicative of a new leadership testing the waters, or was it something else again?

Despite this apparent hardening of its position, it would be fair to say that attitudes to China in India are still on contested ground. This contestation underlines the current ambivalence and sense of caution about the relationship. The feeling is it is a relationship that could go either way, and India would much rather have a stable relationship than an unstable one. The BJP, as it was rising to power in the 1990s, exhibited a stridently nationalist voice, advocating that India should build a fleet sufficient to control the Indian Ocean from "Singapore to Aden."[83] That voice has since been moderated, and the two large Indian parties are now closer together on foreign and security policy in many respects. But in relation to China, the two points of view are not always consonant. The BJP and various commentators associated with it tend to be hard-line on China. The MEA tends to be more moderate on China than the Ministry of Defence—a position increasingly reflected in the secretariat of the Cabinet's Security Committee, if not the prime minister's office. The *Times of India* tends to be more strident in its criticism of China than *The Hindu*. Sometimes different elements within the same ministry speak very differently, depending on circumstances, and the view from Jammu and Kashmir—for example, as expressed by Chief Minister Omar Abdullah—can be very different from that from New Delhi.[84] These different voices in India are also reflected by the different attitudes of various commentators outside India. Some, such as Louise Merrington,[85] have a reasonably optimistic view of the relationship, whereas others, such as Malik, are generally pessimistic. Malik summarizes his position: "On balance, for all the millennial talk about friendship and strategic partnership, little seems to have changed in China's view of India since the 1960s. If anything, the gulf between the two countries—in terms of their perceptions, attitudes, and expectations towards each other—has widened in recent years. . . . Still both exhibit a shared interest in not allowing tensions to overwhelm the relationship as a whole."[86]

Whatever else may be said, it is bound to be the case that the nature of the debate in India on China will be influenced by the rate and manner of China's rise. Should China's rise prove rapid and difficult, the negative voices will quickly gain traction. But there will also be another effect: The "rusted on" doctrine of strategic autonomy, while probably retaining its hortatory value, will become so much hot air in terms of practical policy. In these circumstances, the strategic content of the Indo-US relationship would be bound to deepen.

Although it is too early to comment on the nature of China's power once truly powerful, it does seem to be the case that it is likely to continue to gain power vis-à-vis India. This suggests that over the longer term, India is vulnerable to a rising China. This is potentially troubling to India, especially should Beijing remain assertive on China's key interests and toward perceived competitors such as India.

In this regard, a study by the RAND Corporation (which was, significantly, commissioned by the US Department of Defense) found that in terms of straight line trajectories, China, with an economy more than three times the size of India's at market rates, is growing faster and will therefore continue to widen the gap. What is remarkable about this projection is that even given a low growth scenario for China and a high one for India, China would still have a substantially bigger economy in 2025. According to RAND, China's economic advantage will by 2025 translate into a defense expenditure of between four and seven times India's.[87] The US National Intelligence Council's *Global Trends 2030* document shares this view that China will still be ahead of India by 2030.[88]

There is an argument that sees China being checked in its continued accrual of power vis-à-vis India by its impending demographic problems as its population ages. But the above-cited RAND paper argues that India's dependency ratio will not fall below that of China till 2027. Also, Kundu points out:

> Thus far, available data indicate that India has failed miserably in providing meaningful employment opportunities for its teeming millions. According to India's Planning Commission, the employment elasticity of growth in India in the last decade declined from 0.44 during the first half to an abysmal 0.01 during second half of the decade. If we assume that the average elasticity for the decade is 0.2, and India's workforce increases by roughly 2%

TABLE 4.5 Five Scenarios Comparing Projected GDPs of China and India in 2025 (US$ Billions, Constant 2000 Prices, Market Exchange Rates)

	China	India
GDP in 2007	2,388	771
Average China, Average India	6,489	2,069
Low China, Low India	4,672	1,268
High China, High India	11,263	3,293
Low China, High India	4,672	3,293
High China, Low India	11,263	1,268

Note: Conversion to market rates based on World Bank's world development indicators.

Data source: RAND Corp., *China and India, 2025*, 53, figure 3.5.

every year, the economy has to grow by 10% [per annum] to absorb all the new entrants.[89]

Furthermore, China will doubtless be able to use its enormous capital reserves to substitute capital for labor, just as Japan and Korea have been able to as their populations matured and their labor became more expensive.[90]

As discussed in earlier chapters, risk in India is every bit as pronounced as it is in China when it comes to issues such as water security, climate change, and the challenges of urbanization, infrastructure, health, welfare and education requirements that need to be met if India is to gain leverage from its enormous population. And even though China still has to cross the Rubicon of some kind of democratization process, we should remain conscious of all the impediments associated with India's particular brand of democracy, again as detailed in earlier chapters of this book.

Given the ambivalence in Sino-Indian relations, it would not be surprising if China's comparative rise were to make India edgy and inclined to "call in" its hedge in terms of relations with the United States. India could seek to leverage the US technological superiority through its own relatively cheap productive capability. Coincidentally, such a strategy would harmonize with the current desires of Washington, since one of the great problems the United States faces is China's growing comparative advantage as a source of cheap weapons, technology, and research. An example of Washington's desire to leverage its relationship with India was the offer to provide joint production of the front-line Joint Strike Fighter—an offer India knocked back in favor of the French Rafale.

India's alternative might be eventually to cede position to China on what it considers its core interests, such as the border, South Asia, and the IOR. Comparative accrual of power by China would, moreover, affect India's regional relationships, making it less likely the small powers of the IOR and South/Southeast Asia would seek to use India to balance a rising China. Vietnam's position as China's neighbor would be especially tenuous. Such powers would either tend to look to the United States or be forced to accept China as the regional hegemon.

Given the existence of the strategic autonomy paradigm, however, such circumstances might not be captured in the rhetoric emanating from New Delhi, even were India to sharpen its current tilt to the United States. In making this point, we need to note that the Indo-US strategic relationship is already more developed than *any other* such Indian relationship, as illustrated earlier in this chapter.

But none of the above suggests that a stronger Indo-US relationship, and a concomitant strengthening of the adversarial quality of Sino-Indian relations, is inevitable. Much will depend on how Sino-US relations unfold and on how

China chooses to rise as an Asian power. So this is still a fluid situation—one amenable to policy settings, to how regional security architecture is shaped, and to how the respective leaderships choose to engage with each other into the future. While Sino-US relations will be a key factor in deciding these issues, just how India—the so-called swing state of Asia—decides to insert itself into the Asian security equation will also be significant.

INDIA'S GATHERING CONFIDENCE AS AN ASIAN POWER

India's relationship with those parts of Asia to its east should be viewed in both the context of its continental approach to strategy and the inherent strengths derived from its positioning in the Indian Ocean. The continental posture implies that it would be a poor bet as a balance to China, at least in the shorter term and at least in the Asia-Pacific. Contrary to that, the key strategic position India occupies in the Indian Ocean seems on the surface to offer strategic possibilities for India as it seeks to look east. The fact that India is engaged in a slow accretion of naval power despite its overall continental posture also apparently enhances its strategic potential both as an Indian Ocean power and consequently as an Indo-Pacific power.

What these two apparently contrary trends mean in effect is that India's strategic influence in those parts of Asia to its east will continue to develop, but that East and Southeast Asian powers will approach India more as a hedge against China than as a balance-in-being against China, just as the United States approaches India in this way. Most powers, including Japan and Vietnam, with which India has the closest relations, still have doubts concerning its capabilities as a power in the Asia-Pacific, as distinct from the Indian Ocean domain.

In the past, New Delhi itself has recognized all the pitfalls and paradoxes involved with any assertive role by India in East Asia. In particular, there has been a strong predilection in India not to appear to be siding against China in the region. This is derived from a perception of its own weakness, especially in operating in distant waters, the desire to retain strategic autonomy so as not to be seen as part of any "bloc," and the desire to ensure that India's ambivalent relationship with China is not prematurely forced into an overtly confrontational role. Even as late as 2007, these factors dictated a cautious approach in New Delhi to the so-called quadrilateral proposed by then Japanese prime minister Shinzo Abe and then US vice president Dick Cheney.

Another factor in India's hitherto cautious approach to East and Southeast Asia is that its Look East strategy did not initially progress exactly as would have been hoped when initiated by the Narasimha Rao government in 1991. This is partly due to its genesis: It grew out of the collapse of India's erstwhile friend and major weapons supplier, the Soviet Union, and the parallel collapse of the Indian economy. But India's limitations in East/Southeast Asia, which still to an extent persist, also reflect deeper issues such as its continuing focus on the IOR, Pakistan, Southwest Asia, and the Gulf; its continental posture; and its limited capacity as a soft power. The latter is reflected in the fact that, as pointed out by Daniel Markey and others, India only has about six hundred full-fledged diplomats and is "hobbled" by its selection and training processes and lack of outside expertise.[91] (However, Ian Hall argues that India is seeking to augment its soft power with new-technology approaches to public diplomacy—but with mixed results.[92]) Finally, there is lingering skepticism in Asia that India is committed to the open developmental model that has been so successful in East and Southeast Asia.

India expected an easier ride into Asia than it in fact initially received. In a speech in Singapore in 1994, then prime minister Rao expressed surprise at the subject about which he had been asked to speak—"India's 'New' Relationship with Asia." Rao pointed out that India's influence in Asia was hardly new—indeed, Indian religion and culture lie at the heart of today's Southeast Asia.[93] While Rao's point was true enough, it was largely irrelevant to the states of the Association of Southeast Asian Nations (ASEAN), which were a pragmatic group of countries intent on economic development and hardly concerned with historical links, and which also saw India at that time as a Soviet fellow traveler that had not supported their position on Cambodia following the Vietnamese intervention.

ASEAN skepticism about India's commitment to economic reform was intensified by the fact that the free-trade agreement (FTA) with ASEAN was hard-won. India's farmers were committing suicide at unprecedented levels over supposedly unbridled agricultural imports caused by globalization. The FTA, when it finally emerged in 2009, was not only criticized in India, but also protective of Indian agriculture, especially edible oils. It took over six years to negotiate and will not be fully implemented for nonsensitive goods till 2016 (later for poorer ASEAN countries and India).

When viewed against India's global engagement, its Look East policy has been less pronounced than its rhetorical position suggests, reflecting the broad balance of interests of a potential global player. Indeed, 72.5 percent of India's export trade is still to countries other than East/Southeast Asia, and 67.53 percent of imports is sourced from countries other than East/Southeast Asia.[94] Even though trade with ASEAN has been growing rapidly, ASEAN is now only receiving 12.5 percent of India's exports and supplying only 8.9 percent of imports.[95] Placement of the MEA cadre within the New Delhi headquarters also does not reflect a Look East policy bias, being only twelve of eighty-nine officers specifically servicing a region, or 13.5 percent.[96] In terms of languages spoken (other than official Indian languages, which include English), 401 of the present MEA cadre speak non-East Asian or non-Southeast Asian languages, while only 114 speak East Asian or Southeast Asian languages. A significantly larger number of India's diplomats speak Arabic than Chinese.[97]

Despite these limitations in the conduct of India's Look East strategy, important developments are occurring in India's relations to its east, and significant progress has been made. By the latter 1990s, India's growth rate was approaching East Asian levels. This economic takeoff caused ASEAN to take real notice of India for the first time. India is now much more highly regarded in ASEAN than in the 1990s. It is a member of the ARF and the East Asia Summit (EAS) and participates in the Asia-Europe Meeting (ASEM). Not yet in the Asia-Pacific Economic Cooperation forum (APEC), it has good prospects of eventually joining the grouping. It has extensive defense dealings with Singapore, Australia, Thailand, Japan, Malaysia, Indonesia, and Vietnam. As David Brewster illustrates, it now has a wide range of unfolding activities with East and Southeast Asian countries.[98] Despite the long delay in the FTA, trade between India and ASEAN has been growing handsomely at 21.3 percent per annum in the decade 2001–10. Two-way trade is now $80 billion—matching that of China—and is expected to reach $100 billion by 2015. DFI of $18 billion has flowed into India during this decade, mainly from Singapore. India and ASEAN have just signed an agreement on trade in services, which New Delhi sees as greatly benefiting India.[99]

This recent quickening pace of India's Look East policy raises the important question of just how the "swing state" is likely to insert itself into the rapidly changing Asian power equation. We have argued that so far New Delhi has tended to treat any strategic role for India in Asia with caution, but there is evidence this may be changing.

A ready example of the possible direction of these changes is provided by the Indo-Japanese relationship. For Japan, much of the strategic focus on India relates both to China and to the way India sits in a commanding position in the Indian Ocean. It also relates to the fact that India is strategically linked to Japan's key ally, the United States.

At the strategic level, this "forward policy" on India was especially pronounced under Prime Minister Abe's first premiership from 2006 to 2007. His 2007 attempt to incorporate India, the United States, Australia, and Japan into an effort to contain China—an operation that became known as "the quadrilateral"—was also favored by Vice President Cheney. In the end it failed due to China's vehement response (described further in chapter 6) and the fact that both Canberra and New Delhi got cold feet. But Abe has seemingly renewed the proposal now that he is again prime minister. This has occurred against a backdrop of deteriorating Sino-Japanese relations over the Senkaku/Diaoyu Islands dispute. In an article published in December 2012, Abe wrote, "I envisage a strategy whereby Australia, India, Japan, and the US state of Hawaii form a diamond to safeguard the maritime commons stretching from the Indian Ocean region to the western Pacific."[100]

Abe is being highly specific here in defining the role of the "strategic diamond" as all about maritime security in Japan's vital SLOCs. But as in 2007, at least some of Japan's putative allies will be cautious about appearing to form a balance-in-being against China, lest they prematurely force China into a pattern of opposition and make its rise more difficult. According to Medcalf, "there will be little immediate appetite for its [the quadrilateral's] revival among some participants, notably India and Australia, if they judge that possible benefits in strategic policy coordination are outweighed by the prospective rise in Chinese perceptions, however misplaced, of a containment strategy."[101] This prediction certainly appears to be true of Australia. Its latest defense white paper (2013) appears to backtrack on the one of 2009, which expressed concern about a rising China.[102] Canberra wishes to continue to walk the tightrope between China and the United States and fears any revival of a quadrilateral might unduly unbalance its position to one side of the wire.

This time, however, India's reaction, if judged from progress in the overall relationship with Japan, has been more positive than was the case in 2007. In 2008, Japan signed a security agreement with India—one of only three such agreements, the others being with the United States and Australia. In 2011, the two signed a free-trade agreement. Even though total bilateral trade is only $18.7 billion and weighted heavily in Japan's favor, this is offset by the fact that India is one of the major recipients of Japanese aid, having received $36 billion in the past few years.[103] Tokyo also argues that its FDI in India has increased dramatically and that this effectively offsets the trade imbalance.[104] During Prime Minister Singh's June 2013 visit to Tokyo, the two nations further advanced the bilateral nuclear agreement, which could see a dramatic surge in Japanese investment in India's nuclear technology. Singh's Tokyo visit came hard on the heels of the visit to India of new Chinese premier Li, which sent a message in itself. In the context of its escalating dispute with China over the Senkaku/Diaoyu Islands in 2012, Tokyo further sought to cement strategic relations with India, to coordinate positions in multilateral forums such as the ARF and the EAS, and to develop an ongoing program of strategic dialogue and joint exercising.[105] It remains to be seen, however, whether New Delhi will seek to translate its very warm relationship with Abe's Japan into a multilateral arrangement, as Abe would like.

India has also adopted what at first glance appears to be an unambiguous position in regard to Vietnam. This relationship goes back earlier than Look East and has been driven far more specifically by concern about China than India's other East and Southeast Asia relationships. It is the most overtly strategic of any

Indian relationship in the Asia-Pacific and the one that can most closely be compared with China's relationship with Pakistan.

But for all its antecedents, the relationship still places India in a dilemma, due principally to its continuing strategic weakness in East Asia. For example, in 2011 and again in 2012, Vietnam fell afoul of China over the South China Sea dispute. China cut the seismic cables of Vietnamese oil-exploration vessels on two occasions. India, which has oil and gas exploration licenses off Vietnam, threatened to send naval vessels to protect its interests on the second occasion.[106] The Indian Navy chief, Adm. D. K. Joshi, reportedly said, "When the requirement is there for situations where the country's interests are involved, for example ONGC Videsh, we will be required to go there and we are prepared for that."[107]

This was likely simply posturing: It is doubtful India could do much to counter China so far from its home bases and so near to China's major naval facilities on Hainan Island. Reflecting India's ambivalent position on China and perhaps also its strategic doubts about its ability to operate in the Pacific, the foreign minister, Salman Kurshid, asserted that the South China Sea dispute was a bilateral one between China and Vietnam and not India's business.[108] Still, the incidents illustrated both the danger of the interconnectedness of the Indian Ocean and South China Sea competition and also the fact that India's interests in East Asia have as much to do with its competition with China as with any Look East policy. If anything, the divisive nature of these encounters does more to undermine Look East than to support it.

India's strategic dilemma vis-à-vis Vietnam is also underlined by requests from Hanoi for assistance and how they have been treated by India. For example, in 2011, Vietnam reportedly requested of India transfer of weapons, including the Brahmos cruise missile and naval vessels. According to *The Hindu*, this placed New Delhi in a dilemma because it did not want unduly to antagonize China in the aftermath of the dispute over the oil-search contract.[109] In the event, India locked in to the Russian-Vietnamese arms relationship by providing submariner training for Vietnam's Russian-origin *Kilo*-class submarines. It may also provide pilot training for Vietnam's Su-30s. It has already done so for Malaysia, so could do this without unduly antagonizing China. However, it has apparently balked at providing hardware. So, we must conclude that in strategic terms, the Indo-Vietnamese relationship is a far cry from the Sino-Pakistani relationship, which has involved transfer of strategic material, including nuclear-related material, to Pakistan on many occasions.

And in rational terms, India's strategic doubts, such as they are, are justified. In the final analysis India is both less powerful than China and also more vulnerable to Chinese interference in its backyard than China is to Indian interference in its backyard. These doubts not only reflect geography and respective power, but also the fact that India's continental pull is stronger than China's.

In terms of India and China's tit-for-tat backyard machinations (keeping in mind China's activities in Pakistan and elsewhere in South Asia and India's in Vietnam), India is the far more vulnerable. Not only is it opposed by China's nuclearized friend Pakistan, and not only does China enjoy the strategic advantage on the northern border of far better infrastructure and less exacting terrain in Tibet, but India is especially vulnerable in its Northeast, where separatist movements have been evident since soon after independence. During the 1960s and 1970s, these were assisted from Maoist China. China also attempted to cut India asunder by assisting the Naxalbari (Maoist) revolt in 1967 in a region that lies strategically over the vulnerable so-called Chicken's Neck separating the Northeast from the rest of India. Even today, India would remain highly vulnerable to any Chinese interference in the Northeast in support of separatists or Maoists, the latter having recently moved back into that region.

CONCLUSION

Viewing the ambition and rhetoric of India's foreign focus over the last two decades, it is clear that the nation has a new confidence spurred on by higher economic growth rates and the growing international perception that it will be a very important Asian and global power in the twenty-first century. It is also clear that India prefers to see itself not as a power bounded by its difficult regional circumstances, but as a global player. Within this framework, the political and intellectual mainstream prefers to see India as essentially nonaligned and positioned to play both ends against the middle, as it has now done successfully for many decades, both in the Cold War and afterward. This approach is captured by the frequently used terminology "strategic autonomy."

Yet for all this, India still falls short of true autonomy in two important, closely related aspects. First, the dispositions of India's resources—whether fiscal, security, or diplomatic—do not suggest a nation yet willing or able to play on the world stage or even wider Asian stage. Ambition is one thing, capacity another. Ambition is certainly there: to be the dominant power in the IOR, to be an important player in East and Southeast Asia, and to be a voice in global forums whose power at long last reflects its potential. But the reality is that the pieces are not yet in place to allow this to happen. There is insufficient surplus to devote to a significant reallocation of resources away from inclusive growth and maintaining domestic and neighborhood security toward the kind of diplomatic, aid, and military push that would enable India to meet its aspirations and challenge peer competitors such as China. Continuing poor performance of the Indian state in terms of governance, security, and economic reform exacerbates this tendency by both keeping India pinned down to the home front and demanding resources to meet domestic concerns. Key problems—such as the bottleneck in infrastructure, environmental stress, the heavy subsidy regime, an inefficient state sector, and serious security and governance problems—have yet to be resolved. They all raise the level of risk in India.

And second, peer competitors, especially China, continue both to outgrow India and also to act as players in its South Asian neighborhood and wider Indian Ocean region. This exposure further weakens India and constrains any *genuine* strategic role it may seek or have in East or Southeast Asia.

More seriously for India, however, there is no evidence that any of these mutually reinforcing problems can be quickly or easily solved or that New Delhi has yet put the mechanisms in place to solve them. That is not to say that East and Southeast Asian powers such as Japan and Vietnam do not seriously entertain the idea of using India as a hedge against China, especially in view of India's occupancy of a strategic box seat in the IOR. And in the case of Abe's Japan, there appears to be a desire to go beyond that to something closer to the assertion of a regional balance against China, involving initially Japan, the United States, India, and Australia. Just as the United States is now committed to providing the technology transfer to make India a genuine regional power and thus unsettle China's rise, so too does that now appear to be Japan's broad strategy. Depending on how China chooses to rise in Asia—whether peacefully or in a more threatening manner—these sets of problems are likely in time to derail India's own often-stated predilection to retain its strategic autonomy and sharpen its strategic tilt towards the United States.

In the remaining chapters we explore the kinds of strategies India might adopt to start to break free of the restraints currently pinning it down as a continental power (chapter 5) and how it might choose to insert itself in a positive way into the rapidly evolving Asian power equation (chapter 6).

NOTES

1. Rehman, "India's Aspirational Naval Doctrine," 55.
2. For a good account of this gradual process, see Mohan, *Samudra Mantham.*
3. For India see, for example, Brewster, *India as an Asia-Pacific Power*, 26–28; Mohan, *Samudra Manthan*; DeSilva-Ranasinghe, "Potent and Capable"; and Raghuvanshi, "India to Focus Resources on Naval Operations." For China see Bullock, "China's Bluewater Ambitions," passim.
4. Blagden and Thompson, "Sea Power, Continental Power and Balancing Theory," 190–202, 13, 17.
5. H. J. Mackinder, "the Geographical Pivot of History."
6. As quoted in Bullock, "China's Bluewater Ambitions," 59.
7. Quoted in ibid., 59–60.
8. India's space program has expanded rapidly. Although relatively small at $1.3 billion for 2013, the budget gets considerably more "bang for the buck" than, say, that of the United States due to cost relativities. In 2013, for example, India

planned ten missions on this budget. In late August 2013, India launched its Rukmini military satellite through Arianespace. Rukmini is a geostationary communications and monitoring satellite covering 70 percent of the IOR.

9. Although the government claims it has fallen to 4.9 percent, these claims are based on juggling the fuel subsidy debt. See Kundu, "Subsidy Juggling Trims India's Fiscal Deficit."
10. The share of the navy in the 2012–13 budget estimates is generally put at 19 percent, but this figure does not account for the raised expenditure on defense if we include pensions.
11. See, for example, "India's Navy Boosts Spending 74 Percent." (And indeed, we can add as a postscript that the amount allocated to the navy fell markedly in the 2013–14 budget estimates.)
12. Behera, "DNA Exclusive."
13. Mohanty, *Defence Spending Trends in India*, no pagination.
14. "India to Miss Fiscal Deficit Target."
15. Behera, "DNA Exclusive."
16. Singh, "The Indian Navy's New 'Expeditionary' Outlook."
17. See Government of India, Indian Planning Commission, *Approach Paper to the Twelfth Five Year Plan.*
18. Singh, in "India Union Budget 2012–13."
19. Khilnani et al., *NonAlignment 2.0*, 7.
20. Holmes, Winner, and Yoshihara, *Indian Naval Strategy in the Twenty-First Century*, 23.
21. Ibid.
22. DeSilva-Ranasinghe, "India's Critical National Challenges."
23. World Bank, *Migration and Remittances Factbook 2011.*
24. Government of India, Ministry of Defence (Navy), *Freedom to Use the Seas.*
25. Yardley, "India, Praising U.S. Ties, Defends Buying Iran's Oil."
26. Scott, "India's 'Grand Strategy' for the Indian Ocean," 98.
27. Ibid., 99.
28. Ramachandran, "India Extends Malacca Strait Reach."
29. Ramachandran, "India Navy Pumps Up Eastern Muscle."
30. Quoted in Erickson, "The Growth of China's Navy," 657.
31. Kaplan, *Monsoon*, 283.
32. Lee, "China's Geostrategic Search for Oil," 75–92, 77.
33. India's first indigenous nuclear-powered submarine, the INS *Arihant*, will have twelve K-15 missiles or four K-4 missiles. The former has completed testing and is ready for integration, while the latter is still under development.
34. Ramachandran, "India Navy Pumps Up Eastern Muscle."
35. Selth, "Chinese Military Bases in Burma," 7–9.
36. Rashid, "36th Anniversary of Sino-Bangladesh Ties."
37. Chellaney, "Countering China's 'String of Pearls.'"
38. "China Has No Plan for Indian Ocean Military Bases."

39. The noted scholar on Burma Andre Selth has written extensively debunking the string-of-pearls thesis. His work includes "Burma's Mythical Isles" and "Chinese Military Bases in Burma."
40. Kaplan, *Monsoon*, 11.
41. Mohan, *Samudra Manthan*, location 899 (unpaginated Kindle e-book).
42. Malik, *China and India*, 346.
43. "Chances of Two-Front War with Pakistan, China Remote; but China Threat Real."
44. Herbert-Burnes, "Naval Power in the Indian Ocean," 52.
45. Ibid., 51.
46. Malik, *China and India*, 339.
47. Kaplan, *Monsoon*, 296.
48. Mills and McNamee, "Disaggregating Chinese Actors in Africa," 38.
49. Ibid.
50. Xavier, "India's Strategic Advantage over China in Africa."
51. Singh, "China Base a Threat to Indian Navy?"
52. Government of India, Ministry of Defence (Navy), *Indian Maritime Doctrine INBR [Indian Naval Book of Reference]*, 8.
53. Pant, *The Rise of the Indian Navy*, 3.
54. Government of India, Ministry of Defence (Navy), *Freedom to Use the Seas*, 81–87. Note that this document was first published in 2007 and has subsequently been amended. The 2007 version is apparently no longer available in digitized form.
55. Ibid.
56. Scott, "India's 'Grand Strategy' for the Indian Ocean," 97–129, 98.
57. Deloitte, *Prospects for Global Defence Export Industry in Indian Defence Market*, 8.
58. See, for example, McArdel, "India Eyes Its Cinderella Service."
59. Aviotech, *Indian Naval Acquisitions I*, 7.
60. Erickson, "China Homes In on Pacific Air Superiority."
61. In an earlier draft, the author more seriously questioned the need for the aircraft carrier program and argued it should be terminated in favor of LPDs, shore-based aircraft, and submarines. Naval specialists, however, disputed these findings, and they have not been vigorously pursued.
62. Kaplan, *Monsoon*, 124.
63. Quoted in Malhotra, "Between Delhi and the Deep Blue Ocean."
64. Editorial, *Times of India*, January 18, 1991.
65. Khilnani et al., *NonAlignment 2.0*.
66. Harrison and Kemp, *India and America after the Cold War*, 9.
67. Malik, *China and India*, 337.
68. Cohen and Dasgupta, *Arming without Aiming*, 172.
69. "Indigenous Iron Dome Missile Could Protect India from Cross-Border Threats."
70. "Armed Forces Building Deadly Drone Arsenal, Also Want Combat UAVs."
71. "Giant C-17 Aircraft to Add Strategic Muscle from June."

72. United States Government, Department of Defense, *Report to Congress on U.S.-India Security Cooperation*, 2.
73. Ibid.
74. Ibid., 4.
75. White, *Power Shift*, 31.
76. Quoted in "Rice's Visit Could Take Indo-US Partnership to New Level."
77. "India, China, a Long Way from Border Solution."
78. Malik, *China and India*, 94.
79. Gordon, "Domestic Foundations of India's Security Policy," 8.
80. Government of India, Ministry of External Affairs, *Annual Report for 2004–05*, i.
81. Discussion between the author and a former member of the Cabinet Security Committee Secretariat, New Delhi, 2009.
82. "Chinese Incursion 19 Km, but 750 Sq Km at Stake for India."
83. Bharatiya Janata Party, *Towards Ram Rajya*, 36–37.
84. Compare, for example, the MEA's relaxed view on alleged Chinese incursions in Ladakh to the defense minister's concern at Chinese military modernization, as in "Airspace Violation by Chinese Choppers" and "Indian Chinese Military Modernization—Indian DM." For Abdullah's view, see "CM Abdullah Calls on India to 'Show Some Spine' on China."
85. For a fuller discussion of the various attitudes to China, see Merrington, "Beyond the Protracted Contest."
86. Malik, *China and India*, 88.
87. RAND Corp., *China and India, 2025*, xvii and 53, figure 3.5.
88. United States Government, National Intelligence Council: *Global Trends 2030*.
89. Kundu, "Indian Demographic Dividend Lacks Spark."
90. Gordon, "Sino-Indian Relations and the Rise of China," 51–64.
91. Markey, "Developing India's Foreign Policy "Software,"" 73–96, 74.
92. Hall, "India's New Public Diplomacy," 1089–1110.
93. Muni, "India's 'Look East Policy," 12.
94. Government of India, Department of Commerce, "Direction of Trade Statistics for April–October 2011."
95. Ibid.
96. Government of India, Ministry of External Affairs, *Annual Report for 2011*.
97. Government of India, Ministry of External Affairs, *Annual Report 2010–11*, 210, appendix X.
98. Brewster, *India as an Asia-Pacific Power*, passim.
99. Narayan, *India ASEAN FTA in Services*.
100. Abe, "Asia's Democratic Security Diamond."
101. Medcalf, "Shinzo Abe's Strategic Diamond."
102. See Australian Government, Department of Defence, *Defence White Paper 2013*.
103. Sinha and Nataraj, "Japanese ODA Stimulates Indian Infrastructure Development."
104. "Investments Making Up for Trade Deficit with India."

105. Bagchi, "India, Japan Make Common Cause to Thwart China's Maritime Moves."
106. Perlez, "India and Vietnam Face Off with China in Disputed Waters."
107. "India Sails into Troubled South China Sea."
108. Ibid.
109. "Vietnam's Plea Puts South Block in a Predicament."

CHAPTER 5

THE GOVERNMENT RESPONSE: DOMESTIC GOVERNANCE AND SECURITY

We have argued throughout this volume that domestic security, neighborhood stability, and India's rise as a global power are closely interwoven. Any strategy for India's rise to power will consequently need to contain elements to deal with all three levels of engagement.

Although such a "grand strategy" has never been fully articulated at the government level, the interconnected nature of domestic and foreign strategies is generally recognized. For example, the document *NonAlignment 2.0*, which provides an eloquent statement for a grand strategy for India's rise as an Asian and global power, asserts that "the core objective of a strategic approach should be to give India maximum options in relation to the outside world—that is, to enhance India's strategic space and capacity for independent agency—*which in turn will give it maximum options for its internal development* [emphasis added]."[1] According to this grand strategy, the building blocks of an independent, strong India are clearly defined. Economic development trumps militarism. But economic development must be achieved through inclusive growth, so that the vast bulk of India's huge population is uplifted. Economic development will in turn require open and fair domestic and global markets and a stable international environment. If India is to achieve its desired influence through soft power, it will need to continue to press toward its developmental goals while adhering to its democratic and human rights values, which are unique for such a large country.

Although the goal of seeking "maximum options for internal development" should certainly be pursued, any viable strategy must move below the level of grand strategy to examine the detail of how these grand outcomes might be achieved. But in terms of its analysis of internal security, *NonAlignment 2.0* focuses tightly on energy security, nuclear security, and insurgency in Kashmir, the Northeast, and the Maoist-affected areas. It does not deal substantially with the poor quality of governance in the Indian core, what is wrong with it, and how it might be fixed.[2]

The problem with this focus just on the level of grand strategy is that corruption, poor security, and poor governance are currently preventing the inclusive growth strategy from being adopted in an effective manner, as illustrated in earlier chapters. And without inclusive growth, there can be no true security in the domestic sphere. In turn, without domestic security, cross-border problems and regional interference are bound to multiply.

Our concern with security in this volume therefore of necessity covers nonconventional security issues as well as conventional security. These nonconventional issues include crime, corruption, policing, legal administration, distribution of state benefits, poverty alleviation, environmental issues, population and urbanization stresses, food and water issues, and climate change. Such issues are barely touched upon in *NonAlignment 2.0*, and where they are, the Indian state is seen as capable of dealing with them.[3]

Central to our approach is to argue that the Union government should develop ways of providing additional focus on these lower-order issues of security, such as anticorruption and anticrime measures, internal security, human rights, reform of the police and judiciary, and governance generally. The Union government must find some traction over these issues even though many of them fall predominantly within state government purview. Without leadership from the center, the current drive for greater internal security—especially as it has been developed since the attacks of 26/11—is unlikely to prove sustainable.

The best illustration of the relationship between governance and security is provided by the Maoist revolt. At its heart, this revolt derives from the collapse of institutions designed on the one hand to protect tribal rights and interests in respect to land and compensation, and on the other to provide state services to tribal areas. This institutional failure has occurred at all levels of government. Institutions such as Coal India (a central government agency) and problems of state governments such as those illustrated by the Koda case described in chapter 1 are central to the pervasive corruption in India's coal provinces, which in turn plays an important role in the displacement of tribal populations and malaise behind the Maoist insurrection. Failure to deliver state services such as education, health, and security leave these domains open for exploitation by Maoist groups. The security issues in the Maoist-affected areas in turn draw on central and state resources and negatively affect India's vast minerals and energy provinces, which affects growth, contributing to the classic stagnation-instability vicious circle.

There are other readily available examples of the close connection between poor governance and the failure to provide security not discussed in detail in the present work.[4] There is also ample evidence that India's "million mutinies," to use the term coined by V. S. Naipaul, owe their existence to a significant extent to corruption and poor governance, which derail the very state institutions intended to bring about better nutritional, educational, institutional, justice, and equity outcomes. This general instability within society is in turn linked closely with cross-border problems, especially in Pakistan and Bangladesh, as illustrated in earlier chapters.

The problem of governance thus becomes a central factor limiting India's rise to power. Consequently any strategy seeking to address those limitations needs initially to focus on governance. If India were to become better governed, it would be more robust in the face of regional instability. It would have better managed and less porous borders. It would consequently be less subject to imported problems from the neighborhood. It would provide a regional example and would offer regional ballast for growth and development. In short, India would have hardened itself as a target for interference.

In the present chapter, we explore some possible ways of achieving internal reform. In the succeeding chapter, we examine what might be done in the broader South Asian and global contexts, while keeping in mind that the two sets of prescriptions are really part of a single, broad strategy.

POLICING, SECURITY, AND JUDICIAL REFORM

Counterterrorism and Intelligence Reform

In the aftermath of the 26/11 attacks, major reform of the intelligence processes in India was commenced by the then home affairs minister, P. Chidambaram. In a major speech on December 23, 2009, he said that the improved coordination of the intelligence agencies and reform of the police were essential for achieving better security outcomes in India.[5]

In pursuit of these goals, the MAC and the SMACs were to be established and linked by a dedicated, secure network and operationalized by 2013. In all, thirty locations (including the MAC, the SMACs, and a number of police special branches) are to be linked by this network. This is to be known as the National Intelligence Grid, or NATGRID. The complexities of the NATGRID project have caused a serious lag in implementation, however.[6]

To enable a more rapid response to major terrorist attacks than was achieved on 26/11, National Security Guard (NSG) hubs were established in Hyderabad, Bengaluru, Chennai, and Kolkata, and two additional regional response groups were located in Hyderabad and Kolkata. Each hub is staffed by 250 people.[7] The BSF was significantly upgraded and reequipped, and twenty-nine additional battalions were raised. The CRPF and other central paramilitary forces were also upgraded.

Coastal defenses also came under scrutiny because of the way the 26/11 perpetrators captured an Indian fishing boat and approached Mumbai from the sea. Coordination was strengthened between the coast guard, navy, and coastal police. Sixty-four new coastal police stations were established, and 204 interceptor boats commissioned. Intensified patrolling was imposed. Identity cards were issued to fishermen and in some cases coastal residents.

Following the exposure of serious gaps in the visa system by the Headley case, the Mission Mode Project was designed to provide for online visa and foreigners' registration and tracking, with the objective of creating a secure and integrated service delivery framework for facilitating legitimate travelers and strengthening security.

A new, overarching counterterrorism organization was mandated in 2010, to be called the National Counter Terrorism Centre (NCTC). This was intended to incorporate the IB, the MAC, the NIA, the National Technical Research Organisation, the Joint Intelligence Committee, the National Crime Records Bureau, and the NSG. It was to have an operations division (to include the NSG) and was intended to minimize the current bifurcation between agencies currently controlled by the national security adviser (NSA) and the Ministry of Home Affairs (MHA). It was also to have controversial powers of search and arrest, to be accorded under the Unlawful Activities Prevention Act (UAPA) of 1967. The idea mimicked the post-9/11 US architecture and arose from the early assistance provided by the Federal Bureau of Investigation in the aftermath of 26/11. Implementation is stalled, however, due to opposition from state governments, particularly around the operational powers, which would in effect turn the IB into an operational agency and thus jeopardize its "hands-off" status in respect to political intelligence gathering.[8]

In order to achieve better national investigations outcomes, including for crimes that extend across state boundaries, the Union government established the National Investigation Agency (NIA). The remit of the new organization is to investigate terrorism under UAPA and other illegal activities such as drugs crime, counterfeiting, major organized crime, and money laundering—all crimes that have international or multistate implications.

In the case of the changes to intelligence, a good start has been made, but not all the dots have been connected. The proposed Indian NCTC is stalled. But even should it go ahead, it would be architecturally somewhat different from the US model because it would be hosted by the Department of Home Affairs and not the NSA (the counterpart of the American director of national intelligence). This is significant, since under the Indian model there would be no intelligence "czar" having authority over all Union government intelligence agencies. Thus the domestic agencies involved with intelligence such as the IB and the NIA would be organizationally separated from the foreign intelligence agencies and military agencies (although their intelligence may be fused in the MAC, which would be within the NCTC). Depending on the effectiveness of the operations of the MAC, this potentially provides an area of weakness in the model. It also means that the gap between domestic and external intelligence may not be adequately bridged in the Indian case.

The proposed NCTC has also been heavily criticized from within the existing counterterrorism bodies as "plain silly." Critics maintain that "instead of fixing the problems of the institutions we have, we're committing to spend a fortune on creating yet another bureaucracy." The agencies complain they themselves are seriously under establishment, yet the government is contemplating a new agency.[9] With a looming fiscal deficit and the 26/11 attacks fading in memory, it is difficult to escape the conclusion that despite the continuing push for an NCTC, India is losing steam on its counterterrorism push.

Some additional links will, however, have been achieved by the reforms. The IB, to be represented within the NCTC by the MAC (provided the NCTC is finally approved), will have links into the states via its state offices and the SMACs, which will in turn have links with the state police special branches. But such links will be indirect and incomplete.

The main police body within the NCTC would be the NIA. Despite some recent successes, the NIA is a limited agency that will not have the capacity according to its current legislation to provide the link between the intelligence agencies and state police. The NIA will need to be properly resourced and staffed, which is still not the case. The National Investigation Agency Act (NIA Act) is seemingly generous in providing agency officers with India-wide powers in respect to scheduled offenses.[10] The law states at section 3(3) that "any officer of the Agency of, or above, the rank of Sub-Inspector may . . . exercise throughout India, any of the powers of the officer-in-charge of a police station in the area in which he is present for the time being and when so exercising such powers shall, subject to any such orders [of the central government] as aforesaid, be deemed to be an officer-in charge of a police station discharging the functions of such an officer within the limits of his station."

Sections 6 to 10 give the procedures for putting an investigation into motion. Unfortunately they are somewhat ambiguous and bear some of the hallmarks of hasty drafting. For example, section 8 allows the investigator to investigate any other offense of the "accused" related to the original offense scheduled under the law. It is not clear whether this can only happen after an arrest, but presumably the reference to the accused signifies that this is the case. If so, then that would be a serious limiting factor in the scope of the investigations. Another limiting factor comes about through the system of notification, spelled out in section 6. This stipulates that any scheduled offense reported to any police station in India will be brought to the attention of the state authorities, who will bring it to the attention of the Union government authorities, who will in turn determine if it is a subject of the law and bring it to the NIA for investigation. This convoluted chain of notification could take months.

But the main concern about the NIA Act is that it does not support the intelligence-collection process—which is in turn essential for prevention. It is mainly concerned with an "offense" reported as an FIR. But intelligence is not about offenses or evidence as such (although it can include evidence) but the *analyzed information surrounding offenses and potential offenses.* It is this information surrounding potential offenses that will need to be collected by local-level police and passed upward through the intelligence process. Thus the NIA Act is not an ideal vehicle for either investigations or intelligence. That is not to say, however, that such intelligence will not be passed between the IB, the special branches, the SMACs, and the MAC, but rather that, if it is, it will continue to be a hit-or-miss process. Crucially, the intelligence feed from the grass-roots level will only be as good as the police providing it. And as noted below, nothing in the reform process indicates that state-level policing will be significantly progressed from the present paramilitary thrust under the Police Act of 1861.

To the extent that the MAC, the NIA, the IB, and Union government response agencies such as the NSG will presumably be housed within the NCTC, at least some of the connectivity concerns between intelligence and counterterrorism operations will be met. The weakness in this area arises, however, from the fact that the NSG (as a special-weapons-and-tactics—SWAT—group) is only one small component of counterterrorism response. The other components, such as state police first-response, post facto investigations, consequence management, and deradicalization programs for those arrested, rest predominantly within the state jurisdiction. Also, the intelligence effort surrounding a terrorist event will still have all the problems of coordination and data matching mentioned above.

Mindful of the fact that sound policing must occur from the grass-roots level upward, Chidambaram admonished states to implement what he called "community policing." He also proposed that "to organise and analyse information derived from the community, the State Special Branches should be restructured as a specialised and self-sufficient cadre of the State police in terms of personnel, funds and equipment." To this end, in January 2009 the Union Government "circulated a proposal to restructure the Special Branch in the State police forces. The implementation of the proposal will mark the beginning of a long-haul effort to restructure the intelligence-gathering machinery at the District and State levels."[11] The Union government is also assisting state police to establish 24/7 command-and-control posts and quick-response teams, properly equipped and trained. States were urged to establish antiterrorism units to pre-empt and investigate terrorist attacks where they do not already have them.

In summary, as far as counterterrorism is concerned, while matters have improved since 26/11, there are still some significant problems. Much will depend on the successful introduction of the NCTC, and this is being stymied by central-state jealousies and jurisdictional concerns. In terms of overall security, which includes law and order and policing, there is even less cause to consider that India's manifest problems are being adequately addressed, either in terms of application of new resources or reforms, or the way policing is structured under the existing colonial-era legislation. And as already argued, an effective community-level police force is the front line of any good counterterrorism system.

Reform of the Police

Policing and judicial reform are the areas in which the Union government has had the most difficulty in achieving meaningful change, largely because policing and many areas of the judiciary are subjects reserved for the states under the Constitution. Also, the problem of police corruption in India is so pervasive, the political nexus with police corruption so profound, and the police service so vast and generally benighted that the problem is truly a "wicked" one.

The Police Act of 1861 is currently undergoing a much-needed process of reform, but the process is proving glacial. So far, the Police Act Development Committee has provided a set of recommendations to guide the reform process. At the heart of these recommendations are the suggestions that independence of police from the executive should be enhanced, the constabulary abolished, and the initial rank structure raised, with a three-year intensive-training program at college level. This would be very resource-intensive, but it would also be necessary if the overall quality of policing, particularly community- and street-level policing, is to be improved.[12] Obviously, a far-reaching reform process of this nature would take many years to flow through the system, given the large number of constables already in place under the old system. Moreover, although the recommendations were brought down in 1996, by 2006 they had not been fully implemented, due fundamentally to lack of interest in various state and federal authorities in losing their executive influence over policing—an influence that in many cases proves highly lucrative to corrupt politicians.

Another committee raised by the Ministry of Home Affairs has developed its Model Police Act, published in 2006.[13] Under this act, the rank of constable would be abolished and a police officer would be designated a "civil police officer" after three years of training. Accountability measures would be strengthened through introduction of independent complaints mechanisms. The hold of state governments over police would be reduced by measures such as police boards (to include the leader of the state opposition) and tenured, merit-based appointments for inspectors general of police (commissioners). Although many states have updated their police acts, by no means all have adhered to the tenets of the Model Police Act or recommendations of the Police Act Development Committee in doing so.[14] Presumably they have been restrained for fear of losing control over the police.

Because of these delays, the Supreme Court ordered that the reforms be undertaken. In doing so, the court made seven directives (six directed at the states and one at the Union government). However, by 2012, of India's twenty-eight states, only half had enacted the provisions, and according to some even those enactments are tokenistic.[15] So, the challenge in India is not so much to know what to do about policing but to undertake already-designated reforms. This will take funding and political commitment both at state and Union government levels. But even were the reforms designated so far to be implemented, there are additional matters that would need to be addressed.

Although the Model Police Act deals with the need to upgrade the constabulary, it does not mention the fact that the IPS system, and the state equivalent thereof, currently cast a shadow over the constabulary, as discussed in chapter 1.[16] The problem is that the constabulary is currently in no state to manage without a preselected officer class. It needs to be upgraded before that can happen. But as part of that process, those able, educated men and women recruited as civil police officers (formerly known as constables) need to be given full access to promotion to the officer class, whether it be the state officers or the IPS. Eventual abolition of a separate officer cadre may prove impractical given the vast number of police required in India, but at least the ranks between the officer and nonofficer classes should be made far more fungible as a means of encouraging a better class of person into the constabulary, which badly needs to be upgraded.

None of these recommendations would be cheap, quick, or easy. Both the states and their police services will resist. The Union government will need to ensure that police reform remains a major priority in its security-reform process, that it does not get pushed to one side by other seemingly easier, quick-fix reforms, and that it remains in focus over the long term.

Since policing is reserved for the states under the Constitution, the main lever available to the Union government is the power of the purse. Policing in India—including all levels of state and Union policing—is currently relatively cheap. As illustrated in chapter 4, total spending on policing (Union and states) is currently running at only 37.5 percent of total military spending, or a little under 1 percent of GDP. Given the argument of this book that internal security lies at the heart of both governance and external security, there would be ample scope for a richer India, as growth rates continue to rise, to apply more funds toward policing reform.

To an extent, the Union government is already attempting to use the power of the purse to achieve its goals. It has assisted with funds for the recruitment of four hundred thousand additional state police. It has promulgated guidelines for noncorrupt recruitment and developed an electronic system to ensure "hands-free" and noncorrupt recruitment. This system has already been implemented for central recruitment but is being resisted in a number of states. Utilizing federal funding, an effort has been under way since 2009 to provide a criminal tracking database, known as the Crime and Criminal Tracking and Network System (CCTNS). The project is designed to link India's fifteen thousand police stations and five thousand police offices. But due to its complexity, it has languished, and the completion date is now put at 2015. These initiatives are, however, only a small part of what would be required to reform the constabulary system.

Most important, the Indian culture of internal investigations of complaints against police should not be able to stand alone as the only means of redress. Internal investigation has been shown time and again to be inadequate as a means of stamping out endemic corruption. It certainly has a place, insofar as it would be impossible to investigate all complaints against police by means of an independent commission. But it should be only part of the menu of remedies. Provided they are adequately funded and given an independent investigation arm, the Union-level Lok Pal and states-level Lokayuktas, discussed more fully below, may eventually go some way to providing an external line of investigation of police. However, many of the existing state-level Lokayuktas are themselves dependent on the state police, or special wings thereof, for their investigations.

Judicial System Reform

The continuity of legal reform is absolutely vital to India's governance. The great delays currently being experienced in the courts mean that police tend to take justice into their own hands. There is a consequent loss of accountability and public trust. Such delays also make it far more difficult to address the criminalization of politics, since many of the alleged criminals in the political system are accused awaiting trial and cannot be removed on the basis of adherence to the "innocent until proven guilty" doctrine. Delays also clog the jails. In cases where people are on parole and subsequently found guilty, they endanger the security of citizens. On the other hand, given the low conviction rate, the jailing of those awaiting trial is also likely to be unjust. It is difficult to bring a case to successful conclusion after a delay of ten years or even longer, so such delays are a significant factor in the current low conviction rate.

Against this background, the Union government is engaged in a process of reform of the judicial system that seeks to bring about quicker resolution of cases to reduce the massive backlog and improve judicial access and accountability. This program initially involved a campaign of six months, which was to be extended by a further six months if successful.[17]

The original campaign included the introduction of the Judicial Standards and Accountability Bill of 2010. It sets down accountability standards, makes judges declare assets, and establishes a complaints and investigation mechanism for judicial misconduct. Rs 10 billion was made available to state governments for 2010–11, contingent on states formulating litigation policies to improve outcomes. A further recommendation was made by the Thirteenth Finance Commission to make available to the states Rs 50 billion over five years. Reforms thus generated included computerization of the central and district courts; provision of legal aid for marginalized people; release of prisoners awaiting trial who had served equivalent time to their possible sentences (following which the Union government issued a new directive asking the states to release all such prisoners who had served half the time they would have served if found guilty); creation of a new court, the Gram Nyayalaya, at the *panchayat* level; raising the retirement age of judges from sixty-two to sixty-five; and the raising of Union government support for infrastructure from Rs 1 billion to Rs 5 billion.

Most important, a system of fast-track courts was introduced. According to the BBC, more than a thousand have now disposed of three million cases. Nevertheless, over thirty million cases are pending in high- and district-level courts alone. However, in March 2011, the Union government ceased funding new courts due to financial restraints. There have also been complaints from lawyers and human rights advocates that the fast-track courts can result in miscarriage of justice. In Bihar, which has been most active in their use, only 15 percent of convictions are upheld on appeal.[18] Either way, there is a problem. According to India's Law Commission, "justice delayed is justice denied and at the same time, justice hurried is justice buried."[19]

Against this background of financial limitations on fast-track courts, the scandal over the shocking gang rape and murder of a young woman in Delhi in December 2012 reignited interest in fast-track courts and judicial reform. At the time of writing the Union government has agreed to provide another Rs 800 million to recruit an additional 2000 judges for the fast-track system. The government had also earmarked Rs 28 billion to double the size of the judiciary from 18,871 judges to over 30,000, with the aim of achieving "five-plus free"—that is, free of cases over five years old within five years.[20] The present caseload backlog is fifteen years!

INCLUSIVE GROWTH, ACCOUNTABILITY, AND THE "VIRTUOUS CIRCLE"

Although the UPA is perceived to have a somewhat more leftist orientation than its predecessor, the BJP-led NDA, that government too exhibited a basic commitment to achieving a balanced path to growth. At the time of the UPA victory in

2004, the perception was that the NDA had lost power due to hubris over its India Shining election campaign, which celebrated a "new" India of wealth and power and a rising middle class. The commonly accepted view was that this campaign did not resonate in the rural areas, where 60 percent of Indian voters reside. Subsequent analysis found that the NDA did not lose the election in the rural areas but rather in the big cities.[21] The UPA, however, not only wanted to respond to the apparent concerns of the rural population, but also consisted of an alliance that included leftists of various shades. In order to forge the alliance with leftist parties, the Congress Party was able to put together the Common Minimum Program (CMP)—a deal that involved substantial programs of social uplift.

The UPA has issued a number of documents attempting to chronicle its successes since 2004. Naturally enough, some of this work consists of hagiography, but it may tell us something of value. For example, in its document *Report to the People 2004–2008*, the government emphasized the inclusive-growth mantra. Heavy emphasis was also placed on uplifting minorities, with special sections on Muslims, the Northeast, and Kashmir.[22]

The CMP involved two substantial, flagship social-uplift programs—one the MGNREGS and the other a rural debt-forgiveness program. The CMP also involved a promise by the UPA to revive the then moribund Lok Pal Bill.

By 2009–10, MGNREGS had evolved into a massive, demand-driven program costing $12.6 billion. Plan expenditure on health more than doubled in nominal terms between 2003–4 and 2008–8. Plan expenditure on education increased nearly five times over the same period.[23] By 2013, India was planning a $5 billion initiative to bring free medicine to poor citizens using existing hospitals and clinics, cutting out Western patents and using Indian-sourced generic drugs. Parliamentary reservations for women, the MGNREGS, the passage of the Right of Children to Free and Compulsory Education Act, the passage of the Right to Information Act, and a number of other measures introduced by the UPA also signaled an interest in diffusion of internal tensions through social and economic reform. Special attention was focused on uplifting the Muslim population, identified by the Sachar Committee Report of 2006 as suffering relative deprivation and discrimination.

In India's case, however, pervasive corruption has effectively derailed the grand strategy of inclusive growth. Corruption means that the rupee allocated from the center will fail to reach its intended destination at the grass-roots level. Poverty, illiteracy, poor health, and malnourishment therefore cannot be overcome through application of funding. This contributes to the creation of a vicious circle of poverty, insecurity, and underdevelopment. The initial challenge is therefore to overcome corruption and achieve better governance outcomes in a system that is pervasively corrupt. This in turn poses the question, how can a polity be expected to reform itself—in effect, to pull itself up by its bootstraps—when it is pervasively corrupt?

A country in which the citizens feel that the institutions of state undertake their roles of gathering and dispensing revenue and providing security and justice fairly will be one in which the majority of citizens will see a benefit in adherence to rule of law. Conversely, a country in which the mechanisms of the state are not administered fairly and efficiently will be one in which there is little incentive to adhere to rule of law. In the latter case, what might have been a "virtuous circle" will instead become a vicious circle.

Bo Rothstein argues that the central challenge faced by pervasively corrupt states is to overcome this "beggar thy neighbor" view of the world on the part of the majority of citizens that pervasive corruption produces, rather than simply improving some of the institutions of state. He advocates a "big bang" approach to overcoming corruption on this scale, rather than what he refers to as an incremental, institutional approach as advocated by the World Bank and more generally in the liberal West. He cites the case of Sweden in the nineteenth century, where he says a series of military defeats caused an existential crisis that shocked the system into change. This change involved significant legal and institutional changes over a period of about forty years. These changed Sweden from a "particularist" state, in which preferment was something perceived as the personal fief of royalty and other senior institutions, to a "generalist" meritocracy, in which Weberian definitions of fairness prevailed.[24]

It is undoubtedly the case that Sweden underwent such a relatively quick process of institutional and attitudinal change. But just why it occurred, and the nature of the relationship between the legal and institutional changes and the attitudinal changes of the populace, is more problematic. Other Western European states underwent exactly the same transformation over approximately the same time frame. Great Britain at the beginning of the nineteenth century was characterized by purchased military promotion, "rotten boroughs," and preferment by personal fiefdom every bit as pronounced as in Sweden. So too was France. Britain certainly did not experience the trauma of military defeat or existential crisis at this time, given it was at the zenith of its power. Thus neither the liberal, incrementalist approach nor the big bang theory seem to provide an adequate explanation of how pervasive corruption can be overcome.

What is perhaps missing from the wider explanation is changing social conditions such as far greater access to education and literacy and a bourgeoning and essentially free press. Such outside forces may be capable of acting independently of the corrupt government system to move it from its state of inertia. But an outside force in itself is unlikely to be sufficient. Research has shown that a functioning electoral system is in itself incapable of providing such seeds. What is needed in addition is a set of functioning institutions of state that are not wholly amenable to the dictates of the otherwise corrupt state.[25] The system itself will also need seeds of better governance capable of being nurtured. These include a civil society capable of independent formation and action untrammeled by government, a free or basically free media, a functioning legal process separate from the government, and a populace well-educated and independent enough to act and choose independently of the government. This is not to say democracy is not an important part of the equation—but it is a necessary and not sufficient element.[26]

India has all these institutional benefits, and to an increasing degree its population is better educated and informed. An important factor in this better education and information is rapid growth in the middle class, with estimates ranging from about 70 million to 150 million people.[27] India's rapid acquisition of mobile phones and their interconnectivity to the internet through 2G and now 3G is also a vital factor. As Assa Doron and Robin Jeffrey point out in new research, there are now almost a billion cell phones in India, and they play a crucial role in shaping election outcomes and informing the public of outrages and demonstrations against them, such as occurred in the December 2012 rape case in Delhi.[28] Together these factors operating in India are starting to constitute a virtuous circle, in which corruption is identified and eventually driven out of the system.

Key factors in this virtuous circle are some of the institutions of the state themselves. These include an independent judiciary capable of both noncorrupt and activist interventions, especially at the highest levels of the High Courts and Supreme Court. Some of India's state institutions designed to provide checks and balances are also relatively activist, if underresourced and under attack from vested interests. Examples are the Office of the Comptroller and Auditor General (CAG); the right to information commissioners, at both the Union and state levels operating under the Right to Information Act of 2005; and the Enforcement Directorate (ED) of the Ministry of Finance, which has a mandate to investigate and prosecute money laundering and other financial crimes. Although India has at times attempted to censor the internet and social media,[29] it also possesses vibrant, growing, and essentially independent newspapers, including in the vernacular.[30] And finally, it has committed, active, and independent nongovernment and civil rights sectors.

It is also arguably the case that India is entering a phase in which major reforms are under way of the kind that may one day be seen as constituting a big bang of the kind Rothstein describes in Sweden. Here is Shailaja Chandra on the present process of reform:

> Expectedly, the government response [to Anna Hazare's anticorruption movement] was a slew of anti-corruption bills that have been introduced in Parliament, unheard of in the annals of the past six decades. From 2010, in a span of just two years, as many as 10 anti-corruption bills have been tabled including the disputed Lokpal bill, the forfeiture of benami property, foreign bribery, money laundering, and whistle-blowing bills plus five more—all

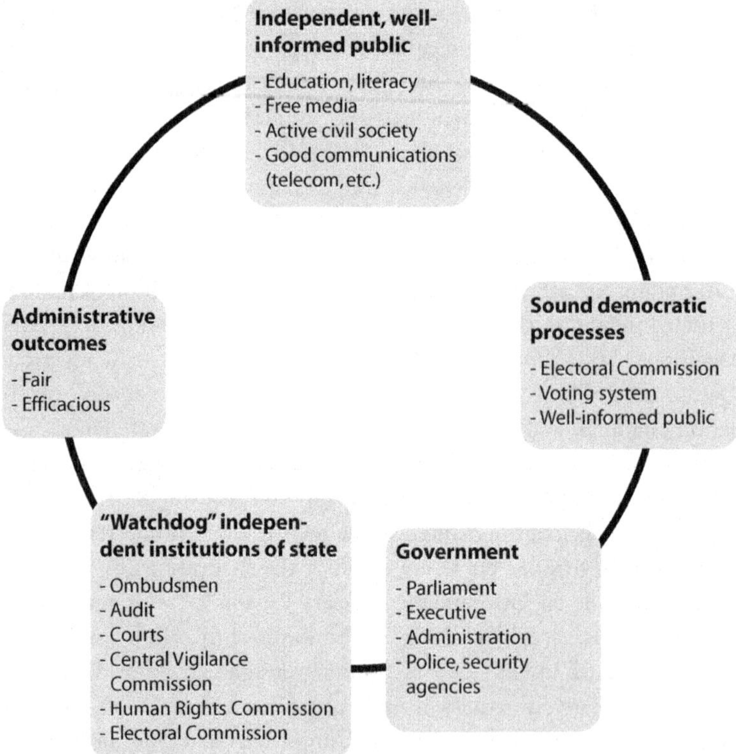

FIGURE 5.1 The Virtuous Circle

> aimed at deterring specific acts of corruption or purporting to give corruption-free public service as a right. And it was not just the Central government that showed this eagerness. Bihar, Rajasthan, Jharkhand and Odisha have actually enacted laws which can result in the attachment of ill-gotten property of public servants—sometimes pending investigation.[31]

Chandra characterizes this as a "good start." But she continues that none of these bills strike at the root of corruption. She argues that the essential problem is the buying of votes through money politics and illegal donations. What is needed, she claims, is enactment of the Registration and Regulation of Political Parties Bill of 2011, which was drafted by a civil society group, the Centre for Standards in Public Life. The bill is intended to establish transparency in donations and outlaw nontransparent contributions, thus attacking the problem of "money politics."[32]

None of this is to argue that India's problems of pervasive corruption and poor governance are going to be overcome in the short term. India is a vast polity with enormous problems to overcome, and "Dhanbad is a long way from Delhi." Those who benefit massively from corruption are bound to kick back against the reform process. But India does have some important building blocks in place to address these problems. In this, it is different from that other highly corrupt, megapopulation country—China.[33]

India's is a vibrant democracy capable of periodically dismissing both state and central governments perceived to be corrupt or inept. Indian democracy is also capable of fostering new political movements against corruption, such as Anna Hazare's Jan Lokpal movement (citizens' ombudsman movement). The movement has adopted some of the traditions of Mahatma Gandhi, replete with fasts by Hazare to force the government's hand. Others, however, accuse him of being an RSS stooge.[34] Whatever the Jan Lokpal movement's political orientation, it has already significantly shaped the Lok Pal Bill introduced in 2011 in response to the CMP. Whatever its flaws, the net result is that the Lok Pal Bill and associated state-level legislation should assist the corruption-fighting capacity of the Indian governance process by giving another hook upon which the public, civil society, and the press can seek to hang the government's dirty linen for all to see.

Another emerging anticorruption movement is Arvind Kejriwal's Aam Aadmi Party (Party of the Common Man). Kejriwal founded it after having split from Anna Hazare's movement. Members have to sign a pledge abjuring the normal trappings of power. The party is entering electoral politics first in Kejriwal's own state of Haryana and in the Union territory of New Delhi. It remains to be seen whether it can perform in India's rough-and-tumble political milieu.

India's challenge is to continue to build on this virtuous circle and work to remove any existing roadblocks that still constrain corruption fighting. Already there has been a significant resistance to the raft of legislation discussed above. The CAG has been especially under fire, as befits an institution that has been at the vanguard of corruption fighting. New legislation is being introduced to remove the single auditor now that he has completed his term and replace him with a commission-like structure. Some see this move as an attempt by a discomforted government to water down the strength of the CAG, even though the outgoing CAG doesn't agree with this view.[35] Another instance of the attempted resistance is the strategy of starving key bodies such as the Right to Information (RTI) Commission of funding so they cannot undertake their work (see below).

A key component in achieving better governance outcomes will be to resist such attempts at resistance and to leverage existing building blocks so that they work together and are mutually supporting. If resistance against the anticorruption institutional base is to be successfully fought, the free press, civil society, and eventually an informed public will need to undertake a massive effort to keep the legislation effective. For example, where corruption or misgovernment is identified by institutions such as the CAG, the free press, the nongovernment sector, or the RTI Commissioners, such instances should be given full publicity by the press and full scope for judicial activism to elicit changes at the governmental levels (including policing). In the case studies in chapter 1, there are several instances of this happening, such as the Koda case, the 2G spectrum scandal, and the Ardash housing scandal in Mumbai. Judicial activism, particularly by the Supreme Court, has often also played a role in bringing greater transparency to these cases, such as in Coalgate. In this way, the existing building blocks can be strengthened and facilitated to operate as a virtuous circle.

In terms of the role of India's press in leveraging the work of anticorruption watchdogs, the courts, and civil society, it is surprising to note that India is ranked by Freedom House at only 79 of 196 countries ranked (196 being least free). Although a significant improvement from the previous year (when India was ranked 131), India is ranked as only "partly free."[36] It seems that the burden of the Freedom House complaint against India in 2012 rested on the attempts of the various levels of government to muffle the voice of the internet.[37] Nevertheless, a ranking of 131 for India is clearly absurd given the vigor and outspoken quality of India's print journalism, and even a ranking of 79 is surprising. This is not a minor issue. The argument of this chapter concerning the virtuous circle hinges substantially on the continuation of a robustly free press in India. Attempts to muffle the internet are certainly a cause for concern and need to be carefully watched and opposed by civil society in India. The fact such attempts are often undertaken at local or state levels rather than the Union level does not mean their impact is any less. But we should also keep in mind that India, unlike many Western countries, still has a diverse and vigorous print medium. This means that there is considerable scope for publicizing problems such as corruption and bringing malfeasance to notice independently of attempts to muffle the internet. That is not to say that reports of corruption in the media alone would be sufficient to stem the tide of corruption in India. Despite all the media coverage of cases mentioned in chapter 1, the corrupt are still apparently as brazen as ever. Rather, the media's role is to expose, so that other elements of the virtuous circle can be brought into play. The virtuous circle is equivalent to a system in which all elements need to be well oiled.

A good example of the operation of this virtuous circle is the use of so-called social audits or MGNREGS in Andhra Pradesh. Uniquely, social audits are built into MGNREGS in section 17 of the act, which mandates they be conducted every six months. The act is also linked to the Right to Information Act of 2005, with a one-week mandated turnaround for RTI requests relating to MGNREGS. In the case of Andhra Pradesh, social audits were institutionalized across the state. The nongovernment sector was commissioned to go into districts to check whether the program had actually distributed employment as it claimed to have done, or whether corruption had either caused the distribution to be distorted in favor of more powerful sectors or caused funds to be diverted. This is a highly labor-intensive role well suited to the nongovernment sector.[38] A study subsequently found a dramatic rise in the awareness of potential recipients of the existence of the program and of their rights under it.[39]

This example suggests the program, which is a key component of the broader strategy of inclusive growth, has been able to leverage from both the activist nongovernment sector and legislation such as RTI to ensure greater probity in management. According to some studies, MGNREGS has also caused a scarcity of agricultural labor and raised its price, suggesting that it has been successful as a means of transferring wealth to the poorer sectors.[40] But on the other hand, a study by the Australian South Asia Research Centre found that transfers to the poor *net of their labor time* are really quite modest, a finding not necessarily inimical to an effect on either poverty or the labor market.[41]

The example of MGNREGS gives pointers to how the Union government might initiate, facilitate, and maintain a virtuous circle including the state; watchdog institutions of state such as the CAG, the ED, and the CVC; legal authorities; and agents of transparency such as NGOs and the free press. But in considering reform of India's accountability mechanisms, the Union government is restrained by the federal structure of the Constitution. Much corruption in India takes place at the state-government level or below. And even where the Union government does have jurisdiction, the focus can be too high up the scale to mitigate or remove everyday corruption.

For example, the powers of the main Union government corruption-fighting agency, the CVC, relate only to central government agencies and relatively senior-level officers at that. The problem with these restrictions is that the vast body of corruption occurs at state level and often at relatively junior levels. As already noted, a grade II clerk in Madhya Pradesh on a salary of Rs 40,000 was found to have assets worth Rs 250 million.[42] Interestingly, this case came to light as a result of an investigation by the Madhya Pradesh Lokayukta Special Police Establishment, which is the investigating arm of the Lokayukta. Unfortunately, the various state-level Lokayukta acts vary in quality. In response to the Jan Lok Pal campaign, the Constitution will be amended to give them uniformity and strength.

According to the CVC commissioner, another problem with the CVC Act is that the CBI, as the CVC investigator, has no power within the states to take up a case. Even where it is invited in, permission is sometimes withdrawn by the state government when the CBI gets onto the trail of an influential offender. The commissioner also points out that the Madhya Pradesh government has barred the CBI from probing IAS, IPS, and Indian Forest Service officers even though they are originally appointed to those categories by the Union.[43]

The debate around the Lok Pal Bill goes to the core of issues of accountability in India. Criticism of the first Lok Pal Bill, originally brought down in 2011 in fulfillment of the commitment under the CMP, focused on the fact the government bill would not give the ombudsman's office its own investigation agency. This omission would effectively keep the CBI, the CVC, and the New Delhi police out of the purview of the Lok Pal's investigations, since they would have to be the investigating agencies on behalf of the Lok Pal. Criticism also focused on the fact that the initial government bill excluded the prime minister and his office from the scrutiny of the Lok Pal. A further criticism related to the fact that state-level Lokayuktas would be tied to the federal legislation.

In subsequent amendments to the bill, the government agreed that the head of the CBI would be selected by committee rather than appointed by the government, thus supposedly avoiding the problem of politicization of the CBI. The Supreme Court also requested that the attorney general prepare a bill to ensure that the CBI remain outside the influence of the government—the Supreme Court having been highly critical of the CBI for consulting the government and being influenced by it in the context of the inquiries into Coalgate.[44] The government also agreed that the CBI's anticorruption wing (which would investigate on behalf of the Lok Pal) would itself be subject to the purview of the Lok Pal, as would the prime minister and his office. Finally, rather than including the states in the federal act, the state governments were given a year to pass new legislation to ensure that their Lokayukta legislation was consistent and adequate.

At the time of writing, the amended bill has been passed by the Lok Sabha but is stalled in the Rajya Sabha, where a committee has made further recommendations. These include bringing the CBI and CVC *to some extent* under the purview of the act, but they also exclude the military. As we have seen, corruption is growing in the military and becoming a significant problem. Under the act as it now stands, the Lok Pal will also have the weakness of the CVC insofar as those it can investigate are confined to the CVC Act categories of public servants—that is, not the lower-grade ones. But to its advantage, the act will contain the coercive powers associated with a normal court under section 27(1). The Lok Pal will thus give the state and Union ombudsmen royal commission–like powers somewhat similar to those of the corruption commissions in Hong Kong and Australia. Following this committee process, Anna Hazare is still criticizing the draft as being too weak because the CVC and CBI are still not fully within the purview of the Lok Pal. However, a former ally of Hazare, the IPS officer Kiren Bedi, has now split from Hazare and asserts the new draft gives most of what the Jan Lok Pal does.[45]

India has a number of other accountability institutions operating at the central level. The National Human Rights Commission is designed to protect the rights of individuals and has the powers of a civil court in respect to all Indian jurisdictions. It may intercede in court processes in relation to human rights and visit institutions to investigate alleged human rights abuses. But its weakness is that it may only make recommendations to governments (although these include recommendations for prosecutions where appropriate). The National Human Rights Commission is also bogged down by the massive workload imposed on it and serious underfunding. It badly needs to be strengthened in terms of both legislation, which requires more robust powers than the right to make recommendations, and funding.

The RTI Act also has its own commissioners and offices at the state and federal levels. The RTI Act is one of the most radical of its kind, but it is currently languishing as an instrument of accountability due to opposition from within governments and from other powerful interests. Even the prime minister, Manmohan Singh, is on record describing it as a "troublesome law."[46] According to the then outgoing Union government information commissioner, Shailesh Gandhi, the law is being killed off by violence (with twelve activists seeking justice under the act murdered between 2008 and 2012), government underfunding, and neglect, which is causing backlogs and delays of the kind experienced in the court system and which is in turn causing the populace to turn away from use of the law. Gandhi said the backlog in the Union commissions was twenty thousand cases and that from twenty-four thousand to forty thousand cases were pending in Maharashtra and Uttar Pradesh alone. He called for continuing public pressure on the government to ensure that the commissions were properly resourced and that the act was not eroded by amendments, which have already been carried out to "defang" the law itself.[47]

The case of the RTI Act provides a classic example of the way in which an act that is initially powerful can be eroded and eventually stymied by bureaucratic and governmental backsliding and opposition from powerful interests. Any government that is serious about accountability needs to protect the act, remove the offending amendments, and ensure that the information commissioners are properly resourced to do their job.

As we illustrated in chapter 1, another development impeding accountability and alienating minorities is the tendency to pass draconian legislation in response to separatism and extremism. One of the worst pieces of legislation impeding accountability is the Armed Forces (Special Powers) Act, or AFSPA. The UPA government at one stage hinted it would reform AFSPA.[48] It is now claiming that the army is resisting any such move and that it cannot proceed.[49] Early in its tenure it abolished the POTA, substituting for that act an amendment to the UAPA, as it had committed to do prior to the 2004 election. As already covered in chapter 1, there are few differences between the two acts. The definition of a terrorist act in the UAPA is similar to that of the POTA, and both are somewhat loose. Detention without trial is also for a similar period of 180 days, although the court can order release of the suspect after 90 days in the UAPA. The presumption of innocence is denied in the case of both acts, and confessions are admissible for the POTA but not for the UAPA.[50]

Given the evidence provided in chapter 1 of abuse of powers by police in counterterrorism operations and of the consequences in terms of radicalization of minorities such as Muslims, the Union government should carefully consider the range of legislation available to it and whether it might be better off, both from a humanitarian and from a counterterrorism point of view, in softening such draconian legislation. Along with police reform, this would go some way to achieving better outcomes in the long process of bringing alienated communities—whether minorities in the heartland or those at the periphery seeking to separate from India—into the mainstream.

DIGITIZATION, TRANSPARENCY, AND SECURITY

Despite its status as a large, poor country, India has a sound record of use of e-government and digitization to achieve transparency and better governance outcomes.

The innovative electronic voting system was first used in 1999. It has not been without its critics, however. Following assertions of inaccuracy and the possibility of vote tampering, the Electoral Commission mandated the introduction of the voter-verified paper audit trail (VVPAT). This has proven complicated to introduce and may well not be in place by the time of the 2014 national election. But at least India is on course to develop a secure, accountable system to ensure better election outcomes, one in which the independence of the Electoral Commission is used to leverage the democratic process. It is noteworthy that there is no equivalent independent authority to oversight elections in the United States, with a consequent mix of sometimes dubious voting systems and frequent gerrymandering.

Another key component of the digitization path to transparency is the establishment of a digitized biometric identity. Such a system is vital to the inclusive growth objective, since much of the routing of the $60 billion of transfers to the poor occurs at the level of establishment of identity. The program, which is known as the Unique Identification (UID) project (or *Aadhaar* project, after the unique identification number), will provide to the entire population of 1.21 billion a unique identification number involving verification through fingerprint and iris scans. The UID registration process is about half accomplished. But it too is not without its critics, who claim that technology is not necessarily neutral and is open to being misused.[51] The program is already being linked to key social-uplift programs such as MGNREGS.

In a replication of successful direct-cash injection programs in Brazil and Mexico, India plans to provide direct injections of cash to circumvent the often corrupt bureaucratic chain, under which Rajiv Gandhi's famous 15 paisa in the rupee allegedly got through to the intended recipient. Pilot cash distribution programs are already using the UID cards. To date, these pay only pensions and scholarships and involve only twenty of the nation's more than six hundred districts. But the direct-cash program will eventually make payments under the food-distribution and fuel-subsidy programs (worth about $14 billion), and the government intends to cover the whole country by the end of 2013. The program has encountered many technical difficulties, not the least of which is establishing bank accounts into which the electronic payments can be made. But the very act of establishing accounts also brings with it empowerment, since only about one-third of Indians have an account. Some say the program is overambitious, while others claim it is a cash giveaway to buy electoral credit for the Congress Party.[52] The most serious criticism claims that such programs work well in countries like Brazil where functioning government services such as for health and education already exist, but that such services hardly function at all in some parts of India, so the program has no foundation on which to build.[53] On the other hand, it offers a real chance of short-circuiting the corrupt and inefficient bureaucratic chain, which involves a host of middlemen.

E-governance is also a tool for transparency in itself. India has developed a national e-governance plan (NeGP). The backbone of the NeGP is the rollout of the Common Service Centres. These are the access points for citizens—250,000 of them across India's 600,000 villages. The intention is that each village will either have a center or be close to one. The Microsoft Corporation reports that "clearly, the government [of India] is taking the e-governance mandate rather seriously, considering that the NeGP was approved only five years back in 2006."[54] E-governance can have substantial benefits in terms of controlling corruption. For example, digitization of land records at Gwalior reportedly for the first time provided graft-free access to land records.[55] The manipulation of land records is one of the major sources of corruption and rural unrest in India.

India also has a number of federal and state-level accountability mechanisms relevant to police and law enforcement. One such measure that is often overlooked is the collection and maintenance of sound law-enforcement and crime statistics. Statistics are fundamental to accountability insofar as citizens are given clear insight into how their services are performing. For example, strong, interlinked statistics between courts and police are capable of providing key information about both court and police performance. It is through the linking of these statistics that they are turbo-charged so that they can be far more exacting as accountability measures.[56]

One early measure the Union government could consider is to fund and oversee in each state periodic crime-victimization surveys designed to give longitudinal and comparative pictures of genuine crime problems. The results of these surveys could also be compared to the results of the existing Indian crime database to determine how effective current collection methods are. They should be widely available to the public, including through the internet.

The central government could also fund yearly publication at the jurisdiction level of statistics relating to complaints brought, complaints upheld, FIRs issued, arrests made, cases brought to court, cases processed in court, numbers of convictions, numbers of acquittals, average time of each court case, and percentage of those charged in relation to those convicted. These data could be published on the internet so that they are readily available, both locally and nationally. They should also be made available at the police-district level in printed form for those with no internet access. NGOs should be used for social auditing of this process, to be funded by the Union government.

ADDRESSING ECONOMIC AND ENVIRONMENTAL CONCERNS

India's economic and environmental strategies need to be highly integrated. This is because to a significant degree the nature of the environmental challenge will be shaped by the type of economic development India pursues and by its success or otherwise. As noted in chapters 2 and 3, environmental challenges are both locally and to a lesser degree internationally driven. They will therefore require solutions at these various levels.

Developmentally India requires massive injections of capital to meet its infrastructure requirements and impending environmental challenges. In particular, labor-intensive industrial development, which will be required to meet the needs of shifting populations from agricultural areas, will require substantial investment in urbanization such as provision of water, energy, transport, and sewage facilities. Industrialization will also require more power generation. Given the needs of India in this area and the problems of the global commons in terms of carbon-dioxide emissions, this will also involve substantial reliance on cleaner energy rather than fossil-based fuels.

This massive requirement for investment is unfortunately needed at a time of relative scarcity of capital through FDI. In a sense, India has missed the boat. East Asian powers such as South Korea, Taiwan, and China managed to catch a wave of international capital and attendant technology transfer generated by the long postwar boom. But since 2008, this boom appears to have come to an end. The West is now capital-starved, and it is the new powers of Asia who are in possession of significant investment capability.

Ironically, India's perceived competitor, China, is in a better position than any other nation to provide it with the capital and expertise necessary to rehabilitate its infrastructure and extend it to support a new wave of urbanization. India should consider doing exactly what China did vis-à-vis the West—that is, use the resources of the perceived competitor (keeping in mind China opened up to FDI and foreign technical assistance relatively soon after the end of the Cultural Revolution) in order to build itself up to a point where it could ultimately compete with the West. To do this, China developed its infrastructure and technology with massive capital injections and technology transfers from the West. This enabled it to industrialize, urbanize, and emerge as the labor-intensive manufacturing powerhouse of the world. Some might argue India could leapfrog the labor-intensive phase and embark directly into an era of hi-tech activity. But it is difficult to see how such activity could accommodate the vast need for jobs as Indians are progressively released from agriculture by agricultural modernization. To adopt this strategy, India would need to set aside its security and trade concerns about China as these were identified in chapter 3.

CONCLUSION

India's internal-security and governance revolutions are now well under way. The current Congress-led UPA government has the overall thrust right—that is, India's future as a power is dependent on better governance and security outcomes at all levels of government. Inclusive growth needs to be encouraged to support social stability, and corruption needs to be tackled to allow for inclusive growth. These interlocking strategies will also be relevant for India's neighborhood relationships. Unless India can deal with dissonance and discontent, it will remain vulnerable to cross-border disruption, will need to spend more on security, and will have less capacity to provide resources for economic development, education, health, and the acquisition of soft and hard power in the region and world.

The current "revolution" is an unfinished one, however. In itself, it is unlikely substantially to achieve its goal of a more secure India. Not surprisingly, it is heavily focused on those areas amenable to the influence of the Union government. But the fundamental issues of security lie lower down in the system. They rest on the ability of police to win the confidence of the people, provide them with security, and act as the eyes and ears of the system in respect to counterterrorism and counterinsurgency. They also depend on the ability of local and district-level courts to deal speedily and justly with cases. Minority communities still need confidence that they will not be discriminated against and subjected to human rights abuses. Most important, fundamental security issues are closely linked to better governance and accountability outcomes at all levels of government. Although India's security revolution may achieve short-term gains, unless these lower-order issues are addressed, it will not prove sustainable.

The two most difficult issues will be the truly difficult problem of police reform and dealing with the reaction to anticorruption measures by those adversely affected, which includes some of the most powerful politicians and officials in the country, as well as myriad operational police and civil servants. Dealing with these problems will require political leadership at the highest levels of Union and state governments and continuing vigilance by civil society groups and the media. Should India be able to improve governance and avoid the resistance of powerful people, it will effectively have hardened itself as a target against cross-border incursion and political mischief from across the region, while at the same time ensuring that its own problems do not feed those from across the borders. By its sheer size it will also provide an example of stability and growth for its neighbors.

But it will need to do more than that. In the following chapter we consider what India might also do to enhance relations within its South Asian neighborhood beyond those actions it might take at home.

NOTES

1. Khilnani et al., *NonAlignment 2.0*, paragraph 9.
2. Ibid., chapter 5.
3. Ibid., 64.
4. For example, it could be argued that to a significant degree the insurrection in Jammu and Kashmir, which commenced in 1990–91, had its genesis in the alleged rigging of the 1987 state assembly election by Rajiv Gandhi in collusion with the Farooq Abdulla of the National Conference. Equally, it could be argued that the Khalistan movement in Punjab was facilitated by the attempts of Indira Gandhi to derail the opposition by supporting the extremist Bhidranwale.
5. Chidambaram, "A New Architecture for India's Security."
6. "Funds for Anti-Terror Infrastructure Not Fully Utilised, No Allocation Cuts."
7. Prior to 26/11, the NSG was located at New Delhi. It was not called in till three hours after the attack, and in all it took the NSG a reported eleven hours to respond. During that time, the inadequately equipped and trained Mumbai police were left to deal with the situation. No equipment was in place on the NSG's aircraft, nor were aircrew available.
8. See Chari, *National Counter Terrorism Centre for India*.
9. "Five Years after 26/11, India Faces Intelligence Famine."
10. Offenses scheduled under the act are terrorism, counterfeiting of currency, human trafficking, illicit drugs trafficking, organized crime, plane hijacking, and violations of the Atomic Energy Act and Weapons of Mass Destruction Act. In addition, all other offenses alleged against the accused under these scheduled offenses may also be investigated. All subsequent references are from the text of the National Investigation Agency Bill as it was passed in the Lok Sabha, which may be found at the South Asia Terrorism Portal website at www.satp.org/satporgtp/countries/india/document/papers/75-c1.htm.
11. Ibid., 4–5.
12. Government of India, Ministry of Home Affairs, Model Police Act 2006.

13. For a critique of the Model Police Act, see Rao, "Presentation on Model Police Act," a PowerPoint presentation by the former secretary of the drafting committee.
14. Ibid.
15. Bipendra, "Retired Cops Push for Police Reforms."
16. Each state police service has an officer cadre that is selected competitively in a manner similar to that of the IPS.
17. The following account, unless otherwise noted, is drawn from "Judicial Reforms of the Govt of India."
18. "Why Bihar Has Most Fast-Track Courts in India."
19. Biswas, "Do India's 'Fast Track' Courts Work?"
20. "Double Strength of Judiciary."
21. Tachil, "India in Transition."
22. United Progressive Alliance, *Report to the People 2004–2008*, passim.
23. Ibid., 4 and 8.
24. Rothstein, "Anti-Corruption," passim.
25. See Saha and Campbell, "Studies of the Effect of Democracy on Corruption." See also Jha et al., "The Role of Bribes in Rural Governance," 30. These researchers found that the introduction of the *panchayat* system and devolution of power to the *panchayats* did not, of itself, improve governance outcomes. It was also necessary to have additional measures to achieve transparency.
26. Some argue that what is needed is not less but rather more democracy. See Vaishnav, "India Needs More Democracy, Not Less."
27. Meyer and Birdsall, *New Estimates of India's Middle Class*, 3. The lower estimate comes from the Centre for Global Development and the upper from the National Council for Applied Economic Research.
28. Doron and Jeffrey, *Cell Phone Nation*. See also Robin Jeffrey, "Hot Election Tip from India."
29. Note, for example, the case in which a twenty-one-year-old Mumbai medical student was arrested (but subsequently released due the outcry) for a relatively mild comment on the Shiv Sena's attempts to shut down Mumbai following the death of Bal Thakeray. See "A Mumbai Student Vents on Facebook, and the Police Come Knocking."
30. Jeffrey, *India's Newspaper Revolution*.
31. Chandra, "Striking at the Roots of Corruption."
32. Ibid.
33. For an exploration of these differences, see Gordon, "India and China: Mega-Population, Mega-Corruption, Mega-Growth."
34. Although some at least see Hazare as a BJP stooge. See Roy, "I'd Rather Not Be Anna."
35. "I Feel Sorry for Kapil Sebal and Company for Their Zero-Loss Theory, GAC Vinod Rai Says."
36. Freedom House, *Freedom of the Press 2013*. For 2012, see "India Ranks 131st in Press Freedom Index."

37. "India Ranks 131st in Press Freedom Index."
38. Ragunathan, "Despite Drawbacks MGNREGS Comes Out on Top in Job Creation."
39. See Aiyer and Samji, "Transparency and Accountability in [MG]NREGA," 18–20.
40. See, for example, a study of a dry district in Karnataka by Harish et al., "Impacts and Implications of MGNREGS on Labour Supply and Income Generation for Agriculture in Central Dry Zone of Karnataka," 485–94.
41. Jha et al., "Net Benefit under National Rural Employment Guarantee Scheme."
42. "This MP Clerk's Salary Is Rs 40,000, Assets 25 Crore."
43. "CVC Seeks Clarity on Mandate to Probe Political Corruption."
44. "Supreme Court Wants Law to Insulate CBI from Interference."
45. "Kiran Bedi Differs with Anna Hazare, Backs Amended Lokpal Bill."
46. Quoted in "India RTI Chief."
47. Ibid.
48. "Cabinet to Decide on AFSPA's Future, Says Chidambarum."
49. "An Abomination Called AFSPA."
50. "Toughening the Law."
51. "World's Biggest Biometric ID Scheme Forges Ahead."
52. "India Aims to Keep Money for Poor out of Others' Pockets."
53. "Will Cash Transfers Work in India?"
54. Microsoft Corporation, "India's E-governance Framework."
55. "Log On for Clean Government."
56. By way of example, in Cambodia there were no adequate court statistics that enabled reconciliation between cases brought and those resulting in a conviction. Consequently, serious corruption in the legal processes did not come to light. Once such statistics were compared, it was evident that very few of the pedophilia cases resulted in convictions, seemingly because of the problem of either corruption among legal officials or the buying-off of witnesses. Knowledge of the author derived from interviews with police, NGOs, and judicial authorities in Cambodia, 2000.

CHAPTER 6

External Strategies and Challenges: From Neighborhood to Region

Previously we discussed the strategies India might adopt to function better domestically. The purpose of those strategies is to "harden" India as a target, achieve better governance outcomes, and allow it to grow economically without undue stress on the population. This activity in the domestic sphere must be the first priority of any strategy for India's rise to power.

The second priority is for India to address the problems of South Asia, insofar as it can. A better-functioning neighborhood would create an India that performs better economically and socially, one more able to engage positively with its neighbors, and one less subject to the spread of cross-border dissonance. Such a neighborhood would also open up new economic vistas. It would give India a springboard from which to launch its wider regional aspirations and achieve inclusive growth.

India's challenges in South Asia are enormous. Many of the problems being experienced by nearby countries are similar to those confronting India. It is difficult enough for India to fix its own problems without having to deal with those of its neighbors.

A third priority is to find ways to look beyond South Asia into the broader region—to the IOR, the Persian Gulf, Central and Southern Asia, Southeast Asia, and East Asia. In terms of this challenge, India needs to leverage the advantage of occupying a box seat dominating the oil SLOCs in ways that don't unduly perturb China and add to the security dilemma already developing in the IOR. It also needs to build on the better domestic economic and governance outcomes considered in the previous chapter in order to enhance its Look East strategy and global position through its enormous soft-power potential.

This chapter considers some of the strategies India might use in order to accomplish these goals. More broadly, the chapter also considers just how India, as a "swing state" in Asia, might seek to insert itself into the currently unstable Asian security architecture.

INDIA AND ITS NEIGHBORHOOD

Indian policymakers have long been aware of the need for their country to perform better in South Asia. The problem has been to know how to do it given the difficult subregional circumstances and India-Pakistan friction. Ashok Beheria, Smriti S. Pattanaik, and Arvind Gupta correctly assert that New Delhi has not yet developed a coherent neighborhood strategy.[1] *NonAlignment 2.0*, cited above, suggests a sensible grand strategy for India's global relations but no practical strategy for South Asia. Certainly this question is in the air, and a number of suggested approaches are cited below.

Foremost among these is that India, as the biggest and most secure South Asian power, should give more to its neighbors than they can or will give back. In short it should act with "strategic altruism."[2] This has been reflected in Indian history by the policies of India's first prime minister, Jawaharlal Nehru. It further progressed as a policy under the so-called Gujral doctrine (named after a former Indian foreign and prime minister, I. K. Gujral), which has been characterized as "non-reciprocal accommodation."[3] As a strategy, it also accords with the international relations theory that "bandwagoning" (that is, the propensity of smaller regional states to go along with a large neighbor as distinct from seeking to balance that neighbor with the help of outside powers) can be induced by strategic altruism. According to E. Sridharan, the United States practiced strategic altruism with considerable success during the Cold War.[4]

A subset of the strategic altruism strategy would be for India to ignore Pakistan, "go around" it as it were, and work toward subregional prosperity with its other South Asian partners, including by the use of strategic altruism. Pakistan would eventually have no choice but to climb aboard the Indian-led juggernaut of South Asian growth.

Both of the above strategies could also incorporate a push from New Delhi to achieve better outcomes within SAARC by seeking to change the organization from one dealing with "soft" issues into one that grapples with real economic, social, and political problems. Some strategies for accomplishing this are suggested below. But given the history of SAARC, it would be unwise to expect too much from the organization.

Alternatively, India could simply ignore South Asia as a whole and go around it on the global level, thus sidestepping the need to "control," or at the very least "neutralize," its neighborhood—a need that seems in history to have been necessary for most emerging powers. According to this argument, eventually India would possess so much regional and global critical mass that its small neighbors would have no choice but to buckle under to its sphere of influence.

Finally, some suggest that India should use its democratic and human rights example as an exemplar to other South Asian countries to turn a subregion of dissonance into one of cooperation and prosperity. Although Ali Ahmed favors such an approach, he also cautions that time will be needed "for liberal-rationalism in other [non-Indian South Asian] states to find favour."[5]

None of these strategies, except that of ignoring South Asia and seeking to act on the wider regional and global stages, is mutually exclusive. The likely outcome is that India will pursue a number of them, at least in some measure. The questions that therefore arise are ones of emphasis rather than choice. Moreover, the pursuit of inclusive growth and improved governance in the domestic sphere, as advocated in chapter 5, would serve as a foundation for all other external strategies. An India that is strong domestically and growing robustly would be an India better placed to compete with China as an investor in South Asia. It could use its critical mass even more effectively to ensure all South Asian states could rise on the same tide. It would be less subject to being sucked into the vicious circle of cross-border dissonance that is so much a feature of present-day South Asia.

The strategy of inclusive growth is a crosscutting one, however. It requires domestic activity, such as pursuing policies favoring growth and achieving better governance and distribution outcomes. It also requires strategies in foreign policy, such as choosing to refrain from developing a powerful and expensive force-projection capability and avoiding actions that might trigger subregional or regional tension or even conflict. As argued in earlier chapters, inclusive growth is a strategy with which India is already engaged, at least in the broadest sense of always spending under three percent of GDP on defense and seeking to spread the benefits of economic liberalization. Within this broad framework, however, more could be done domestically to encourage growth through further liberalization and to address corruption and governance issues insofar as they distort efforts to redistribute some of the benefits of growth. In terms of international strategies (the subject of this chapter), more could be done to capture investment capital from East Asia (especially from China) for infrastructure and to shape the strategic environment and foster subregional growth and confidence.

In discussing such strategies, we will first examine India's options in South Asia and then possible scenarios in the wider region, including the IOR. But when it comes to South Asia, India's most intractable problem is to know what to do about Pakistan.

DEALING WITH PAKISTAN

If India's Pakistan problem could be solved, much else in South Asia would fall into place. Although other South Asian countries have close relations with China, these relationships do not have the strategic depth of the China-Pakistan relationship. No other South Asian country shares a territorial dispute with India of the intensity of the Kashmir dispute. Three South Asian countries—Sri Lanka, Nepal, and Bhutan—have deep cultural-religious ties with India, and Afghanistan shares a strategic concern about Pakistan.[6] In most cases the trading relationship has developed further than it has between India and Pakistan, where mutual hostility and suspicion have tainted what could otherwise be a more healthy relationship.

Without the toxic Pakistan-India relationship, SAARC would have better prospects of providing a much-needed strategic and economic bridge between the countries of South Asia. In saying this, we do not necessarily seek to contradict Michael's position as stated in chapter 2—namely, that the real problem with SAARC is India's pursuit of soft regionalism. Rather, we would argue that one of the reasons for India's adoption of that model is to prevent Pakistan and other powers from ganging up on it within a SAARC framework designed to give them real power. But as matters stand, SAARC can probably only progress at the pace India-Pakistan relations will allow, and that has been glacial. This is a serious regional impediment, since SAARC has an enormous agenda of potential work, such as improving cross-border transport, addressing issues of regional crime and terrorism, fostering closer economic relations, and helping to address cross-border environmental issues.

Much therefore hangs on achieving a more functional relationship between India and Pakistan. But can it be done, and if so, how?

If the India-Pakistan relationship is the key to unlocking the potential of South Asia, some have argued that a resolution of the Kashmir issue is the key to unlocking India-Pakistan relations. Ganguly asserts that "few other conflicts in the post–World War II era, with the possible exception of the Arab-Israeli dispute, have proved as intractable."[7] He attributes this intractability to the different interpretations of state between India and Pakistan. According to him, this difference means that the existence of an India-dominated Kashmir, with its Muslim majority, amounts to an affront to the very raison d'être of Pakistan. In turn this is translated into irredentist demands by Islamabad. Ganguly says that given these circumstances, Westphalian concepts of state dictate that neither feels able to cede territory.[8]

On its part, New Delhi fears that erosion of Indian sovereignty in Kashmir could be a thin end of the wedge in relation to demands for independence in its Northeast. Any decision to divide Kashmir on ethno-religious lines would also, in New Delhi's view, seriously undermine India's secular position.[9] Moreover,

India is the status quo power in Kashmir. It controls the coveted Vale of Kashmir, while Pakistan is the revisionist power seeking to control it. India therefore has no incentive to give ground on the status quo.

Pakistan's Muslim interpretation of statehood, on the other hand, means that any government in Islamabad that were to give up the claim to Indian Kashmir could be subject to serious censure from the religious interests that remain powerful political forces in Pakistan, as already discussed in chapter 2 in terms of Musharraf's "October surprise" peace offer. Additionally, the controlling elites of Pakistan, especially the army and feudal elements, gain credibility they would not otherwise have from the ongoing dispute over Kashmir and antagonism toward India. The focus on India has arguably diverted Pakistan from a social revolution or even substantial social reform.

Because of these resistances on both sides of the border, some kind of major political rapprochement between India and Pakistan, quite apart from any settlement of the Kashmir dispute, would probably be needed for significant progress on Kashmir to occur.

Pakistan, moreover, does not speak with a united political voice. Rather, it has a range of actors within and outside exercising degrees of control through undue influence or use of violence, such that some are now even countenancing civil war in Pakistan.[10] Such actors (more fully discussed in chapter 3) range from the Pakistani Taliban, which would overthrow the state and establish a Taliban-like emirate; to "friendly" Islamist groups operating across the border into Afghanistan, such as the Haqqani network; to separatist groups in Baluchistan and Sind; to violent, anti-Shiite groups such as Lashkar-i-Jhangvi, based in Punjab—to name a few. This diverse array of forces, combined with dysfunctional and corrupt mainstream politics, an assertive army, and a failing economy, mean that Pakistan is a difficult country in which to achieve political stability, at least in the short term. Rapprochement with India may have to wait upon a more settled domestic environment in Pakistan. And in that regard, matters could get worse before they get better.

Given this pessimistic account, is there anything India could or should do to provide a circuit breaker?

Pakistan has consistently said it wishes to resume the so-called composite dialogue with India—that is, the dialogue in which a multiplicity of subjects can be discussed, including Kashmir. Although India has engaged in more limited talks, on its part New Delhi has resisted any full-scale resumption of the dialogue. It has done so on the grounds that Pakistan has never brought the perpetrators of 26/11 to justice.

India, as the status quo power, has no incentive to give ground on Kashmir. It requires no further territory in Kashmir beyond the LOC—simply that it be allowed to retain what it already has. On the other hand, India does want the violent campaign of cross-border *jihad* directed against it by groups like the LeT, the JeM, and the HuJI to be limited by the Pakistani authorities. Although Pakistan claims it can do nothing in this regard, India counterclaims that both leaders and alleged perpetrators are functioning in Pakistan without hindrance from the authorities.

Meanwhile, India has concluded that it can give ground in some areas, especially trade-related ones and people-to-people relations. Given a more open relationship in these areas, New Delhi is of the view that, over time, confidence may create a better environment in which to conduct eventual discussion on more difficult issues such as Kashmir.

This broad strategy is probably correct. But, in addition, India should certainly not do anything that would destabilize Pakistan. Pakistan might currently be a difficult neighbor, but a Pakistan collapsing as a state would be far worse, unleashing forces that could impact negatively throughout South Asia for generations. On these lines, India should also have an eye out for a genuine attempt on the part of a Pakistani leader to forge a rapprochement with India. India's difficulty will come should another attack be mounted from Pakistan of the seriousness of the attacks of 26/11. Any attack on Pakistan that followed could unleash the "law of unintended consequences," possibly leading to the serious destabilization of Pakistan, which would certainly not be in India's interest.

GOING AROUND PAKISTAN: ACTION IN SOUTH ASIA

The policy of ignoring the troubled South Asian neighborhood and developing an international role on the world stage is not a viable option for India. The problems of South Asia have first to be alleviated if India is fully to realize its global potential. This will in turn involve focusing on the comprehensive domestic and neighborhood policies discussed in chapter 5 and in the present chapter.

India is just too vulnerable in South Asia to ignore its circumstances there. It has perforce to work on the neighborhood because, as matters now stand, a peer competitor such as China can make too many difficulties for it there should relations continue to be vexatious or deteriorate. Also, troubled neighbors can further disrupt India itself, for example through cross-border terrorism; illegal migration; the spread of crime; the leakage of weapons, explosives, and people across porous borders; the failure of South Asia to achieve economic liftoff; and the diversion of funds needed for border and regional security. Squabbles between neighbors can also reverberate into international forums—prime examples among many available being the periodic importation of the India-Pakistan dispute over Kashmir into the United Nations and the way the India-Pakistan dispute was initially a factor in keeping India out of East Asian forums such as APEC.

Given the troubled status quo between India and Pakistan and given India's need to work on South Asia as a whole, it makes sense to continue that work elsewhere in South Asia pending better relations between India and Pakistan, rather than simply trying to sidestep South Asia as a whole. Indeed, a South Asia experiencing growth and prosperity would be one in which Pakistan would wish to be more heavily engaged. Given it would be one in which India was already interdependent with its neighbors (other than Pakistan), greater Pakistani involvement in South Asia would, as a result, mean greater Pakistani involvement with India.

Enhanced cooperation within South Asia would also have the advantage of leveraging the subregion's considerable comparative advantage as the next great labor-intensive manufacturing powerhouse of the world. But to do this, infrastructure—including urban infrastructure, transport infrastructure, and power generation and distribution—needs to be greatly improved across the region. For trade to develop, common attitudes to rule of law, crime, and mutual legal cooperation also need to be developed. In terms of these requirements, there is considerable scope for greater coordination to achieve better outcomes for the entire subregion.

For example, South Asia could jointly work on harnessing the vast hydroelectric potential of the Himalayas and developing shared electricity grids to distribute the resulting power. There is considerable scope for rehabilitating the cross-border transport links severed at the time of the breakup of the British Raj. Should Indo-Pakistani relations improve, all South Asia could benefit from the subregion's proximity to the oil and natural gas producers of the Gulf and Central Asia through current proposals for pipelines linking South Asia to the Gulf and Central Asia. Since most regional nations have English in common, the subregion could emerge as one of the most important global information-technology (IT) hubs. Common approaches could be developed to important international concerns, for example the better protection of guest workers from South Asia working in the Gulf. Educational institutions could make considerable gains by regional cross-fertilization, possibly under the auspices of SAARC. Important environmental concerns could be tackled jointly, especially through regional hydroelectric plans and the sharing of other clean-energy technologies. Improved subregional security would enhance domestic security in all countries, which would in turn foster economic growth and well-being. Cross-border trade under SAFTA would be enhanced by more open borders, more efficient and transparent border regimes, more commonality in rule of law, and better transport infrastructure.

There are already a number of initiatives to improve coordination of information and communications technology (ICT), but they are uneven in their cover and half-baked. SAARC selected "Information, Communication and Media" as one of its areas of cooperation in 1997. This decision was followed by meetings of SAARC communications ministers, the establishment of a working group, and subsequent development of a plan of action. One important issue identified for the agenda of the working group was the establishment of effective systems for telecommunications among SAARC countries.[11] Other suggestions, not necessarily to be undertaken by SAARC, include the establishment of a South Asian IT institute to train, research, and share information. Under the South Asia Subregion Economic Cooperation (SASEC, which includes only India, Nepal, Bhutan, and Bangladesh), a master plan has been developed to include the South Asian Information Highway Project, designed to better integrate member countries on the internet and reduce costs. It is a component of a wider strategy—the SASEC Master Plan, formulated in 2001. The Asian Development Bank and the United Nations Educational, Scientific, and Cultural Organization have picked up some of the funding of this plan.[12]

There are thus many important initiatives, but very little follow-up work has been undertaken to implement them. Commentators in New Delhi might argue differently, however. They might claim that India is already adopting the strategy of going around Pakistan to develop the South Asian subregion. The UPA government made such a claim in its *Report to the People*.[13] But when we examine India's aid and investment programs in detail, we cannot identify any substantial and sustained application of aid, technology, or capital within the subregion.

At first glance, India's direct aid contribution to South Asia is relatively handsome given its own high levels of poverty (see table 6.1). Of the total aid program of 3422.87 *crore* ($633 million) in 2011–12, 84 percent was earmarked for South Asia (including Afghanistan). Two countries that could be considered "special," however, make up the lion's share of this amount. Aid to Afghanistan was Rs 2.9 billion, and Bhutan received a massive Rs 20.3 billion. A case can be made to discount most of these amounts. As discussed in chapter 3, Afghanistan is seen in New Delhi as a component in the strategic competition with Pakistan and also as a potential source of violent jihadist blowback against India in the post-NATO environment. The considerable aid provided to it by India has a distinct strategic purpose. Bhutan is a tiny, landlocked, strategically important mountain kingdom (population 687,000) that exists on heavy subsidies from India—a situation inherited from the British. If these amounts were to be subtracted, then the remaining sum expended in South Asia would be quite modest—a mere Rs 5.640 billion (about $105 million).

India's total direct-aid program of $633 million compares poorly with China's aid program, which the Congressional Research Service estimated was $25 billion in 2007.[14] Even accounting for the fact that China's economy is over thrice the size of India's, the proportion spent by India is not nearly as great, and deducting the special expenditure in Afghanistan and Bhutan, the expenditure elsewhere in South Asia is minimal. It would seem from these data that there is considerable scope for additional Indian aid to South Asia.

TABLE 6.1 Principal Destinations of India's Technical Cooperation Programs as in Revised Estimates 2011–12

Country	Technical Cooperation Budget (in *Crore* of Rupees)	Percentage of India's Total Aid and Loan Budget
Bhutan	2,030.00	59.31
Afghanistan	290.00	8.47
Maldives	273.00	7.98
Nepal	150.00	4.38
African countries	124.00	3.62
Sri Lanka	133.00	3.89
Burma	111.82	3.27
Eurasian countries	30.00	0.88
Bangladesh	8.00	0.23
Latin American countries	0.50	0.10
Mongolia	2.00	0.06
Others	270.55	7.90
Total	3,422.87	100

Source: Government of India, Ministry of External Affairs, *Annual Report 2011–12*, 209, appendix XV.

It is also noteworthy that Pakistan received no Indian aid. Even in the context of the devastating floods that struck Pakistan in 2010, Islamabad reportedly refused Indian offers of assistance.[15] But even were Indian assistance to Pakistan feasible in nonsensitive areas, it is doubtful such assistance would do a great deal to untangle the knot of suspicion between the two. For India and Pakistan, a political breakthrough apparently has to precede an economic breakthrough.

India's relatively small contribution of Rs 80 million (about $1.6 million) to Bangladesh in direct aid is far more surprising, especially since the year of reporting, 2011–12, was one in which a supposedly "pro-India" Awami League government was in power in Dacca. In addition to this minimal aid, however, India gives Bangladesh access to significant lines of credit and concessional garment imports. For example, India's Exim Bank has provided Bangladesh with a line of credit of $800 million for imports of Indian goods and services.[16] India also gave Bangladesh permission to allow eight million Bangladeshi garments into India duty-free.[17] This was eventually extended to forty-six lines of garments to be allowed duty-free, leading to a rapid increase in imports, with an expected $2 billion worth to be shipped by 2015. But Indian garment makers and cloth manufacturers have become alarmed, arguing that the Bangladeshi facility gives Chinese textile manufacturers free entry into the Indian market.[18] The real issues are that Bangladesh's wage structure is lower, its labor market more flexible, and India is facing emerging infrastructure bottlenecks. Although such initiatives offer great promise of closer economic relations within South Asia, India will probably only be so generous in this area since it still has a large population—mostly women—dependent on the industry and since the garment industry is an important political lobby.

In addition to its modest aid program of Rs 1.5 billion to Nepal (about $30 million), New Delhi has also provided lines of credit of $350 million for an agreed program of construction of roads, railways, and power grids between India and Nepal.[19] As with Pakistan, however, India's long-term aid and trade relationship with Nepal is made more difficult by mutual suspicion and charges of Indian "interference," as explored in chapter 2. But unlike the case of Pakistan, it would pay India to persist with Nepal in the most sensitive way it can.

Sri Lanka is probably the South Asian country with which India has best prospects. Since 2000, India and Sri Lanka have had a free-trade agreement. Trade has boomed since the end of the civil war, jumping to $5.1 billion in 2011–12.[20] The trade asymmetry between the two in India's favor has been dealt with by a series of special conditions that favor Sri Lanka, known as the special and differential treatment. But notwithstanding, India imposed a series of restraints on sensitive areas, especially *vanaspati* (vegetable oil reconstituted as ghee), and trade is still heavily in India's favor. Given the basically sound relations between the two, the small flow of aid, at only Rs 1.3 billion (about $26 million), is surprising. As well as direct aid, however, India has allocated significant lines of credit to Sri Lanka amounting to over $1 billion for accessing Indian imports and constructing the Southern Railway.[21] Despite periodic hiccups in the relationship, for example in relation to the perception in electorally important Tamil Nadu that the rights of Tamils are being eroded by the Rajapaksa government as described in chapter 2, it would seem that there is much more New Delhi could do to foster relations with Colombo, even if it means taking a relatively small hit in its overall trade balance.

In short, there is considerable scope for India to be far more proactively involved with neighborhood countries other than Pakistan, particularly through generous application of aid and technical assistance, which is currently minimal, and more open trading regimes. Indeed, it is perplexing why India has not been more fully involved with its close neighbors in this way.

SOUTH ASIA AS A SPRINGBOARD TO LOOK EAST

As well as acting to improve its situation in South Asia, India also needs to find ways to achieve better outcomes in terms of the Look East strategy, which, as we observed in chapter 4, is not all it could be. One option that could have the result both of improving India's South Asian positioning and also giving it a better base in South Asia from which to achieve greater economic and soft-power influence in Southeast Asia is to leverage from its existing Look East strategy to achieve far better economic integration between South Asia and Southeast/East Asia. Such integration could be developed through better land transport links, both within and between South Asia and East/Southeast Asia. These links could include the development of investment corridors, especially from Southeast Asia and southern China, through Bangladesh, and on into India, or through India's northeastern states and into the rest of India.

Already proposals are being developed along these lines, but they suffer because of lack of coordination and different visions of what might be involved.

India has tended to act with suspicion concerning developments that involve crossing Bangladesh into Southeast Asia. As discussed in chapter 3, India is also wary of FDI from China, both in general and in terms of so-called sensitive industries and areas. Such sensitive areas include India's Northeast. In terms of development of land transport links, India favors development of the route through its northeastern states over a route that would first pass through Bangladesh before entering Southeast Asia and China. India is pursuing the northeastern route through the Trilateral Highway Agreement (India, Burma, and Thailand) and a component of the Trans Asian Railway (a component of which also runs through Bangladesh). As Laldinkima Sailo argues, Indian reluctance to develop the Northeast has now given way to a strategy of development of the region as an integral part of the Look East strategy. India sees the transport links as integral to development in the Northeast.[22] Panchali Saikia points out, however, that the route covers difficult, mountainous terrain beset by separatist and guerrilla operations both in India and Burma. It also raises concerns around increased drug and weapons smuggling.[23]

On its part, Bangladesh favors developing land routes directly into China and Southeast Asia to leverage its growing economic relationship with China independently of any links that might originate in India. Bangladesh and China have reportedly agreed to develop road and rail connections between Kunming and Chittagong and to build a deep-water port at Sonadia (near Cox's Bazaar) to connect with this route.[24]

Although any route from India to East and Southeast Asia passing through Bangladesh would not necessarily preclude the northeastern India route, the benefits of a major link through Bangladesh for a more open and economically integrated South Asia should not be ignored and should be fully supported by India along with a northeastern Indian route. Recently both sides have shown signs of being more favorably inclined to such an arrangement. India is now looking to transport food into its Northeast via Bangladesh's Ashuganj port (a river port in Chittagong District), which it is seeking to develop through a line of credit, rather than the current arduous route through the Chicken's Neck. India is also seeking to modernize its major customs posts on the land border with Bangladesh in order to increase the flow of trade—a necessary precondition for any viable land route into Southeast Asia via Bangladesh. Both sides are moving to allow trucks to move directly from destination to destination without having first to unload.[25]

Given Bangladesh's potential as a center for labor-intensive manufacturing, the development of land links through it into India could be associated with an investment corridor, developed jointly by India, Bangladesh, Southeast Asian countries, and other investors such as China and Japan. Nepal and Bhutan, two land-locked countries, could also be linked with this route or perhaps with the route through India's Northeast. Such a development would give a boost to India's FTA with ASEAN and help better integrate Bangladesh into South Asia. Bangladesh also seems willing to foster such connections. According to the *Daily Star*, "Bangladesh and China agreed [recently] to actively participate in and promote Bangladesh, China, India and Myanmar (BCIM) regional economic cooperation."[26]

Of course, the development of this kind of linkage does not come without problems and risks. All such developments bring greater spread of crime, especially smuggling of illicit drugs, weapons, and people, and the spread of terrorism and diseases such as HIV/AIDS. Mitigation of these problems would imply both better governance in India (for example, more effective and honest border controls) and also a better regime of law-enforcement cooperation throughout the affected countries. On the latter, there is as yet no effective system of mutual legal assistance treaties (MLATs) within SAARC or between SAARC countries and Southeast Asia. India and Thailand have only just signed an MLAT after two decades of negotiations. Given the way two-way criminality is spreading from India into Southeast Asia and vice versa, this situation needs urgent attention.[27] These potential problems would need to be addressed by the introduction of more practical models of regionalism than the soft variety so far favored by India.

India has also assisted with the development of two subregional initiatives linking South Asian and Southeast Asian countries. The Bay of Bengal Initiative for Multi-Sectoral Technical and Economic Cooperation (BIMSTEC) is a grouping of India, Thailand, Bangladesh, Burma, and Sri Lanka, and the Mekong-Ganga Group (MGG) links India with the Mekong Countries (China, Laos, Vietnam, Thailand, and Burma). These groupings have, on the whole, not been very effective.[28] But it is interesting that, with the exception of Sri Lanka in the case of BIMSTEC, they are broadly coterminous with the countries to be linked through the new Asian land routes. It seems that there would be considerable scope to build on this fortuitous circumstance to improve the regional links between South and Southeast Asia, especially since "connectivity" is one of the three "C" goals of the Greater Mekong Sub-Region group—the other two being improved "competition" and enhanced "community." According to the Greater Mekong Sub-Region model, the main strategic thrust is to develop a sense of community alongside the development of infrastructure projects so that the infrastructure projects actually have some commitment and do not languish.[29] There is no reason why this successful model could not be adopted both by BIMSTEC and the MGG.

Another regional association providing a potential bridge between South Asia and Southeast Asia / Southern China is the Bangladesh-China-India-Myanmar Forum for Regional Cooperation (BCIM), which first met in 2002. If anything, the BCIM has more robust possibilities than BIMSTEC, since it includes the regional giant, China. Yet like BIMSTEC, as far as New Delhi is concerned, it has essentially been on a back burner while India, with its minimalist diplomatic capability, attempts to swim in bigger ponds, including those consisting of the Asia-Pacific and globally focused forums. According to Shastri Ramachandran, forums such as the BCIM and BIMSTEC are the key to a more successful Look East policy.[30] They should receive far more attention and resources from India than they now do.

INDIA IN EAST ASIA

Just as India needs a step-by-step policy toward South Asian integration, so too does its Look East policy need first to engage in a genuine Look East strategy with India's "near east," including its own northeastern states, Bangladesh, Myanmar, and the links to and through those places and on into Southeast Asia and Southern China. In the words of the former Indian senior diplomat, Ambassador Eric Gonsalves, to truly look east "requires India to: one, mesh with our neighbours to the East in the most advantageous way; two: address with care and attention—when opportunity is knocking—relations with our other South Asian neighbours; three, build up the Northeast as a much-needed economic bulwark for buttressing the security posture which, at present, relies on scorched earth policies on the border; four: work on the connectivity that underlies all these processes."[31]

This is no simple task. Four developments will be imperative: a better working relationship with Bangladesh, the development of land transport routes and investment corridors out of India and on into Southeast Asia and China, working toward a situation in which both India and China are able to set aside border and other competition sufficiently to allow for open integration of this vital part of the world, and, finally, fostering of a collective regime capable of meeting the transnational challenges that invariably accompany more open borders and increased trade. The last of these will involve a more effective governance regime in India itself, as well as more resolute efforts to develop a collective regime through regional, subregional, and bilateral links.

In some ways, the prospects for greater integration across this part of Asia are good. Burma, hitherto a point of intense competition between India and China, is both proceeding to partially democratize and also seeking a more balanced relationship between China and India as part of that process. Bangladesh is somewhat problematic, as noted in chapter 2. Just as it did with Burma, India is increasingly competing with China in Bangladesh to provide aid and investment. But also as discussed above, India has not so far applied the level of resources to Bangladesh that it could, given the size of its economy. In this process, BIMSTEC, but particularly the BCIM, which includes China, could prove important forums for developing better common means of addressing the transnational problems that always surround such opening up of borders and increases in trade.

Further afield in Asia, India's strategy of seeking to participate fully in the Asia-Pacific regional organizations such as the ARF, ASEM, the EAS, and eventually APEC is a positive one. India as a future leading power offers significant leavening of the Asian power equation and brings to the fore the possibility of a genuine multilateral balance emerging in Asia. As a massive and basically successful democracy, India has soft-power potential in Southeast and East Asia that could be a vital component in the development of the region and in providing a soft-power balance to China's growing hard-power and financial soft-power influence. In a situation in which the West is in apparent comparative decline, the rise of a powerful, vigorous democracy such as India could provide an important human rights voice in "the Asian Century."

But as with the construction of a successful strategy in South Asia, India's strategy in East and Southeast Asia is dependent on substantial efforts to reform governance at home. As matters now stand, India's reputation in Asia is somewhat tarnished by what is seen as its poor governance record, lack of sustained and sustainable economic progress, the difficulty of working with it on either a government-to-government or business-to-business basis, restraints on capital flows, and excessive red tape. A better-functioning India at home would obviously be a better-functioning India abroad. A stronger economy would be more competitive in the capital and investment market. It would be an economy better able to compete with China in supporting the economies of smaller subregional and regional countries. It would be more able to sustain the development of India's soft power, which has enormous global potential.

Rather than seeking a chimerical strategic role in the Asia-Pacific (a point further discussed below), India should be looking to pluck the low hanging soft-power fruit available to it in Asia. To begin, this could involve the rapid upgrade of its pitifully inadequate diplomatic service, which, as mentioned in chapter 4, numbers only about six hundred full-fledged diplomats. This compares very poorly with the foreign services of other leading Asian powers such as China. According to Oliver Stuenkel: "In a recent op-ed in the *Times of India*, [international affairs analyst] Kanti Bajpai . . . decried the situation. . . . If the Indian foreign ministry continues to grow at the current pace, it will have 1200 diplomats by 2040—yet by this time, China will have 10,000 diplomats to represent it around the world. The number of U.S. diplomats already far exceeds 10,000 today."[32]

Moreover, again as indicated in chapter 4, there is no actual reflection of India's supposed Look East orientation in the disposition of its resources. New diplomats, preferably with Asian language skills, urgently need to be located in embassies from Beijing to Jakarta. Trade and cultural representation also need to be upgraded. But none of this will achieve much if the soft power "front end" is not connected to a better-functioning home bureaucracy and a less restricted and corrupted economy.

Another aspect of India's Look East policy that needs careful attention is its role vis-à-vis China. As described above, some countries are prepared to see India as a hedge against China's rise, just as India is hedging in its relationship with the United States. Japan under Prime Minister Abe's first government fell into that category. Vietnam is also inclined in that direction. Thailand and Singapore see India in that light, although to a lesser degree. Australia is more wary, depending as it does on China for its trade and economic well-being.

This presentation of India as a hedge against China is not necessarily the best way to pursue the Look East policy, however. Look East, in its fundamentals, involves greater economic and regional integration. This is essentially a process of building rather than dividing and separating. That is not to say strategic issues will not be in play, but rather that they should be kept separate from any Look East strategy and the organizational base upon which it depends, whether it be BIMSTEC, the ARF, the EAS, or, when India joins, APEC.

The reason for this will become more apparent when we discuss India's role in a future Asian security architecture. Such an architecture will not necessarily be able to rely on traditional balance-of-power arrangements or even concert-of-power arrangements. If it is to be successful, it will also depend on the maintenance of a forward momentum with the current building blocks approach, the ever-increasing interdependence of the nations of the region, and the support these constructs can provide to the subtle, difficult task of power balancing.

INDIA AND INDIAN OCEAN REGIONALISM

Just as India's concerns about Pakistan and China have colored its approach to subregional formations such as SAARC and BIMSTEC, so too have they affected the way India has approached regionalism in broader constructs such as some of those of the IOR. Unlike the smaller subregional organizations in and around South Asia, however, the quality of the association within the IOR, the Indian Ocean Rim Association (IORA), has far-reaching international strategic implications.

For all its concrete activities in support of nonconventional security objectives in the IOR, such as assistance in the 2004 tsunami and bilateral pursuit of pirates,

India has on the whole chosen not to join international attempts to build security and confidence in the region. It has declined to join the anti–nuclear smuggling Proliferation Security Initiative (PSI). It is not a member of Combined Task Force 151 (CTF-151—the antipiracy initiative). It has also continually blocked the emergence of a viable IOR regional association.

There are two interpretations of this Indian preference. First, as we discussed in chapter 4, dominant regional powers will usually seek to downplay multilateral forums and collective security, especially within their own region.

A second, related interpretation is that India wishes to keep Pakistan, and increasingly China, out of such forums. In the case of SAARC, it cannot do this in respect to Pakistan, since SAARC exists *qua* its South Asian coverage. But India can define the ground rules of SAARC to ensure it remains an essentially weak regional organization. We argued above that there is probably not much that can be done about this in relation to SAARC until India-Pakistan relations improve. In the case of the IORA, however, the situation is different. The IOR is less well-formed as a region. But it is also special because of its role as "the great connector" for world trade, especially the trade of vital energy flows into East Asia. India has not only been able to keep Pakistan out of the IORA, but also to ensure that the organization is a weak one.

In view of these concerns to keep Pakistan out, India effectively scuttled the attempt by Australia's foreign minister Gareth Evans in 1995 to set up a comprehensive security mechanism in the IOR. New Delhi did this largely because it saw the 1995 Perth initiative by Evans as cutting across the so-called Mauritius Process initiated by New Delhi a few months earlier. The Mauritius Process was a narrowly based, first-track mechanism designed to keep Pakistan and like-minded countries such as China out. It was also intended to impose the kind of soft regionalism favored by India.[33] At the time, the Perth process (known as the International Forum on the Indian Ocean Region—IFIOR) was criticized by India because it dealt with security issues—albeit nonconventional ones.[34]

The successor organization of the Mauritius Process, what is now known as the IORA, first met in 1997 and has effectively been kept on a drip feed since. In the words of then Indian minister of state for external affairs Shashi Tharoor, "the [IORA] organization is lean to the point of emaciation, with just half a dozen staff (including the gardener!) in its Mauritius secretariat."[35] Although China is now a dialogue partner, it has also been kept out of the organization proper. Even the United States has only just been admitted as a dialogue partner. Iran had reportedly hitherto kept it out, but India recently prevailed on Tehran to reverse this position.[36] When Pakistan requested to join in 2005 and again in 2007, these requests were resisted on the grounds that Pakistan had not then accorded most-favored-nation (MFN) status to India.[37] With a newly elected government in

Pakistan, there are now renewed hopes that Pakistan's previous announcement it would accord MFN status to India can be honored, which could go some way to opening the door to Pakistan's entry to the IORA.

India also established the Indian Ocean Naval Symposium (IONS), which first met in 2008. The organization takes a low-key approach to maritime security, focusing on open discussion in working groups and less controversial aspects of maritime security, especially nonconventional security such as piracy. Meetings take place biannually and are hosted by the forthcoming chair. The IONS does not include non–Indian Ocean powers. Although it is a useful confidence-building and to a lesser extent information-sharing forum, it does not yet provide a true problem-solving capability. Its deliberations have not so far blossomed into decisive joint action on any of the difficult security issues confronting the IOR, and its discussions are restricted to nonconventional security threats, which means it is unable directly to address the pressing security dilemma developing in the Indian Ocean between India and China explored in chapter 4. (However, by addressing nonconventional security issues, it could have the indirect effect of partially alleviating China's concerns about the security of its SLOCs.)

India also established the Milan naval exercise, which it conducts biannually with South Asian nations (but not Pakistan to date) and Southeast Asian nations, usually in the northeastern Indian Ocean. Although called an exercise, Milan is essentially a get-together of various navies in order to promote goodwill and confidence.

And finally, as we have seen, India sponsored a subregional grouping focusing on the northeastern quadrant of the Indian Ocean, BIMSTEC. The purpose of BIMSTEC is economic rather than strategic, and Indonesia is a notable omission given its key location on the Strait of Malacca.

India's response to the need of confidence-building measures and multilateral institutions in the IOR leads us to conclude, along with Mohan, that "Delhi seems far more comfortable in multilateral military institutions set up under its leadership rather than those where the agenda and direction are set by the others."[38]

If India is to achieve greater subregional harmony and all that goes with it, this attitude deserves further consideration in New Delhi. In particular, India needs to explore with China its perceived security needs in the Indian Ocean region and how they might be met. Nothing would be lost thereby, and China could acquire a sense of being part of a collective security effort. That could, in turn, help to reverse the developing security dilemma in the IOR, according to which China feels that its flows of vital oil and gas could be threatened by India or by India and the United States in combination. China would consequently be less inclined to develop its security interests throughout the region—interests that could one day be called in to support protection of its SLOCs. The problem is that such behavior on the part of China creates its own insecurity in India. As discussed in chapter 4, India feels increasingly surrounded in what it believes to be its IOR and South Asian backyards.

The other element in India's approach to regionalism as it applies to the IOR touches upon its general approach to security in the IOR, again as described in chapter 4. According to this approach, the IOR is seen as a backyard in which India should strive for sea denial, even sea control in some areas. That is understandable given India's history of invasion from the sea and heavy dependence on SLOCs, especially for essential energy requirements. But the strategy itself of seeking sea denial, sea control, and strategic dominance crowds out the prospect of collective security for the IOR.

In terms of grand strategy, however, seeking to dominate the IOR and determine the nature of any collective regimes may cut across the goal of achieving inclusive growth. As we saw, inclusive growth and its concomitants—a receptive international environment for growth and a consequent policy of not seeking to rock the strategic boat—are already part of India's core strategy.

Clearly, India would not accept the risk of relying solely on collective security in the IOR. But there may be strategies New Delhi could adopt that would enable India to hedge in terms of maintaining sufficient strategic and military capability, while also allowing for further positive developments in fostering collective security. Just as both Washington and New Delhi see the Indo-US relationship as a hedge against a difficult rise of China, so too could India's Indian Ocean interests be developed in the same way.

Nothing would be lost, for example, in accepting a more forward role for the outside powers in the IORA or allowing the organization gradually to develop beyond soft regionalism. With a focus on economic development and maintaining security against nontraditional threats such as piracy, smuggling, climate change, illegal migration, and transnational crime, there would be logic in including not only littoral states, but also all major users of the ocean. Such an approach would ipso facto involve both Pakistan and China. But given the nature of the organizations concerned and their focus on nonconventional security, it would not give them carte blanche to develop their strategic assets in the region or gang up on India. Nor would it necessarily prevent the Indian hedge of developing its naval assets—although, as we have noted above, such an approach does to an extent complicate the process of achieving better collective security.

The IONS could also be similarly configured to accept extraregional Indian Ocean users such as China and the United States. It could also be progressed from a mere discussion forum to an organization that actually plans joint activities to manage and improve the maritime space in the IOR, including in areas such as search-and-rescue coordination, disaster relief, and antipiracy and antismuggling activities.

After all, China has accepted an invitation to participate in 2014 in Exercise RIMPAC, which takes place biennially off Hawaii. There is no reason why China should not be invited to participate in the Milan multilateral exercise. The argument that it is not an Indian Ocean power will not wash: India, which is not a Pacific power, participated in the 2012 Exercise RIMPAC.

Were India to put out feelers toward an expanded and more effective collective-security mechanism, it is possible that the security dilemma building in the Indian Ocean might be arrested. If not, it is likely further to gain momentum, consuming more and more resources and eventually jeopardizing the inclusive-growth strategy.

INDIA, CHINA, AND THE FUTURE OF ASIAN SECURITY ARCHITECTURE

In the early part of the twenty-first century, the Sino-US relationship will be the most important bilateral relationship in terms of driving the security agenda and dictating the security architecture in Asia. This relationship will be the key to determining the nature of China's rise and the type of power it will become. That will, in turn, dictate both the nature of Asian security and the character of other bilateral relationships such as the one between India and China. That is not to say Sino-Indian relations do not have their own history and momentum, but rather that should China's rise be essentially peaceful and stable, the Sino-Indian relationship would have far better prospects of itself being peaceful and stable. Nor is it to argue that one day the Sino-Indian relationship might not be the most important in Asia. However, that time is still some way off.

The US role in East and Southeast Asia has hitherto been one of offshore balancing. The system according to which this has occurred has been variously labeled the "hub and spokes" model or the "San Francisco system." Either way, what is involved is an emphasis on *bilateral* rather than multilateral relationships between the United States and its friends and allies in Asia. Any form of multilateral balance has mostly been avoided, lest it take on the character of an attempt to contain China. And containment of China is generally agreed to be a bad thing, lest the United States and its friends and allies make of China that which they fear most—an out-and-out enemy—which nobody would want, at least not until it is more evident what kind of power China will be. This form of offshore balancing is of necessity a subtle exercise—one that could quickly slide into a process of containment.

Equally, as the late Coral Bell pointed out about the Cold War, power balances are also capable in the right hands of evolving into a "concert of powers." Indeed, Bell characterized the long concert of nineteenth-century Europe as being an evolution of British offshore balancing within Europe, so there is both a model and precedent, at least according to her.[39] White also advocated a concert of powers for Asia as a possible means of peacefully inducting a rising China. Both Bell and White assert India has a role in an Asian concert, along with China, the United States, Russia, and Japan.[40]

Under a concert of powers, a small group of countries (say, about four or five) effectively acts like a club to maintain the core needs for peace and stability in the region within which it operates. There are no written rules to this club, but should any one power seek to become hegemonic or challenge the status quo, it would know that the others would quickly band together against it and make its life uncomfortable. A concert of powers therefore usually represents an *incipient* power balance rather than a balance *in being*.

Emphasis on balance of power as a driving force of concert-of-powers theory would tend to the view that the concept is fundamentally a neorealist one. Following Kenneth Waltz, neorealists argue that power balancing will likely reestablish a rough status quo to offset the rise of a significant power like China. It is this *potential* that gives rise to the possibility of an emerging concert.[41] Although admitting the possibility of miscalculation, neorealists assert that power balancing tends to maintain peace, since the costs of war for any side in a balanced situation are too high. The neorealist roots of concert-of-power theory lie in the fact that the theory holds that the powers in the concert need to be approximately equal in order to balance each other's presence and that they constitute an incipient balance capable of countering any single power that seeks to overthrow what is understood to be the order underlying the concert.

Given the view that a concert of powers is an incipient power balance, it follows that should any two or more powers move too close within the concert, the concert would tend to slide into a conventional power balance or even containment. The concert of powers is thus inherently unstable and difficult to maintain, especially where one power continues to rise within the concert, as China is rising today. Moreover, adherents of the idea of a "Concert of Asia" maintain that there is a historical precedent in the successful concert of Europe, which achieved peace for a hundred years until the start of the First World War. They also maintain that this model is applicable to modern-day Asia.[42] Many scholars, however, take a different view. According to Acharya, "the [European] system worked well between 1815 and 1823, but experienced a steady decline thereafter."[43] Carsten Holbraad argues that the reality of the times interacted closely with the norms of the concert, if not actually driving them.[44]

Moreover, Asia's situation is different given the fact of a rapidly rising China. Nor do we today have the vast outlet of energy and acquisition afforded by the colonial grab that characterized nineteenth-century Europe. Concerts also tend to be inherently unstable unless underwritten by strong cultural and strategic understanding among their members, which is certainly not the case in contemporary Asia.[45] Any Concert of Asia that may emerge is therefore likely to be unstable. Any role for India in it will consequently also need to be played out in carefully maintained sets of circumstances. For example, if China were to continue to grow rapidly relative to India—a possibility explored more fully in chapter 4—then India may consequently be forced into a closer strategic relationship with the United States.

White argues that India would be a good candidate for a Concert of Asia because it will never be an ally of the United States. Rather, as a potential leading global power, it would prefer to remain equidistant between the other leading powers.[46] It is probably true that India will never be an "ally" of the United States in the formal sense of the word—that is, be signatory to an alliance. But this does not mean that in some circumstances India would not be driven toward a closer strategic relationship with the United States, such that its role in any concert could be jeopardized. How might this occur?

We have argued throughout this volume that strategic developments are hostage to regional and even local geostrategic factors as much as regional and local factors are hostage to global factors. Indeed, the relationships are ones of complexity—complexity that requires both regional analysis and global strategic understanding in order to describe.

In the context of India's rise as an Asian power, the above consideration plays out not just in terms of India's emerging role on the wider Asian stage, but also the processes involved in its reaching that stage in the first place as a genuine player. Thus its strategic relationships and its character and capability as a power will be determined as much by its domestic and neighborhood performance as by the way other powers such as China and the United States play their respective roles in the broader regional and global domains. Indeed, India's own actions and strategies will also determine whether it will be an essentially strong power or remain within the "weak-strong" paradigm that has dogged it for decades.[47]

This understanding of how India might strengthen its domestic domain and rise to power in its neighborhood and region becomes central to our understanding of India's possible role in an Asian concert—indeed of India's possible strategic and economic roles in Asia itself. As discussed in the previous chapters, an India that is unable to achieve governance and economic reform, that continues to be dogged by its neighborhood ills and dragged back into continental forms of security, that needs to contest Chinese and other "interference" in its neighborhood, and that gains its strength from its capacity to control shipping lanes of vital energy into China (possibly in collusion with the United States) will not be an India capable of a truly independent role in Asian security or an Asian concert.

An India, moreover, that continues to fall back economically in relation to China will feel deeply insecure, especially should China continue to probe it in respect of its vital interests. In regard to the latter, while China's behavior, once truly powerful, is still unknown, we also note that a China that remains highly insecure about flows of its vital energy supplies and other commodities across the Indian Ocean will be a China less disposed to rely on collective security and more disposed to take a realpolitik approach to security in general. This latter approach would also entail strategies to test India in its weakest points, for instance in its vulnerable Northeast, as a means of countering possible Indian testing of China's vulnerable energy SLOCs.

But of course, India and China are not the only factors in the Asian security equation. As discussed above, the Sino-US relationship will be the seminal one, at least in the earlier decades of the "Asian century." While the United States has been basically disposed to follow its subtle policy of offshore balancing in terms of bilateral interests, it does from time to time slide toward multilateralism. One such incident occurred during the abortive attempt under the influence of then Japanese prime minister Abe and then US vice president Cheney in 2007. What they tried to construct amounted to a power balance against China involving the United States, Japan, Australia, and India—the so-called quadrilateral. This was an attempt to induct India into the existing trilateral dialogue of the United States, Japan, and Australia.

This effort, however, illustrates the problem with an actual multilateral balance, as distinct from an incipient one. What happened was that China commenced to issue threats about the proposal, citing it as a direct strategic challenge. Beijing protested formally to the four powers, and the Xinhua News Agency asserted that "any grouping without China is ridiculous, irresponsible and impractical and marks formation of a small NATO to resist China."[48] Both Australia and India sought to distance themselves from the proposal, concluding that the time was not yet ripe for any balance in being against China.[49] Better to wait to assess whether there was still a reasonable prospect for a peaceful rise of China in Asia. The then Australian prime minister, Julia Gillard, announced during her 2011 visit to Beijing that Australia rejected the need to "contain" China.[50]

It is noteworthy from the above account of the abortive quadrilateral that it actually unfolded somewhat differently from the way concert-of-powers theory would suggest. Theory would have it that a non–status quo actor would be constrained in its behavior by fear of the formation of a balance in being as opposed to an incipient balance. While there has been little subsequent evidence that Beijing in any way constrained its normal behavior as a result of the episode, there is plenty of counterevidence that two of the proponents of the quadrilateral were forced by Beijing to constrain theirs, at least for a time. In fact, what transpired was as much about fear of derailing the relationship with China and China's peaceful rise as it was about constraining China through the threatened quadrilateral. Or was it the case that the quadrilateral was never intended to be actualized and that it was simply an example of skillful use of incipient power balancing? Given the main proponents—Abe and Cheney—this seems unlikely.

Since that time, the Barack Obama administration has unveiled its pivot to Asia, which would appear to involve a refocusing on Asia and a diminution of resources in the Middle East and Southwest Asia with the wind-down in Iraq and Afghanistan.

President Obama has been adamant that the pivot, which is now mostly referred to as a "rebalance," is not an attempt to balance or contain China. Beijing, however, has refused to believe these denials; indeed, according to some accounts, their very frequency makes China suspicious.[51] In terms of the effect of the pivot policy on the general disposition of Asian security, several developments have occurred. First, there is skepticism in Asia about the capacity of the United States successfully to pivot to Asia in the first place, given the ongoing exigencies in the Middle East, including the continuing nuclearization of Iran and the destabilizing civil war in Syria. Second, there is concern that, despite the US denials, the pivot is very much about containing China and that therefore America's allies will be forced eventually to choose between the two. This latter concern has certainly played out in relation to India's approach to the pivot. Although, as Muni points out, India is responsive to the pivot, believing it is a way of providing a continuing balance against China's rise, New Delhi does not wish the policy to be driven forward by Washington at the expense of India's traditional policy of strategic autonomy or for it to drive a wedge between India and China. New Delhi is also concerned that the policy may upset the relationships between China and Washington's allies and friends, thus upsetting the peace and stability so badly needed for India's development. So, according to India, the policy of pivot needs to maintain the tradition of subtle power balancing for it to be effective. But again, as pointed out by Muni, India finds itself between a rock and a hard place on the pivot. For India, the worst outcome would be a so-called G2 (Group of Two) involving China and the United States, which would severely limit India's options as a developing power. The pivot is preferable, yet tricky.[52] For India, a concert of powers would be the best outcome of all since it would maintain New Delhi's current policy of strategic autonomy. Yet for all the reasons mentioned above, the idea of a concert of powers, while aspirational, remains difficult and even doubtful. But India would have the best prospects of being a part of a concert of near equals if it is able to act to address its domestic, neighborhood, and regional ills, thus remaining strong enough to be an independent player in any concert than may evolve.

Given the uncertainties surrounding the concert idea, to what should India aspire and how should it act to bring it about? If India really wishes to maintain a policy of strategic autonomy (which would in turn assist its putative role in any Asian concert), it needs to do the following.

First, India should seek to garner genuine strength. This involves, first, being strong at home, which is a form of "target hardening" that would make it less pervious to the exigencies of the cross-border problems that currently reverberate throughout South Asia and that draw in outside powers such as China. Economic, bureaucratic, and governance reform would also make India a far more attractive partner to South, Southeast, and East Asian powers.

Second, India should take far more concerted action to create a more functional, better-integrated South Asia. This may initially involve a strategy of going around Pakistan in South Asia, but it also entails cooperative action elsewhere in South Asia to assist regional development and integration, including in ways that better integrate the region with East and Southeast Asia and assist the drawing in of capital from those comparatively capital-rich locations. To assist in these processes, India needs to abandon its insistence on soft forms of regionalism and seek to construct out of SAARC, BIMSTEC, and other subregional associations more active, problem-solving organizations capable of channeling investment resources and addressing cross-border restraints. This kind of regionalism would have far better prospects of providing a bridge for transport, cooperation, trade, and investment between India and its eastern partners—in other words, cater for a genuine Look East policy.

Third, India also needs to cultivate genuine, inclusive collective security in the IOR. As in South Asia, regionalism needs to be configured to solve real problems in practical ways instead of being designed to keep genuine multilateralism at bay. As for the Indian Ocean, genuine, practical regionalism that includes recognition of the Indian Ocean's role as the "great connector" for nonlittoral users, and not just as an "Indian lake," could go at least some way to mitigating the worrying security dilemma developing in the IOR. Equally, a more defensive strategy on the part of India in regard to its naval development and especially use of carrier battle groups, as briefly mooted in chapter 4, could support genuine collective security in the IOR, provide additional funding for the necessary reforms required for stability at home, and enable development of a defensive submarine capability and land-based air capability.

Finally, India should recognize that its strengths in Asia to its East are not strategic, except for its role in the IOR. Just as China is strategically disadvantaged by its location vis-à-vis India in the IOR, so is India strategically disadvantaged by its location vis-à-vis China in the Asia-Pacific. Raw attempts seemingly to balance China, for example in Vietnam, will simply not bear fruit. Sensitive policymakers in New Delhi are well aware of this. On entering the Pacific sphere, Indian naval forces not only lose their natural advantages in the IOR, but also unnecessarily adversely affect the strategic disposition and enhance the overall strategic competition with China. This is not to say that India should not Look East—far from it. It is, rather, to make the obvious point that India should play to its strategic and soft-power strengths according to their best disposition in the respective spheres in which they are operating.

Crucially, if the dispositions in the Asia-Pacific are fraught with risk—as we have argued that they are—a stronger, more stable, and more economically effective India would be a far better contributor to the current range of efforts to make of the Asia-Pacific an economically and politically interdependent region capable of absorbing China's peaceful rise and accommodating a range of powers such as India.

NOTES

1. Behuria et al., "Does India Have a Neighbourhood Policy?," 229–46.
2. Jones, "South Asia," 183–93, 191.
3. Behuria et al., "Does India Have a Neighbourhood Policy?," 238.
4. Sridharan, *International Relations Theory and South Asia*, 8.
5. Ahmed, "South Asia at the Crossroads," 335–45, 345.
6. Many would also argue, with some justification, that Pakistan and Bangladesh share important cultural and linguistic ties with India. While accepting this, we have not included them because of the fact that religious differences often appear to obstruct closer relationships and undermine cultural factors.
7. Ganguly, *Conflict Unending*, 1.
8. Ibid., 4–6.
9. For these concerns, see Prime Minister Singh's response to the Musharraf offer, as reported in Waldman, "India's Offer for Peace Talks on Kashmir Is Sweetened with Aid."
10. Dasgupta, "How Will India Respond to Civil War in Pakistan?"
11. South Asian Association for Regional Cooperation, "Areas of Cooperation."
12. Aktar and Arinto, *Digital Review of Asia Pacific 2009–10*, 122.
13. United Progressive Alliance, *Report to the People: 2004–2008*, 51.
14. United States Government, Congressional Research Service, *China's Foreign Aid Activities in Africa, Latin America and Southeast Asia*. We need to note, however, that China's official figure is far lower, and it is difficult to quantify China's aid since it does not count its aid according to the Development Assistance Committee of the OECD rules.
15. Bagchi, "India Ready to Give More Aid but Pakistan Silent."
16. Exim Bank of India, *Exim Bank's Cooperative Lines of Credit*.
17. United Progressive Alliance, *Report to the People: 2004–2008*.
18. "Bangladesh Garment Exports to India Sees a Big Spurt."
19. Exim Bank of India, *Exim Bank's Cooperative Lines of Credit*.
20. "India, Sri Lanka Boost Trade, Investment Ties."
21. Exim Bank of India, *Exim Bank's Cooperative Lines of Credit*.

22. Sailo, "Northeast India–Southeast Asia Connectivity," passim.
23. Saikia, *Connecting South Asia.*
24. "China Ready to Work on Ctg-Kunming Road Link."
25. "Pragmatism over Politics."
26. Rashid, "36th Anniversary of Sino-Bangladesh Ties."
27. See Gordon, "Regionalism and Cross-Border Cooperation against Crime and Terrorism in the Asia-Pacific Region," 75–102.
28. Saikia, *Connecting South Asia.*
29. Ibid.
30. Ramachandran, "India Has a 'Look East' Policy Too."
31. Quoted in ibid.
32. Stuenkel, "How Many Diplomats Does an Emerging Power Need?"
33. See Michael, *India's Foreign Policy and Regional Multilateralism*, 113–44.
34. In 1994–95, the author was commissioned to provide academic research for the IFIOR process. He subsequently published this research as a book on the IOR. See Gordon, *Security and Security Building in the Indian Ocean Region.* For the description of the IFIOR process, see pages 202–3. The Indian criticism took the form of interventions within the IFIOR conference itself, which was attended by the author.
35. Quoted in Michael, *India's Foreign Policy and Regional Multilateralism*, 141.
36. Luke, "IOR-ARC Expands."
37. At least that was the excuse provided to the author by a senior member of the Indian Ministry of External Affairs in a discussion in 2012.
38. Mohan, "From Isolation to Partnership," 11.
39. Bell, "Kissinger in Retrospect," 207.
40. Bell, *Living with Giants*, 35–36, and White, *Power Shift*, 31.
41. Waltz, "Anarchic Orders and Balances of Power," 98–130.
42. White, *Power Shift*, passim, and Bell, *Living with Giants*, passim.
43. Acharya, "A Concert of Asia?," 85.
44. Holbraad, *The Concert of Europe*, 13.
45. Gordon, "The Quest for a Concert of Powers in Asia,"35–55.
46. White, *Power Shift*, 31.
47. For a description of India as a "weak-strong" state, see Gordon, "Domestic Foundations of India's Security Policy," 11–16.
48. Xinhua, August 24, 2007, quoted in D. S. Rajan, Intellibriefs.
49. Brewster, "The Australia-India Security Declaration," 3.
50. "Julia Gillard Rejects Need to Contain China."
51. Liu, "China Sees Threat in US Pivot to Asia."
52. Muni, "Obama Administration's Pivot to Asia and India's Role," passim.

Conclusion

India aspires to be a global power, and it certainly has that capability over the longer term. But policymakers in New Delhi will have to take a different tack to allow India to continue to seek an independent role among nations, as befits a potential leading global power.

India's primary challenges lie in the domestic sphere of activity. They relate to issues of governance and particularly the need to deal with the pressing problem of corruption, which is undermining India's core strategy of inclusive growth. India's poor state of governance also leaves it vulnerable to cross-border problems within its difficult South Asian milieu. To address these domestic-level issues, India needs to reinforce the virtuous circle that is inherent in its liberal and democratic structures and traditions.

To accomplish this, India should ensure that the mechanisms of governance designed to support transparency, such as the CAG, the CVC, right to information commissioners, the National Human Rights Commission, and Lok Pal (once introduced) are well resourced, well supported, and removed from political interference. The judicial system is a key mechanism both for supporting security and for providing transparency. Government needs to press ahead forthrightly with the processes of judicial reform already engaged.

Other nongovernment entities also supporting transparency should be supported and protected. These include the media, the internet, and civil society groups. Nascent efforts to muzzle the internet should be nipped in the bud, if necessary using Union powers and legislative processes. Civil society groups should be supported in their role of providing social audit of public programs, ensuring transparency, and where possible providing key services such as health and education in circumstances in which governments are failing to fulfill these roles.

Addressing problems of policing in India will be vital to the overall effort to achieve better governance and security. This would involve a major push to improve the constabulary service, achieve better interjurisdictional coordination, better link police with the counterterrorism and intelligence mechanisms, and ensure that every police service has an independent process for considering complaints, appointing senior personnel, and managing transfers. Public security will also be enhanced by still better coordination of intelligence services, including through a new effort to ensure the NCTC comes to fruition. Greater resources should be applied to flagging efforts to achieve better data flows within and between police and intelligence agencies. A national counterterrorism plan should be negotiated between the different levels of government, and regular exercises should be undertaken to ensure that it works in actual situations.

Governments at all levels should further support processes of e-governance as a transparency measure by urgently fixing the current problems with the electronic voting system; assessing current direct cash-payment initiatives and, if successful, extending them to further subjects for payment and additional jurisdictions; progressing and generally supporting the UID program; ensuring that crucial records such as land ownership and MGNREGS data are posted electronically on a nationwide basis; posting crime data, including results of victimization surveys, publicly on the internet; and ensuring that records of cases brought and disposed of in each jurisdiction are available publicly on the internet.

Draconian legislative provisions such as UAPA and AFSPA, which have often been misused in ways that alienate minorities, should be modified. Policies of inclusive growth to strengthen and uplift minorities, especially Muslims, should be pursued vigorously.

India's economic development and the associated strategy of inclusive growth are also jeopardized by bottlenecks in infrastructure and the failure to press ahead with economic reform. Emerging environmental problems relating to atmospheric and local pollution, shortage of potable water, and inadequate urban infrastructure will also impede sustainable growth.

To address these problems, India should consider garnering higher levels of FDI from Asia, including from its perceived competitor, China, just as China used capital and technology from the West in its program of modernization. Improved infrastructure will not in itself be sufficient to improve the economy without further economic reform, including through reforms of agriculture and of the current restrictive labor laws and creating a freer environment for FDI and technology transfer.

India's cumbersome laws and negative investment and business environment also constrain its otherwise enormous potential to develop its soft power as a means of engaging with Asia and other global centers of economic power. All too often India is considered "too hard," either as an investment destination or as a partner in diplomacy. A significant effort to present a more welcoming front would almost instantaneously unlock the considerable goodwill toward India throughout the Asia-Pacific.

India's secondary challenge is to find ways to transform its South Asian neighborhood into a more benign and stable platform from which to emerge as a potential power in the wider regional and global domains. Essential to this project is the task of "target-hardening" the nation by effectively engaging in the domestic strategies mentioned in the previous paragraphs. This is because South Asia, almost more than any other subregion, suffers from enmeshed dissonance. India can, through its critical mass, help untangle this Gordian knot by improving its own governance and thus removing the points of vulnerability that provide a hook upon which cross-border dissonance and interference from outside the subregion can take hold.

Equally, however, it will be necessary for India to find ways effectively to go around Pakistan and invigorate South Asia and SAARC. A positively enmeshed South Asia would be one that would have greater capacity eventually to engage Pakistan. Meanwhile, it is critical for India to refrain from any action that might destabilize an already fragile Pakistan. New Delhi will also need to be sensitive to any genuine attempts at rapprochement that might emanate from Islamabad.

Critical to the task of rehabilitating South Asia will be the fostering of projects better to free up trade and physically link the economies of the subregion in terms of transport, telecommunications, and energy infrastructure. These activities in South Asia should be integral to a program to link South Asia with its Southeast and East Asian neighbors through enhanced infrastructure and creation of a cross-regional "epistemic" community linking the two subregions. Greater economic integration will also necessitate more effective subregional programs to address the kind of cross-border issues so often associated with economic integration, such as cross-border crime, the spread of illicit drugs, people smuggling and trafficking, fraud, cybercrime, and money laundering. SAARC and subregional platforms such as BIMSTEC should be strengthened to assist India's regional goals. To do this, India will need to dispense with its policy of soft regionalism toward these institutions and apply far more aid and technical assistance than the very limited assistance it has provided so far. Overall India's aid program is very small if its aid to Afghanistan and Bhutan is discounted, and these two countries are arguably special cases.

Neighborhood-focused programs might include the creation of shared electricity grids to harness the enormous hydroelectric potential of the Himalayas, provided it can be done without undue environmental stress; shared energy pipelines from the Gulf and Central Asia over Pakistan, provided the security situation can be eased between India and Pakistan; shared approaches to some of South Asia's most pressing environmental problems, such as urbanization, pollution, water scarcity, and "green energy" production and distribution; joint development of cross-border communication links, including telecommunications, roads, and railways; shared key educational institutions; shared approaches to dealing with cross-border problems, including drug smuggling, human trafficking, international fraud and cybercrime, terrorism, and arms smuggling; and shared programs to build on India's ICT strengths and the English-language skills of the region to make South Asia an important ICT hub.

In those parts of Asia to India's East, India should support its own Look East policy by progressing intra–South Asian transport and infrastructure links and ensuring that such links are in turn connected to Southeast Asia and East Asia. Subregional associations such as BIMSTEC, the MGG, and BCIM could provide useful platforms to assist this process, since they happen to be coterminous with the areas to be linked. Bangladesh and India's Northeast both offer excellent bridges for such connectivity, and Bangladesh in particular should be developed as an investment corridor into Southeast Asia. As part of this process, India should make a major effort to develop Bangladesh as a key relationship, including through much higher levels of aid and technical assistance. But activity on this scale would also involve acceptance of China's role as a provider of technology and capital and destination of some of the planned links.

In terms of India's performance in its wider region—especially the IOR and the Asia-Pacific—India needs first to deal with the troubling security dilemma developing in the IOR between itself and the United States on the one hand and China on the other. To do this it may need to dispense with long-held policies that treat the IOR as a strategic backyard. This would initially involve permitting a more constructive and inclusive regionalism to flourish. This kind of regionalism would be capable of assisting the IOR to address its manifest nonconventional security problems. It would include China and other external users such as the United States and Japan. Pakistan would be encouraged to participate, especially should it fulfill its undertaking to accord MFN status to India. The IORA should be upgraded from a soft regional organization to one capable of tackling nonconventional security problems such as piracy, transnational crime, oceanic research in relation to climate change, SLOC protection, search-and-rescue support, littoral economic development (especially among the poorest nations of the littoral), and the problems of small island states, including in relation to climate change.

Second, India could consider meeting its defense needs in the Indian Ocean without recourse to developing its anticipated fleet of three expensive carrier battle groups. Although two may already be locked in, the third could be set aside to provide additional resources for submarines and other defensive elements such as land-based aircraft. Any such decision could be reassuring to other littoral powers and nonlittoral users of the Indian Ocean and thus assist in the fostering of a more effective cooperative framework.

India should recognize that although it is strategically advantaged as the sole power of potential in the IOR and because of its position athwart East Asia's vital energy SLOCs, it is equally strategically disadvantaged in the Asia-Pacific. In that strategic domain it is not only still being outstripped by China, but also suffers the exact same strategic impediment as China in the Indian Ocean—that of distance. Moreover, China is much better placed to make tit-for-tat mischief in India's backyard than India is in China's. New Delhi should recognize this strategic disadvantage and not seek to act as a strategic player in the Asia-Pacific. Rather, it should rely on building upon its considerable soft-power potential—a potential that would be greatly enhanced should India engage in the type of reforms to its domestic polity suggested here.

Although India's relationship with the United States is increasingly of a strategic nature, it will likely continue to fall short of an "alliance." India does not wish to sacrifice its long-standing policy of strategic autonomy. Nor would it wish to provoke a difficult rise of China. In view of the sensitivity of the relationship with the US vis-à-vis China, India prefers to keep it in the form of a "hedge." Washington is also conscious of the need not to provoke China. Its intention is to support India through technology transfer in both civilian and military spheres. It would also like to improve India's military doctrine and organizational capacity so the two armed forces can operate jointly if ever the need should arise. These cautious strategies on both sides are sensible at least pending development of a better understanding of just how China might seek to rise as an Asian power.

Should India not be able to carry out the governance reforms suggested in this book and other economic reforms suggested elsewhere, it is likely China will continue to draw away economically and militarily. India would also remain relatively exposed in its South Asian setting to outside interference. While this would not necessarily mean that the Sino-Indian bilateral relationship would deteriorate, it would present strategic challenges for India and could cause it to move closer to the United States, thus threatening its policy of strategic autonomy and also its potential role as a swing state in Asia.

Ironically, in order fully to realize its potential and emerge as a truly global power, India has first to neutralize threats originating in South Asia by concentrating on the domestic and neighborhood arenas of activity. India will perhaps never be a Eurasian power in the sense that Russia and China are. But it could be a far more open and vigorous trading, financing, and soft-power nation and even eventually a true maritime nation. Its goal to be a global player would be realized not necessarily or solely in terms of military assets, but more in terms of other global skills such as owning and managing an extensive merchant marine; possessing vigorous, globally connected financial, commercial, industrial, research, and educational sectors; and developing as a trading and investment partner with the quality of rule of law that is needed to play a genuine global economic role.

Bibliography

Abe, Shinzo. "Asia's Democratic Security Diamond." Project Syndicate, London School of Business. December 27, 2012. Accessed June 23, 2013. www.project-syndicate.org/commentary/a-strategic-alliance-for-japan-and-india-by-shinzo-abe.

"An Abomination Called AFSPA." *The Hindu*, February 12, 2013. Accessed February 21, 2013. www.thehindu.com/opinion/lead/an-abomination-called-afspa/article4404804.ece.

Acharya, Amitav. "A Concert of Asia?" *Survival* 41, no. 3 (Autumn 1999).

"Afghanistan Favors India and Denigrates Pakistan." *New York Times*, October 4, 2011. Accessed October 4, 2012. www.nytimes.com/2011/10/05/world/asia/afghanistan-curries-favor-with-india-and-denigrates-pakistan.html.

"After Keeping India in Dark on Dam, China Promises No Harm." *Times of India*, February 5, 2013. Accessed February 5, 2013. http://timesofindia.indiatimes.com/world/china/After-keeping-India-in-dark-on-dam-China-promises-no-harm/articleshow/18342898.cms.

"After Owaisi, It's Togadia's Turn to Make Hate Speech." *The Hindu*, February 5, 2013. Accessed April 18. 2013. www.thehindu.com/news/national/after-owaisi-its-togadias-turn-to-make-hate-speech/article4383110.ece.

"Agricultural Distress Main Reason for Farmers' Suicide, Says Study." *The Hindu*, January 29, 2013. Accessed April 29, 2013. www.thehindu.com/news/national/tamil-nadu/agriculture-distress-main-reason-for-farmers-suicide-says-study/article4354419.ece.

Ahmed, Ali. "South Asia at the Crossroads." *South Asian Survey* 16, no. 2.

Ahmed, Ishaq. *India's Infrastructure Needs*. ISAS Brief no. 249. Singapore: National University of Singapore, 2012.

Ahmed, Tufail. *Enquiry and Analysis Series Report 816*. Middle East Media Research Institute. March 12, 2012. Accessed June 6, 2012. www.memri.org/report/en/0/0/0/0/0/840/6208.htm.

"Airspace Violation by Chinese Choppers." *Times of India*, August 30, 2009.

Aiyer, Yamini, and Salimah Saniji. "Transparency and Accountability in NREGA: A Case Study of Andhra Pradesh." Centre for Policy Research, New Delhi. Accountability Initiative: Engaging Accountability. Working paper series. Accessed

June 28, 2011. http://docs.google.com/viewer?a=v&q=cache:WRjJ6wT9usYJ:indiagovernance.gov.in/download.php?filename%3Dfiles/31_1244199489.pdf+results+of+social+audits+in+india+Andhra+Pradesh&hl=en&gl=us&pid=bl&srcid=ADGEESgIB3MaRjULiGcmn4ukP7Iar80DHKipJK7_SaovfnCfGuzLFGaHvqbVOCH5BS4sD4gNIAPx_kkjCNk94BEsgEMSmIr-hgV92oWILi1NK1ENPePOPzj5euErnpy49a2GQB872biT&sig=AHIEtbS_8EVqLVhLcNe9tw6NuPhQPyzhlQ.

Aktar, Shahid, and Patricia Arinto, eds. *Digital Review of Asia Pacific 2009–10*. New Delhi: Sage, 2009. Accessed May 22, 2013. http://books.google.com.au/books?id=R4u48rbqEe0C&pg=PA285&dq=digital+review+of+Asia+Pacific+2009-10&hl=en&sa=X&ei=zRGcUbOHM6msiAeD-4GoBw&ved=0CD0QuwUwAA#v=onepage&q=digital%20review%20of%20Asia%20Pacific%202009-10&f=false.

Amnesty International. Public statement, March 3, 2008. AI Index ASA 20/003/2008.

Andhra Pradesh Government, Andhra Pradesh Police. OCTOPUS unit charge sheet. Completed for the Hyderabad High Court concerning the IM accused in the twin blasts of 2007. Author's files.

Anonymous. "The LM2500 Demonstration." *Asia-Pacific Defence Forum*. Winter 1991–92.

"Another Shrine Charred in J and K." *Times of India*, July 16, 2012. Accessed July 16, 2012. http://timesofindia.indiatimes.com/india/Another-shrine-charred-in-JK-triggers-protest/articleshow/14974479.cms.

"Antrix Led to Revenue Loss of 1.9 Crore." *Business Standard*, March 28. 2011. Accessed March 28, 2011. /www.business-standard.com/india/news/%5Cantrix-led-to-revenue-lossrs-19-cr%5C/429093/.

"Antrix Showered Gold Coins on DOS, ISRO Officials." *Times of India*, February 16, 2011. Accessed March 28, 2011. http://articles.timesofindia.indiatimes.com/2011-02-16/india/28550997_1_gold-coins-antrix-devas-isro-chairman.

Ara, L. A., and M. M. Raheman. *The Competitiveness and Future Challenges of Bangladesh in International Trade*. www.wto.aoyama.ac.jp/file/090126laila_paper.pdf.

Arakotaram, Karan. "The Rise of the Kashmiriyat: People-Building in 20th Century Kashmir." *Columbia Undergraduate Journal of South Asian Studies* 1, no. 1 (Fall 2009). www.columbia. Accessed July 2, 2012. http://www.columbia.edu/cu/cujsas/Volume%20I/Karan%20Arakotaram%20-%20Kashmiriyat.pdf.

Arif, G. M. "Recruitment of Pakistani Workers in the Gulf." International Labour Office, Geneva. Working Paper no. 64 (July 2009), xi. Accessed June 12, 2012. www.ilo.org/wcmsp5/groups/public/---ed_norm/---declaration/documents/publication/wcm_041928.pdf.

"Armed Forces Building Deadly Drone Arsenal, Also Want Combat UAVs." *Times of India*, February 5, 2013. Accessed February 5, 2013. http://timesofindia.indiatimes.com/india/Armed-forces-building-deadly-drone-arsenal-also-want-combat-UAVs/articleshow/18341063.cms.

Arora, Vishal, and Vijay Sinha. "Bhutan Switches Focus to China." *Asia Times Online*, November 20, 2012. Accessed April 29, 2013. www.atimes.com/atimes/South_Asia/NK20Df01.html.

"Arrests Follow India Mob Attack." BBC News, February 24, 2008. Accessed January 19, 2010. http://news.bbc.co.uk/go/pr/fr/-/2/hi/south_asia/7261586.stm.

Asfar, Rita, "Population Movement in the Fluid, Fragile and Contentious Borderlands between Bangladesh and India." Paper presented at the Migration in South Asia Conference, University of Manchester, July 2008.

Asia/Pacific Group on Money Laundering (Financial Action Task Force). *APG Mutual Evaluation Report on India, March 2005*. Accessed February 3, 2009. www.apgml.org/documents/docs/8/India%20ME1%20-%20Final.pdf.

———. *Mutual Evaluation Report: Anti–Money Laundering and Combating the Financing of Terrorism: India*. Paris: FATF, 2010. www.fatf-gafi.org/media/fatf/documents/reports/mer/MER%20India%20full.pdf.

Asia-Pacific Human Rights Network. "Gujarat Riots Point to Need for Police Reform." http://www.hrw.org/reports/2002/india/India0402-03.htm and http://www.hrw.org/reports/2002/india/India0402-06.

Asian Human Rights Commission. "Stop Talking and Start Acting." December 22, 2010. Accessed April 19, 2013. AHRC-STM-267-2010. www.humanrights.asia/news/ahrc-news/AHRC-STM-267-2010/.

Association for Democratic Reform. "Reference Material." Accessed June 7, 2010. http://adrindia.org/criminalization-of-politics.html.

"ATS Arrests Man Who Arranged Fake Passports for D-Company." *Times of India*, January 21, 2010. Accessed January 22, 2010. http://timesofindia.indiatimes.com/city/lucknow/ATS-arrests-man-who-arranged-fake-passports-for-D-company/articleshow/5482437.cms.

Australian Government, Australian Crime Commission. *Illicit Drug Report 2007–08*. Accessed January 7, 2010. www.crimecommission.gov.au/publications/iddr/2007_08.htm.

Australian Government, Department of Defence. *Defence White Paper 2013*. www.defence.gov.au/whitepaper/.

Aviotech. *Indian Naval Acquisitions I: Defense Ship-Building in India, 2011*. Accessed February 7, 2012. www.aviotech.com/Aviotech_Thought_Leadership_Series_Naval_Shipbuilding_December_2011-2.pdf.

Babbage, Ross, and Sandy Gordon, eds. *India's Strategic Future: Regional State or Global Power?* London: Macmillan, 1992.

Bagchi, Indrani. "India, Japan Make Common Cause to Thwart China's Maritime Moves." *Times of India*, January 29, 2013. Accessed February 2, 2013. http://articles.timesofindia.indiatimes.com/2013-01-29/india/36615613_1_maritime-dialogue-india-and-japan-joint-naval-exercises.

———. "India Ready to Give More Aid but Pakistan Silent." *Times of India*, August 17, 2010. Accessed August 18, 2010. http://timesofindia.indiatimes.com/india/India-ready-to-give-more-aid-but-Pak-silent/articleshow/6322057.cms.

Bagchi, Suvojit. "Tension among Mumbai's Muslims." BBC News, July 17, 2006. Accessed December 1, 2007. www.bbc.co.uk/go/pr/fr/-/2/hi/South_Asia/5187100.stm.

Bagwati, Jagdish. *In Defense of Globalization*. New York: Council on Foreign Relations, Oxford University Press, 2004.

Bajpai, Kanti. "India's Strategic Culture." In *South Asia in 2020: Future Strategic Balances and Alliances*, edited by Michael R. Chambers. Carlisle, PA: Strategic Studies Institute, 2002.

"Bangladesh Anger over India Torture Video." BBC News, January 19, 2012. Accessed May 4, 2012. www.bbc.co.uk/news/world-asia-india-16625104.

"Bangladesh Garment Exports to India Sees a Big Spurt." *Business Line*, November 28, 2011. Accessed July 12, 2013. www.thehindubusinessline.com/industry-and-economy/article2668611.ece.

Basham, A. L. *The Wonder That Was India*. London: Fontana, 1971.

Basu, Kaushik. "India's Dilemmas: The Political Economy of Policymaking in a Globalised World." *Economic and Political Weekly* 48, no. 5 (February 2, 2008).

Beckley, Michael. "China and Pakistan: Fair-Weather Friends." *Yale Journal of International Affairs*, March 2012. Accessed October 5, 2012. http://yalejournal.org/wp-content/uploads/2012/04/Article-Michael-Beckley.pdf.

Behera, Laxman K. "DNA Exclusive: Slump Hits Defence Budget." *DNA*, September 3, 2012. Accessed November 13, 2012. http://www.dnaindia.com/india/report_dna-exclusive-slump-hits-defence-budget_1735970.

"Behind Reality Rush in Haryana, a Guilt-Edged Licence Raj." *The Hindu*, February 4, 2013. Accessed April 19, 2013. www.thehindu.com/news/national/behind-realty-rush-in-haryana-a-giltedged-licence-raj/article4375630.ece.

Behuria, Ashok K., Smriti S. Pattanaik, and Arvind Gupta. "Does India Have a Neighbourhood Policy?" *Strategic Analysis* 38, no. 2 (March 2012).

Bell, Coral. "Kissinger in Retrospect: The Diplomacy of Power-Concert." *International Affairs* 53, no. 2 (April 1977).

———. *Living with Giants: Finding Australia's Place in a More Complex World*. Canberra: Australian Strategic Policy Institute, 2005.

Bhagwati, Jagdish, and Arvind Panagariya. *Why Growth Matters: How Economic Growth in India Reduced Poverty and the Lessons for Other Developing Countries*. New York: Council on Foreign Relations, 2013.

Bharatiya Janata Party. *Towards Ram Rajya*. New Delhi: Friends Publishers, 1991.

Bipendra, N. C. "Retired Cops Push for Police Reforms." TwoCircles.net, September 20, 2012. Accessed January 2013. http://twocircles.net/2012sep26/retired_cops_push_police_reforms_launch_movement.html.

Bisht, Medha. "Diversion of the Yarlung Tsangpo: A Probability Analysis." IDSA Comment. Accessed September 26, 2012. www.idsa.in/idsacomments/DiversionofYarlungTsangpo_MBisht_111109.

Biswas, Soutik. "Do India's 'Fast Track' Courts Work?" BBC World Service, January 9, 2013. Accessed January 17, 2013. www.bbc.co.uk/news/world-asia-india-20944633.

Blagden, David W., and Jack S. Thompson. "Sea Power, Continental Power and Balancing Theory." *International Security* 36, no. 2 (Fall 2011).

Brantlinger, Patrick. *Rule of Darkness: British Literature and Imperialism, 1830–1914*. Ithaca, NY: Cornell University Press, 1988.

Brass, Paul R. *The Production of Hindu-Muslim Violence in Contemporary India*. Seattle, WA: University of Washington Press, 2003.

———. "Response to Ashutosh Varshney." Mail Archive. www.mail-archive.com/sapac@www.residentlounge.com/msg00137.html.

Brewster, David. "The Australia-India Security Declaration: The Quadrilateral Redux?" *Security Challenges* 6, no. 1 (Autumn 2010).

———. *India as an Asia-Pacific Power*. Oxford and London: Routledge, 2012.

British Council. *Pakistan: The Next Generation*. Islamabad: British Council, 2009.

"BSF Maps Vulnerable Spots along Border with Pak, Bangladesh." *Times of India*, September 5, 2012. Accessed April 24, 2013. http://articles.timesofindia.indiatimes.com/2012-09-05/india/33614963_1_border-outposts-india-bangladesh-border-bsf-officer.

Bullock, Christopher R. "China's Bluewater Ambitions: The Continental Realities of Chinese Naval Strategies." *Conflict and Security*, Summer/Fall 2002.

Bunscombe, Andrew, and Omar Wariach. "India Is Stealing the Water of Life, Says Pakistan." *The Independent*, March 26, 2009. Accessed December 3, 2009. file:///Users/sandy/Desktop/india-is-stealing-water-of-life-says-pakistan-1654291.html.

"Burning Gujarat." Gujaratplus.com. www.gujaratplus.com/riots_gal/. Accessed March 22, 2014.

Buzan, Barry. "Asia: A Geopolitical Reconfiguration." Accessed October 27, 2013. www.ifri.org/downloads/barrybuzanengpe22012.pdf.

Buzan, Barry, and Ole Waever. *Regions and Powers: The Structure of International Security*. Cambridge: Cambridge University Press, 2003.

"Cabinet to Decide on AFSPA's Future, Says Chidambarum." *OneIndia*, March 3, 2010. April 8, 2010. http://news.oneindia.in/2010/04/03/cabinetto-decide-on-afspas-future-says-chidambaram.html.

"CAG Vinod Rai: Government's 'Brazenness' in Decision-Making Is 'Appalling.'" *Indian Express*, November 7, 2012. Accessed April 18, 2013. www.indianexpress.com/news/cag-vinod-rai-governments-brazenness-in-decision-making-is-appalling/1028213.

Camilleri, Joseph A. *Regionalism in the New Asia-Pacific Order: The Political Economy of the Asia-Pacific Region*. Cheltenham, UK: Edward Elgar, 2003.

"Canberra, India 'Water Down' UN Resolution on Sri Lankan Human Rights." *The Australian*, March 23, 2013. Accessed April 28, 2013. www.theaustralian.com.au/news/world/canberra-india-water-down-un-resolution-on-sri-lankan-human-rights/story-e6frg6so-1226603760908.

Centre for Media Studies. *India Corruption Study: 2008*. New Delhi: Transparency International India, 2008.

"Centre Wades into Barelvi-Wahabi Duel?" *Times of India*, April 25, 2012. Accessed June 21, 2012. http://articles.timesofindia.indiatimes.com/2012-04-25/india/31398556_1_shrine-hazratbal-barelvi-sect.

"Chances of Two-Front War with Pakistan, China Remote; but China Threat Real." *Economic Times*, October 15, 2012. Accessed November 8, 2012. http://articles.economictimes.indiatimes.com/2012-10-15/news/34473120_1_china-and-pakistan-military-nexus-extensive-rail-network.

Chandra, Shailaja. "Striking at the Roots of Corruption." *The Hindu*, November 27, 2012. Accessed May 2, 2013. www.thehindu.com/opinion/lead/striking-at-the-root-of-corruption/article4137685.ece.

Chari, P. R. *National Counter Terrorism Centre for India: Understanding the Debate*. IPCS Brief no. 181, March 2012. Accessed January 14, 2013. www.ipcs.org/pdf_file/issue/IB181-Chari-NCTC.pdf.

Chaterjee, Debalina. "Kalashnikov Culture in Pakistan." *South Asia Defence and Strategic Review*, May 25, 2012. Accessed June 6, 2012. www.defstrat.com/exec/frmArticleDetails.aspx?DID=347.

Chaudhary, Krishman Bir. "India's Farming Crisis." *New Agriculturalist*, n.d. Accessed July 13, 2012. www.new-ag.info/en/view/point.php?a=45.

Chauhan, Neeraj. "Atif Showed Gujarat Riot Visuals to Provoke Youngsters." *Indian Express*, September 25, 2008. Accessed December 9, 2009. www.indianexpress.com/news/atif-showed-gujarat-riot-visuals-to-provoke/365539/.

Chellaney, Brahma. "Countering China's 'String of Pearls.'" *Washington Times*, May 6, 2013. Accessed June 21, 2013. www.washingtontimes.com/news/2013/may/6/countering-chinas-string-of-pearls/.

———. *Water: Asia's New Battleground*. Washington, DC: Georgetown University Press, 2011.

"Cheque Payments in Kalaignar Money Transfer Nailed Kanimozhi." *Oneindia News*, May 21, 2011. Accessed June 10, 2011. http://news.oneindia.in/2011/05/21/chequepayments-in-kalaignar-money-transfer-nailedkanimoz-aid0126.html.

Chidambaram, P. "A New Architecture for India's Security." Intelligence Bureau Centenary Endowment Lecture. *Outlook India*, December 23, 2009. Accessed January 22, 2010. www.outlookindia.com/article.aspx?263495.

"China Has No Plan for Indian Ocean Military Bases." *The Hindu*, September 4, 2012. Accessed October 30, 2012. www.thehindu.com/opinion/interview/article3855313.ece.

"China Ready to Work on Ctg-Kunming Road Link." *Financial Express*, October 19, 2012. Accessed June 28, 2013. www.thefinancialexpress-bd.com/index.php?ref=MjBfMTBfMTlfMTJfMV8yXzE0NzQ4MA.

"China's Murder Rate Decreases as Arrests Jump." *Shanghai Daily*, May 17, 2006. Accessed April 8, 2009. In *Wikipedia*, "List of Countries by Intentional Homicide Rate." http://en.wikipedia.org/wiki/list_of_countries_by_murder_rate#cite_ref-compcriminology_50_7.

"China's Tourism Plan Quells Brahmaputra Dam Fears." *The Hindu*, June 24, 2012. Accessed October 2, 2012. www.thehindu.com/news/international/article3566337.ece.

"Chinese Incursion 19 Km, but 750 Sq Km at Stake for India." *Times of India*, May 3, 2013. Accessed May 2, 2013. http://timesofindia.indiatimes.com/india/Chinese-incursion-19km-but-750-sq-km-at-stake-for-India/articleshow/19826487.cms.

"Chittagong Arms Were for ULFA." *The Hindu*, March 8, 2009. Accessed March 8, 2009. www.hindu.com/2009/03/08/stories/2009030855661200.htm.

Chockalingham, K. "Criminal Victimization in Four Major Cities in Southern India." *Forum on Crime and Society* 3, nos. 1 and 2 (December 2003).

Clarke, Ryan. *Crime-Terror Nexus in South Asia: States, Security and Non-State Actors*. Oxford: Routledge, 2011.

"Climate Goal Is Supported by China and India." *New York Times*, March 9, 2010. Accessed July 16, 2012. www.nytimes.com/2010/03/10/science/earth/10climate.html.

"CM Abdullah Calls on India to 'Show Some Spine' on China." *Times of India*, December 14, 2011.

Cohen, Stephen P. *Shooting for a Century: The India-Pakistan Conundrum*. Washington, DC: Brookings Institution Press, 2013.

Cohen, Stephen, and Sunil Dasgupta. *Arming without Aiming: India's Military Modernization*. Washington, DC: Brookings Institution Press, 2010.

Coll, Steve. *Ghost Wars: The Secret History of the CIA, Afghanistan, and bin Laden, from the Soviet Invasion to September 10, 2001*. New York: Penguin, 2004.

Comptroller and Auditor General, Government of India. Various reports. www.cag.gov.in/.

"Cops Claim Bangladeshi Student Body Guided Sabarmati Tunnel Diggers." *Times of India*, March 13, 2013. Accessed April 29, 2013. http://articles.timesofindia.indiatimes.com/2013-03-13/ahmedabad/37682020_1_crime-branch-sabarmati-central-jail-chhota-chakkar.

Cortright, David, and Amitabh Matoo. "Carrots and Cooperation: Incentives for Conflict Resolution in South Asia." In *The Price of Peace: Incentives and International Conflict Resolution*, edited by David Cortright. Lanham, MD, and Oxford: Rowman & Littlefield, 1997.

"CVC Seeks Clarity on Mandate to Probe Political Corruption." *The Hindu*, November 8, 2012. Accessed May 8, 2013. www.thehindu.com/news/national/cvc-seeks-clarity-on-mandate-to-probe-political-corruption/article4077599.ece.

Dalrymple, William. *The Last Mughal: The Fall of a Dynasty; Delhi, 1857*. London: Bloomsbury, 2006.

Darul Uloom Deoband website. Accessed June 6, 2012. www.darululoom-deoband.com/english/index.htm.

Dasgupta, Sunil. "How Will India Respond to Civil War in Pakistan?" *East Asia Forum*, 25 (February 2013). Accessed March 4, 2013. www.eastasiaforum.org/2013/02/25/how-will-india-respond-to-civil-war-in-pakistan/.

Datta, Surjit. "The Asian Transition and India's Emerging Strategy." In *Global Power Shifts and Strategic Transition in Asia*, edited by N. S. Sisodia and V. Krishnappa, 25–26. New Delhi: Academic Foundation, 2009.

"Decoding Koda." *Tehelka* 6, no. 46 (November 21, 2009). Accessed June 8, 2011. www.tehelka.com/story_main43.asp?filename=Bu211109decoding_koda.asp.

Deloitte. *Prospects for Global Defence Export Industry in Indian Defence Market.* 2010. http://defense-aerospace.com/dae/articles/communiques/DeloitteIndiaDefence.pdf.

DeSilva-Ranasinghe, Sergei."India's Critical National Challenges." Future Directions International, October 12, 2011. Accessed November 28, 2011. www.futuredirections.org.au/publications/indian-ocean/255-indias-critical-national-challenges.html.

———. "Potent and Capable: India's Transformational 21st Century Navy." Future Directions International. Accessed November 29, 2012. www.futuredirections.org.au/publications/south-west-asia/508-potent-and-capable-indias-transformational-21st-century-navy.html.

Destradi, Sandra. *Indian Foreign and Security Policy in South Asia: Regional Power Strategies.* London: Routledge, 2012.

"'DNA' Exclusive: Slump Hits Defence Budget." DNA (website), September 3, 2012. Accessed February 24, 2014. www.dnaindia.com/india/report_dna-exclusive-slump-hits-defence-budget_1735970.

"Doha Round Must Consolidate Progress Made So Far." *Times of India*, May 25, 2011. Accessed July 13, 2012. http://articles.timesofindia.indiatimes.com/2011-05-25/india-business/29581327_1_doha-round-development-dimension-wto-director-general.

Doherty, Ben. "Sinking into Deep Despair of a Drug Epidemic." *Sydney Morning Herald*, March 11, 2013.

Doniger, Wendy. *The Hindus: An Alternative History.* New Delhi: Penguin/Viking, 2009.

Doron, Assa, and Robin Jeffrey. *Cell Phone Nation.* New Delhi: Hachette, 2013.

"Double Strength of Judiciary: CJI." *Times of India*, February 28, 2013. Accessed May 8, 2013. http://articles.timesofindia.indiatimes.com/2013-02-28/india/37352638_1_chief-justices-law-ministry-cji.

D'Souza, Shantie Mariet, and Bibhu Prasad Routray. *Violence in Assam: Resource Wars, Illegal Migration or Government Deficit?* ISAS Brief no. 250 (September 6, 2012).

Dubey, Muchkund. "The World's Reaction to Gujarat." *The Hindu*, May 14, 2002. Accessed November 7, 2011. www.cscsarchive.org:8081/MediaArchive/liberty.nsf/(docid)/7249126E357648C1E5256BBF00290856.

"ED, CBI to Visit UK, Isle of Man for Alleged Money Trail." *Economic Times*, June 8, 2011. Accessed June 8, 2011. http://economictimes.indiatimes.com/news/politics/nation/2g-scam-ed-cbi-to-visit-uk-isle-of-man-for-alleged-money-trail/articleshow/8768795.cms.

Editorial, *Times of India*, January 18, 1991.

eLegalix. Allahabad High Court Judgment Information System. Accessed November 7, 2011. http://elegalix.allahabadhighcort.in/elegalix/DisplayAyodhyaBenchLandingPage.do.

Erickson, Andrew S. "China Homes In on Pacific Air Superiority." *Asia Times Online*. Accessed March 9, 2013. www.atimes.com/atimes/China/CHIN-01-060313.html.

———. "The Growth of China's Navy: Implications for Indian Ocean Security." *Strategic Analysis* 32, no. 4 (July 2008).

Exim Bank of India. *Exim Bank's Cooperative Lines of Credit*. Periodically updated. Accessed October 28, 2013. www.eximbankindia.in/sites/all/themes/exim/files/locstat.pdf.

Fawn, Rick, ed. *Globalising the Regional, Regionalising the Global*. Cambridge: Cambridge University Press, 2009.

Federation of American Scientists. "Pakistan's Nuclear Weapons: A Brief History of Pakistan's Nuclear Program." 2002. Accessed August 20, 2008. www.fas.org/nuke/guide/pakistan/nuke/index.html.

Financial Action Task Force. "FATF Statement re AML Strategic Deficiencies." June 21, 2013. Accessed July 9, 2013. www.knowyourcountry.com/pakistan1111.html.

"Five Years after 26/11, India Faces Intelligence Famine." *The Hindu*, February 27, 2013. Accessed May 9, 2013. www.thehindu.com/news/national/five-years-after-2611-india-faces-intelligence-famine/article4456325.ece.

"Fleeing Hindus Seek Shelter." *The Pioneer*, November 22, 2011. http://archive.dailypioneer.com/index.php?option=com_k2&view=item&id=50531:fleeing-hindus-seek-shelter&Itemid=549&tmpl=component&print=1

"Foreign Hand behind Balochistan Unrest, NA committee Told." *Dawn*, October 6, 2011. Accessed April 24, 2013. http://dawn.com/2011/10/06/foreign-hand-behind-balochistan-unrest-na-committee-told/.

Freedom House. *Freedom of the Press 2013*. Accessed May 8, 2013. www.freedomhouse.org/report/freedom-press/freedom-press-2013.

French, Patrick. "The Princely State of India." *Outlook Magazine*, January 17, 2011. Accessed June 14, 2011. www.outlookindia.com/article.aspx?269931.

"From Hawala Scam to Coalgate: Full Circle for Supreme Court." *The Hindu*, May 3, 2013. Accessed May 8, 2013. www.thehindu.com/opinion/op-ed/from-hawala-scam-to-coalgate-full-circle-for-supreme-court/article4677411.ece.

Fund for Peace. "Failed State Index 2010." Accessed June 24, 2010. www.fundforpeace.org/web/index.php?option=com_content&task=view&id=99&Itemid=140.

"Funds for Anti-Terror Infrastructure Not Fully Utilised, No Allocation Cuts." *The Hindu*, March 1, 2013. Accessed May 8, 2013. www.thehindu.com/news/national/funds-for-antiterror-infrastructure-not-fully-utilised-no-allocation-cuts/article4463561.ece.

Gandhirajan, C. K. *Organized Crime*. New Delhi: APH Publishing, 2004.

Ganguly, Sumit. *Conflict Unending: India-Pakistan Tensions since 1947*. New York: Columbia University Press, 2001.

Ganguly, Sumit, and S. Paul Kapur, eds. *Nuclear Proliferation in South Asia: Crisis Behaviour and the Bomb*. Oxford and New York: Routledge, 2009.

Ghosh, Palash. "What Are India and Pakistan Really Fighting About?" *International Business Times*, December 27, 2013. Accessed February 22, 2014. www.ibtimes.com/what-are-india-pakistan-really-fighting-about-1520856.

"Giant C-17 Aircraft to Add Strategic Muscle from June." *Times of India*, March 12, 2013. Accessed May 2, 2013. http://articles.timesofindia.indiatimes.com/2013-03-12/india/37649986_1_c-130js-c-130j-super-hercules-medium-lift-fleet.

Gordon, Sandy. "Domestic Foundations of India's Security Policy." In *India's Strategic Future*, ed. Babbage and Gordon.

———. "Globalisation and Economic Reform in India." *Australian Journal of International Affairs* 51, no. 1 (1997).

———. "India and China: Mega-Population, Mega-Corruption, Mega-Growth." *East Asia Forum*, May 11, 2011. Accessed January 10, 2013. www.eastasiaforum.org/2011/05/10/mega-population-mega-corruption-mega-growth/.

———. "India's Growing Problem with Illicit Drugs." *South Asia Masala*, February 18, 2010. Accessed March 6, 2013. http://asiapacific.anu.edu.au/blogs/southasiamasala/2010/02/18/indias-growing-problem-with-illicit-drugs/.

———. "India's Political Economy: Classic Strategies No Longer Apply." *East Asia Forum*, October 14, 2011. Accessed August 1, 2012. www.eastasiaforum.org/2011/10/14/india-s-political-economy-classic-strategies-no-longer-apply/.

———. *India's Rise as an Asia-Pacific Power: Rhetoric and Reality*. Australian Strategic Policy Institute (Canberra: ASPI, 2012).

———. *India's Rise to Power in the Twentieth Century and Beyond*. Houndmills, UK: Macmillan, 1995.

———. "Nation, Neighbourhood and Region: India's Emergence as an Asian Power." *South Asian Survey* 17, no. 2 (2010).

———. "The Quest for a Concert of Powers in Asia." *Security Challenges* 8, no. 1 (Summer 2012).

———. "Regionalism and Cross-Border Cooperation against Crime and Terrorism in the Asia-Pacific Region." *Security Challenges* 5, no. 4.

———. "Resources and Instability in South Asia." *Survival* 35, no. 2 (Summer 1993).

———. *Security and Security Building in the Indian Ocean Region*. Canberra: Strategic and Defence Studies Centre, Australian National University, 1996.

———. "Sino-Indian Relations and the Rise of China." In *Rising China*, ed. Huisken.

Goswami, Namrita. *Bangladeshi Illegal Migration into Assam: Issues and Concerns from the Field*. IDSA Issues Brief. Accessed January 21, 2010. www.idsa.in/issuebrief/BangladeshiIllegalMigrationintoAssam_ngoswami_140110.

Government of India. Census of India 2011. Accessed June 16, 2011. http://censusindia.gov.in/Census_Data_2001/India_at_glance/rural.aspx.

Government of India, Department of Commerce. "Direction of Trade Statistics for April–October 2011." Accessed February 9, 2012. www.commerce.nic.in/ftpa/rgnq.asp.

Government of India, Indian Planning Commission. *Approach Paper to the Twelfth Five Year Plan*. Accessed November 7, 2012. http://planningcommission.nic.in/plans/planrel/12appdrft/appraoch_12plan.pdf.

———. "Mid-Term Appraisal of the Tenth Five Year Plan (2002–2007)." Accessed December 18, 2009. http://planningcommission.gov.in/plans/mta/midterm/english-pdf/chapter-17.pdf.

Government of India, Ministry of Defence. Annual Reports. http://mod.nic.in/aboutus/welcome.html.

Government of India, Ministry of Defence (Navy). *Freedom to Use the Seas: India's Maritime Military Strategy*. 2011. Accessed February 3, 2012. http://indiannavy.nic.in/maritime_strat.pdf.

———. *Indian Maritime Doctrine INBR [Indian Naval Book of Reference]* 8. New Delhi: Ministry of Defence, n.d. but probably 2005.

Government of India, Ministry of External Affairs. *Annual Report for 2004–05*. New Delhi: Ministry of External Affairs, n.d.

———. *Annual Report 2010–11*. Accessed December 19, 2012. www.jeywin.com/wp-content/uploads/2010/08/2010-2011-Annual-Report-of-Ministry-of-External-Affairs-in-English.pdf.

———. *Annual Report for 2011*. Accessed February 9, 2012. mea.gov.in/staticfile/organisation.pdf.

———. *Annual Report 2011–12*. Accessed July 2013. http://mea.gov.in/Uploads/PublicationDocs/19337_annual-report-2011-2012.pdf.

Government of India, Ministry of Home Affairs. *Annual Report for 2008–09*. Accessed December 12, 2009. www.mha.nic.in/pdfs/AR(E)0809.pdf.

———. Model Police Act 2006. www.mha.nic.in/padc/The%20Model%20Act,%202006%2030%20Oct.pdf.

Government of India, Ministry of Home Affairs, Bureau of Police Research and Development. "Data on Police Organisations in India, 2012." Accessed February 11, 2013. http://bprd.nic.in/showfile.asp?lid=1047.

Government of India, Ministry of Home Affairs, Narcotics Control Bureau. *Annual Report 2008*. http://narcoticsindia.nic.in/ANNUAL%20REPORT%202008%20PDFF.pdf.

———. *Annual Report 2009*. http://narcoticsindia.nic.in/ANNUAL%20REPORT%202009%20PDFF.pdf.

Government of India, Ministry of Home Affairs, National Crime Records Bureau. "Snapshots' (1953–2007)." In *Crime in India 2007*. Accessed April 8, 2009. www.ncrb.nic.in/cii-2007/Snapshots%201953-2007.pdf.

———. *Crime in India 2007*. Accessed January 29, 2009. http://ncrb.nic.in/crimeinindia.htm.

Government of India, Prime Minister's High Level Committee (Sachar Committee). *Social, Economic, Educational Status of the Muslim Community of India: A Report*. New Delhi, 2006. Accessed February 22, 2008. www.godgraces.org/files/Muslim%20Report.pdf.

"Govt Looks for Ways to Cover Trade Gap with China." *Business Standard*, July 16, 2012. Accessed July 16, 2012. http://business-standard.com/india/news/govt-looks-for-ways-to-cover-trade-gapchina/480554/.

Gray, Colin S., and Geoffrey Sloan. *Geopolitics, Geography and Strategy*. Oxford: Frank Cass, 1999.

Greenpeace. *Safeguard or Squander: Deciding the Future of India's Fisheries*. Accessed September 5, 2012. www.greenpeace.org/india/Global/india/report/Safeguard-or-squander-deciding-the-future-of-india's-fisheries.pdf.

Guha, Ramachandran. "Democratic to a Fault?" *Prospect Magazine*, January 25, 2012. Accessed February 17, 2012. www.prospectmagazine.co.uk/2012/01/democratic-to-a-fault-ramachandra-guha-indias-future/.

"Gujarat Riots in Pictures." *Milli Gazette*. Accessed June 6, 2012. www.milligazette.com/gujarat/012.htm.

"Gujarat Riots Point to Need for Police Reform." Asia-Pacific Human Rights Network. Accessed December 2, 2009. file:///Users/sandy/Desktop/gujarat%20riots%20point%20to%20need%20of%20police%20reform.

Gupta, Akhil. "Narratives of Corruption: Anthropological Accounts of the Indian State." *Ethnography* 6, no. 5 (2005).

"Hafiz Saeed Seeks to Exploit Shinde's 'Hindu Terror' Remarks, BJP Launches All-Out Attacks." *Times of India*, January 21, 2013. Accessed January 23, 2013. http://timesofindia.indiatimes.com/india/Hafiz-Saeed-seeks-to-exploit-Shindes-Hindu-terror-remarks-BJP-launches-all-out-attack/articleshow/18116395.cms?prtpage=1.

Hagerty, Devin T. "The Kargil War: An Optimistic Assessment." In *Nuclear Proliferation in South Asia*, ed. Ganguly and Kapur, 100–16.

Hall, Ian. "India's New Public Diplomacy: Soft Power and the Limits of Government Action." *Asian Survey* 52, no. 6 (November–December 2012).

Hanauer, Larry, and Peter Chalk. *India's and Pakistan's Strategies in Afghanistan*. Santa Monica, CA: RAND Corp., 2012.

Haqqani, Hussain. "The Ideologies of South Asian Jihadi Groups." Carnegie Endowment. Accessed April 29, 2013. http://carnegieendowment.org/files/Ideologies.pdf.

Harish, B. G., N. Nagaraj, M. G. Chandrakanth, P. S. Srikantha Murthy, P. G. Chengappa, and G. Basavaraj. "Impacts and Implications of MGNREGA on Labour Supply and Income Generation for Agriculture in Central Dry Zone of Karnataka." *Agricultural Economics Research Review* 24 (2011).

Harrison, Selig S., and Geoffrey Kemp. *India and America after the Cold War*. Report of the Study Group on US-Indian Relations in a Changing International Environment. Washington, DC: Carnegie Endowment, 1993.

"Hasan Ali Earned Commission in Boeing-AI Deal: ED Report." *Economic Times*, May 20, 2011. Accessed May 27, 2011. http://economictimes.indiatimes.com/news/politics/nation/hasan-ali-earned-commission-in-boeing-ai-deal-ed-report/articleshow/8471968.cms.

Herbert-Burnes, Rupert. "Naval Power in the Indian Ocean: Evolving Roles, Missions and Capabilities." In *India Ocean Rising: Maritime Security and Policy Challenges*, ed. Michel and Sticklor.

"Hindu Temples, Homes Attacked across Bangladesh." *Times of India*, March 13, 2013. Accessed March 14, 2013. http://timesofindia.indiatimes.com/world/south-asia/Hindu-temples-homes-attacked-across-Bangladesh/articleshow/18954491.cms.

Holbraad, Carsten. *The Concert of Europe: A Study in German and British International Theory 1815 1914*. London. Longman, 1970.

Holmes, James R., Andrew C. Winner, and Toshi Yoshihara. *Indian Naval Strategy in the Twenty-First Century*. Oxford: Routledge, 2009.

Homer-Dixon, Thomas, and Jessica Blitt, eds. *Ecoviolence: Links among Environment, Population and Security*. Lanham, MD: Rowman & Littlefield, 1998.

Huisken, Ron, ed. *Rising China: Power and Reassurance*. Canberra: ANU E Press, 2009.

Human Rights Watch. "Anti-Terrorism Legislation." India Human Rights Press Backgrounder. November 20, 2001. Accessed November 29, 2007. www.hrw.org/backgrounder/asia/india-bck1121.htm.

———. "Broken System: The Deteriorating State of the Indian Police." August 4, 2009. Accessed June 27, 2011. www.hrw.org/es/node/84624/section/6.

"Hunger Back to 1990 Levels in South Asia." *Times of India*, June 23. 2010. Accessed June 23, 2010. http://timesofindia.indiatimes.com/articleshow/6080627.cms?prt.

Huntington, Samuel. *Political Order in Changing Societies*. New Haven: Yale University Press, 1968.

"I Am Not the Hawala Kingpin, I Was Just Branded One." Interview of H. Ameerdeen. *Outlook India*, June 11, 1997.

"I Feel Sorry for Kapil Sebal and Company for Their Zero-Loss Theory, GAC Vinod Rai Says." *Times of India*, May 20, 2013. Accessed June 24, 2013. http://articles.timesofindia.indiatimes.com/2013-05-20/india/39391719_1_cag-vinod-rai-audit-reports-media-policy.

"IM Men Got 10 Lakh for Pune Blast." *Times of India*, September 16, 2012. Accessed September 18, 2012. http://articles.timesofindia.indiatimes.com/2012-09-16/india/33879739_1_ats-probe-im-men-blasts.

"India Aid Programme Beset by Corruption: World Bank." BBC News, May 18, 2011. Accessed May 19, 2011. www.bbc.co.uk/news/world-south-asia-13447867.

"India Aims to Keep Money for Poor Out of Others' Pockets." *New York Times*, January 5, 2013. Accessed February 7, 2013. www.nytimes.com/2013/01/06/world/asia/india-takes-aim-at-poverty-with-cash-transfer-program.html?pagewanted=all&_r=0.

India Armed Violence Assessment. Issues Brief no. 1. September 2011. IAVA-IB1-states-of-armed-violence.pdf.

"India, China, a Long Way from Border Solution." *Indian Express*, n.d. Accessed December 3, 2012. http://m.indianexpress.com/news/-india-china-long-way-from-border-solution-/1039182/.

"India Does Not See Doha Round Concluding before 2013." *Wall Street Journal*, September 23, 2011. Accessed July 13, 2012. www.livemint.com/2011/09/23192313/India-does-not-see-Doha-round.html.

"India Faces Growing Chinese Hostility after 26/11." *Business Line*. www.thehindubusinessline.com/todays-paper/tp-opinion/article1044695.ece?ref=archive.

"India Is a Major Drugs Hub: US." *Economic Times*, September 18, 2007. Accessed January 6, 2010. www.unodc.org/india/en/rajiv_quoted_et.html.

"India Lost 26,000 cr to Grey Markets Says a Study." *The Hindu*, January 15, 2013. Accessed April 19, 2013. www.thehindu.com/business/india-lost-rs-26000-cr-to-grey-markets-says-a-study/article4309859.ece.

"India Ninth-Most Corrupt Country." *Economic Times*, December 10, 2010. Accessed March 23, 2011. http://articles.economictimes.indiatimes.com/2010-12-10/news/27614571_1_corrupt-country-transparency-international-petty-corruption.

"Indian Police Reform Gains Ground." Deutsche Welle. Accessed March 29, 2010. www2.dw-world.de/southasia/South_Asia/1.234779.1.html.

"Indian State Empowers Poor to Fight Corruption." *New York Times*, December 2, 2010. Accessed June 28, 2011. www.nytimes.com/2010/12/03/world/asia/03india.html.

"India Ranked 94th in Corruption Perception Index Ratings Says Transparency International." *Indian Express*, April 15, 2013. Accessed April 15, 2013. www.indianexpress.com/news/india-ranked-94th-in-corruption-peAs.

"India Ranks 131st in Press Freedom Index: Internet 'Partly Free.'" *Times of India*, November 21, 2012. Accessed May 8, 2013. http://articles.timesofindia.indiatimes.com/2012-11-21/india/35256765_1_india-ranks-google-transparency-internet-freedom.

"India RTI Chief: Information Law under Threat." BBC, July 5, 2013. Accessed February 1, 2013. www.bbc.co.uk/news/world-asia-india-18718581.

"India Sails into Troubled South China Sea." IPS News Service, February 24, 2013. Accessed June 25, 2013. www.ipsnews.net/2013/02/india-sails-into-troubled-south-china-sea/.

"India Seen as an Attractive Destination for Foreign Direct Investment." *Economic Times*, July 9, 2012. Accessed April 30, 2013. http://economictimes.indiatimes.com/opinion/editorial/india-seen-as-an-attractive-destination-for-foreign-direct-investment/articleshow/14761742.cms.

"India's Immense 'Food Theft' Scandal. BBC News, February 22, 2011. Accessed June 27, 2011. www.bbc.co.uk/news/world-south-asia-12502431

"India's Navy Boosts Spending 74 Percent: Plans to Buy 46 Ships, Pay for Car rier." *Defense News*, March 26, 2012. Accessed October 26, 2012. www.defensenews.com/article/20120326/DEFREG03/303260003/India-8217-s-Navy-Boosts-Spending-74-Percent.

"India, Sri Lanka Boost Trade, Investment Ties." *Hindustan Times*, November 25, 2012. Accessed February 27, 2013. www.hindustantimes.com/business-news/WorldEconomy/India-Sri-Lanka boost- -trade-investment-ties/Article1-964159.aspx.

"India to Have 15 Crore Pending Cases by 2040, Report Says." *Times of India*, January 17, 2013. Accessed May 8, 2013. http://articles.timesofindia.indiatimes.com/2013-01-17/india/36393546_1_crore-cases-judges-per-million-population-civil-case.

"India to Miss Fiscal Deficit Target." *Wall Street Journal*, September 18, 2012. Accessed October 26, 2012. http://online.wsj.com/article/SB10000872396390443816804578003522176287106.html.

"Indigenous Iron Dome Missile Could Protect India from Cross-Border Threats." *Times of India*. Accessed November 23, 2012. www.iofsbrotherhood.org/site/forum/messages.php?webtag=WEBTAG&msg=21987.1.

"Inside China: Indian Ocean Fortress." *Washington Times*, September 5, 2012. Accessed April 28, 2013. www.washingtontimes.com/news/2012/sep/5/inside-china-indian-ocean-fortress/?page=all.

International Crisis Group. *Afghanistan: The Long, Hard Road to the 2014 Transition*. Asia Report no. 236. October 8, 2012. Accessed October 9, 2019. www.crisisgroup.org/~/media/Files/asia/south-asia/afghanistan/236-afghanistan-the-long-hard-road-to-the-2014-transition.pdf?utm_source=afghanistanreport&utm_medium=3&utm_campaign=mremail.

"Investments Making Up for Trade Deficit with India: Japan." *Economic Times*, June 5, 2013. Accessed June 24, 2013. http://articles.economictimes.indiatimes.com/2013-06-05/news/39764398_1_maruti-suzuki-india-trade-deficit-cepa.

"Irregularities Found in Coal Blocks Allocation: CBI Tells Court." *The Hindu*, January 24, 2013. www.thehindu.com/news/national/irregularities-found-in-coal-blocks-allocation-cbi-tells-court/article4340815.ece. Accessed January 24, 2013.

Jalal, Ayesha. *Partisans of Allah: Jihad in South Asia*. Cambridge, MA: Harvard University Press, 2008.

Jamestown Foundation. "Lashkar-e-Taiba's Financial Network Targets India from the Gulf States." www.jamestown.org/single/?no_cache=1&tx_ttnews%5Btt_news%5D=35221.

Jauregui, Beatrice Anne. "Shadows of the State, Subalterns of the State: Police and 'Law and Order' in Postcolonial India." PhD diss., Department of Anthropology, University of Chicago, 2010.

Jeffrey, Robin. "Hot Election Tip from India." *The Hindu*, February 7, 2013. Accessed May 16, 2013. www.thehindu.com/todays-paper/tp-opinion/hot-election-tip-from-india/article4387683.ece.

———. *India's Newspaper Revolution: Capitalism, Politics and the Indian Language Press, 1977–99*. London: Hurst, 2000.

———. *What's Happening to India? Punjab, Ethnic Conflict and the Test for Federalism*, 2nd ed. London: Macmillan, 1994.

Jesani, Amar. "Medical Professionals and Interrogation: Lies about Finding the Truth." *Indian Journal of Medical Ethics* 10, no. 4 (October/December 2006). Accessed December 2, 2006. www.ijme.in/144ed116.html.

Jha, Raghbendra, Raghav Gaiha, and Manoj J. Pandey. "Determinants of Employment in India's National Rural Employment Guarantee Scheme." ASARC Working Paper no. 2010/17. https://crawford.anu.edu.au/acde/asarc/pdf/papers/2010/WP2010_17.pdf.

———. "Net Benefit under National Rural Employment Guarantee Scheme." ASARC Working Paper no. 2010/12. Accessed February 6, 2013. https://crawford.anu.edu.au/acde/asarc/pdf/papers/2010/WP2010_12.pdf.

Jha, Raghbendra, Hari Nagarajan, and Kailash C. Pradhan. "The Role of Bribes in Rural Governance: The Case of India." Australia South Asia Research Centre. Working paper pending publication.

Johnson, Chalmers. *Blowback: The Costs and Consequences of American Empire*. New York: Metropolitan Books, 2000.

Johnson, Don, and Jean Elliott Johnson. *Through Indian Eyes*. New York: Apex, 2008.

Jolly, Asit. "The Wahhabi Invasion." *India Today*, December 23, 2011. Accessed June 6, 2012. http://indiatoday.intoday.in/story/saudi-charities-pump-in-funds-through-hawala-channels-to-radicalise-kashmir-valley/1/165660.html.

Jones, Peter. "South Asia: Is a Regional Security Community Possible?" *South Asian Survey* 15, no. 2 (2008).

Joseph, Josy. "Securitization of Illegal Migration of Bangladeshis to India." Institute of Defence and Strategic Studies, Singapore. Working Paper no. 10, January 2009.

Joshi, Monaj. *Lost Rebellion: Kashmir in the Nineties*. New Delhi: Penguin, 1999.

———. "US, India and Af-Pak Endgame." *India Today*, May 5, 2012. Accessed October 4, 2012. http://indiatoday.intoday.in/story/us-india-and-afghanistan-pakistan-endgame/1/187448.html.

"A Journalist Who Cracked the Gujarat Fake Encounter Ease." *Rediff*, April 25, 2007. Accessed January 19, 2010. www.rediff.com///news/2007/apr/25spec.htm.

"JPC Clean Chit to PM: It's Raja Who 'Misled' Him." *The Hindu*, April 19, 2013. Accessed April 19, 2013. www.thehindu.com/news/national/jpc-clean-chit-to-pm-its-raja-who-misled-him/article4631034.ece?homepage=true.

"Judge, Family Have NREGS Job Card." *Times of India*, December 16, 2010. Accessed June 28, 2011. http://articles.timesofindia.indiatimes.com/2010-12-16/india/28239524_1_nizamabad-district-judge-job-card.

"Judicial Reforms of the Govt of India." Forum for Fast Justice. Accessed January 31, 2013. www.fastjustice.org/judicial_reforms_undertaken.html.

"Julia Gillard Rejects Need to Contain China." *The Australian*, April 27, 2011. Accessed April 27, 2011. www.theaustralian.com.au/national-affairs/julia-gillard-rejects-need-to-contain-china/story-fn59niix-1226045266144.

"Jundal Reveals Source behind Procuring 10 Indian SIM Cards for 26/11 Gunmen." *Times of India*, July 13, 2012. Accessed September 18, 2012. http://articles.timesofindia.indiatimes.com/2012-07-13/india/32663192_1_sim-cards-syed-zabiuddin-ansari-abu-jundal.

Kamran, Tahir. "Salafi Extremism in the Punjab and Its Transnational Impact." In *Communalism and Globalisation in South Asia and Its Diasporas*, edited by Deanna Heath and Chandana Mathur. London and New York: Routledge, 2011.

Kaplan, Robert D. *Monsoon: The Indian Ocean and the Future of American Power*. New York: Random House, 2010.

Kar, Dev. *The Drivers and Dynamics of Illicit Financial Flows from India: 1948–2008* Washington, DC: Global Financial Integrity, 2010.

Kautilya. *Arthasastra*. Translated by R. Shamasastry, 3rd ed. Mysore: Wesleyan Mission Press, 1929.

Kautilya. *Arthashastra*. Chapter 2, "Peace and Exertion," in Book VI, "The Source of Sovereign States." Accessed January 28, 2009. www.bharatadesam.com/literature/Kautilya_arthashastra/artashastra_6.php.

Khan, Shaheen Rafi. "Can Illegal Trade between Pakistan and India Be Eliminated?" Sustainable Development Policy Institute (Pakistan). *Research and News Bulletin* 12, no. 3 (May–June 2005). Accessed January 28, 2009. www.sdpi.org/help/research_and_news_bulletin/may_june_05/can_illegal_trade%2.0.htm.

Khilnani, Sunil, Rajiv Kumar, Pratap Bhanu Mehta, Prakash Menon, Nandan Nilenkani, Srinath Raghavan, Shyam Saran, and Siddharth Varadarajan. *NonAlignment 2.0: A Foreign and Strategic Policy for India in the Twenty First Century*. New Delhi: Centre for Policy Research, 2012.

Khurana, Mridu Lal. "India's 1984 Anti-Sikh Riots: Waiting for Justice." *Time*, October 28, 2009. Accessed March 29, 2010. www.time.com/time/world/article/0,8599,1931635,00.html.

"The Killing of a Young Boy." *The Hindu*, February 19, 2013. Accessed April 28, 2013. www.thehindu.com/opinion/op-ed/the-killing-of-a-young-boy/article4428792.ece.

"Kiran Bedi Differs with Anna Hazare, Backs Amended Lokpal Bill." NDTV, February 1, 2013. Accessed February 13, 2013. www.ndtv.com/article/india/kiran-bedi-differs-with-anna-hazare-backs-amended-lokpal-bill-325221?h_related_also_see.

Kohli, K. K. "Maritime Power in Peace and War: An Indian View." *African Security Review* 5, no. 2, 1996.

KPMG. "Survey on Bribery and Corruption: Impact on Economy and Business Environment." Accessed March 23, 2011. www.KPMG_Bribery_Survey_Report_new.pdf.

Krepon, Michael. "The Perils of Proliferation in South Asia." *Arms Control Today*, April 2010. Accessed October 3, 2013. www.armscontrol.org/act/2010_04/BookReview#5.

Kumar, Anand. "Illegal Bangladeshi Migration to India: Impact on Internal Security." *Strategic Analysis* 35, no. 1 (January 2011). Accessed July 14, 2012. http://dx.doi.org/10.1080/09700161.2011.530988.

Kumar, Rajiv, and Raja Menon. *The Long View from Delhi: To Define the Indian Strategy for Foreign Policy*. New Delhi: Academic Foundation Delhi, 2011.

Kundu, Kunal Kumal. "Indian Demographic Dividend Lacks Spark." *Asia Times Online*, February 20, 2013. Accessed July 11, 2013. www.atimes.com/atimes/South_Asia/SOU-01-200213.html.

———. "Subsidy Juggling Trims India's Fiscal Deficit." *Asia Times Online*, June 7, 2013. Accessed June 9, 2013. www.atimes.com/atimes/South_Asia/SOU-05-070613.html.

Lahiri-Dutt, Kuntala. "Indus Floods, 2010: Why Did the Sindhu Break Its Agreement?" *South Asia Masala*, September 1, 2010. Accessed August 7,

2012. http://asiapacific.anu.edu.au/blogs/southasiamasala/2010/09/01/indus-floods-2010-why-did-the-sindhu-break-its-agreement/.

Lal, Rollie. "South Asian Organised Crime and Terrorist Networks." *Orbis* 49, no. 2 (Spring 2005).

Lall, B. R. *Who Owns CBI?: The Naked Truth*. New Delhi: Manus, 2007.

"Land Scam General." *Sunday Times* (London), February 2, 2010. Accessed June 8, 2011. www.timesonline.co.uk/tol/news/world/asia/article7011587.ece.

Lannoy, Richard. *The Speaking Tree: A Study of Indian Culture and Society*. London: Oxford University Press, 1971.

"Lashkar-e-Taiba Has Dedicated Internet team: Abu Jundal." *Economic Times*, July 2, 2012. Accessed July 2, 2012. http://economictimes.indiatimes.com/news/politics/nation/lashkar-e-taiba-has dedicated-internet-team-abu-jundal/articleshow/14573585.cms.

Lee, John. "China's Geostrategic Search for Oil." *Washington Quarterly* 35, no. 3 (Summer 2012). Accessed July 11, 2013. http://csis.org/files/publication/twq12SummerLee.pdf.

Liu, Natalie. "China Sees Threat in US Pivot to Asia." Voice of America, June 7, 2013. Accessed June 10, 2013. www.voanews.com/content/china-sees-threat-in-us-pivot-to-asia/1677768.html.

"Log On for Clean Government." *Times of India*, January 23, 2013. Accessed May 8, 2013. http://articles.timesofindia.indiatimes.com/2013-01-23/india/36504913_1_biometric-attendance-system-e-governance-babus.

London School of Economics. "India: The Next Superpower?" March, 2012. Accessed March 24, 2012. www2.lse.ac.uk/IDEAS/publications/reports/SR010.aspx.

Luke, Leighton. "IOR-ARC Expands: US and Comoros Join." Future Directions International. November 7, 2012. Accessed June 3, 2013. www.futuredirections.org.au/publications/indian-ocean/29-indian-ocean-swa/781-ior-arc-expands-us-and-comoros-join.html.

Mackinder, H. J. "The Geographical Pivot of History." *Geographical Journal* 23, no. 4 (April 1904).

"Major Drugs Haul in India's Punjab." BBC News, March 8, 2013. Accessed April 18, 2018. www.bbc.co.uk/news/world-asia-india-21711057.

"Major Sameer Visited 26/11 Control Room, Confirms Zabuiddin." *The Hindu*, July 5, 2012. Accessed September 18, 2012. www.thehindu.com/news/national/article3606201.ece.

Maley, William. "Afghanistan in 2011: Positioning for an Uncertain Future." *Asian Survey* 52, no. 1 (January–February 2012).

Malhotra, Jyoti. "Between Delhi and the Deep Blue Ocean." *The Hindu*, December 17, 2012. Accessed February 2, 2013. www.thehindu.com/opinion/op-ed/between-delhi-and-the-deep-blue-ocean/article4206875.ece.

Malik, Mohan. *China and India: Great Power Rivals*. Boulder, CO, and London: First Forum, 2011.

"Manipur Drug Trafficking Case to Be Handed Over to CBI." *The Hindu*, March 6, 2013. Accessed March 6, 2013. www.thehindu.com/news/national/other-states/manipur-drug-trafficking-case-to-be-handed-over-to-cbi/article4479714.ece.

Markey, Daniel. "Developing India's Foreign Policy 'Software.'" *Asia Policy*, no. 8 (July 2009): 73–96.

Marshall, Michael. "Frozen Jet Stream Leads to Floods, Famine and Disease." *New Scientist* 207, no. 2773 (August 14, 2010).

"Masjid Blast: Cops on Toes to Find Last Bomb." *Times of India*, May 22, 2007. Accessed August 12, 2013. http://timesofindia.indiatimes.com/india/Masjid-blast-Cops-on-toes-to-find-last-bomb/articleshow/2065645.cms?

McArdel, Jennifer. "India Eyes Its Cinderella Service." *Maritime Security Review*, April 20, 2012. Accessed November 14, 2012. www.marsecreview.com/2012/04/cinderella-service/?pfstyle=wp.

McKinsey Global Institute. *India's Urban Awakening: Building Inclusive Cities, Sustaining Economic Growth*. N.p.: McKinsey Global Institute, 2010.

"MEA Added to Confusion over 2008 Hoax Call to Zardari." *The Hindu*, March 23, 2011. Accessed October 3, 2011. www.thehindu.com/news/the-india-cables/mea-added-to-confusion-over-2008-hoax-call-to-zardari/article1562663.ece.

Medcalf, Rory. "Shinzo Abe's Strategic Diamond." *The Diplomat*, January 15, 2013. Accessed June 25, 2013. http://thediplomat.com/flashpoints-blog/2013/01/15/shinzo-abes-strategic-diamond/.

Méon, Pierre-Guillaume, and Khalid Sekkat. "Does Corruption Grease or Sand the Wheels of Growth?" *Public Choice*, no. 122 (2005).

Merrington, Louise. "Beyond the Protracted Contest: Redefining the Sino-Indian Relationship." PhD thesis, Australian National University, 2011.

Meyer, Christian, and Nancy Birdsall. *New Estimates of India's Middle Class*. Centre for Global Development. Accessed May 17, 2013. www.cgdev.org/doc/2013_MiddleClassIndia_TechnicalNote_CGDNote.pdf.

Michael, Arndt, ed. *India's Foreign Policy and Regional Multilateralism*. Houndmills UK: Palgrave Macmillan, 2013.

Michel, David, and Richard Sticklor, eds. *India Ocean Rising: Maritime Security and Policy Challenges*. Washington, DC: Stimson Center, 2012.

Microsoft Corporation. "India's E-governance Framework." Accessed May 8, 2013. www.microsoft.com/india/msindia/perspective/e_governance.aspx.

Miller, Benjamin. *States, Nations and Great Powers: The Sources of Regional War and Peace*. Cambridge: Cambridge University Press, 2007.

———. "States, Nations, and the Regional Security Order of South Asia." In *South Asia's Weak States*, ed. Paul.

Mills, Greg, and Terence McNamee. "Disaggregating Chinese Actors in Africa." *East Asia Forum* 4, no. 2 (April–June 2012).

"MLAs' Fortunes Grow More Than All Other Investments." *Times of India*, May 19, 2011. Accessed June 7, 2011. http://articles.timesofindia.indiatimes.com/2011-05-19/india/29560028_1_recontesting-fund-manager-mutual-funds.

Mohan, C. Raja. "From Isolation to Partnership: The Evolution of Indian Military Diplomacy." ISAS Singapore Working Paper no. 144 (February 20, 2012).

———. "India and the Balance of Power." *Foreign Affairs* 85, no. 4 (July/August 2006).

———. *Samudra Mantham: Sino-Indian Rivalry in the Indo-Pacific*. Washington DC: Carnegie Endowment for International Peace, 2012 (e-book version).

Mohanty, Deba R. *Defence Spending Trends in India*. Observer Research Foundation. Accessed November 3, 2010. www.observerindia.com/cms/export/orfonline/modules/analysis/attachments/defence_1333106028570.pdf.

"Monsoon or Later." *The Economist*, July 28, 2012.

Mufti, Shahan. "Funding the Pakistan Taliban." *Global Post*, August 7, 2009. Accessed July 16, 2013. www.globalpost.com/dispatch/taliban/funding-the-pakistani-taliban.

"Multinational Crackdown on Computer Con Artists." *New York Times*, October 3, 2012. Accessed April 24, 2009. www.nytimes.com/2012/10/04/business/multinational-crackdown-on-computer-con-artists.html?_r=0.

"Mumbai Cops Goof Up: 7/11 Accused Acquitted." *Times of India*, May 12. 2009. Accessed January 6, 2010. http://timesofindia.indiatimes.com/India/Mumbai-cops-goof-up-711-accused-acquitted/articleshow/4511603.cms.

"A Mumbai Student Vents on Facebook, and the Police Come Knocking." *New York Times*, November 20, 2012. Accessed May 17, 2013. www.nytimes.com/2012/11/21/world/asia/india-police-arrest-student-over-facebook-post.html?_r=0.

Muni, S. D. "India's 'Look East' Policy: The Strategic Dimension." ISAS Working Paper no. 121 (February 1, 2011).

———. "Obama Administration's Pivot to Asia and India's Role." ISAS Working Paper no. 159 (August 29, 2012).

———. "Problem Areas in India's Neighbourhood Policy." *South Asian Survey* 10, no. 2 (2003).

"Musharraf's Kashmir Solution Hypothetical: Aziz." *The Hindu*, November 1, 2004. www.hindu.com/thehindu/holnus/001200411011050.htm.

Nair, Padmaja. "The State and Madrasas in India." Religion and Development Research Program, Working Paper no. 15 (2009). Accessed June 6, 2012. http://epapers.bham.ac.uk/1567/1/Nair_Madrasas_India.pdf.

Narayan, S. *India ASEAN FTA in Services*. ISAS Brief no. 126 (December 21, 2012).

National Investigation Agency Bill. South Asia Terrorism Portal. Accessed January 20, 2010. www.satp.org/satporgtp/countries/india/document/papers/75-c1.htm.

National Law Institute University, Bhopal. "Criminalisation of Politics in India: A Study of Politicians in the 15th Lok Sabha with Criminal Records." Accessed June 14, 2011. www.scribd.com/doc/20133814/Criminalization-of-Politics-in-India-A-project-study.

Nayar, Baldev Raj. "Economic Globalization and State Capacity in South Asia." In *South Asia's Weak States*, ed. Paul.

———. "A World Role: The Dialectics of Purpose and Power." In *India: A Rising Middle Power*, edited by John W. Mellor. Boulder, CO: Westview, 1979.

Nye, Joseph S. *Soft Power: The Means to Success in World Politics*. New York: PublicAffairs, 2004.

"The $100 M Global Scam." *Sydney Morning Herald*, March 6, 2011. Accessed April 19, 2013. www.smh.com.au/business/the-100m-global-scam-20110305-1biyh.html.

"On Line Terror Plot: Bangalore Jihadis Took Inspiration from al Qaida's On line Magazine." *Times of India*, September 3, 2012. Accessed September 4, 2012. http://articles.timesofindia.indiatimes.com/2012-09-03/india/33562741_1_online-magazine-karnataka-terror-plot-al-qaida.

"Over 30% of MPs, MLAs Face Criminal Charges." *The Hindu*, July 22, 2013. www.thehindu.com/news/national/over-30-of-mps-mlas-face-criminal-charges/article4938403.ece.

Palit, Amitendu. *China-India Economics: Challenges, Competition and Collaboration*. New York: Routledge, 2012.

Pant, Harsh V. "The Pakistan Thorn in China-India-US Relations." *Washington Quarterly* 35, no. 1 (Winter 2012).

———, ed. *The Rise of the Indian Navy: Internal Vulnerabilities, External Challenges*. London: Ashgate, 2012.

Pasupuleti, Sudershan, Eric G. Lambert, Shanhe Jiang, Jagadish V. Bhimarasetty, and K. Kaishankar. "Crime, Criminals, Treatment and Punishment: An Exploratory Study of Views among College Students in India and the US." *Journal of Contemporary Criminal Justice* 25, no. 2 (March 2009).

Patil, Sanjay. *Feudal Force: Reform Delayed; Moving from Force to Service in South Asian Policing*. Commonwealth Human Rights Initiative. 2008. Accessed December 18, 2009. www.humanrightsinitiative.org/publications/police/feudal_forces_reform_delayed_moving_from_force_to_service_in_south_asian_policing.pdf.

Paul, T. V. *International Relations Theory and Regional Transformation*. Cambridge: Cambridge University Press, 2012.

———. "State Capacity and South Asia's Perennial Insecurity Problems." In *South Asia's Weak States*, ed. Paul.

———, ed. *South Asia's Weak States: Understanding the Regional Insecurity Predicament*. Stanford, CA: Stanford University Press, 2010.

Perlez, Jane. "India and Vietnam Face Off with China in Disputed Waters." *Sydney Morning Herald*, December 6, 2012. Accessed December 23, 2012. www.smh.com.au/world/india-and-vietnam-face-off-with-china-in-disputed-waters-20121205-2avjj.html.

Pinglay, Prachi. "Police Slated over Mumbai Attacks." BBC News, June 16, 2009. Accessed January 6, 2009. http://news.bbc.co.uk/go/pr/fr/-/2/hi/south_asia/8103528.stm.

"PMO Hits Out at Modi's Bid to Rake Up Sir Creek on Poll-Eve." *The Hindu*, December 12, 2012. Accessed April 25, 2013. www.thehindu.com/news/national/pmo-hits-out-at-modis-bid-to-rake-up-sir-creek-on-polleve/article4192308.ece.

"Potential for a Mining Boom Splits Factions in Afghanistan." *New York Times*, September 8, 2012. Accessed April 29, 2013. www.nytimes.com/2012/09/09/world/asia/afghans-wary-as-efforts-pick-up-to-tap-mineral-riches.html?_r=0.

Pradhan, R. D. *1965 War: The Inside Story*. New Delhi: Atlantic Publishers, 2007.

"Pragmatism over Politics." *Business Standard*, October 9, 2013. Accessed October 9, 2013. www.business-standard.com/article/current-affairs/pragmatism-over-politics-113100500576_1.html.

"Protesters at Shahbagh in Bangladesh Backed by India." *Times of India*, February 26, 2013. Accessed April 25, 2013. http://articles.timesofindia.indiatimes.com/2013-02-26/india/37308683_1_bangladeshi-youth-shahbagh-protesters.

Raghuvanshi, Vivek. "India to Focus Resources on Naval Operations." *Defense News*, October 24, 2012. Accessed December 23, 2012. www.defensenews.com/article/20121024/DEFREG03/310240004/India-Focus-Resources-Naval-Operations.

Ragunathan, A. V. "Despite Drawbacks MGNREGS Comes Out on Top in Job Creation." *The Hindu*, January 29, 2013. Accessed August 22, 2013. www.thehindu.com/news/states/tamil-nadu/despite-drawbacks-mgnregs-comes-out-on-top-in-job-creation/article4354758.ece?homepage=true.

Rajagopalan, Rajesh, and Varun Sahni. "India and the Great Powers: Strategic Imperatives, Normative Necessities." *South Asian Survey* 15, no. 5 (2008).

Rajan, D. S. Intellibriefs. August 29, 2007. Accessed April 7, 2011. http://intellibriefs.blogspot.com/2007/08/china-media-fears-over-india-becoming.html.

Rajan, K. V. "Renewing SAARC." Regional Conference on "New Life within SAARC." Institute of Foreign Affairs (Nepal), 2005. Accessed February 4, 2009. www.ifa.org.np/document/saarcpapers/rajan.pdf.

Ramachandran, Shastri. "India Has a 'Look East' Policy Too." *World News*, April 30, 2012. Accessed June 7, 2013. www.international.to/index.php?option=com_content&view=article&id=5891:india-has-a-look-east-policy-too&catid=80:politics&Itemid=120.

Ramachandran, Sudha. "India Extends Malacca Strait Reach." Foundation for National Security Research. August 8, 2012. Accessed November 13, 2012. www.fnsr.org/india-extends-malacca-strait-reach.php.

———. "India Fishing for Trouble in Sri Lanka." *Asia Times Online*, February 23, 2011. Accessed September 5, 2012. www.atimes.com/atimes/South_Asia/MB23Df04.html.

———. "India Navy Pumps Up Eastern Muscle." *Asia Times Online*, August 20, 2011. Accessed October 30, 2012. www.atimes.com/atimes/South_Asia/MH20Df02.html.

Raman, B. "Evolution of Militancy in Indian Muslim Community." South Asia Analysis Group Paper no. 4605 (July 19, 2011). Accessed November 22, 2011. www.southasiaanalysis.org/\paper4605.html.

———. "India and Jihadi Terrorism during 2009." *Sri Lankan Guardian*, January 3, 2010. Accessed January 5, 2010. www.srilankaguardian.org/2010/01/india-jihadi-terrorism-during-2009.html.

"Rana, Headley Implicate Pak, ISI in Mumbai Attack during ISI Chief's Visit to US." *Times of India*, April 12, 2012. Accessed March 5, 2013. http://articles.timesofindia.indiatimes.com/2011-04-12/us/29409412_1_rana-and-headley-isi-tahawwur-hussain-rana.

RAND Corp. *China and India, 2025: A Comparative Assessment*. Santa Monica, CA: RAND Corp., 2011. Accessed February 20, 2011. http://www.rand.org/content/dam/rand/pubs/monographs/2011/RAND_MG1009.pdf.

———. (G. Treverton, Karla J. Cunningham, Jeremiah Goulka, Greg Ridgeway, and Anny Wong). *Film Piracy, Organized Crime, and Terrorism*. Santa Monica, CA: RAND Corp., 2009.

Rao, U. N. B. "Presentation on Model Police Act." Accessed January 16, 2010. http://74.125.95.132/search?q=cache:O7lQeju2TrsJ:www.commoncauseindia.org/whatsNew/PresentationonModelPoliceActU_N_B_Rao.ppt+india+model+police+act&cd=5&hl=en&ct=clnk&gl=au.

Rao, V. Venkateswara. "Black, Bold and Bountiful." *Hindu Business Line*, August 13, 2010. Accessed May 30, 2011. www.thehindubusinessline.in/2010/08/13/stories/2010081350370900.htm.

Rashid, Harun. "36th Anniversary of Sino-Bangladesh Ties." *Daily Star*, October 19, 2011. Accessed June 7, 2013. http://archive.thedailystar.net/newDesign/news-details.php?nid=207045.

Redfield, Robert. *Peasant Society and Culture*. Chicago: University of Chicago Press, 1956.

Rehman, Iskander. "India's Aspirational Naval Doctrine." In *Rise of the Indian Navy*, ed. Pant.

"Relations between India and Sri Lanka Sour." *New York Times*, September 5, 2012. Accessed April 25, 2013. http://india.blogs.nytimes.com/2012/09/05/relations-between-india-and-sri-lanka-sor/.

"Renuka, Tyler Deny Links with Hasan Ali Khan." CNN-IBN, May 28, 2011. Accessed June 7, 2011. http://ibnlive.in.com/news/renuka-tytler-deny-links-with-hasan-ali-khan/155036-37-64.html.

"Revealed: Quattrocchi, Chadda Bribed in Bofors Deal." *Rediff*, January 3, 2011. Accessed June 3, 2011. www.rediff.com/news/slide-show/slide-show-1-revealed-quattrocchi-chadda-bribed-in-bofors-deal/20110103.htm.

"Rice's Visit Could Take Indo-US Partnership to New Level." *Times of India*, March 30, 2005. Accessed November 8, 2012. http://articles.timesofindia.indiatimes.com/2005-03-30/edit-page/27837301_1_global-power-strategic-partnership-united-states-and-india.

Ripsman, Norris M., and T. V. Paul. *Globalization and the National Security State*. Oxford: Oxford University Press, 2010.

Rothstein, Bo. "Anti-Corruption: The Indirect 'Big Bang' Approach." *Review of International Political Economy* 18, no. 2 (May 2011).

Roul, Animesh. "Lashkar-e-Taiba's Financial Network Targets India from Gulf States." *Terrorism Monitor* 7, no. 19 (July 2, 2009). Accessed June 13, 2012. www.jamestown.org/single/?no_cache=1&tx_ttnews%5Btt_news%5D=35221.

Roy, Arundhati. "I'd Rather Not Be Anna." *The Hindu*, August 21, 2011. Accessed May 20, 2013. www.thehindu.com/opinion/lead/article2379704.ece.

———. *Listening to Grasshoppers: Field Notes on Democracy*. New Delhi: Hamish Hamilton, 2009.

Roy, M. K. "The Indian Navy from the Bridge." *Proceedings*, March 1990.

"Rs 1k cr CWG Loss Could Have Been Education Bonanza." *Times of India*, March 28, 2011. Accessed March 28, 2011. http://timesofindia.indiatimes.com/india/Rs1k-cr-CWG-loss-couldve-been-education-bonanza/articleshow/7803078.cms.

Rush, Howard, Chris Smith, Erika Kraemer-Mbula, and Puay Tang. *Crime Online: Cybercrime and Illegal Innovation*. CENTRIM, University of Brighton, Research Report. July 2009. Accessed March 4, 2010. http://eprints.brighton.ac.uk/5800/.

SAARC Fifteenth Summit, Declaration. Colombo, 2008. Accessed February 4, 2009. http://saarc-sic.org/_adm/editor/summits_15.php.

"SAARC Secys [*sic*] Meet in July to Review Measures, Policies." *Financial Times*, June 30, 2012. www.thefinancialexpress-bd.com/more.php?news_id=134958&date=2012-06-30. Accessed March 22, 2014.

Sagar, Rahul. "State of Mind: What Kind of Power Will India Become?" *International Affairs* 84, no. 4 (2009).

Saha, Shrabain, and Neil Campbell. "Studies of the Effect of Democracy on Corruption." Paper prepared for the 36th Australian Conference of Economists, September 2007. Accessed May 13, 2013. www.ecosoc.org.au/files/File/TAS/ACE07/presentations%20(pdf)/Saha.pdf.

Sahni, Varun. "Regional Dynamics of Emerging Powers: Power/Control or Leadership/Consent?" In *International Relations Theory and South Asia*, ed. Sridharan.

Saikia, Panchali. *Connecting South Asia: Experimenting with the Greater Mekong Sub-Regional Model*. Issues Brief. Institute of Peace and Conflict Studies, New Delhi. Accessed March 22, 2014. http://www.ipcs.org/issue-brief/india/connecting-south-asia-experimenting-with-the-greater-mekong-sub-regional-189.html.

Sailo, Laldinkima. "The Great 'Exodus': Violence in Assam and Its Aftermath." ISAS Insights no. 187 (September 6, 2012).

———. "Northeast India–Southeast Asia Connectivity: Barrier to Bridge." ISAS Working Paper no. 162 (November 16, 2012).

"Santokben, Godmother." *Outlook India*, March 8, 1999. Accessed July 4, 2011. www.outlookindia.com/article.aspx?207083.

"Saudi-Based NRIs Funded Mumbai Blasts: ATS." *Times of India*, August 2, 2006. Accessed October 30, 2013. http://timesofindia.indiatimes.com/home/specials/Saudi-based-NRIs-funded-Mumbai-blasts-ATS/articleshow/1838830.cms.

Schmitt, Eric. "Many Sources Feed Taliban's War Chest." *New York Times*, October 19, 2009.

Scott, David. "India's 'Grand Strategy' for the Indian Ocean: Mahanian Visions." *Asia-Pacific Review* 13, no. 2 (2006).

Selth, Andrew. "Burma's Mythical Isles." *Australian Quarterly* 80, no. 6 (November–December 2008).

———. "Chinese Military Bases in Burma: The Explosion of a Myth." Griffith Asia Institute, Regional Outlook. Accessed November 29, 2012. www.griffith.edu.au/__data/assets/pdf_file/0018/18225/regional-outlook-andrew-selth.pdf.

Sempa, Francis P. *Geopolitics: From the Cold War to the 21st Century*. Brunswick, NJ: Transaction, 1989.

Sen, Amartya, and Jean Drèze. *An Uncertain Glory: India and Its Contradictions*. London: Penguin, 2013.

Sen, Ronojoy. "The Delhi Rape Crisis: Observations on Middle Class Activism in India." ISAS Brief no. 266 (January 24, 2013).

"Senior Police Officer Arrested in Gujarat Riots Case." *Rediff*, February 8, 2009. Accessed January 2010. www.rediff.com/news/2009/feb/08godhra-top-cop-held-in-riots-case.htm.

Sethi, Harsh. "No Room for Nuance in This Fragile Republic." *The Hindu*, January 28, 2013. Accessed January 28, 2013. www.thehindu.com/opinion/op-ed/no-room-for-nuance-in-this-fragile-republic/article4351057.ece?homepage=true.

"A Sieve of a Scheme?" *Outlook India*, April 19, 2010. Accessed June 28, 2011. www.outlookindia.com/printarticle.aspx?264994.

Singh, Abhijit. "The Indian Navy's New 'Expeditionary' Outlook." National Maritime Foundation. Accessed October 7, 2013. http://maritimeindia.org/article/indian-navys-new-expeditionary-outlook.

Singh, Mandip. "China Base a Threat to Indian Navy?" *The Diplomat*, December 17, 2011. Accessed December 23, 2012. http://thediplomat.com/2011/12/17/china-base-a-threat-to-india-navy/.

Singh, Nina, and Daniel Keniston. "Telling It Like It Is." *Karmayog*. www.karmayog.org/police/police_22362.htm.

Singh, Parvinder. "India Union Budget 2012–13." *OneWorld South Asia*, March 16, 2012. http://southasia.oneworld.net/news/india-union-budget-2012-13-2013-a-quick-view-of-agriculture-and-social-sector-trends#.UJnpKo5C8po.

Singh, Sinderpal, *India in South Asia: Domestic Identity Politics and Foreign Policy from Nehru to BJP*. London: Routledge, 2013.

Sinha, Rohit, and Geethanjali Nataraj. "Japanese ODA Stimulates Indian Infrastructure Development." *East Asia Forum*, June 18, 2013. Accessed June 24, 2013. www.eastasiaforum.org/2013/06/18/japanese-oda-stimulates-indian-infrastructure-development/.

Sinha, Uttam Kumar. "India and Pakistan: Introspecting the Indus Treaty." *Strategic Analysis* 32, no. 6 (November 2008).

Skrikrishna Commission Report. Sabrang Communications. Accessed November 3, 2011. www.sabrang.com/srikrish/sri%20main.htm.

"Smuggling Fake Currency from Pakistan to India Is a Terrorist Act: NIA." *Times of India*, December 11, 2012. Accessed April 25, 2013. http://articles.timesofindia.indiatimes.com/2012-12-11/india/35748489_ 1_willful-circulation-ficn-fake-indian-currency-notesSouth.

"Software Deal Used a Cover for Helicopter Bribes." *Times of India*, February 14, 2013. Accessed April 18, 2013. http://articles.timesofindia.indiatimes.com/2013-02-14/india/37098831_1_software-exports-payment-iaf-chief-sp-tyagi.

South Asian Association for Regional Cooperation. "Areas of Cooperation: Information, Communication and Media." Accessed May 22, 2013. http://saarc-sec.org/areaofcooperation/cat-detail.php?cat_id=56.

South Asia Terrorism Portal. Accessed November 24, 2009. www.satp.org (various).

"'Spam Capital' India Arrests Six in Phishing Probe." BBC News, January 3, 2012. Accessed May 4, 2012. www.bbc.com/news/technology-16392960.

Sridharan, E. "International Relations Theory and South Asia: Security, Political Economy, Domestic Politics, Identities, and Images." In *International Relations Theory and South Asia*, ed. Sridharan.

———, ed. *International Relations Theory and South Asia.* New Delhi: Oxford University Press, 2011.

"Sri Lankan Reporter Shot in Colombo." *Financial Times* (Asia), February 17, 2013. Accessed April 28, 2013. www.ft.com/intl/cms/s/0/87f0172e-78b8-11e2-8cdb-00144feabdc0.html#axzz2RjQDglW4.

Stiglitz, Joseph. *Globalization and Its Discontents.* New York and London: Norton, 2002.

Stuenkel, Oliver. "How Many Diplomats Does an Emerging Power Need?" *Post-Western World.* Accessed May 31, 2013. www.postwesternworld.com/2012/10/14/how-many-diplomats-does-an-emerging-power-need/.

"Supreme Court Wants Law to Insulate CBI from Interference." *The Hindu*, May 9, 2013. Accessed May 9, 2013. www.thehindu.com/news/national/supreme-court-wants-law-to-insulate-agency-from-interference/article4696677.ece.

"Surgical Strikes Are Feasible Militarily: Army Chief." *Indian Express*, February 8, 2009. Accessed October 2, 2012. www.indianexpress.com/news/surgical-strikes-are-feasible-militarily-army-chief/420738/3.

Swami, Praveen. "The Indian Mujahidin and Lashkar-i-Tayyiba's Transnational Networks." *CTS Sentinel*, June 15, 2009. Accessed June 14, 2012. www.ctc.usma.edu/posts/the-indian-mujahidin-and-lashkar-i-tayyiba%E2%80%99s-transnational-networks.

———. "The Terror Commander in the White Kufi Hat." *The Hindu*, April 4, 2012. Accessed April 26, 2012. www.thehindu.com/news/article3278239.ece.

———. "The Well-Tempered Jihad: The Politics and Practice of Post-2002 Islamist Terrorism in India." *Contemporary South Asia* 16, no. 3 (September 3, 2008).

Tachil, Tariq. "India in Transition: Do Policies Matter in Indian Elections?" Center for Advanced Studies of India. Accessed July 14, 2010. http://casi.ssc.upenn.edu/iit/thachil.

"Take Steps to Curb Terror Funding, America Tells India." *Economic Times*, March 2. 2009. Accessed January 11, 2010. http://economictimes.indiatimes.com/News/PoliticsNation/Take-steps-to-curb-terror-funding-America-tells-India/articleshow/4210150.cms.

"Taliban Spread Terror as New Gang in Town." *New York Times*, March 28, 2013. Accessed June 19, 2013. www.nytimes.com/2013/03/29/world/asia/taliban-extending-reach-across-pakistan.html?pagewanted=all&_r=0.

Tanham, George K. *India's Strategic Culture: An Interpretive Essay.* Santa Monica, CA: RAND Corp., 1992.

Tankel, Stephen. *Storming the World Stage: The Story of Lashkar-e-Taiba.* New York: Columbia University Press, 2011.

Taylor, McComas. "Mythology Wars: The Indian Diaspora, 'Wendy's Children' and the Struggle for the Hindu Past." *Asian Studies Review* 35, no. 2 (June 2011).

Tellis, Ashley J. *India as a New Global Power*. Washington, DC: Carnegie Endowment, 2005. Accessed July 5, 2013. http://carnegieendowment.org/files/Tellis.India.Global.Power.FINAL.pdf.

"The Terror Transporters of India." *Rediff*, April 27, 2012. Accessed April 26, 2013. www.rediff.com/news/slide-show/slide-show-1-the-terror-transporters-of-india/20120427.htm.

"This MP Clerk's Salary Is Rs 40,000, Assets Rs 25 Crore." *Times of India*, February 6, 2013. Accessed April 19, 2013. http://articles.timesofindia.indiatimes.com/2013-02-06/india/36948551_1_properties-bairagarh-sq-ft.

"3 Cops to Protect Each VIP, Just 1 Policeman for 761 Citizens." *Times of India*, February 8, 2013. Accessed February 8, 2013. http://timesofindia.indiatimes.com/india/3-cops-to-protect-each-VIP-just-1-policeman-for-761-citizens/articleshow/18391600.cms.

"332 Deaths in Custody during Islamic Insurgency, Kashmir Police Say." *International Herald Tribune*, February 21, 2008. Accessed February 22, 2008. www.iht.com/articles/2008/02/21/asia/kashmir.php.

Timmons, Heather. "Can India 'Fix' Afghanistan?" *New York Times*, June 7, 2012. Accessed October 4, 2012. http://india.blogs.nytimes.com/2012/06/07/can-india-fix-afghanistan/.

"Top Uttar Pradesh Bureaucrat Removed for Alleged Links with Hasan Ali." *India Daily*, April 16, 2011. www.theindiadaily.com/top-uttar-pradesh-bureaucrat-removed-for-alleged-links-with-hasan-ali/.

"Toughening the Law." *India Today*, January 9, 2009. Accessed April 8, 2010. http://indiatoday.intoday.in/site/Story/24801/IN%20THIS%20ISSUE/Toughening+the+law.html.

Tow, William. "Setting the Context." In *Security Politics in the Asia-Pacific: A Regional-Global Nexus?*, edited by William Tow. Cambridge: Cambridge University Press, 2009.

"Transfer of Jobs to Asian Workers Feeds Discontent." *Asian Wall Street Journal*, March 4, 2011. Accessed June 12, 2012. http://online.wsj.com/article/SB10001424052748704858404576134610056742244.html.

Tripathi, Anurag. "The Easy Way to Arms and Violence." *Tehelka* 5, no. 3 (January 26, 2008). Accessed January 29, 2010. www.tehelka.com/story_main37.asp?filename=Ne260108the_easy.asp.

Tripathi, Narendra Kumar. "Hydropower in Asia: Spinning a Dependence and Interdependence Binary." *South Asian Survey* 17, no. 2 (2010).

"26/11 Probe: Poor Crime Scene Management Say Experts." *The Hindu*, November 19, 2009. Accessed June 6, 2010. http://beta.thehindu.com/news/article51268.ece.

"2G Scam: ED to Attach Rs 2340 cr of Unitech Properties." *Times of India*, April 28, 2011. Accessed June 8, 2011. http://articles.timesofindia.indiatimes.com/2011-04-28/india/29482642_1_unitech-wireless-swan-telecom-spectrum-scam.

"2G Scam: 32 Accounts with Dodgy Transfers under Lens." *Times of India*, June 9, 2011. Accessed June 9, 2011. http://timesofindia.indiatimes.com/india/2G-scam-32-accounts-with-dodgy-transfers-under-lens/articleshow/8782402.cms.

"2G Scam: Witnesses to Be Examined from June 29." *The Hindu*, June 8, 2011. Accessed June 8, 2011. www.hindu.com/2011/06/08/stories/2011060866211800.htm.

"2008: Extremist Recruitment on the Rise in South Punjab Madrassahs." Cable reproduced in full in *Dawn*, May 22, 2011.

United Kingdom Government, Department of Public Prosecutions. "Conviction Rate Increases." *DPP Journal*, June 29, 2009. www.cps.gov.uk/news/journals/dpps_journal/conviction_rate_increases/.

United Nations Committee on Economic, Social and Cultural Rights. "The Marginalised Status of Muslims in Gujarat." Accessed April 11, 2012. www2.ohchr.org/english/bodies/cescr/docs/info-ngos/Gujarat_India40.pdf.

United Nations High Commissioner on Refugees. Minorities at Risk Project. "Chronology for Hindus in Bangladesh, 2004." Accessed April 3, 2012. www.unhcr.org/refworld/docid/469f3869c.html.

United Nations Office on Drugs and Crime. "Executive Summary." *South Asia Regional Profile 2005*. Accessed January 6, 2010. www.unodc.org/pdf/india/publications/south_Asia_Regional_Profile_Sept_2005/10_india.pdf.

———. *World Drug Report 2008*. Accessed January 6, 2010. www.unodc.org/documents/wdr/WDR_2008/WDR_2008_eng_web.pdf.

———. *World Drug Report 2009* (Vienna: UNODC, 2009).

United Progressive Alliance. *Report to the People: 2004–2008*. New Delhi: Ajanta Offset, 2010.

United States Government, Congressional Research Service. *China's Foreign Aid Activities in Africa, Latin America and Southeast Asia* (summary). Accessed February 27, 2013. www.fas.org/sgp/crs/row/R40361.pdf.

———. *Islamic Religious Schools, Madrasas: Background*. Report to Congress, October 29, 2003. Accessed September 26, 2012. www.policyalmanac.org/world/archive/madrasas.pdf.

———. (John Rollins, Liana Sun Wyler, and Seth Rosen). *International Terrorism and Transnational Crime: Threats, Policy and Considerations*. January 5, 2010. Accessed January 19, 2010. www.fas.org/sgp/terror/R41004.pdf.

United States Government, Department of Defense. *Report to Congress on U.S.-India Security Cooperation*. November 2011. Accessed November 8, 2012. www.defense.gov/pubs/pdfs/20111101_NDAA_Report_on_US_India_Security_Cooperation.pdf.

United States Government, Department of State. *Country Reports on Terrorism 2007*, chapter 2, "South and Central Asia Overview." Accessed April 3, 3009. www.state.gov/s/ct/rls/crt/2007/103709.htm.

———. *The Trafficking in Persons Report 2009*, as in *Nepal Monitor*, June 17, 2009. Accessed March 4, 2010. www.nepalmonitor.com/2009/06/human_trafficking_in.html.

———. 2012 INCSR, Report on India. Accessed June 17, 2013. www.state.gov/j/inl/rls/nrcrpt/2012/vol1/184100.htm.

United States Government, National Intelligence Council. *Global Trends 2030: Alternative Futures*. Accessed June 25, 2013. http://globaltrends2030.files.wordpress.com/2012/11/global-trends-2030-november2012.pdf.

United States Government, US District Court, Southern District of New York. Facsimile indictment of Bashir Noorzai dated January 6, 2005. Accessed March 4, 2010. www.investigativeproject.org/documents/case_docs/691.pdf.

Unnithan, Sandeep. "Why We Can't Get Him." *India Today*, May 27, 2011. Accessed April 30, 2012. http://indiatoday.intoday.in/story/india-unable-pressurise-pakistan-to-deport-dawood-ibrahim/1/139519.html.

"US Embassy Cables: India 'Unlikely' to Deploy Cold Start against Pakistan." *The Guardian*, November 30, 2010. Accessed October 3, 2012. www.guardian.co.uk/world/us-embassy-cables-documents/248971.

Vaishnav, Milan. "India Needs More Democracy, Not Less." Carnegie Endowment. Accessed August 22, 2013. http://carnegieendowment.org/2013/04/11/india-needs-more-democracy-not-less/fz38.

Varshney, Ashutosh. "Aligarh Is Not India." *India Today*, November 10, 2003.

———. *Ethnic Conflict and Civic Life: Hindus and Muslims in India*. London: Yale University Press, 2002.

"Vietnam's Plea Puts South Block in a Predicament." *The Hindu*, November 9, 2011. Accessed June 25, 2013. www.thehindu.com/news/national/vietnams-plea-puts-south-block-in-a-predicament/article2610605.ece.

"Vision of Humanity." Global Peace Index. Accessed April 3, 2009. www.visionofhumanity.org/gpi/results/rankings.php.

"V. K. [Singh] Scents a Chinese Tunnel." *The Telegraph*, June 5, 2012. Accessed October 9, 2012. www.telegraphindia.com/1120605/jsp/frontpage/story_15571405.jsp#.UHOnVY5C8po.

Waldman, Amy. "India's Offer for Peace Talks on Kashmir Is Sweetened with Aid." *New York Times*, November 18, 2004. www.nyt.com/2004/11/18/international/asia/18kashmir.html?oref=login&pake.

Waltz, Kenneth N. "Anarchic Orders and Balances of Power." In *Neorealism and Its Critics*, edited by Robert O. Keohane. New York: Columbia University Press, 1986.

Water Resources Group, *Charting Our Water Future: Economic Frameworks to Inform Decision-Making*." 3030 Water Group. Accessed July 2, 2013. Charting Our_Water_Future_ExecSummary.pdf.

Weiner, Myron. *The Politics of Scarcity: Public Pressure and Political Response in India*. Chicago: University of Chicago Press, 1962.

Whalley, John, and Tanmaya Shekhar. "The Rapidly Deepening India-China Economic Relationship." CESIFO Working Paper no. 3183 (September 2010). Accessed July 16, 2012. www.ifo.de/portal/pls/portal/docs/1/1185240.PDF.

"What Is Devas Multimedia? *The Hindu*, February 7, 2011. Accessed March 28, 2011. www.thehindu.com/news/national/article1162745.ece.

"What the Hell Is Going On: Supreme Court on Hasan Ali." *Times of India*, March 4, 2011. Accessed June 9, 2011. http://articles.timesofindia.indiatimes.com/2011-03-04/india/28659062_1_interrogation-black-money-hasan-ali-khan.

White, Hugh. *Power Shift: Australia's Future between Washington and Beijing*. Melbourne: Black Inc., 2010.

"Why Bihar Has Most Fast-Track Courts in India." BBC News. Accessed May 6, 2013. www.bbc.co.uk/news/world-asia-india-21320104.

"Why the Indian Mujahideen Is Keeping a Low Profile." *Rediff*, April 27, 2012. Accessed April 26, 2013. www.rediff.com/news/report/why-the-indian-mujahideen-is-keeping-a-low-profile/20120413.htm.

"Will Cash Transfers Work in India?" BBC News, November 28, 2012. Accessed May 6, 2013. www.bbc.co.uk/news/world-asia-india-20521937.

"With Few Muslims in Civil Services, Sponsors Chip In." *Thaindian News*, June 3, 2008. Accessed March 26, 2010. www.thaindian.com/newsportal/uncategorized/with-few-muslims-in-civil-services-sponsors-chip-in_10055925.html.

World Bank. "Anti-Money Laundering and Combating the Financing of Terrorism: Pakistan." Mutual Evaluation Report, July 9, 2009. Accessed July 9, 2013. https://openknowledge.worldbank.org/bitstream/handle/10986/12243/700310ESW0P1110an0MER0final0version.pdf?sequence=1.

———. "Bangladesh and Maldives Respond to Climate Change Impacts." December 7, 2012. Accessed June 20, 2013. www.worldbank.org/en/news/press-release/2012/12/07/bangladesh-maldives-respond-to-climate-change-impacts.

———. *Economic Growth in South Asia: Promising, Un-equalising, . . . Sustainable?* Washington DC: World Bank, 2006.

———. "India: Foreign Trade Policy." Accessed July 12, 2012. web.worldbank.org/WBSITE/EXTERNAL/COUNTRIES/SOUTHASIAEXT/EXTSARREGTOPINTECOTRA/0,,contentMDK:20592520~menuPK:579454~pagePK:34004173~piPK:34003707~theSitePK:579448,00.html.

———. "India's Poor Yet to Reap Full Benefits of Its Anti-Poverty Programs." World Bank Report, May 18, 2011. Accessed June 30, 2011. www.worldbank.org/WBSITE/EXTERNAL/COUNTRIES/SOUTHASIAEXT/EXTSAREGTOPPOVRED/0,,contentMDK:22917236~menuPK:493447~pagePK:2865114~piPK:2865167~theSitePK:493441,00.html.

———. *Managing Climate Risk: Integrating Adaptation into World Bank Group Operation*. Report no. 37462. Washington, DC: International Bank for Reconstruction and Development, World Bank, 2006. Accessed June 22, 2012. www-wds.worldbank.org/external/default/WDSContentServer/WDSP/IB/2006/09/28/000090341_20060928112135/Rendered/PDF/374620Managing0Climate0Risk01PUBLIC1.pdf.

———. *Migration and Remittances Factbook 2011*, 2nd ed. Accessed February 17, 2012. http://siteresources.worldbank.org/INTLAC/Resources/Factbook2011-Ebook.pdf.

World Justice Project. "Rule of Law Index." Accessed April 18, 2013. http://worldjusticeproject.org/country/india.

"World's Biggest Biometric ID Scheme Forges Ahead." BBC News, February 13, 2012. Accessed February 7, 2013. www.bbc.co.uk/news/world-asia-india-16979875.

Wu, Mark. "Antidumping in Asia's Emerging Giants." *Harvard International Law Journal* 53, no. 1 (Winter 2012).

Xavier, Constantino. "India's Strategic Advantage over China in Africa." *IDSA Comment*, June 30, 2010. Accessed November 29, 2012. www.idsa.in/idsacomments/IndiasstrategicadvantageoverChinainAfrica_cxavier_300610.

Yardley, Jim. "India, Praising U.S. Ties, Defends Buying Iran's Oil." *New York Times*, February 12, 2012. Accessed February 12, 2012. www.nytimes.com/2012/02/12/world/asia/india-trumpets-ties-with-us-amid-iran-oil-deal.html.

Yousaf, Mohammed, and Mark Adkin. *The Bear Trap: Afghanistan's Untold Story*. London: Leo Cooper, 1992.

Yusuf, Huma. "Conflict Dynamics in Karachi." United States Institute for Peace, 2012. Accessed October 4, 2013. www.usip.org/sites/default/files/resources/PW82.pdf.

Yusufzai, Ashfaq. "Across Afghan Border, a Smugglers' Market." *Asia Times Online*, August 7, 2007. Accessed February 9, 2009. www.atimes.com/atimes/South_Asia/IH07Df01.html.

About the Author

Alexander "Sandy" Gordon has a BA from the University of Sydney and a PhD from Cambridge University. He has worked as an academic at the University of New South Wales (ADFA), Wollongong University, and the Australian National University, from where he retired as professor in 2011. His academic specialities cover India, South Asia, the Indian Ocean, and transnational crime. As a public servant, he worked in Australia's Office of National Assessments, in the Australian Agency for International Development, as executive director of the Asian Studies Council, and as head of Intelligence, Australian Federal Police.

He is the author of a number of books on India and the Indian Ocean region.

INDEX

Aam Aadmi Party (Party of the Common Man), 169
Abdulla, Farooq, 178n.4
Abdullah, Omar, 140
Abe, Shinzo, 143, 145–46, 195, 202–3
Acharya, Amitav, xxvi, 200
Adarsh Housing Society scam, 12
Adwani, L. K., 46
Afghanistan
  borders of, 73n.2
  direct aid from India to, 188–89
  global competition in South Asia and, 92–96
  Islam and the Soviet invasion, 81
  Islam and the U.S. invasion, 81–82
  jihad against the Soviets, 84
  mujahideen, funding of, 84–85
  opium grown in, 65–66
  Pakistan border, conflict over, 45
Afghan National Army (ANA), 93
Afghan National Police (ANP), 95
Afghan Trade and Transit Agreement (ATTA), 64
Africa, Sino-Indian competition in, 127
Agusta Westland, 10
Ahl al-Hadith, 57, 61, 83–86
Ahmed, Ali, 183
Ali, Sameer, 58
All India Anna Dravida Kazhagam (AIADMK), 50
al-Qaeda
  in Afghanistan, 81
  as globalized concern, 87
  Karachi, senior members captured in, 72
  LeT and, 59
  online magazine, 87
  the Taliban and, 66
  U.S. ability to defeat, Indo-Pakistani relations and, 80
Ameerdeen, H., 18–19
Amnesty International, 63
Andhra Pradesh, 16, 170
Andhra Pradesh Minorities Commission, 30
Ansari, Syed Zabiuddin (Abu Jundal), 58, 87
anticorruption movement, 169–70
Antrix, 13
Arakotaram, Karan, 108n.20
Armed Forces (Special Powers) Act (AFSPA), 173, 208
arms and explosives smuggling, 67–68
Arunachal Pradesh, 104, 118, 137–39
ASEAN Regional Forum (ARF), xxv–xxvi, 145–46
Asia-Europe Meeting (ASEM), 145
Asian Development Bank, 188
Asian Human Rights Commission, 28
Asian security architecture, future of, 199–205
Asia-Pacific Economic Cooperation forum (APEC), 145, 186
Asia/Pacific Group on Money Laundering (APG), 16, 68

Assam
illegal migration into, 66–67
independence movement in, 45
population pressure in, 70
Association for Democratic Reform (ADR), 21
Association of South East Asian Nations (ASEAN), 47, 144–45, 192
Australia
China, dependency on, 195
China, the quadrilateral and relations with, 146, 202
Indian Ocean, presence in, 122
Australian Crime Commission, 26
Australian South Asia Research Centre, 16, 171
Aviation Research Centre, 33
Awami League, 49, 51

Babri Masjid, destruction of, 46, 48, 52–56
Babur, Zahir-ud-din Muhammad, 52
Bajpai, Kanti, xviii, 194
Bajran Dal, 60
Baloch Liberation Army, 51
Banerjee, Mamata, 106
Bangladesh
the Assam independence movement and, 45
Babri Masjid destruction, violence following, 54
borders of, 73n.2
China, road and rail connections agreements with, 191
Chinese trade with, 124
climate change, vulnerability to, 105–6
domestic politics and cross-border tensions, 49
Farakka Barrage, impact of, 46
Global Peace Index ranking, 23
illegal migrants into India from, 66–67
Indian aid to, 189–90
Indian competition with China in relations with, 194
the Indian Mujahideen and, 60
smuggling of arms through, 55
as a terrorist haven, 61
Bangladesh-China-India-Myanmar Forum for Regional Cooperation (BCIM), 193–94, 210
Banna, Hassan al-, 82
Basham, A. L., 5
Basu, Kaushik, 107n.4
Bay of Bengal Initiative for Multi-Sectoral Technical and Economic Cooperation (BIMSTEC), xxv, 192–94, 197, 209–10
Beckley, Michael, 109n.45
Bedi, Kiren, 172
Behera, Laxman K., 117
Beheria, Ashol, 182
Bell, Coral, 199–200
benami, 11
Bengali National Party, 49
Bhai, Amir. *See* Ameerdeen, H.
Bhakti Movement, 52
Bharatia Janata Party (BJP)
economic nationalism, Swadeshi Jagran Manch and, 99
foreign and security policy, position on, 140
Gujarat, governing party at time of riots in, 56
Hindu identity, political appeal to, 46, 53
illegal migration as a concern of, 67
Kalam chosen as president by, 53
terrorist training camps, accusation of running, 60
Bhosale, Shivaji, 53
Bhutan
direct aid from India to, 188–89
domestic politics and cross-border tensions, 50
India, close relations with, 124
Bihar
corruption in MGNREGS, loss to the exchequer from, 16
fast-track courts, convictions upheld from, 164
illegal production of cigarettes in, 17
bin Laden, Osama, 91
BJP. *See* Bharatia Janata Party
Blitt, Jessica, 70

blowback, 79, 82, 84–85, 188
Bofors AB, 9–10
Bofors bribery scandal, 9–10
Bombay, impact of decolonization, 46. *See also* Mumbai
Border Security Force (BSF), 34, 65, 157
Brass, Paul, 3, 40n.144
Brewster, David, 145
"British India," 1–2
Bullock, Christopher R., 112
Burma, 25, 73n.2, 124, 193–94
Buzan, Barry, xx, xxixn.3

Cabinet Committee on Security (CCS), 33
Cabinet Secretariat, 33
CAG. *See* Comptroller and Auditor General, Office of the
Calcutta, impact of decolonization, 46
Cambodia, 180n.56
caste politics, 3
caste structure, corruption as a means of upward mobility in, 6
cell phones, 167
Central Bureau of Investigation (CBI)
  Adarsh Housing Society scam, actions regarding, 12
  Bofors bribery scandal, actions regarding, 10
  Coalgate scandal, actions regarding, 14
  2G telecommunications scam, actions regarding, 10–11
  Lok Pal Bill and, 172
  money laundering, investigation of, 18–19
  politicization of, 28
  right of transfer, misuse of, 27
  states, lack of power to take up a case within, 171
  structure of society and, 5
Central Paramilitary Forces, 34
Central Reserve Police Force (CRPF), 28, 157
Central Vigilance Commission (CVC), 13, 171–72, 207
Centre for Standards in Public Life, 168
Chandra, Shailaja, 167–68
Chattisgarh, loss to the exchequer from corruption in MGNREGS, 16
Chellaney, Brahma, 104, 125
Cheney, Dick, 143, 145, 202–3
Chennai, high-level political involvement with gangs in, 22
Chidambaram, P., 29, 33, 35, 118, 157, 160
China, People's Republic of
  Bangladesh, road and rail agreements with, 191
  border dispute with India, 137–38
  capital and expertise, as source of, 176–77
  climate change, concerns regarding, 103–5
  direct-aid contributions from, 188
  diversity of views in India on, 139–40
  economic globalization, comparison to India regarding impact of, 99–103
  evolving four-way relationship with India, Pakistan, and the United States, 88 (*see also* global power competition, four-way relationship of India, Pakistan, the United States and China)
  India, rivalry with, 80
  India, trade relationship with, 101–2
  Indo-U.S. relations and, 135–43
  murder rate in, 24
  Panchsheel multilateralism with India, 47
  Sino-Indian competition in the Indian Ocean, 123–28, 197
  space, prospective future control of, 113
  strategic analytical approach, as an example of, xix
  United States, relationship with and the security architecture of Asia, 199, 202
  United States, South Asia and the rivalry with, 80
China Institute for Strategic Studies (CISS), 91
Chinese Sinohydro Company, 104
chowkidar, 1, 27
Churchill, Winston, 96
climate change, 103–6
Clinton, Bill, 134

Coalgate scandal, 14, 28
Coal India Ltd., 121, 156
Cohen, Stephen P., 49, 134–35
Cole, Bernard, 112
colonial era, policing as a legacy of, 27–28
Combined Task Force 151 (CTF-151), 196
Common Minimum Program (CMP), 165
Common Service Centres, 175
Commonwealth Games (CWG) scandal, 12–13
Commonwealth Human Rights Initiative, 27
communal conflict, 40n.144, 41n.145
communalism, 3
Comptroller and Auditor General, Office of the (CAG)
  Commonwealth Games scandal, 13
  efforts to rein in, 169
  2G telecommunications scam, 10–11
  ISRO Antrix-Devas scandal, 13
  reform, role in, 167, 207
concert-of-power theory, 199–203
Congressional Research Service, U.S. (CRS)
  China's direct-aid program, estimate of, 188
  criminal gangs and terrorists, links between, 33
Congress Party
  coalition building by, 50
  Common Minimum Program, 165
  economic liberalization by, 99
Constitution of 1950, 2
continental power
  characteristics of, 112
  India as, 112–13, 148–49 (*see also* security; strategic autonomy)
corruption
  benefits and costs of, 3–4
  bribes, number of households paying, 36n.32
  cultural interpretations of, 4–6
  development and problems of, 7, 35
  extent and indicators of, 7–9
  informal rules surrounding, 5–6
  megacorruption
    Adarsh Housing Society scam, 12
    Bofors bribery scandal, 9–10
    Coalgate scandal, 14, 28
    Commonwealth Games (CWG) scandal, 12–13
    2G telecommunications scam, 10–11
    Hooda government in Haryana, 7–8
    ISRO Antrix-Devas scandal, 13
    Koda corruption scandal, 7, 11–12, 17, 156
  modernization and, 6–7
  money laundering as vital for, 16–18 (see also *hawala*; money laundering)
  nexus of politicians, police, criminals and (*see* nexus, the)
  overcoming pervasive, 165–74
  public services, ranking of corrupt, 8–9
  social protection programs and, 14–16, 35, 165
  the virtuous circle driving out, 167–72
counterterrorism
  abuse of legislation authorizing, 62–63
  intelligence reform and, 157–61, 208
  policing and, 29–33, 35
  reform of mechanisms for, 35
crime and criminals
  conviction rate for, 31
  counterterrorism and, 32–33
  cross-border in South Asia (*see* South Asia, cross-border crime)
  level of in India, 23–26
  murder rate, 23–24
  the nexus, as one component of (*see* nexus, the)
  politics and, 21–22
  statistics and victimization surveys as accountability mechanisms, 175–76
  terrorism and, 55
  underreporting of, 24–25
Crime and Criminal Tracking and Network System (CCTNS), 163
culture
  political (*see* political culture)
  strategic, strategy distinguished from, xviii

currency swaps, 17
cybercrime, 68–69

dabar, 5
Dalai Lama, 138–39
Dalrymple, William, 82
Darul Uloom, 87
Dasgupta, Sunil, 134–35
Datta, Surjit, xxiv
D Company, 32–33, 54–55, 64, 69
Defense, U.S. Department of, 135
Defense Policy Group, 135
democratic politics. *See* politics
democratization, pace and negative effects of, 2–3
Deng Xiaoping, xix
Devas Multimedia, 13
developmental strategy. *See* inclusive growth
dharma, 4
digitized biometric identity, 174
DMK. *See* Dravida Munnetra Kazhagam
Doniger, Wendy, 4
Doron, Assa, 167
Dravida Munnetra Kazhagam (DMK)
 corruption of politicians in, 11
 Sri Lankan human rights issue, domestic politics and, 97
 Sri Lankan Tamil cause, domestic politics and support for, 50–51
Drèze, Jean, 7
D'Souza, Shanthie Mariet, 70
Durand, Mortimer, 45
Durand Line, 45, 92

East Asia, India's Look East strategy and, 143–48, 190–95
East Asia Summit (EAS), xxv–xxvi, 145–46
economic growth
 inclusive growth, policy of (*see* inclusive growth, policy of)
 rates of, 2
ED. *See* Enforcement Directorate
e-governance, 175, 208
Electoral Commission, 174
electoral politics, organized crime and, 22
electronic voting system, 174
encounter killings, 6
energy, 121
Enforcement Directorate (ED)
 the Koda corruption scandal and, 11
 Ministry of Finance as host for, 33
 money laundering and, 17, 20–21, 167
 right of transfer, misuse of, 27
environmental problems
 climate change, 103–6
 economic strategies and infrastructure investment, integration with, 176–77
 globalization and, 80
 Sino-Indian relations and, 103–5
 in South Asia, 70–72, 105–6
Evans, Gareth, 196
Exercise RIMPAC, 199

Faisal, Prince Turki al-, 84
Farakka Barrage, 46
fast-track courts, 164
Federal Bureau of Investigation, 158
Federation of Indian Chambers of Commerce and Industry, money "lost" to grey markets, 17
Financial Action Task Force, 68
firearms trafficking, 67–68
fish stocks and fishermen, 71
Fonseca, Sarath, 97
Food Security Bill, 15
Foreign Contribution Regulation Act (FCRA), 85
foreign direct investment (FDI) model, 99, 102, 208
France, 166
Freedom House, 170
free press. *See* media, the
free-trade agreement (FTA) with ASEAN, 144–45, 192
French, Patrick, 5
Fund for Peace, Pakistan as failed state, 48

Gandhi, Indira
 assassination of, 31
 dabar held by, 5

Gandhi, Indira *(Cont.)*
"foreign hand," communal problems blamed on, 51
Khalistan movement facilitated by, 178n.4
Tamil cause, support for, 50
Gandhi, Mahatma, 60, 169
Gandhi, Rajiv
Bofors bribery scandal, cleared of wrongdoing in, 10
money laundering, involvement in, 19
percentage of expenditure that reaches intended target, 4, 174–75
rigging of 1987 election, 178n.4
Gandhi, Shailesh, 173
Gandhirajan, C. K., 22
Ganguly, Sumit, xxiv, 184
Gillard, Julia, 202
Global Financial Integrity (GFI), extent of illicit movement of funds overseas, 17
globalization
complex impact of, 79–82
economic, contested role in India of, xxii–xxiii
foreign trading relations, inclusive growth and, 100–102
international trade, South Asian countries and, 98–99
the internet and, 87
Islamic fundamentalism as reaction to, history of, 82–83
of the labor market, 86
location and, xxi–xxii
militant Islam and, 82–88
negative effects of, xvii, xxii, 48
the state and, xvii
Global Peace Index, 23
global power competition, 79–82
environmental concerns and Sino-Indian relations, 103–6
four-way relationship of India, Pakistan, the United States and China, 88
Afghanistan and, 92–96
the attacks of 26/11 and its aftermath, 88–92
Sri Lankan Civil War, end of, 96–98
Islam and, 81–82
Sino-Indian relations, economic globalization and, 99–103
South Asia's negative strategic enmeshment and, xxv–xxvi
Godse, Nathuram, 60
Gonsalves, Eric, 193
Gotru, Nirmala, 22
governance
corruption (*see* corruption)
future of India and problems of, xviii, 7, 157, 207
inclusive growth compromised by problems of, xviii, 14–16
modernization and standards of, 6–7
policing and, 26–29 (*see also* police and policing)
reform of, 207
counterterrorism and intelligence, 157–61
e-government and digitization to improve transparency, 174–76
environmental concerns, integration of economic strategies with, 176–77
the judicial system, 163–64
the police, 161–63
security and, 156–57 (*see also* security)
strategy in East and Southeast Asia and need for reform of, 194
water problems and, 71
Government of India Act of 1935, 2
Gram Nyayalaya, 164
Great Britain, 166
Greater Mekong Sub-Region group, 192–93
Guha, Ramachandran, xxii, 7
Gujarat
anti-Muslim riots of 2002, political manipulation of police bias and, 32
"encounters," police killings in, 32
organized crime and electoral politics in, 22
riots of February 2002, 56–57
Gujarat Muslim Revenge Force, 57
Gujral, I. K., 182
Gujral doctrine, 182

Gulf Wars, 132–33
Gupta, Akhil, 7
Gupta, Arvind, 182

Hadood Ordinance, 84
Hagerty, Devin T., xxiv, xxxn.32
Hall, Ian, 144
Haqqani network, 61, 81, 93, 185
Hari Singh, Maharaja, 43
Harkat-ul-Jihad al-Islami (HuJI), 60
Haryana
  corruption in, 7–8
  water rights given to, 110n.80
hawala
  corruption and, 12
  criminal networks and terrorists, use by, 64
  the Jain case, 17–19
  the Khan case, 19–21
  money laundering and the nexus, connection to, 16–18
  money laundering and "triangle" between Mumbai, Karachi, and Dubai, 68
  roots and banking function of, 37n.68
  steps in transaction through *hawala* dealers, 38n.74
Hawkins, Charles E., 112
Hazare, Anna, 169, 172
Headley, David, 58
Hedgewar, Keshav Baliram, 53
Hinduism
  domestic politics in India and, 46, 51
  as a fragmented faith, 53
  globalization and the rise of Hindu politics, 87–88
  Indian identity and, 52–53
  tension with Muslims exacerbated by police, 31
Hindu Right
  anti-Muslim sentiment, political use of, 62
  illegal migration as a concern of, 67
  terrorism and, 60
  See also Bharatia Janata Party
Holbraad, Carsten, 200
Holmes, James R., 120
Homer-Dixon, Thomas, 70
HuJI, 186
Hu Jintao, 128, 137
Human Rights Watch, 27–28, 63
Hyderabad, investigations of bombings in, 30

Ibrahim, Dawood, 20, 32–33, 54–55, 87
illegal migration, 66–67
IM. *See* Indian Mujahideen
inclusive growth, policy of
  Common Minimum Program (CMP), programs of, 165
  as a core strategy, xvii–xviii, 198
  as a cross-cutting strategy, 183
  foreign trading relations and, 100
  goals and significance of, 14
  Indian government spending and, 119–20
  See also social protection programs
Income Tax Department, the Koda corruption scandal and, 12
India Armed Violence Assessment project, 24
Indian Mujahideen (IM)
  attacks by and investigations of, 30
  Gujarat riots, recruiting based on footage of, 57
  Gulf experience of, 86
  as homegrown group, 61
  terrorist attacks and consequent casualties, statistics on, 75n.60
  terrorist attacks and radicalizing of, 40n.129, 54, 75n.55
  violent jihadist attacks by, 59–60
Indian Narcotics Control Bureau (NCB), rate over time of opiates seizures, 25
Indian Ocean, area of. *See* Indian Ocean Region
Indian Ocean Naval Symposium (IONS), xxv, 197–98
Indian Ocean Region (IOR)
  the China factor in Indo-U.S. relations in, 135–43
  failure of SAARC, India's weak regionalism and, 47

Indian Ocean Region (IOR) *(Cont.)*
geostrategic advantages in, 122–23
India's cautious regional action in, 111–12
India's naval ambitions in, 128–32
Indo-U.S. relations in, 132–35
potential threats, as a source of, 120–22
regionalism in, India's support of weak, 123
regional strategies for, 195–99, 204, 210
Sino-Indian competition in, 123–28, 197
Indian Ocean Rim Association for Regional Cooperation, xxv
Indian Ocean Rim Association (IORA), xxv, 123, 195–98
Indian Planning Commission, poor performance of legal and security sectors as impediment to development, 35
Indian Police Commission, 29
Indian Police Service (IPS), 28, 162
Indian Space Research Organisation (ISRO), 13
Indo-Bangladesh relations
Assam independence movement and, 45
Farakka Barrage and, 46
Indonesia, 47
Indo-U.S. nuclear agreement, 133–34
infrastructure investment, need for massive, 176–77
intellectual property crime, 68–69
Intelligence Bureau (IB), 34, 158–60
intelligence fusion centers, 41n.154
International Crisis Group, 95
International Forum on the Indian Ocean Region (IFIOR), 196
International Narcotics and Law Enforcement Affairs, U.S. Bureau for, *hawala* transfers for legally derived remittances, 17
internet
Indian diaspora, rise of, 87–88
violent jihadist ideas and, 87
Inter-Services Intelligence Directorate (ISI), 45, 58–60, 84–85, 93
Iran, 94, 196
ISI. *See* Inter-Services Intelligence Directorate
Islam
globalization and militant, 82–88
global power competition and, 81–82
Pakistan, as basis of origin for, 45–46
Wahhabi and Salafist versions of, influx into South Asia of, 82–85
See also Muslims
Islami Chhatra Sangh, 60
Israel, 134
ISRO Antrix-Devas scandal, 13

Jadeja, Santokben, 22
Jain, J. K., 18–19
Jain, S. K., 18–19
Jain *hawala* case, 17–19
Jaish-e-Mohammed (JeM), 54, 61, 83, 85, 89, 108n.9, 186
jajmani system, 1
Jamaat-ud-Dawa, 83, 85, 87
Jammu, Hindu and Ladakhi minorities in, 2
Jan Chetna Manch (Organization of People's Awareness), 104
Jan Lok Pal, 172
Jan Lokpal movement, 169
Japan, 143, 145–46, 149, 195
Jauregui, Beatrice Anne, 5–6
Javed, Mohammad, 71
Jeffrey, Robin, 3, 167
JeM. *See* Jaish-e-Mohammed
Jha, Raghbendra, 3, 9, 15–16
Jharkhand, the Koda corruption scandal in, 11–12
jihad
international against the West, 89
terrorism in India and (*see* terrorism, violent jihadist in India)
violent
blowback and the rise of, 79, 83–86
the internet and the rise of, 87
Jinnah, Mohammed Ali, 49, 85, 108n.15
Joint Intelligence Committee, 33, 158
Joshi, D. K., 147
Joshi, Rita Bahuguna, 22

Judicial Standards and Accountability Bill of 2010, 164
judiciary, the
- backlog of cases, police and public taking law into their own hands due to, 32, 163
- corruption, activism in fighting, 11–12, 170
- money laundering, activism in fighting, 20
- police reform, action regarding, 29, 162
- politicization of the CBI, frustration with, 28, 172
- reform of the judicial system, 163–64, 207

jugaad, 6

Kalam, Abdul, 53
Kalmadi, Suresh, 13
Kamran, Tahir, 83
Kanimozha, 11
Kaplan, Robert D., 85, 96, 123, 125, 127, 132
Kapoor, Deepak, 90
Karachi, as bellwether for urban decay, 72
Karunanidhi, Muthuvel, 51
Karzai, Hamid, 95
Kasab, Ajmal, 58
Kashmir
- Hindu and Ladakhi minorities in, 2
- India-Pakistan conflict over, 43–45, 48
- India-Pakistan relations, as the key to, 184–86
- separatist movement in Indian, 85

Kashmiris, 2
Kashmiriyat, 2, 85, 108n.20
Kautiliya (Chanakya), 46–47, xxxn.31
Kejriwal, Arvind, 169
Kenya, 127–28
Khan, A. Q., 84
Khan, Hasan Ali, 19–21
Khan *hawala* case, 19–21
Khashoggi, Adnan, 20
Khidmat Foundation, 85
Khilnani, Sunil, xviii–xix, xxixn.5
Kissinger, Henry, xxiii
Koda, Madhu, 11–12, 21, 22
Koda corruption scandal, 7, 11–12, 17, 156
Kolkata. *See* Calcutta
Kondapalli, Srikanth, 102
Krishna, 73n.24
Kumar, Anand, 66–67, 76n.89
Kumar, V. Vasanth, 16
Kundu, Kunal Kumal, 141–42
Kurshid, Salman, 147

Lakhvi, Zakir ur Rehman, 58
Lall, B. R., 19
Lashkar-e-Taiba (LeT), xxiii–xxiv, 54–55, 57–61, 83, 85–89, 87, 108n.9, 186
Lashkar-i-Jhangvi, 51, 83, 185
Law Commission, 164
Laws of Manu, 2
Lee, John, 123
Liechtenstein Global Trust Bank (LGT Bank), 19–20
Li Keqiang, 140, 146
literacy, 2
location
- globalization and the significance of, xxi–xxii
- trajectory of emerging powers, role in determining, xxiii–xxiv

Lokayuktas, 163, 171–72
Lok Pal, 163, 207
Lok Pal Bill, 165, 169, 171–72
Lok Sabha, MPs charged with serious crimes, 22
Look East strategy, xxv, xxviii, 143–45, 190–95, 210
loyalty, Indian view of, 19

Mackinder, H. J., 112
Madagascar, 128
Madhya Pradesh
- CBI, limitations placed on, 171
- corruption in, 8
- corruption in MGNREGS, loss to the exchequer from, 16

Mahabharata, 2
Mahan, Alfred Thayer, 112

Maharashtra, the Adarsh Housing Society scam, 12
Maharashtra Anti-Terrorism Squad (ATS), 57, 86
Mahatma Gandhi National Rural Employment Guarantee Scheme (MGNREGS)
  anomalies uncovered by audits, 15–16
  checks and balances built into, 15
  cost of, 120
  effectiveness of, disparate reports on, 171
  electronically posting data, 208
  evolution into a demand-driven program, 165
  social audits of, 170–71
  social uplift program, as key, 174
Mahmood, Fasih, 87
Majid, Tariq, 91
Malagoan, 41n.145
Malaysia, 147
Maldives, Republic of the, 73n.2, 128
Maley, William, 95
Malik, Mohan, 125, 134, 138, 140
Maoist insurgencies/revolt
  better governance and development outcomes, resolution depends on, 119
  Chinese assistance for, 148
  corruption as a cause of, 45
  failed governance as cause of, 7, 35, 156
Maran, Dayanidhi, 11
Markaz, 57
Markey, Daniel, 144
Maududi, Abu A'la, 82
Mauritius, 127
Mauritius Process, 196
Mayawati, 5
McKinsay et alia, water deficit in India, report on, 70–71
McKinsey Global Institute, urbanization, report on, 2, 72, 99
Medcalf, Rory, 146
media, the
  corruption, fighting, 9, 13, 170
  freedom of the press, ranking of, 170
  insensitivity of bureaucrats in dealing with, 13
megacorruption. *See* corruption, megacorruption
Mekong-Ganga Group (MGG), 192–93, 210
Mengistu Haile Mariam, 98
Menon, Shiv Shanker, 132
Merrington, Louise, 140
MGNREGS. *See* Mahatma Gandhi National Rural Employment Guarantee Scheme
Michael, Arndt, xxiv, 47, 184
Microsoft Corporation, 175
migration, illegal, 66–67
Milan naval exercise, 197, 199
military, the
  in Bangladesh, 49
  carrier battle groups in the Indian Ocean, 210
  defense spending, 113–19
  Gulf Wars and fall of Soviet Union, lessons derived from, 133
  Indian navy, present and planned assets in, 130–31
  military-to-military relationship of India and the U.S., 135
  modernization of, corruption and, 35
  modern weapons and the globalization of warfare, xxi–xxii
  naval effort in the Indian Ocean, 128–32
  naval power, aspirations to become, 112–13
  nuclearization, asymmetrical warfare and impact of, xxiv
  in Pakistan, 49
  proxy war, evolution of, xxii
  space, control of and future power projection, 113
  See also security
Miller, Benjamin, xxi, 80–81
Ministry of Defence (MOD)
  China, position on, 140
  corruption in, 10
  Defence Intelligence Agency, 33
Ministry of External Affairs (MEA)
  China, position on, 140
  investment in Afghanistan, 93

Look East policy, personnel specialties and, 144–45
strategic autonomy, reiteration of, 138–39
Ministry of Finance, Enforcement Directorate, 33. *See also* Enforcement Directorate
Ministry of Home Affairs (MHA)
Intelligence Bureau (IB), 34, 158–60
Maoist revolt and failure of development efforts, 35
the Model Police Act, 161–62
ratio of policeman/woman to citizens, 29
Mir, Sajid, 58
Mission Mode Project, 158
Model Police Act, 161–62
modernization
rapid process of, 2
standards of governance and, 6–7
unintended effects of, 2–3
Modi, Narendra, 51, 56–57
Mohammed, Khalid Sheikh, 72
Mohan, C. Raja, xxix, 125, 197
Mohanty, Deba R., 117
money laundering
corruption, as means of hiding, 16–18
as cross-border crime in South Asia, 68
hawala and (*see hawala*)
morality, corruption and Hindu notions of, 4–6
Multi-Agency Centre (MAC), 34, 157–60
Mumbai
Gujarat riots, terrorist violence as revenge for, 74–75n.46
rioting following destruction of Babri Masjid, 53–55
terrorist targeting of, 61
26/11 attacks, 58–59
See also Bombay
Muni, S. D., 47, 203
murder rate, 23–24
Musharraf, Pervez, 49, 185
Muslims
ghettoization of communities in western India, 57
law enforcement authorities and, 62
poor socioeconomic status in India, 61–62
radicalizing young through the internet, 87
violence between movements of, 83
violent jihadist terrorism in India (*see* terrorism, violent jihadist in India)
See also Islam
mutual legal assistance treaties, 192

Naipaul, V. S., 157
Nandy, Ashish, 6
Nasheed, Mohamed, 128
Nasreen, Tasmina, 54
National Counter Terrorism Centre (NCTC), 158–61, 208
National Crime Records Bureau, 158
National Democratic Alliance (NDA), 165
national e-governance plan (NeGP), 175
National Election Watch, 21
National Human Rights Commission, 172–73, 207
National Intelligence Grid (NATGRID), 157
National Investigation Agency Act (NIA Act), 159–60
National Investigation Agency (NIA), 34, 65, 158–60
National Security Act, 63
National Security Adviser (NSA), 33, 158
National Security Council (NSC), 33
National Security Guard (NSG), 34, 157–58, 160, 178n.7
National Technical Research Organisation, 33, 158
Naxalite revolt. *See* Maoist insurgencies/revolt
Nehru, Jawaharlal, xviii, 138, 182
neighborhood
as context for India's rise to power, questions regarding, xxi
issues concerning, xx
location, globalization and the significance of, xxi–xxii

neighborhood *(Cont.)*
redefining to go around Pakistan, xxv
South Asia (*see* South Asia)
trajectory of emerging powers, role of location in determining, xxiiii–xxiv
See also region and regionalism
Nepal
China and, 124–25
domestic politics and cross-border tensions, 50
Indian aid to, 190
smuggling across border with India, 55
New Framework Agreement, 135
nexus, the
in Gujarat, 22
as the heart of India's corruption problem, 7
the Koda corruption scandal and, 12
money laundering and *hawala*, connection of, 16–18 (see also *hawala*; money laundering)
relationship of politicians, police, and criminals, 3
NonAlignment 2.0, xviii–xx, 120, 132–33, 138–39, 155–56, 182
non-reciprocal accommodation, 182
Noorzai, Haji Bashir, 66
North Atlantic Treaty Organization (NATO), 94–95
North-South Transport Corridor, 94
Nye, Joseph S., xxi

Obama, Barack, 203
Operation Cold Start, 90
Operation Parakram, 89
Owaisi, Akbaruddin, 56

Pakistan
Afghan border, conflict over, 45
Babri Masjid destruction, violence following, 54
borders of, 73n.2
change in, the mujahideen and, 84–85
climate change, vulnerability to, 105
domestic politics and cross-border tensions, 49
ethnic fault lines and the Bangladeshi independence movement, 43
evolving four-way relationship with India, the United States and China, 88 (*see also* global power competition, four-way relationship of India, Pakistan, the United States and China)
Federally Administered Tribal Areas (FATA), 92
Global Peace Index ranking, 23
Ibrahim's refuge in, 55
Indian aid, absence of, 189
Indian Ocean Rim Association, exclusion from, 196–97
India's strategy of going around, xxv, 186–90
Kalashnikov culture in, 84
Kashmir, conflict with India over, 43–45, 48
LeT in, 58–59, 61
money laundering in, 68
population growth and problems of, 47–48
population of, 73n.9
religious basis for division from India, 45–46
strategies for improving the relationship with, 184–86
tensions between Muslim sects in, 83
terrorist attacks in India, support for, 61
26/11 attacks, involvement in, 58–59
Pakistani Taliban, 64
Pakistan People's Party, 49
panchayat, 1, 15, 22, 179n.25
Panchsheel multilateralism, 47
Pande, Prashant Chandra, 74n.43
Panetta, Leon, 93
Panikkar, K. M., 120
Pant, Harsh V., 92, 128
Parthasarathy, G., 91
Pattanaik, Smitri S., 182
Paul, T. V., xvii, xxiii
PDS. *See* Public Distribution System
Pearl, Daniel, 72

Planning Commission, Eleventh Plan, "inclusive growth" and access to essential services by the impoverished, 6–7
Police Act Development Committee, 161–62
Police Act of 1861, 27, 29, 30, 161
police and policing
anti-Muslim bias, 62
bias in, 31–32
counterterrorism and, 29–33
governance and, 26–29
Gujarat riots, complicity in, 56–57
intelligence reform and counterterrorism efforts, 157–61
poor police performance, factors ensuring, 27–29
Provincial Armed Constabulary (PAC), 28
public opinion of, 26–27
reform of, 161–63, 207–8
security concerns and failures of, 34–35
political culture, conceptions of corruption and, 4–6
political institutions
authority and power, ideas of, 5
diversity of, 1
as elements of the virtuous circle driving out corruption, 167–68
Lok Sabha, members inheriting seats in, 5
politics
crime and, 21–22
domestic and cross-border tensions, 49–51
the police and, 27–28
population
diversity of, 1
of Pakistan, 73n.9
power
Hindu interpretations of, 5
measures of, xxi
Prabakaran, Velupillai, 97
Pradhan, R. D., 91
Prevention of Money Laundering Act, 17–18
Prevention of Terrorism Act (POTA), 63, 173–74
Proliferation Security Initiative (PSI), 196
Provincial Armed Constabulary (PAC), 28
Public Distribution System (PDS), percentage of food actually reaching intended target, 15
Punjab
addiction in, 25
water rights, loss of, 110n.80

quadrilateral, the, 145–46, 202–3
Quattrocchi, Ottavio, 10, 19

Radia, Niira, 10
Rai, Vinod, 10
Raja, A., 11
Rajagopalan, Rajesh, xxiii
Rajapaksa, Mahinda, 51, 96
Rajasthan
corruption in MGNREGS, loss to the exchequer from, 16
semifeudal principalities of, 2
underreporting of crime in, 25
Ram, 52–53, 73n.24
Ramachandran, Shastri, 193
Raman, B., 30, 52, 54
RAND Corporation
growth of Chinese and Indian economies, projections of, 141
Pakistan's retaliatory options against India in Afghanistan, discounting of, 94
Rao, P. V. Narasimha, 18–19, 144
Rao, Rama, 19
Rapid Response Force (RRF), 28
Rashtriya Swayamsevak Sangh (RSS), 53, 60
Rath Yatra, 46
Redfield, Robert, 74n.27
region and regionalism
alternative strategies to go around Pakistan, xxiv–xxv, 186–90
East Asia and the Look East strategy, xxv, 143–48
failure of in South Asia, xxiv–xxv

region and regionalism *(Cont.)*
the Indian Ocean (*see* Indian Ocean Region (IOR))
issues concerning, xx
limits on India's ability to act on the level of, 111–12
soft regionalism, xxiv, 111, 123 (*see also* South Asian Association for Regional Cooperation (SAARC))
soft regionalism, need to move away from, 204
South Asia (*see* South Asia)
See also neighborhood
Registration and Regulation of Political Parties Bill of 2011, 168
Rehman, Iskander, 111
religion, division of India and Pakistan on the basis of, 45–46
Reporters Without Borders, 97
Representation of the People Act of 1951, 22
Research and Analysis Wing (RAW), 33
Rice, Condoleeza, 90, 136
Right of Children to Free and Compulsory Education Act, 165
Right to Information Act, 165, 167, 170
Right to information (RTI) Commission, 169
Ripsman, Norris M., xvii
Rothstein, Bo, 3–4, 166–67
Routray, Bibhu Prasad, 70
Roy, Arundhati, 3
RTI Act, 173
rural-debt forgiveness program, 165

SAARC. *See* South Asian Association for Regional Cooperation
SAARC Convention on Mutual Legal Assistance in Criminal Matters, 69
SAARC Regional Convention on Narcotic Drugs and Psychotropic Substances, 69
SAARC Regional Convention on Suppression of Terrorism, 69
SAARC Regional Convention on Terrorism, Additional Protocol to, 69
Sachar Committee Report, 31, 56, 165
Saeed, Hafiz, 58–60, 87
Sagar, Rahul, xviii
Sahni, Varun, xxiii
Saikia, Panchali, 191
Sailo, Laldinkima, 191
Sampoorna Grameena Rozgra Yojana, 15
Sangh Parivar (Hindu Family), 54
Saudi Arabia, 84, 85–86
Savarkar, Vinayak Damodar, 52–53
Scott, David, 122, 129
security
architecture of security organizations, 33–34
Asian security architecture, future of, 199–205
aspirations and realities regarding, 148–49
concerns, Chinese investment and, 102
continental form of, xxvi
continental power, India as, 111–13
counterterrorism, 29–33 (*see also* counterterrorism)
East/Southeast Asia, India's Look East strategy and, 143–48
energy needs and, 121
governance and, 156–57
inclusive growth approach and, 119–20
the Indian Ocean
the China factor in Indo-U.S. relations in, 135–43
dilemma in the Indian Ocean Region, 112
geostrategic advantages in, 122–23
India's naval ambitions in, 128–32
Indo-U.S. relations in, 132–35
potential threats, as a source of, 120–22
Sino-Indian competition in, 123–28
intelligence agencies, 33–34
neighborhood conditions and, xvii
performance of policing agencies and, 34–35
policing (*see* police and policing)
spending for defense and, 113–19
"strategic autonomy" (*see* strategic autonomy)
See also military, the; strategic thought

Selth, Burma Andre, 151n.39
Sen, Amartya, 7
Seychelles, 127–28
Shanghai Cooperation Organization (SCO), 95
Sharma, Anand, 100
Shinde, Shushil Kumar
Shiva, 73n.24
Shiv Sena, 53–55
Sikhs, police bias against, 31
Singapore, 145, 195
Singapore Ports Authority (SPA), 126
Singh, Manmohan, 133, 138–39, 146, 173
Sir Creek, 51, 71
Small Arms Survey, 24
social protection programs
  Common Minimum Program (CMP), 165
  corruption and, 14–16, 35, 165
  Mahatma Gandhi National Rural Employment Guarantee Scheme (MGNREGS) (*see* Mahatma Gandhi National Rural Employment Guarantee Scheme (MGNREGS))
  Public Distribution System (PDS) (*see* Public Distribution System (PDS))
  spending on, 119–20
sodium pentothal, 31
South Asia
  challenges in, 181
  climate change, expected impact of, 105–6
  contested borders in, 43–46
  cross-border crime, 64–65
    arms and explosives smuggling, 67–68
    cooperation against, 69–70
    cybercrime and intellectual property crime, 68–69
    illicit drug smuggling, 65–66
    money laundering, 68 (*see also* money laundering)
    people trafficking, 66–67
  decolonization, problematic legacy of, 45–48
  direct aid contribution from India, 188–89
  domestic politics and cross-border tensions in, 49–51
  environmental problems, 70–72, 103–6
  globalization, impact of (*see* globalization)
  global power competition, impact of (*see* global power competition)
  map of, 44
  neighborhood-wide change, necessity of, xxiv
  potential, failure to realize, 72
  religious basis for partition of British India, impact of, 45–46
  strategies for achieving better outcomes in, 182–83, 209–10
    Look East strategy, India's "near east" and, 193–95
    Look East strategy, leveraging to improve integration with Southeast/East Asia, 190–93
    Pakistan, dealing with, 184–86
    Pakistan, dealing with other countries and going around, 186–90
South Asia Free Trade Agreement (SAFTA), 98, 187
South Asian Association for Regional Cooperation (SAARC)
  cross-border crime, failure to cooperate against, 69
  failures of, consequences of, 47–48
  failures of, reasons for, xxiv
  India-Pakistan relations and, 184, 196
  information and communications technology, improving coordination of, 187–88
  mutual legal assistance treaties, absence of, 192
  real problems, pushing to deal with, 182, 209
  South Asian and global trade, 98–99
South Asian Information Highway Project, 188
South Asia Subregion Economic Cooperation (SASEC), 188
South Asia Terrorism Portal (SATP), 23

Southeast Asia, India's Look East strategy and, 143–48, 190–93
South-North Water Transfer Scheme, 103–4
Soviet Union. *See* Union of Soviet Socialist Republics
Space, Department of, 13
space program, 149–50n.8
Sridharan, E., xxx–xxxin.33, 182, xxixn.2
Srikrishna Commission, 32, 54
Sri Lanka
  domestic politics and cross-border tensions, 50–51
  Global Peace Index ranking, 23
  global power competition and the end of the Civil War, 96–98
  Indian aid to, 190
stability-instability paradox, xxiv
state, the
  corruption, achieving policy objectives and, 3–4 (*see also* corruption)
  globalization and, xvii
  Kashmir conflict and interpretation of, 184–85
  structure of society and, 5
  See also governance
State, U.S. Department of
  heroin/opium seizures, statistics on, 25
  illicit drugs, India as a hub for, 25
  terrorism, collection of data on deaths caused by, 23
state-nation incongruence, 80–81
Steel Authority of India Ltd., 93
Stimson Center, 127
strategic altruism, 182
strategic autonomy
  as a core strategy, xvii
  domestic and neighborhood consolidation as priority for achieving, xxvi–xxvii
  focus on lower-order issues, need for, xix–xx
  reiteration of, 138–39
  steps to maintain a policy of, 204–5
strategic thought
  China as an example, xix
  "grand strategy" for India, xviii–xix
  lower-order issues, need to focus on, xix–xx
  strategic culture distinguished from, xviii
  three strands of Indian, xviii
  See also security
Students Islamic Movement of India (SIMI), 54, 59–61, 86
Stuenkel, Oliver, 194–95
Subsidiary Multi-Agency Centres (SMACs), 34, 157, 159–60
super security complex, xx
Swami, Praveen, 52, 86–87
Sweden, 166
Swiss Bankers Association, amount of illicit funds from India in Swiss banks, 19
Syed, Ahsan Ali, 21

Taliban
  Afghan refugees as breeding ground for, 84
  al-Qaeda, harboring of, 81
  China and, 95
  Deobandi Islam, adherents of, 83
  in Karachi, 72
  Pakistan and, 92–93
  Pakistani, 64, 185
  as rulers in Afghanistan, 66
Tamil Nadu
  farmer suicides in, 100
  Sri Lanka-India relations and, 71, 190
  the Sri Lankan Civil War and, 50
  underreporting of crime in, 24–25
Tanham, George K., xviii
Tapuriah, Kashinath, 20
Taylor, McComas, 87–88
Tehrik-i-Taliban Pakistan, 51
Telecommunications, Department of (DOT), 2G telecommunications scam, 10–11
Tellis, Ashley J., xx, xxxn.13
terrorism
  cooperation against in South Asia, 69–70
  counterterrorism, policing and, 29–33 (*see also* counterterrorism)

criminals and, 55
deaths caused by, data on, 23
financing of, *hawala* and, 16
the Hindu Right and, 60
in India, nature of, 61–63
investigations of, 30–31
Muslim acts of, high impact of, 45
narco-terrorism, Afghanistan as a center of, 66
Operation Parakram in response to, 89
substate actors and the effects of neighborhood, xxiii–xxiv
violent jihadist in India, 51–52, 61–63
Babri Masjid, destruction of, 46, 48, 52–53
Gujarat riots, 56–57
Gulf funding and connections for, 86–87
the Indian Mujahideen (IM), 59–60 (*see also* Indian Mujahideen (IM))
Mumbai rioting following destruction of Babri Masjid, 53–55
26/11 attacks, 58–59, 61, 88–92
See also war on terrorism
Terrorism and Disruptive Activities Act (TADA), 62–63
Thailand, 195
Tharoor, Shashi, 196
Togadia, Praveen, 56
Trans Asian Railway, 191
transnational crime. *See* South Asia, cross-border crime
Travencore, highly developed state of, 2
tribal populations, 2
Trilateral Highway Agreement (India, Burma, Thailand), 191
26/11 attacks
global power competition and, 88–92
India-Pakistan relations and, 58–59, 61
24/7 reporting, 48
2G telecommunications scam, 10–11

UBS. *See* United Bank of Switzerland
Uganda, 127
Union of Soviet Socialist Republics
Afghanistan, invasion of, 81, 84
Ethiopia, human rights abuses ignored in, 97–98
fall of, India and, 133
Pakistan, human rights abuses ignored in, 98
Unique Identification (UID) project, 174–75, 208
United Arab Emirates (UAE), 85
United Bank of Switzerland (UBS), 20–21
United Liberation Front of Assom (ULFA), 45
United Nations, India-Pakistan conflict over Kashmir, 43–44
United Nations Educational, Scientific, and Cultural Organization (UNESCO), 188
United Nations High Commissioner for Refugees (UNHCR), 54
United Nations Millennium Development Goals Report, 47
United Nations Office on Drugs and Crime, 25
United Progressive Alliance (UPA)
leftist orientation and inclusive growth, 164–65
minority government status as restraint, 99
United States
Afghanistan, invasion of, 81–82
Afghan mujahideen, funding of, 84
Asia, pivot to, 203
Asian security architecture and, 199–200, 202–3
defense spending, 114, 118
evolving four-way relationship with India, Pakistan, and China, 88 (*see also* global power competition, four-way relationship of India, Pakistan, the United States and China)
Indian Ocean Rim Association, admission as dialogue partner, 196
Indo-U.S. relations, Asian security architecture and, 201
Indo-U.S. relations, the China factor in, 135–43

United States (Cont.)
Indo-U.S. relations, the Indian Ocean and, 132–35
murder rate in, 23
Persian Gulf presence, 121
world trade negotiations, critical of BRICs in, 100
Unlawful Activities Prevention Act (UAPA), 63, 158, 173–74, 208
urbanization, 2, 71–72
US National Intelligence Council, shocks to be faced by South Asian nations, 48
US Pacific Command (USPACOM), 132, 134
Uttar Pradesh
caste politics in, 3
corruption, "good" and "bad" money within, 6
corruption in MGNREGS, 15–16
food distributed by PDS that is stolen in, 15
political grounds for criminal charges in, 22
splendidness of ruler, vestiges of belief in, 5

Varshney, Ashutosh, 3, 40n.144, 52–53
Vietnam, 142–43, 146–47, 195
violence
jihad and (*see* jihad, violent; terrorism, violent jihadist in India)
level of in India, 23–26
violent jihad. *See* terrorism, violent jihadist in India
virtuous circle, 167–72
Vishnu, 73n.24
Vishwa Hindu Parishad (World Hindu Council), 54
voter-verified paper audit trail (VVPAT), 174

Waever, Ole, xx, xxixn.4
Waheed, Mohammed, 128
Waliullah, Shah, 82–83
Walz, Kenneth, 200
warfare. *See* military, the
war on terrorism
global power competition and, 106
negative effects of, 48
the 26/11 attacks and, 89
Weiner, Myron, 3
welfare programs. *See* social protection programs
White, Hugh, 136, 200–201
Winner, Andrew C., 120
World Bank
corruption, incremental approach to overcoming, 166
food disseminated for the poor that reaches intended target, 4
illegal trade in South Asia, 64
MGNREGS, praise for, 16
Pakistan, money laundering in, 68
Public Distribution System, report on, 15
social protection programs, percentage of GDP devoted to, 15
World Health Organization, murder rate based on health reporting, 24
World Hindu Council, Bajran Dal, 60
World Trade Organization (WTO), 100–102
Wu, Mark, 102

Yoshihara, Toshi, 120
Yusuf, Huma, 72

Zakat and Ushr Ordinance of 1980, 83
Zardari, Asif Ali, 90
Zia-ul-Haq, Muhammad, 83–84, 98

CPSIA information can be obtained at www.ICGtesting.com
Printed in the USA
BVOW08*1755140715

408283BV00003B/10/P